Abrams' Angiography

Cumulative Index

Abrams' Angiography

Cumulative Index

Little, Brown and Company
BOSTON   NEW YORK   TORONTO   LONDON

ISBN 0-316-08443-3

Printed in the United States of America

EB-M

Editorial: Nancy E. Chorpenning, Deeth K. Ellis
Production Services: Julie Sullivan
Indexer: AlphaByte, Inc.
Production Supervisor: Michael A. Granger
Designer: Marty Tenney
Cover Designer: Louis C. Bruno, Jr.

How to Use the Cumulative Index

The page numbers in the cumulative index that are preceded by a "III" refer to pages in *Abrams' Angiography: Interventional Radiology*. All other page numbers refer to volumes I and II of *Abrams' Angiography*.

Contents

Volume I

I. General Considerations

1. **Historical Notes**   3
   HERBERT L. ABRAMS

2. **Radiographic Contrast Agents: History, Chemistry, and Variety**   13
   MICHAEL A. BETTMANN

3. **Physiologic Effects and Systemic Reactions**   22
   MICHAEL A. BETTMANN

4. **The Emergency Treatment of Reactions to Contrast Media**   34
   STANLEY BAUM

5. **Diagnostic Pharmacoangiography**   49
   DOUGLAS C. B. REDD

6. **Rapid Film Changers**   66
   KURT AMPLATZ

7. **Angiographic Equipment**   86
   MELVIN R. JUDKINS, BARRY T. KATZEN, AND MICHAEL S. VAN LYSEL

8. **Catheters, Methods, and Injectors for Superselective Catheterization**   155
   CONSTANTIN COPE AND STANLEY BAUM

9. **Magnification Angiography**   176
   RICHARD H. GREENSPAN AND STANLEY BAUM

10. **Principles of Magnetic Resonance Angiography**   188
    FELIX W. WEHRLI

11. **Vascular Sonography**   205
    JOSEPH F. POLAK

II. The Central Nervous System

12. Cerebral Vascular Angiography: Indications, Technique, and Normal Anatomy of the Head 241

CHRISTOPHER J. MORAN, DANIEL K. KIDO, AND DEWITTE T. CROSS III

13. Abnormalities of Cerebral Vessels 284

DEWITTE T. CROSS III, DANIEL K. KIDO, AND CHRISTOPHER J. MORAN

14. Spinal Angiography 356

ROBERT W. HURST

III. The Thorax

Section A: Thoracic Aortography

15. Technique, Indications, and Hazards of Thoracic Aortography and the Normal Thoracic Aorta 391

HERBERT L. ABRAMS AND GUNNAR JÖNSSON

16. Patent Ductus Arteriosus 415

JOHN B. MAWSON AND J. A. GORDON CULHAM

17. Coarctation of the Aorta 434

RACHEL R. PHILLIPS AND J. A. GORDON CULHAM

18. Aorticopulmonary Window (Aortic Septal Defect) 464

J. A. GORDON CULHAM

19. Aneurysms of the Thoracic Aorta 467

PATRICIA ANN RANDALL AND ROBERT J. ASHENBURG

20. Dissecting Aortic Aneurysm 493

HERBERT L. ABRAMS AND KRISHNA KANDARPA

21. Blunt Trauma to the Thoracic Aorta and Brachiocephalic Arteries 521

YORAM BEN-MENACHEM AND RICHARD G. FISHER

22. Additional Applications of Thoracic Aortography 540

HERBERT L. ABRAMS

Section B: Coronary Arteriography

23. Technique of Coronary Arteriography   556

DAVID C. LEVIN

24. Complications of Coronary Arteriography   572

JOHN E. ARUNY

25. Normal Coronary Anatomy   583

SVEN PAULIN

26. Angiography in Coronary Disease   635

HERBERT I. ABRAMS, KRISHNA KANDARPA, AND JOHN E. ARUNY

27. Coronary Collateral Circulation   700

SVEN PAULIN

28. Pitfalls in Coronary Arteriography   726

DAVID C. LEVIN

29. Anomalies and Anatomic Variations of the Coronary Arteries   740

DAVID C. LEVIN

30. Coronary Arteriography Following Bypass Surgery   756

DIANA F. GUTHANER, MICHAEL R. REES, AND LEWIS WEXLER

Section C: Pulmonary Arteriography

31. Pulmonary Arteriography: Indications, Technique, Normal Findings, and Complications   768

ROBERT E. BARTON, PAUL C. LAKIN, AND JOSEF RÖSCH

32. Pulmonary Arteries: Congenital and Acquired Abnormalities   786

PAUL C. LAKIN AND JOSEF RÖSCH

33. Developmental Anomalies of the Pulmonary Arteries   822

PAUL R. JULSRUD

34. The Physiologic and Microstructural Basis for Radiologic Findings in the Normal and Disturbed Pulmonary Circulation   849

MORRIS SIMON

Section D: The Venous Systems of the Thorax and Abdomen

35. Anomalous Pulmonary Venous Connection   868

PAUL R. JULSRUD AND KENNETH E. FELLOWS

36. The Vertebral and Azygos Veins   891

HERBERT L. ABRAMS AND MICHAEL F. MEYEROVITZ

37. The Superior Vena Cava   915

MICHAEL A. BETTMANN

38. The Inferior Vena Cava   932

ERNEST J. FERRIS AND HEMENDRA R. SHAH

Section E: The Thoracic Outlet

39. Parathyroid Angiography   976

MARCELLE J. SHAPIRO AND JOHN L. DOPPMAN

40. Arteriography of Thoracic Outlet Syndrome   995

ERICH K. LANG, JANIS GISSEL LETOURNEAU, AND DEBORAH G. LONGLEY

Index to Volumes I and II   [1]

Volume II

IV. The Abdomen and Pelvis

Section A: Lumbar Aortography

41. Abdominal Aortography   1013

MARTIN C. CRAIN AND MARK W. MEWISSEN

42. Complications of Angiography and Interventional Radiology   1024

JONATHAN M. LEVY AND SAMUEL J. HESSEL

43. The Abnormal Abdominal Aorta: Arteriosclerosis and Other Diseases   1052

MICHAEL J. HALLISEY AND STEVEN G. MERANZE

44. Aneurysms of the Abdominal Aorta   1073

DANA R. BURKE

Section B: Renal Angiography

45. Renal Angiography: Techniques and Hazards; Anatomic and Physiologic Considerations   1101

ERIK BOIJSEN

46. Renal Tumor Versus Renal Cyst   1132

HERBERT L. ABRAMS AND CLEMENT J. GRASSI

47. Angiography of Renal Infection   1178

MORTON A. BOSNIAK, MARJORIE A. AMBOS, AND RICHARD S. LEFLEUR

48. Angiography of Hydronephrosis   1202

MORTON A. BOSNIAK, RICHARD S. LEFLEUR, AND MARJORIE A. AMBOS

49. Anomalies and Malformations   1217

ERIK BOIJSEN

50. Angiography and Embolization in Renal Trauma   1230

RICHARD G. FISHER AND YORAM BEN-MENACHEM

51. Renal Arteriography in Hypertension   1244

HERBERT L. ABRAMS AND CLEMENT J. GRASSI

52. Renal Venography   1290

HERBERT L. ABRAMS AND BENJAMIN B. FAITELSON

53. Renal Transplantation   1325

RICHARD D. SHLANSKY-GOLDBERG

Section C: Adrenal Angiography

54. The Roles of Angiography in Adrenal Disease   1352

STEVEN B. OGLEVIE AND JOSEPH J. BOOKSTEIN

Section D: Pancreatic, Hepatic, and Splenic Arteriography

55. Pancreatic Angiography   1383

ERIK BOIJSEN

56. Portal and Pancreatic Venography   1422

ANDERS LUNDERQUIST AND KRASSI IVANCEV

57. Hepatic Arteriography   1433

STANLEY BAUM

58. Splenic Arteriography   1457

HERBERT L. ABRAMS AND MICHAEL F. MEYEROVITZ

59. Splenoportography and Portal Hypertension   1497

GEOFFREY A. GARDINER, JR. AND INGEMAR BERGSTRAND

60. Arterial Portography   1527

KLAUS M. BRON AND RICHARD A. BAUM

Section E: Mesenteric Arteriography

61. Superior Mesenteric Angiography   1549

ERIK BOIJSEN

62. Inferior Mesenteric Arteriography   1587

HERBERT L. ABRAMS AND MICHAEL F. MEYEROVITZ

63. Mesenteric Ischemia   1615

SCOTT J. BOLEY AND LAWRENCE J. BRANDT

Section F: Bladder and Pelvic Arteriography

64. Pelvic Angiography   1636

ERICH K. LANG

Section G: Retroperitoneal Angiography

65. Retroperitoneal Arteriography in Adults   1669

DAVID C. LEVIN

V. The Extremities and Lymphangiography

Section A: Angiography of the Extremities

66. Artiography of the Patient with Previous Aortoiliac Interventions   1681

ANDREW B. CRUMMY AND JOHN C. MCDERMOTT

67. Femoral Arteriography   1697

JOSEPH F. POLAK

68. Venography   1743

MICHAEL A. BETTMANN

69. Arteriography of the Upper Extremity 1755
ARNOLD CHAIT

70. Angiography of Dialysis Shunts 1767
ARNOLD CHAIT

71. Angiography of Bones, Joints, and Soft Tissues 1779
CHARLES J. TEGTMEYER, DAVID J. SPINOSA, AND ALAN H. MATSUMOTO

72. Peripheral Vascular Magnetic Resonance Angiography 1822
RICHARD A. BAUM AND JEFFREY P. CARPENTER

73. MR Venography in the Detection of Venous Thrombosis 1837
GEORGE A. HOLLAND AND MARYELLYN GILFEATHER

Section B: Lymphangiography

74. Technique and Complications of Lymphangiography 1864
WALTER A. FUCHS

75. Normal Radiologic Anatomy of the Lymphatics and Lymph Nodes 1871
WALTER A. FUCHS

76. The Thoracic Duct 1891
GEORGE A. HOLLAND AND ALEXANDER ROSENBERGER

77. Lymphangiopathies 1907
WALTER A. FUCHS

78. Benign Lymph Node Disease 1923
WALTER A. FUCHS

79. Malignant Metastatic Disease 1927
WALTER A. FUCHS

80. Malignant Lymphomas 1940
RONALD A. CASTELLINO

Index to Volumes I and II [1]

Interventional Radiology

I. General Considerations

1. Mechanisms of Balloon Angioplasty and Restenosis   3

    GARY J. BECKER AND BRUCE F. WALLER

2. Balloon Angioplasty Catheters   24

    GARY J. BECKER

3. Atherectomy Catheters   44

    JOSEPH L. SKEENS AND MICHAEL D. DAKE

4. Agents for Small-Vessel and Tissue Embolization   52

    MICHAEL C. SOULEN

5. Mechanical Embolic Agents   55

    JEFFREY S. POLLAK AND ROBERT I. WHITE, JR.

6. Principles of Regional Chemotherapy   80

    MICHAEL J. PENTECOST

7. Vascular Stents   85

    GARY J. BECKER

8. Principles of Selective Thrombolysis   119

    JOSEPH J. BOOKSTEIN AND KARIM VALJI

9. Thrombolysis: Clinical Applications   132

    KARIM VALJI AND JOSEPH J. BOOKSTEIN

10. Percutaneous Suction Thromboembolectomy   160

    ROBERT E. LAMBIASE, GARY S. DORFMAN, AND TIMOTHY P. MURPHY

11. Percutaneous Image-Guided Biopsy   166

    JEFFREY S. MOULTON

12. Intravascular Biopsy   195

    JOSEPH BONN

13. **Interventional Radiology and the Cancer Patient**   201

MICHAEL J. PENTECOST

14. **Preintervention Assessment**   204

KLEMENS H. BARTH

15. **Intraprocedure Management**   211

KLEMENS H. BARTH, ALAN H. MATSUMOTO, AND STEVEN V. LOSSEF

16. **Postintervention Care**   219

KLEMENS H. BARTH

II. Revascularization of the Aorta and Its Branches

17. **Percutaneous Aortoiliac Intervention in Vascular Disease**   225

KENNETH S. RHOLL

18. **Femoropopliteal Revascularization**   262

ERIC C. MARTIN

19. **Infrapopliteal Revascularization**   284

MARCY B. JAGUST AND THOMAS A. SOS

20. **Renal Angioplasty**   294

CHARLES J. TEGTMEYER, ALAN H. MATSUMOTO, AND ALLEN M. JOHNSON

21. **Endovascular Interventions for Chronic Mesenteric Ischemia**   326

ALAN H. MATSUMOTO, CHARLES J. TEGTMEYER, AND J. FRITZ ANGLE

22. **Extracranial Brachiocephalic Angioplasty**   339

DONALD E. SCHWARTEN

23. **Transluminal Placement of Endovascular Stent-Grafts for the Treatment of Thoracic Aortic Aneurysms**   356

MICHAEL D. DAKE

24. **Coronary Angioplasty and Related Techniques**   366

HOWARD C. HERRMANN AND JOHN W. HIRSHFELD, JR.

III. Interventional Radiology of the Gastrointestinal System

25. Arteriographic Diagnosis and Treatment of Gastrointestinal Bleeding 389
STANLEY BAUM

26. Embolotherapy of Hepatic Arterial Injuries 422
RICHARD G. FISHER AND YORAM BEN-MENACHEM

27. Interventional Therapies for Hepatic Malignancy 436
MICHAEL J. PENTECOST

28. Benign Biliary Obstruction 455
ROY L. GORDON

29. Malignant Obstruction of the Hepatobiliary System 472
ANTHONY C. VENBRUX AND FLOYD A. OSTERMAN, JR.

30. Percutaneous Cholecystostomy 483
CONSTANTIN COPE

31. Percutaneous Removal of Biliary Calculi 491
CONSTANTIN COPE

32. Liver Transplantation: Associated Interventions 509
ALBERT B. ZAJKO AND PHILIP D. ORONS

33. Interventions in Portal Hypertension 525
ZIV J. HASKAL

34. Percutaneous Gastrostomy and Gastrojejunostomy 547
DANIEL PICUS AND ERIC S. MALDEN

IV. Interventional Radiology of the Genitourinary System

35. Nephroureteral Obstruction 561
PARVATI RAMCHANDANI

36. Renal Calculus Disease 587
PARVATI RAMCHANDANI

37. The Lower Genitourinary Tract 614
FLAVIO CASTAÑEDA AND JOSÉ M. HERNANDEZ-GRAULAU

38. Interventions in Urinary Diversions   645

PARVATI RAMCHANDANI

39. Renal Cysts and Urinomas   658

MICHAEL D. DARCY

40. Selective Salpingography and Fallopian Tube Recanalization   672

AMY S. THURMOND

41. Varicocele   678

RICHARD D. SHLANSKY-GOLDBERG

42. Penile Vascular Catheterization in Diagnosis and Therapy of Erectile Dysfunction   705

JOSEPH J. BOOKSTEIN AND KARIM VALJI

43. Recanalization of Dialysis Fistulas   726

ANNE C. ROBERTS AND KARIM VALJI

V. Interventional Radiology of the Central Nervous System

44. Revascularization in the Central Nervous System   745

ROBERT W. HURST

45. Neurointerventional Radiology: Intraaxial Embolotherapy of the Central Nervous System   765

TONY P. SMITH AND RANDALL T. HIGASHIDA

46. Neuroendovascular Therapy of Intracranial, Extraaxial Lesions   789

PETER KIM NELSON, AVI SETTON, AND ALEJANDRO BERENSTEIN

VI. Interventional Radiology of the Thorax

47. Transcatheter Bronchial Artery Embolization for Inflammation (Hemoptysis)   819

MATTHEW A. MAURO AND PAUL F. JAQUES

48. Interventional Radiology of Thoracic Abscesses   829

GILES W. BOLAND AND STEVEN L. DAWSON

49. Pulmonary Arteriovenous Malformations   837

ROBERT I. WHITE, JR. AND JEFFREY S. POLLAK

VII. Interventional Radiology of Trauma

50. Arteriography and Transcatheter Treatment of Extremity Trauma 857

MICHAEL D. KATZ AND SUE E. HANKS

51. Angiographic Management of Hemorrhage in Pelvic Fractures 869

JOHN A. KAUFMAN AND ARTHUR C. WALTMAN

52. Transcatheter Arterial Embolization in the Management of Splenic Trauma 884

GEORGE I. GETRAJDMAN AND SALVATORE J. A. SCLAFANI

53. Arteriography and Transcatheter Embolization in the Management of Renal Trauma 892

SUE E. HANKS AND MICHAEL D. KATZ

VIII. Pediatric Interventional Radiology

54. Pediatric Interventional Angiography 903

J. A. GORDON CULHAM

IX. Abscess Drainage

55. Percutaneous Treatment of Abdominal Abscesses 925

PETER J. EISENBERG AND STEVEN L. DAWSON

56. Percutaneous Drainage of Pelvic Abscesses and Fluid Collections 939

GREGORY J. SLATER AND STEVEN L. DAWSON

X. Miscellaneous Applications of Interventional Radiology

57. Percutaneous Vascular and Nonvascular Foreign Body Retrieval 959

FREDERICK S. KELLER, JOSEF RÖSCH, AND RICHARD A. BAUM

58. Venous Access 969

MATTHEW A. MAURO AND PAUL F. JAQUES

59. Vena Cava Filters 982

TIMOTHY P. MURPHY, GARY S. DORFMAN, AND ROBERT E. LAMBIASE

60. Abnormal Arteriovenous Communications 998

ROBERT J. ROSEN

Cumulative Index

Cumulative Index

ABCs of basic life support, 36
Abdomen and pelvis, 1011–1677
    abscess in. *See* Abdominal abscesses
    angiography in
        adrenal, 1352–1382. *See also* Adrenal
            glands
        bladder and pelvic, 1636–1668. *See
            also* Pelvic angiography
        hepatic, 1433–1456. *See also* Hepatic
            arteriography
        mesenteric, 1549–1635. *See also* Mes-
            enteric angiography
        pancreatic, 1383–1548. *See also* Pan-
            creatic angiography
        pelvic, 1636–1668
        renal, 1101–1351. *See also* Renal angi-
            ography
        retroperitoneal, 1669–1677
        splenic, 1457–1496. *See also* Splenic
            arteriography
    anomalous pulmonary venous connec-
        tion in, 868–890. *See also* Anoma-
        lous pulmonary venous connection
    arterial portography in, 1527–1548. *See
        also* Arterial portography
    biopsy complications in, 1035
    complications of procedures for, 1035–
        1036
    inferior vena cava in, 932–975. *See also*
        Inferior vena cava (IVC)
    large systemic venous systems of, 868–
        975
    lumbar aortography in, 1013–1100. *See
        also* Lumbar aortography
    lymphangiography in, 1864–1952. *See
        also* Lymphangiography
    portal and pancreatic venography in,
        1422–1432
    splenoportography and portal hyperten-
        sion in, 1497–1526. *See also* Spleno-
        portography
    superior vena cava in, 915–931. *See also*
        Superior vena cava (SVC)
    vascular sonography of masses in, 230
    vertebral and azygos veins in, 891–
        914. *See also* Vertebral and azygos
        veins
Abdominal abscesses
    complications of, 1035–1036
    etiology of, III:925
    hepatic, III:929–931
    in pancreatic disease, III:932–936
    percutaneous drainage of, III:925–938
        diagnosis and, III:925–928
        in lesser sac abscesses, III:936
        liver abscess in, III:929–931
        morbidity and mortality in, III:928–
            929
        in pancreatic disease, III:932–936
        in perirenal abscesses, III:936
        in psoas abscesses, III:936–937
        splenic abscess in, III:931–932
        surgical and medical treatment versus,
            III:925
    pseudocysts and, III:933, III:934–935
    splenic, III:931–932

Abdominal angina, 1631–1634
    inferior mesenteric arteriography in, 1600
Abdominal angiography. *See* Abdomen and
    pelvis
Abdominal aorta. *See also* Aorta
    abnormal, 1052–1072. *See also* Arterio-
        sclerosis, of abdominal aorta
    anatomy of, 1015, 1017–1023
    aneurysms of. *See* Abdominal aorta aneu-
        rysms
    angiography after interventions of,
        1681–1863. *See also* Aortoiliac dis-
        ease, angiography of extremities
        after interventions for
    aortography and. *See* Abdominal aortog-
        raphy
    arteriosclerosis and other diseases of,
        1052–1072. *See also* Arterioslero-
        sis, of abdominal aorta
    branches of
        anatomy of, 1015, 1017–1023
        paired lateral, anatomy of, 1018, 1021
        segmental, anatomy of, 1021
        sonography of, 213–214, 228–230
    coarctation of, 437
    cut film angiography of, 22–23
    digital subtraction angiography of, 22
    infrarenal
        fusiform aneurysm of, 1074
        postoperative narrowing of, 1070
    injuries to brachiocephalic arteries and,
        522
    iodine content in angiography of, 22–23
    plaque in, stenting for, III:99
    postoperative narrowing of, 1070
    sonography of, 213, 214, 228–230
        in postoperative and postintervention
            follow-up, 230
Abdominal aorta aneurysms, 1073–1100
    acute vascular occlusion and, 1602–
        1603
    in arteriosclerosis and other diseases,
        1058, 1059, 1060, 1073
    chronic intestinal ischemia and, 1631
    clinical presentation of, 1077–1081
    endoluminal grafting with fluoroscopic
        guidance in treatment of, 1093–
        1095
    etiology of, 1073, 1074
    genetics in, 1073
    incidence of, 1073–1074
    in inferior vena cava obstruction, 961
    inflammatory, 1074–1077, 1080
    multiple, 1091
    mycotic, 1077, 1080
    pathology of, 1074–1077, 1078
    preoperative evaluation of, 1074–1075,
        1076, 1082–1095
        angiography in, 1074–1075, 1086–
            1091
        choice of method in, 1091–1093
        computed tomography in, 1074–
            1075, 1076, 1081, 1082–1086,
            1091, 1093
        magnetic resonance imaging in, 1091,
            1092–1093

spiral volumetric computed tomogra-
    phy in, 1091, 1093, 1094
ultrasonography in, 1076, 1084–
    1085, 1090–1091
radiographic evaluation of, 1081–1096
    detection and serial evaluation in,
        1081–1082, 1083, 1084–1085
    in postoperative complications, 1095–
        1096, 1097, 1098
    preoperative, 1074–1075, 1076,
        1082–1095. *See also* Abdominal
        aorta aneurysms, preoperative evalua-
        tion of
    in suspected leaking or rupture, 1094,
        1095, 1096
    rupture of, 1079–1080, III:688
        death from, 1073
        evaluation of suspected, 1094, 1095,
            1096
        in suspected leaking or rupture, 1094,
            1095, 1096
    saccular, 1074–1075, 1078
        infrarenal, 1080
        mycotic, 1080
    screening for, 1096–1098
    sonography of, 207, 228–229
    syphilitic, 1077, 1078, 1080–1081
    ureteral strictures after repair of, III:578
Abdominal aortography, 1013–1023
    in abdominal aorta aneurysms, 1074–
        1075, 1086–1091
    in agenesis of kidney, 1316
    anatomy in, 1015, 1017–1023
    in bronchial artery embolization, III:823
    catheterization in
        superselective, 158
        transaxillary, 1016
        transfemoral, 1013–1016
        translumbar, 1016–1017
    in donor angiography before renal trans-
        plantation, 1326
    historical notes on, 8
    in neurogenic tumor of kidney, 1166
    in renal pelvic tumors, 1161
    in renal transplantation angiography,
        1328
Abdominal pain. *See also* Pain
    in dissecting aneurysms, 496, 497
Abdominal trauma, ureteral strictures after,
    III:578
Abdominal veins in tumor, large draining,
    1782
Aberrant arteries, 1217
    subclavian, as coarctation of aorta vari-
        ant, 439–440
ABI. *See* Ankle-brachial index (ABI)
Ablation. *See* Embolization
Abnormalities. *See* Anomalies and malfor-
    mations
ABO blood incompatibility, III:518
Abrams HL, 556, 635, 893, 1587
    biplane image-amplified cineangiography
        introduced by, 9
    in percutaneous transfemoral selective
        coronary arteriography develop-
        ment, 10

3

Abrodil, 7, 14, 15
Abscesses
abdominal. *See* Abdominal abscesses
adrenal gland, 1379
Brodie, 1783
hepatic, 1438, 1440–1441
after arteriography, III:434
percutaneous drainage of, III:929–931
lesser sac, III:936
lymph node, 1925
mediastinal, III:832–835
pancreatic, 1401, 1402, 1408, 1409, 1413, 1414–1415, III:932–936
pelvic, percutaneous drainage of, III:939–955. *See also* Pelvic abscess percutaneous drainage (PAD)
percutaneous drainage of, III:923–955
abdominal, III:925–938. *See also* Abdominal abscesses, percutaneous drainage of
fluid collections in, III:939–955. *See also* Pelvic abscess percutaneous drainage (PAD)
pelvic, III:939–955. *See also* Pelvic abscess percutaneous drainage (PAD)
postprocedural care for, III:219–221
perineal, III:632
perinephric, 1185, 1190–1191, 1676
perirenal, III:936
periurethral, III:618
psoas, III:936–937
pulmonary, 802, III:829–831
renal. *See* Renal abscess
retroperitoneal, 1676
in spleen, 1491–1492, III:931–932
subphrenic, III:926–927
thoracic, III:829–836
Absence
of cisterna chyli, 1898, 1899
of inferior vena cava, 898, 900, 904–908, 947, 949
of innominate vein, 899, 900, 908
of kidney, 1222
of left main coronary artery, 564–565, 726–727, 751–752
of pulmonary valve, 828–829
of renal veins, 1313–1315, 1316
Absolute ethanol
in arteriovenous malformations, III:1013, III:1015
in varicocele percutaneous embolization, III:696
in venous malformations of extremities, III:1024–1026, III:1027
Acalculous cholecystitis, percutaneous cholecystostomy in, III:485
ACAS (Asymptomatic Carotid Artery Surgery), III:340
Accessory left gastric artery, 1463
Accessory renal arteries, 1217–1221, 1224
hydronephrosis and, 1210, 1213–1215
normal arteriography of, 1245–1246, 1258, 1263
right lower pole, 1089
Accessory spleen, 1405, 1471
Accordion catheter in percutaneous nephrostomy, III:566

Accustick dilator
in pelvic percutaneous abscess drainage, III:952
in percutaneous cholecystomy, III:484
ACE (angiotensin-converting enzyme) inhibitors. *See* Angiotensin-converting enzyme (ACE) inhibitors
Acetaminophen
idiosyncratic reactions to urokinase and, III:155
in pleurisy, III:852
before thrombolytic therapy, 1043
Acetyl salicylic acid before pediatric angioplasty, III:911
Acetylcholine (ACh), 59
in erection evaluation, III:708, III:709
glucagon and, 61–62
metabolism of, 49
in pancreatic angiography, 1392
ACh. *See* Acetylcholine (ACh)
Acidosis, metabolic, prevention of, 39, 45
ACOM (anterior communicating artery), 314, 315
Acquired pulmonary abnormalities, 799–819
aortic arch aneurysm in, 818
atelectasis in, 816–818
Behçet disease in, 819
embolism in, 805–810, 811, 812
emphysema in, 801, 802, 803
heart disease in, 799–801
heart failure in, 818–819
hypertension in, 800, 801
hypervascularity in, 786, 815–816
hypovascularity in, 786, 816
intrathoracic tumors in, 810–813, 814, 815
kyphoscoliosis in, 818–819
lung cancer in, 810–813, 814, 815
obliterative pulmonary diseases in, 801–803, 804–806
pneumothorax in, 816–818
primary hypertension in, 813–815
Rasmussen aneurysms in, 819
secondary pulmonary hypertension in, 815
Takayasu arteritis in, 819
Acquisition frame rates, 135
ACR (American College of Radiology) standards, 1024, 1025
ACR-NEMA (American College of Radiology and National Electrical Manufacturers Association), digital angiography and, 148
Acrylic adhesives in arteriovenous malformations, III:1015–1016
of extremities, III:1020
ACT. *See* Activated clotting time (ACT)
ACTH. *See* Adrenocorticotropic hormone (ACTH)
Actinomycin-D, III:1033
Activase. *See* Alteplase
Activated clotting time (ACT), III:126
after infrapopliteal revascularization, III:286, III:290
in carotid angioplasty, III:342
in coronary angioplasty, III:368
in pulse-spray thrombolysis, III:126, III:732

Activated partial thromboplastin time (aPTT)
in intraarterial chemotherapy, III:1034
in pulse-spray thrombolysis, III:126
Acute intraarterial thrombolytic therapy in central nervous system, III:745–751, III:752, III:753
Acute Physiology and Chronic Health Evaluation (APACHE), III:536
Acute tubular necrosis (ATN) from thrombolysis complications, III:250
Adamkiewicz, artery of, 361, 363
Adams-DeWeese clips, III:983
ADC (analog-to-digital conversion), 142–143
Addison disease, 1378–1379
Adenine nucleotides, 24
Adenocarcinoma
of adrenal glands, 1359
of colon. *See* Colon, adenocarcinoma of
of lung, 814
of pancreas, III:187–188
renal, 1137. *See also* Renal cell carcinoma
of small bowel, 1577–1578
Adenoma
adrenal
aldosteronism in, 1361
angiography in, 1358, 1359, 1373–1374, 1375
in Cushing syndrome, 1364, 1367
of colon, villous, 1604
hepatic, 1443–1445
mediastinal. *See* Mediastinal adenomas
pancreatic
microcystic, 1405
occult, 1403
parathyroid. *See* Parathyroid adenomas
renal, 1161–1163, III:190
thyroid, 233, color plate 12
Adenomyosarcoma of kidney, 1132. *See also* Wilms tumor
Adenopathy, paraaortic, 962
Adenosine, III:216
Adenoviral vectors for genes, III:16, III:17
Adhesions
pelvic, III:397, III:399
superior mesenteric angiography in, 1579
Adhesives
acrylic. *See* Acrylic adhesives in arteriovenous malformations
in arteriovenous malformations, III:1015–1016
of extremities, III:1020
calibrated leak balloon with, III:65
in cerebral arteriovenous malformations, III:778
Admission chest film in blunt trauma, 524
Adrenal arteries
inferior, 1352, 1353, 1354
collateral circulation in renal ischemia and, 1277, 1278, 1283
middle, 1352, 1353
in renal angiography, 1124
superior, 1352, 1353
Adrenal glands, 1352–1382
in Addison disease, 1378–1379
adenoma of
aldosteronism in, 1361
angiography in, 1358, 1359, 1373–1374, 1375
in Cushing syndrome, 1364, 1367

in adrenogenital syndromes, 1368–1369
in aldosteronism, 1359–1364
anatomy of, 1352–1353
angiographic techniques for, 1353–1356, 1357, 1358
  arteriography in, 1353–1354
  complications of, 1356
  normal angiogram and, 1356, 1357, 1358
  venous sampling in, 1355
arteries of. *See* Adrenal arteries
arteriographic appearance of, versus phrenic artery extravasation, III:393, III:394
biopsy of, III:189–190
carcinomas of, 1373, 1374
  cortical, 1368, 1376–1378
  in Cushing syndrome, 1368
  magnetic resonance imaging in, 1359
  metastatic, from lung cancer, 1673, 1674
central veins of, 1352–1353
computerized tomography of, 1357–1358
  in bilateral masses, 1362–1364
  in Cushing syndrome, 1364–1368
cysts of, 1375–1376, 1377
  adrenal angiography in, 1375–1376, 1377
hemorrhages in, 1379–1380
hyperplasia of
  in adrenogenital syndromes, 1368–1369
  in Cushing syndrome, 1364, 1366
infectious processes of, 1379
in localization of adrenal remnants, 1376
magnification angiography of, 186
in neuroblastomas and ganglioneuromas, 1376, 1378
nonfunctioning tumors of, 1359, 1373–1374, 1375
normal, 1356, 1357, 1358
pheochromocytomas of, 1369–1373
  complications of angiography and, 1356
scintigraphy of, 1356–1357, 1364
  in adrenogenital syndromes, 1368–1369
sympathicoblastoma of, 1936
transcatheter ablation of, 1380
tumors of, renal carcinoma versus, 1302
ultrasonography of, 1359
venography of, 1354–1355
  normal, 1358
  in pheochromocytomas, 1373
Adrenal remnants, localization of, 1376
Adrenal veins, 1292, 1295, 1296, 1298, 1354–1355
  for inferior vena cava collateral circulation, 957
Adrenergic blockers
  in pancreatic angiography, 1394
  in pheochromocytoma, 1356, 1372, 1373
Adrenergic receptors
  catecholamines and, 52
  vascular response to, 51
Adrenergic stimulators in pancreatic angiography, 1394
Adrenocorticotropic hormone (ACTH)
  in Cushing syndrome, 1364

inferior petrosal venous sampling for, 253
Adrenogenital syndromes, 1368–1369
Adson maneuver, 998, 1005, 1007
Adult respiratory distress syndrome (ARDS), III:250
Aethoxysklerol, III:696
Afferent arteries in renal angiography, 1118
Agenesis of kidney, 1222
  renal venography in, 1313–1315, 1316
Agfa-Gevaert cine films, 107
Agfa-Gevaert film processor, 107
Agitation, cine film processing and, 109
AICAs (anterior inferior cerebellar arteries), 278
AIDS-related cholangiopathy, III:470
Air embolism, 1035
  as lung biopsy complication, III:185
  in pulmonary arteriovenous malformation embolotherapy, III:850–851
  venous access catheters and, III:979
Air gap between film and object of study in magnification angiography, 177, 178
Airway
  in emergency treatment, 36, 38–39, 47–48
  esophageal, 38
  obstruction of upper, 36
Akinesia, left ventricular, 561, 640
Alagille syndrome, 831
ALARA (as low as reasonably achievable) standards, 137
Albeatici S, 1497, 1527
Albuterol, 30, III:216, III:217
Alcohol. *See also* Ethanol embolization
  in celiac ganglion block, III:201
  in pediatric embolization, III:906, III:907–908
  in renal cyst sclerosis, III:663, III:665
Aldosterone, hypertension and, 1244
Aldosterone antagonists, 1306
Aldosteronism, 1359–1364
Aldosteronoma, 1361–1364
Algorithm
  for bladder outflow obstruction diagnosis, III:627
  data compression, on-line digital recording and, 148
  diagnostic
    for peripheral vascular disease, 1834
    in traumatic thoracic aorta aneurysms, 483
  Lossy compression, 148
  ray-tracing, 199
Aliasing, 191
  in Doppler imaging, 209–210, color plates 1 and 2
Alignment of x-ray beam with intensifiers, 127
Alkaloids, ergot, 55–56
Alkylating agents, III:81
Allen maneuver, 998–999
Allergic reaction
  after thrombolytic therapy, 1042
  to contrast media. *See* Contrast media, allergic reaction to
  history of, III:206
  to methylparaben, III:214
  preintervention assessment and, III:209

Allografts
  liver. *See* Liver, transplantation of
  renal. *See* Renal transplantation
Almen T, 15–20
Alpha-adrenergic blockers
  in autonomic hyperreflexia, 1036
  in benign prostatic hyperplasia, III:626–627
  in pancreatic angiography, 1394
  in pheochromocytoma, 1356, 1372, 1373
Alpha-adrenergic receptors
  catecholamines and, 52–53
  dopamine and, 61
  imidazoline derivatives and, 52
  vascular response to, 51
Alpha$_2$-antiplasmin, III:123
  plasmin neutralization by, III:121
Alpha$_2$-macroglobulin, III:123
5-Alpha-reductase inhibitor, III:627, III:628
Alport syndrome, 1226, 1227
Alprostadil, 60
Alteplase, III:121. *See also* Tissue-type plasminogen activator (tPA)
ALU (arithmetic logic unit), 144
Alveolar edema in pulmonary venous hypertension, 863–864
Alveolar pressure, 854–855
Alwens W, 4
Ambos classification of dissecting aortic aneurysms, 495
Amebic hepatic abscesses, III:930–931
American Association for the Surgery of Trauma Organ Injury Scaling Committee, III:422, III:428
American College of Radiology (ACR), standards for diagnostic arteriography of, 1024, 1025
American College of Radiology and National Electrical Manufacturers Association (ACR-NEMA), digital angiography and, 148
American Urological Association (AUA)
  Guidelines Panel Review of, III:595
  symptom score evaluation of, III:626
Ameuille P, 7
Amicar. *See* Aminocaproic acid (ECAP)
Aminocaproic acid (ECAP), 1651, III:403, III:826
Aminoglycosides, III:562–563
Aminophylline, 48, III:216, III:217
Amiodarone, 1031
Amipaque. *See* Metrizamide
Amobarbital, III:825
Ampicillin
  interventional radiology and, III:209
  percutaneous nephrostomy and, III:563
  prostatic urethroplasty and, III:628
Amplatz K, 556
Amplatz catheters, 556–558
  in coronary artery bypass grafts, 760, 761
Amplatz coil positioner, III:60, III:61
Amplatz filter, magnetic resonance venography and, 1852
Amplatz guidewire in percutaneous gastrostomy, III:549, III:551
Amplatz injector, 171, 172
Amplatz large-field film changer, 82

Amplatz needle in bladder procedures, III: 614, III:618–619
Amplatz see-through film changers, 77–78, 79, 80
Amplatz snare, complications with, 1044
Amplatz stainless steel spiders, III:61
Amplatz technique in coronary arteriography, 557, 570
Amplatz vena cava filters, III:987, III:994
Amplifiers for electrocardiography, 118
Ampullaceous cisterna chyli, 1885, 1888
Ampullaceous dilation of terminal portion of thoracic duct, 1896
Ampullaceous trunks of thoracic duct, 1888, 1889
Amputation, limb, 246
Amyloidosis, 1491
Amytal in provocative tests, III:776, III: 777
Analog-to-digital conversion (ADC), 142–143
Analysis console for vascular intervention angiography, 135
Anaphylaxis, III:217
    in allergic reaction to lymphangiography contrast media, 1868
    in coronary arteriography complications, 579
    in systemic reactions to contrast agents, 29, 49, 1024–1025
Anaplastic small-cell lung cancer, III:177
Anastomoses
    Blalock-Taussig. *See* Blalock-Taussig procedure
    central artery, 1067
    in coarctation of aorta repair, 453, 454, 455
    in coronary artery bypass grafts, 757, 758, 759
        distal, 757, 759, 763
        proximal, 762
    in coronary artery stenosis, angiographic pitfalls and, 723
    in Crohn disease surgery, leakage of, III: 942–943
    dialysis shunt, complications of
        arterial, 1768–1770, 1771
        venous, 1773, 1774
    extremity angiography in evaluation of, 1690
    gastric, ulcers in, III:405, III:411
    interarterial coronary, 711–712, 714–718
    Kugel's, 714–715
    in liver allograft
        aneurysms and pseudoaneurysm of, III:512–513
        bile leakage from, III:521, III:522
        preparation of, III:509–510
    lymphaticovenous, 1909, 1931
    pseudoaneurysms of, after aneurysm repair, 1095, 1098
    in renal artery stenosis, 1284–1287
    in renal transplantation, 1325–1331
        renal artery stenosis and, 1339–1341
    satellite circulation for, 701
    subclavian pulmonary artery, 549–551
        thoracic aortography for evaluation of, 549–551
    tubocornual, in fallopian tube obstruction, III:672

ureteroenteral, strictures in continent diversions from, III:649, III:652–653
ureteroileal, strictures from, III:649, III: 650–652
urinary tract, dehiscent
    percutaneous nephrostomy in, III:563
    ureteroneocystostomy site, III:583–584
venous, for stenoses in dialysis fistula, III:733–734, III:736
Anatomy
    of abdominal aorta, 1015, 1017–1023
    of bones, joints, and soft tissues in extremities, 1779–1780
    of bronchial arteries, III:820–822
    of coronary arteries. *See* Coronary arteries
    of femoral arteries, 1697–1703
    of genitourinary system in varicocele, III:678–686, III:687
    of hepatic arteries, 1434–1436
    in hepatobiliary obstruction from malignancy, III:473–476
    in inferior mesenteric angiography, 1588–1590
    of inferior vena cava, abnormal, 941–947
    of intracranial, extraaxial lesions, III: 791–795, III:799–800, III:809–812
    of left ventricle, ischemic heart disease and, 120
    of lymphatics and lymph nodes, 1871–1890. *See also* Lymphatics
    in pancreatic angiography, 1383–1389, 1390, 1391
    of pancreatic veins, 1426–1427, 1428
    in patent ductus arteriosus, 416–417
    of penile artery, III:711
    in peripheral vascular magnetic resonance angiography, 1826–1828
    of portal vein, 1422–1424, 1425
    pulmonary
        in arteriovenous malformations, III: 838–840, III:841–845
        developmental anomalies and, 824
        in partial anomalous pulmonary venous connection, 881–883
        physiology and microstructure in, 850, 851, 852
        in anomalous pulmonary venous connection, 871–873
    renal
        in angiography, 1113–1125. *See also* Renal angiography, anatomy in
        interventional radiology and, III:892
        percutaneous stone removal and, III: 597, III:598
    of splenic artery, 1017, 1020, 1457–1458
    splenoportography, 1498, 1501–1506, 1507, 1514
        changes in, 1512–1526
        cirrhosis of liver and, 1512–1521
        extrahepatic vascular, 1498, 1501–1504, 1505–1506
        intrahepatic vascular, 1504, 1506, 1507, 1514
        in malignant tumors, 1522–1524, 1525–1526

in superior mesenteric angiography, 1549–1555
    arterial, 1549–1552, 1553–1555
    venous, 1552–1555
of superior vena cava, 915–916
of thoracic outlet, 995–996, 1883–1889, 1891–1892
    radiologic, 1892–1897
Ancillary equipment, ceiling suspension of, 105
Anderson RK, 892
Anectine. *See* Succinylcholine chloride
Anemia
    pulmonary hypervascularity in, 815–816
    splenomegaly in, 1467
Anesthesia
    in extracorporeal shock wave lithotripsy complications, III:608
    in interventional radiology for urethral lesions, III:618
    local. *See* Local anesthesia
    in pediatric interventional angiography, III:903
    in percutaneous pelvic abscess drainage, III:947
    for thoracic aortography, 391–392
    hazards and, 398
Aneurysm
    aortic
        abdominal, 1073–1100. *See also* Abdominal aorta aneurysms
        after coarctation of aorta therapy, 455–456, 459
        arch, 818
        dissecting, 493–520. *See also* Dissecting aneurysms, of aorta
        ductus diverticulum, III:361
        of intrathoracic branches, 489
        in superior vena cava obstruction, 916, 923, 924
        thoracic. *See* Thoracic aortic aneurysms
    aortic sinus, ruptured, 396
    arteriovenous, congenital, 1731–1733
    of carotid-cavernous artery, fistulas in, III:802
    of celiac artery, 1631
    of central nervous system. *See* Cerebral aneurysm
    cerebral. *See* Cerebral aneurysm
    classification of, 467, 468
    in coronary disease, 645, 653
    defined, 467
    in dialysis shunt complications, 1771, 1772, 1773
    of ductus arteriosus, 420–421
    false. *See* False aneurysms
    femoral arteriography in, 1723–1726
    of hepatic artery anastomosis in liver allograft, III:512–513
    historical notes on study of, 8, 10
    inferior mesenteric angiography in, 1601, 1602
    intracranial. *See also* Cerebral aneurysm
        complications of embolization in, 1032
        rupture of, III:753–757, III:758. *See also* Cerebral aneurysm
    of jejunal artery, 1414
    lymphatic, of thoracic duct, 1901

mechanical embolic agents for, III:72–74
of middle meningeal artery, 352
peripheral artery
   in extremities, 1709–1711
   pulmonary, 843, 845
   racemose, 1731–1733
   Rasmussen, 819
renal artery
   after renal transplantation, 1344–1346, 1347, 1348
   dissecting, 1251–1253, 1270–1271
   hypertension and, 1251–1253, 1264–1266, 1270–1271
   with medial fibroplasia, 1254, 1255
   sonography of, 216, color plate 7
   in spinal dural arteriovenous fistulas of type II and III, 379, 382
   splenic artery, 1474–1475, 1476, 1477
   in pancreatitis, 1412, 1413, 1414
   splenoportography and, 1500
of subclavian artery in thoracic outlet syndrome, 996, 997
superior mesenteric vessels and, 1570–1571, 1572
   chronic intestinal ischemia and, 1631
thoracic aortic. *See* Thoracic aortic aneurysms
ventricular, as indication for angiography, 637
Aneurysmal bone cysts, 1797–1798
   embolization in, III:905
Angina. *See also* Angina pectoris
   abdominal, 1631–1634
   intestinal, 1631–1634
      inferior mesenteric arteriography in, 1600
Angina pectoris
   balloon angioplasty in, III:373
      restenosis after, III:8, III:14
   coronary arteriography in, 636–638, 689–690
      morphology and, 661
      normal, 662
      Prinzmetal variant angina and, 636, 638, 685–686, 732–733
   incapacitating, as indication for coronary arteriography, 636
   mild
      but with likelihood of three-vessel or left main disease, 636
      in young adults or patient with poor family history, 638
      with normal resting and exercise electrocardiogram, 662
   Prinzmetal variant, 636, 638, 685–686, 732–733
   vasospasm and, 686, 687, 732–733
   unstable, coronary arteriography and, 636, 661
Angiocardiography. *See also* Coronary arteriography
   in coarctation of aorta, 435, 436, 444–447, 448, 449
   in pseudocoarctation of aorta, 553
   in thoracic aortography, 393
   truncus arteriosus of, 549
Angio–Conray 80%, 170
Angiodysplasia. *See also* Vascular ectasia
   arteriography in, III:415–417, III:418
   carotid-cavernous fistulas in, III:802

of cecum and ascending colon, 184, III:414–417, III:418
magnification angiography of, 184
mesenteric angiography in
   inferior, 1608–1611
   superior, 1550–1551, 1564–1565, 1571–1573
pancreatic, 1406
Angiofibroma
   juvenile, 339–340
   nasopharyngeal, III:905
Angiography. *See also* Arteriography; Venography
   of abdomen and pelvis. *See* Abdomen and pelvis
   adrenal, 1352–1382. *See also* Adrenal glands
   after renal transplantation. *See* Renal transplantation, angiography in
   aortography in. *See* Aortography
   in arteriovenous malformations, III:1007, III:1009, III:1010
   of bones, 1779–1821. *See also* Bone, angiography of
   in bronchial artery embolization, III:820–III:824
   in carotid-cavernous fistulas, III:803–807
   central nervous system. *See* Central nervous system
   of cerebral plexiform nidus aneurysms, III:776, III:777
   in cerebral vessel vasospasm, III:755
   complications of. *See* Complications
   coronary. *See* Coronary arteriography
   for dialysis fistula blood flow analysis, III:739
   drugs in, 49–65. *See also* Pharmacoangiography
   in dural arteriovenous malformations, III:801
   equipment for. *See* Equipment, angiographic
   of extremities. *See* Extremities
   history of, 3–12
   joints in. *See* Joints
   in liver transplantation complications, III:509
   lymphatic system in, 1864–1952. *See also* Lymphangiography
   magnetic resonance. *See* Magnetic resonance imaging (MRI)
   magnification. *See* Magnification angiography
   mesenteric, 1549–1614
      bradykinin and, 62
      inferior, 1587–1614. *See also* Inferior mesenteric angiography
      superior, 1549–1586. *See also* Superior mesenteric angiography
   pancreatic, 1383–1548. *See also* Pancreatic angiography
   of parathyroid. *See* Parathyroid angiography
   pediatric interventional, III:901–921. *See also* Pediatrics, interventional angiography in
   in pelvic fractures, III:870–877, III:878
   in preinterventional assessment, III:206
   in pulmonary arteriovenous malformations, III:838, III:839–845

renal. *See* Renal angiography
retroperitoneal, 1669–1677
in sarcomas, III:1031
soft tissue in. *See* Soft tissue
before subclavian, innominate, and vertebral artery angioplasty, III:761
of superior vena cava. *See* Superior vena cava (SVC)
vertebral, 933
Angiography trays, prepackaged, 242
Angioma
   cavernous, 1731
      spinal angiography in, 385
   of cecum, 1550–1551
   cutaneous, spinal dural arteriovenous fistulas of type II and III and, 377
   metameric, 369
   pancreatic, 1404, 1406
      islet-cell tumors versus, 1403, 1404
   superior mesenteric angiography in, 1550–1551, 1564–1565, 1570–1573
Angiomyolipoma, renal, 1163–1165
Angioneurotic edema, III:217
Angiopeptin, III:15
Angioplasty. *See also* Percutaneous transluminal angioplasty (PTA)
   balloon. *See* Balloon angioplasty
   of brachiocephalic vessels
      for cerebral ischemia, III:757–763
      extracranial. *See* Extracranial brachiocephalic arterioplasty
   of carotid arteries, III:760–761
   in chronic mesenteric ischemia, 1633–1634
   complications of, 1039–1041, III:254–256
   coronary arteriography and, 684
   extracranial brachiocephalic. *See* Extracranial brachiocephalic arterioplasty
   extremity angiography and, 1682, 1684, 1685, 1689, 1690
   femoral arteriography after, 1713, 1719, 1721, 1723, 1724
      projections for, 1709
   in femoropopliteal revascularization. *See* Femoropopliteal revascularization
   of innominate artery, III:761–763
   in intracranial post-subarachnoid hemorrhage vasospasm, III:753–757, III:758
   laser. *See* Laser angioplasty
   monitoring requirements for, III:367–368
   of nonorifice cervical vertebral stenoses, III:350
   pediatric, III:910–916, III:917
      complications of, III:916
      indications for, III:911–916, III:917
   percutaneous transluminal. *See* Percutaneous transluminal angioplasty (PTA)
   pseudoaneurysms after, 1693, 1694
   of subclavian artery, III:761–763
   tibial, III:284–293
   transluminal. *See* Percutaneous transluminal angioplasty (PTA)
   vascular sonography after, 226–227, 228, color plates 1 and 2
   of vertebral artery in occlusive disease, III:761–763

Angiosarcoma
    of extremities, 1806
    hepatic, 1450
Angioscopy, percutaneous, of inferior vena
        cava, 940–941
Angioserograph, extra–large-field
Angiostat, III:53
Angio-table (AOT) cut film changer, 73
Angiotensin, 54–55
    action of, 52
    in endometrial carcinoma, III:82
    in renal angiography, 1104, 1110
    in renin-angiotensin system, 1244
Angiotensin I, 54–55
Angiotensin II, 51, 54–55
Angiotensin amide, 55
Angiotensin-converting enzyme (ACE)
        inhibitors, 51, 1339
    hypertension during therapy with, III:
        295, III:296
    before renal angioplasty, III:295, III:
        296, III:305
    in restenosis after balloon angioplasty,
        III:15
Angiovist. *See* Sodium diatrizoate
Angle of radiographic tube, 95–96
Angle correction in Doppler imaging,
        208–209
Angled catheter in transaxillary procedures,
        1016
Angular artery, 271
Anisoylated plasminogen streptokinase com-
        plex (APSAC), III:122, III:127
Ankle, cross section above, 1827
Ankle-brachial index (ABI), 579
    in extremity trauma, III:858
    revascularization and
        femoropopliteal, III:265–270, III:
            275–276
        infrapopliteal, III:284
Anode angle of radiographic tube, 96
Anodica spot-film cameras, 101
Anomalies and malformations. *See also* Con-
        genital abnormalities
    aortic arch, 396, 547–548
    arteriovenous. *See* Arteriovenous malfor-
        mations (AVMs)
    of coronary arteries, 740–749
    inferior mesenteric arteriography in,
        1609
    of inferior vena cava
        abnormal anatomy and, 943–947,
            948
        types of, 945–947
    internal iliac vein, 1849
    intracranial, complications of emboliza-
        tion in, 1032
    magnification angiography in, 180, 181
    of portal vein, 1422, 1425
    pulmonary
        developmental, 822–848. *See also* Pul-
            monary developmental anomalies
        lung sequestration and, 549, 550
        venous. *See* Anomalous pulmonary
            venous connection
    renal, 1217–1229. *See also* Renal anoma-
        lies and malformations
    of thoracic duct, 1898, 1899, 1901
Anomalous origin
    of coronary arteries, 833, 837, 838
        from pulmonary artery, 799, 800

    of hepatic arteries, 1543–1544
    of pulmonary arteries, 832–833,
        836
Anomalous pulmonary venous connection,
        868–890
    partial, 879–887
        anatomy of, 881–883
        angiography of, 882, 886–887
        clinical aspects of, 884
        embryology of, 881, 882
        physiology of, 883–884
        plain films of, 883, 884–886
    total, 868–879, 880, 881
        anatomy in, 871–873
        angiography in, 877–881
        cardiac, 871–873
        cardiac catheterization in, 878
        clinical aspects of, 873–874
        embryology of, 868–871
        infracardiac, 873
        left-sided, 871
        mixed, 873
        nonobstructed, 875
        obstructed, 874–875
        physiology of, 873
        plain films of, 874–878
        prominent venous structures in, 872,
            875–878
        right-sided, 871
        supracardiac, 871
Antecubital vein
    pulmonary arteriography approach and,
        771
    pulse-spray pharmacomechanical throm-
        bolysis for, III:150
    retrograde catheterization of, 933
Antegrade approach
    for femoral arteriography, 1705
    in femoropopliteal revascularization, III:
        263–264
    in nephrotomography for urinomas, III:
        668, III:669
    in percutaneous catheterization of ure-
        teroileal anastomotic strictures, III:
        650
    for pyelography in hydronephrosis,
        1202, 1203
    in ureteral stenting, III:574–576
    for urography in hydronephrosis, 1210–
        1211
Anthracyclines, III:81
Anthron catheters, III:1034
Antiandrogens in prostatic hyperplasia, III:
        627–628
Antianginal drugs, 60
Antibiotics
    in abdominal abscesses, III:925
    in breast carcinoma, III:82
    in cholecystotomy, III:483
    in nephrostomy, III:562–563, III:572
    before partial splenic ablation, 1492
    in pelvic abscess drainage, III:947
    preintervention assessment and, III:208–
        209
    prostatic biopsy and, III:636
    prostatic urethroplasty and, III:628
    in regional chemotherapy, III:81
    in seminal vesicle interventions, III:640
    in transjugular intrahepatic portosystemic
        shunt, III:532
Anticipation time, 72

Anticoagulation. *See also* Heparin
    contraindications to, vena cava filters
        and, III:986
    detachable balloons in embolization and,
        III:68
    infrapopliteal revascularization and, III:
        290
    intraaxial embolotherapy for central ner-
        vous system and, III:765–766
    in superior vena cava obstruction treat-
        ment, 927
    thrombolysis in aortoiliac disease and,
        III:234
Antidiuretic hormone, 55. *See also* Vaso-
        pressin
Antiemetics, III:214
Antihistamines
    in contrast media reactions, 30, 1868
    idiosyncratic reactions to urokinase and,
        III:155
    for interventional radiology procedures,
        III:212, III:213
    thrombolytic therapy and, 1043
Antihypertensives
    interventional radiology in, III:214–215
    renal angioplasty and, III:305–306
    renin determination and, 1306, 1308
    reserpine as, 59
Antimalarials, 49
Antimetabolites, III:80–81
Antineoplastic agents
    in regional chemotherapy, III:80–84
    in restenosis after balloon angioplasty,
        III:15
Antiplatelet medications, 927
    after infrapopliteal revascularization, III:
        290
    in pulse-spray thrombolysis, III:127, III:
        128, III:137
    in restenosis after balloon angioplasty,
        III:15
    revascularization preparation and, III:
        230
    in thrombolysis action, III:126, III:127.
        See also Thrombolysis
    uses of, III:137
Antispasmodics, infrapopliteal revasculariza-
        tion and, III:290
Antithrombin agents, 1623, III:137. *See
        also* Thrombolysis
Aorta
    abdominal. *See* Abdominal aorta
    aneurysm of. *See* Aneurysm, aortic
    and aortic branches, revascularization of,
        III:223–385
        for chronic mesenteric ischemia, III:
            326–338. *See also* Mesenteric is-
            chemia
        coronary angioplasty in, III:366–385.
            See also Coronary angioplasty
        endovascular stent-grafts for thoracic
            aortic aneurysms in. *See* Thoracic
            aortic aneurysms, stent-grafts for
        extracranial brachiocephalic arte-
            rioplasty in, III:339–355. *See also*
            Extracranial brachiocephalic arte-
            rioplasty
        femoropopliteal, III:262–283. *See also*
            Femoropopliteal revascularization
        infrapopliteal revascularization in, III:
            284–293

percutaneous aortoiliac intervention in. *See* Percutaneous aortoiliac intervention
renal angioplasty in. *See* Renal angioplasty
stent-grafts for thoracic aortic aneurysms in, III:356–365
aorticopulmonary window and, 464–466, 796, 798
ascending, 406–408
  in aortic arch anomalies, 547
  blunt trauma to, 527
  dilatation of, in coarctation of aorta, 447, 449
  dimensions of, 540
  dissection of, in coronary arteriography complications, 578
  in infant, 403
atherectomy for, catheter in, III:49
blunt trauma to, 521–539. *See also* Blunt trauma, to aorta and brachiocephalic arteries
Carrel patch of, 1325, 1326
coarctation of, 434–463
  abdominal, III:913
  angiocardiography and aortography in, 435, 436, 444–447, 448, 449
  aorticopulmonary window and, 464, 796, 798
  arch development and, 435–437
  atresia of aortic arch and, 446, 447
  chest x-ray in, 441, 442, 443
  clinical presentation of, 438–439, 440, 441
  collateral circulation and, 437–438, 447, 449, 450
  in complete aortic occlusion, 1061
  complications of, 440
  definition of, 434
  dissecting aortic aneurysms and, 493
  echocardiography in, 441–444
  epidemiology of, 435
  incidence of, 434
  in infant, 411, 434, 435
  investigation methods for, 441–452
  lesions associated with, 435
  magnetic resonance imaging in, 447–452
  normal narrowing of isthmus versus, 402, 404, 410, 411, 445
  in older child or adult, 434
  percutaneous transluminal angioplasty in, 457–460
  surgical treatment of, 452–455
  thoracic, 396, 435
  variants of, 437
collateral circulation in renal ischemia and, 1277, 1283
coronary artery bypass graft origin from, 756, 757
descending, 408
  in aortic arch anomalies, 547, 548
  blunt trauma to, 527–528
  in infant, 403–404
diameter of, 412
diffuse intimal thickening of, 412
dissecting aneurysms of, 493–520. *See also* Dissecting aneurysms, of aorta
ductus arteriosus and, 417
in inferior vena cava obstruction, 959, 961, 962

insufficiency of, 397, 543–546, 547
isthmus of
  coarctation of aorta and, 445, 450, 451
  embryology of, 436
  hourglass configuration of, 447
  in infant, 403, 410
  normal narrowing of, 402, 404, 410, 411, 445
  pathologic narrowing of, 445, 447, 450, 451
  transection of, in blunt trauma to aorta and brachiocephalic arteries, 523, 528, 529, 530
kinking of, 553
left-to-right shunts from, into pulmonary arteries, 796
lymph nodes in region of, 1879–1881
normal vascular sonography flow patterns in, 213–214
occlusion and stenosis of. *See* Aortic stenosis
paired lateral branches of, 1018, 1021
in persistent circumaortic venous ring, 947, 950
postoperative abdominal arteriography of, 1069, 1070
pseudocoarctation of, 437, 553
  thoracic aortography in, 396
recoarctation of, 449, 454, 455
  after percutaneous transluminal angioplasty, 459
renal artery directly from, 1217, 1219, 1220
in single coronary artery anomalies, 748
thoracic
  aneurysms of, 467–492. *See also* Thoracic aortic aneurysms
  coarctation of, 396, 435
  tortuosity of, in arteriosclerotic disease, 1058, 1059
  trauma to, thoracic aortography in, 397
  wall of, 412, 467
Aortic aneurysm. *See* Aneurysm, aortic
Aortic arch
  aneurysm of, 818
  anomalies of, 547–548
    aortography in, 249, 396, 547–548
  blunt trauma to, 527
  in child and adult, 408
  coarctation of aorta and
    atresia in, 446, 447
    deformities in, 441, 443
    development in, 435–437
    in infant, 437, 443, 445, 446
    notching and, 441, 443
  double, 548
    Edwards' hypothetical, 415, 416
  in infant, 403, 410, 437, 443, 445, 446
  interrupted, aorticopulmonary window and, 464
  left, 548
  thoracic aortography of
    in anomalies, 396
    technique for, 249
  transverse, hypoplasia of, 437, 443, 445, 446
Aortic arch syndrome, 397
Aortic branches, revascularization of. *See* Aorta, and aortic branches, revascularization of

Aortic bulb
  in child and adult, 406, 409
  in infant, 401
  normal anatomy of, 591, 593
Aortic catheterization catheter for superselective catheterization, 156–158
Aortic diverticulum, retroesophageal, 548
Aortic grafts, 549
Aortic hump sign, 499, 500, 501, 503
Aortic lymph nodes and vessels, 1931
  testicular tumor malignant metastatic spread to, 1930, 1935
Aortic patch in donor liver preparation, III:509
Aortic plexus of sympathetic nervous system in inferior vena cava obstruction, 958
Aortic ring, 503
Aortic root
  anatomy of, 591–603
  in child and adult, 406
  in infant, 401
Aortic septal defect, 464–466
  thoracic aortography in, 396
Aortic silhouette in infant, 401–404, 405
Aortic sinuses
  in infant, 401
  ruptured aneurysm of, 396
Aortic spindle
  described, 410
  ductus diverticulum versus, 410–411
Aortic stenosis, 397, 540–545
  in brachiocephalic branch, 543, 552, 553
  cardiac catheterization in, 543
  congenital, 540
  dissecting aortic aneurysms and, 493
  gadolinium-enhanced 3D-TF MR angiography in, 1831
  in mesenteric branch, 214, 229–230
  sonography of, 229
    mesenteric branch in, 214, 229–230
  subvalvular, 540–543
  supravalvular, 542, 544–545
    with congenital coronary atresia, 744–745
Aortic valves
  abnormalities of, with supravalvular lesions, 542
  bicuspid
    coarctation of aorta with, 434, 435, 447
    dissecting aortic aneurysms and, 493
  incompetence of, dissecting aortic aneurysms and, 503
  silent regurgitation in, 546
Aorticopulmonary (AP) window, 464–466
  developmental anomalies and, 829, 830
  pulmonary arteriography in, 796, 798
Aortitis, syphilitic, 486–487
Aortobifemoral grafts
  femoral arteriography after, 1719, 1721
  thrombolysis of, in pelvic intraarterial fibrinolytic therapy, 1640, 1641
Aortocaval fistula, 962
Aortoenteric fistula, 1069, 1070
  after aneurysms repair, 1095–1096
  after aortoiliac interventions, 1692–1693
Aortofemoral bypass, 1053, 1060, 1061

Aortography
  abdominal, 1013–1023. *See also* Abdominal aortography
  acetylcholine and, 59
  in aorticopulmonary window, 464–466
  in coarctation of aorta, 435, 436, 444–447, 448, 449
  in dissecting aortic aneurysms, 500, 503–509, 510–515
  in femoral arteriography, filming equipment for, 1706
  historical notes on, 6, 8, 9, 10
  intravenous, in dissecting aortic aneurysms, 500, 503
  lumbar, 1013–1100. *See also* Lumbar aortography
  in patent ductus arteriosus, 417, 424, 425, 426
  renal
    catheters for, 1102
    in restenosis after balloon angioplasty, III:11
  spinal angiography and, 367
  of thorax. *See* Thoracic aortography
Aortoiliac angioplasty. *See* Percutaneous aortoiliac intervention
Aortoiliac disease
  angiography of extremities after interventions for, 1681–1696
    aortoenteric fistulas and, 1692–1693
    arteriovenous fistulas and, 1693
    aspiration of paraprosthetic fluid and, 1694, 1695
    failure of prosthetic materials and, 1693–1695
    in graft thrombosis, 1682, 1684, 1685, 1689, 1690
    in immediate problems, 1689–1690
    infected grafts and, 1686, 1691–1692
    in late postoperative problems, 1690
    magnetic resonance imaging and, 1695
    paraprosthetic enteric fistulas and, 1692–1693
    progression of disease and, 1682, 1685, 1687–1689, 1690–1695
    pseudoaneurysms and, 1686, 1691–1694
    technique for, 1681–1689
  arteriosclerotic
    chronic thrombosis in, 1060–1061
    endarterectomy in, 1053
    occlusive, 1052, 1060
  percutaneous intervention in, III:225–261. *See also* Percutaneous aortoiliac intervention
  peripheral vascular magnetic resonance angiography in, 1831–1833
Aortoiliac steal syndromes, 1634
Aortoiliofemoral obstruction, chronic, 1066
AOT (angio-table) cut film changer, 73
AP (aorticopulmonary) window, 464–466
  developmental anomalies and, 829, 830
  pulmonary arteriography in, 796, 798
APACHE (Acute Physiology and Chronic Health Evaluation), III:536
Aperture of camera in video systems for digital angiography, 139–140
Apex of heart, epicardial collaterals at, 704, 707

Aplasia
  of coronary artery, 596, 598
  of kidney, 1222
  of left pulmonary artery, 799
  in lymphedema, 1907, 1908, 1909
APMC (anterior pontomesencephalic cerebellar) vein, 279, 280
Appendiceal arteries, 1020
Apron for radiation monitoring, 128
APSAC (Anisoylated plasminogen streptokinase complex), III:122, III:127
aPTT. *See* Activated partial thromboplastin time (aPTT)
Apudomas, III:451–452
Aramine. *See* Metaraminol
Arch, aortic. *See* Aortic arch
Archival storage in digital angiography, 148–149
Arcuate arteries in renal angiography, 1114, 1115, 1117, 1118, 1120
  for chronic glomerulonephritis, 1269
Arcuate veins, displacement of, 1317
ARDS (adult respiratory distress syndrome), III:250
Argatoban, III:126, III:137
Argon in laser systems, III:380, III:381
  in femoropopliteal angioplasty, III:280, III:281
Arithmetic logic unit (ALU), 144
Arm
  lymph nodes of, 1881–1882
  lymphangiography of, 1866
  normal ultrasonography flow patterns in, 212
Arritechno 35 camera, 100
Arrow International arterial blood containment device, 157
ARROW-Fischell Pullback Atherectomy Catheter, III:293
Arteria accessoria, 600
Arteria anastomotica auricularis magna, 710
Arteria intermedia, 589
Arteria magna in thoracic aortic aneurysms, 477
Arteria pancreatica magna, 1459, 1460, 1463
Arteriae coronariae, 586
Arterial blood containment device, 156–157
Arterial blood gases in pulmonary arteriovenous malformations, III:838
Arterial inflow stenoses in dialysis fistula, III:734–735
Arterial occlusion and stenosis
  iatrogenic
    from cerebral angiography, 246
    from coronary artery catheterization, 579
  vascular sonography in, 214–215, color plate 3
    Doppler gate location and, 207–208, 209
Arterial portography, 1527–1548
  abnormal, 1532–1541
    in extrahepatic obstruction, 1535, 1536, 1537
    in intrahepatic obstruction and collaterals, 1532–1535
    in patent but nonvisualized splenoportal axis, 1539–1541

  in prior splenectomy, 1535–1537
  in surgical shunts, 1537–1538, 1539
  catheters and catheterization in, 1529
  complications of, 1530
  computerized tomography during, 1541–1545
  contraindications to, 1530
  contrast and filming in, 1529
  delayed scanning in, 1545
  in hepatic malignancy, III:438
  indications for, 1531
  new methods in, 1545–1546
  normal, 1531–1532
  patient preparation for, 1528–1529
  pharmacoangiography in portal system in, 1530
  position and film position in, 1529–1530
  principles of, 1527–1528
  technique of, 1528–1530
Arterial puncture
  in coronary arteriography, 558–560
  double wall, 248
  single wall, 248
  for superselective catheterization, 156–158
Arterial ring of Vieussens, collaterals of, 703–704, 706–708
Arterial sheaths. *See* Sheaths
Arterial spasm. *See* Vasospasm
Arterial steals in dialysis shunt complications, 1776–1778
Arterial thrombosis. *See* Thrombosis
Arteries
  of Adamkiewicz, 361, 363
  of Bühler, 1458, 1459
  of conus medullaris, 361
  coronary. *See* Coronary arteries
  in gray scale imaging, 206
  ischemic time and repair of, 1728
  pancreatic, 1383–1389, 1390, 1391
  of Riolan, 1458, 1460
Arteriocaliceal fistula after transplant, 1346–1347
Arteriography. *See also* Angiography
  after infrapopliteal revascularization, III:286–289
  coronary. *See* Coronary arteriography
  in extremity trauma, III:857–868
    guidelines for conservative management versus, III:859–860
    history of, III:857
    indications for, III:857–859
    technique for, III:860–861
    transcatheter management and, III:861–867
  in gastrointestinal bleeding, III:389–421. *See also* Gastrointestinal system, arteriography in
  hepatic, 1433–1456. *See also* Hepatic arteriography
  penile, III:710–712, III:713–716
  in portography, 1527–1548. *See also* Arterial portography
  postoperative aortic, 1069, 1070
  renal. *See* Renal arteriography
  in renovascular hypertension diagnosis, III:112
  splenic. *See* Splenic arteriography
  in splenoportography, 1497–1526. *See also* Splenoportography

thyroid, superior, 983
transaxillary, complications of, 1031
transbrachial, complications of, 1030
venous malformations and, III:1023, III:1024, III:1026
Arteriolae rectae, 1118
Arteriolar nephrosclerosis, 1260–1261
Arterioplasty, extracranial brachiocephalic, III:339–355. *See also* Extracranial brachiocephalic arterioplasty
Arteriosclerosis. *See also* Atherosclerosis obliterans
    of abdominal aorta, 1052–1072
        aneurysms in, 1058, 1059, 1060, 1073
        angiographic signs of, 1053–1060
        aortoiliac occlusion and, 1063–1069
        chronic aortoiliac thrombosis in, 1060–1061
        collateral pathways in, 1056, 1060, 1061–1069
        complete aortic occlusion in, 1061, 1062–1063
        diffuse segmental vascular narrowing in, 1053–1054, 1055, 1056
        diffusely dilated vessels in, 1058, 1059
        dissecting aneurysms and, 493, 494
        eccentric changes in contrast column density in, 1056, 1057–1058
        filling defects in contrast column in, 1056, 1057
        irregular vascular contours in, 1054, 1056
        lumbar arteries in, 1064, 1067, 1068, 1069
        occlusions in, 1058–1060
        parietal collateral network in, 1063, 1065, 1067–1069
        plaque in, stenting and, III:99
        postoperative aortic arteriography in, 1069, 1070
        projections for variations in, 1057–1058
        systemic-systemic collateral network in, 1063, 1065, 1067–1069
        tortuous vessels in, 1058, 1059
        vessel wall calcification in, 1056, 1057
        visceral-systemic collateral network in, 1056, 1061, 1062–1063, 1066–1067
        in younger person, III:225–226
    brachiocephalic angioplasty and. *See* Extracranial brachiocephalic arterioplasty
    in cerebral vessels, 285–297
        aneurysms and, 320–321
        angiography technique in, 250
    in dialysis shunt complications, 1769
    ectatic, 1716
    in left coronary artery, 662–677, 682–683
    in mesenteric vessels, 1399, 1631–1632
        inferior mesenteric angiography in, 1593–1601, 1602
        with ischemia, III:326
    in pelvic arteries, 1637, 1638–1640
    plaque in. *See* Plaque
    progression of, extremity angiography in evaluation of, 1682, 1685, 1687–1689, 1690–1695

renal
    angioplasty results in, III:308–311, III:312. *See also* Renal angioplasty
    renovascular hypertension and, 1250, 1251, 1278, III:294
    semiselective renal angiography in, 1116, 1117
    in splanchnic arteries, 1399
        chronic intestinal ischemia and, 1631–1632
    in splenic artery, 1473–1474
    in subclavian artery, 1007
    in superior mesenteric artery obstruction, 1566–1567
    in thoracic aorta aneurysms, 473–477. *See also* Thoracic aortic aneurysms
    in upper extremity vessels, 1758–1759, 1765
Arteriovenous communications, abnormal, III:998–1030
    arteriovenous fistulas in, III:1000–1003, III:1004, III:1005. *See also* Arteriovenous fistula
    arteriovenous malformations in, III:1003–1022. *See also* Arteriovenous malformations (AVMs)
    hemangiomas in, III:998–1000. *See also* Hemangioma
    superior mesenteric angiography in, 1550–1551, 1564–1565, 1568, 1570–1573
    venous malformations in, III:1022–1029
Arteriovenous fistula, III:1000–1003, III:1004, III:1005. *See also* Arteriovenous malformations (AVMs)
    in angiography complications
        from cerebral angiography, 246
        in coronary arteriography, 578
        in embolization procedures, 1032
        at puncture site, 1027, 1028
    carotid-cavernous, 347
    of central nervous system, direct, III:781
    diagram of pathophysiology of, III:1001
    in extremity trauma, III:857–858
        arteriography technique for, III:860
        self healing of, III:859
        transcatheter management and, III:861–867
    femoral arteriography in, 1729–1730
    hemodialysis, percutaneous suction thromboembolectomy for thrombosed, III:163
    in hepatoma, 1448–1449
    inferior mesenteric arteriography in, 1609
    intradural. *See* Spinal dural arteriovenous fistulas
    in liver, III:425–426, III:428, III:431
    metal-based mechanical embolic agents for, III:58, III:59, III:61, III:62, III:74
    pediatric embolization in, III:908, III:909
    as percutaneous stone removal complication, III:602
    peripheral artery, femoral arteriography in, 1709–1711
    postoperative, after bypass vein graft, 223, 227
    pulmonary
        arteriography in, 770, 794–797
        hypervascularity in, 815–816

renal
    after renal transplantation, 1344–1346, 1347, 1348
    after trauma, 1231, 1235, 1239, 1240, III:895–896, III:897, III:898
    classification of, 1266
    hypertension and, 1266–1268
    in renal cell carcinoma, 1144, 1146, 1151
    splenic, 1475–1477, 1478
    in superior mesenteric artery, 1568
    in tumor, 1781–1782
Arteriovenous malformations (AVMs), III:1003–1022. *See also* Arteriovenous fistula
    cerebral, III:775–784
        aneurysms in, 314. *See also* Cerebral aneurysm
        angiography for diagnosis of, 251
        complications of embolization of, 1032
        direct arteriovenous fistulas in, III:781
        interaxial embolotherapy in, III:775–784
        intraoperative studies in, 252–253
        nidus, III:775–779
        postembolization care in, III:782–784
        radiosurgery for, III:779–781
        vein of Galen, III:782, III:783, III:784
    classification of, III:999
    clinical features of, III:1006
    diagnostic studies of, III:1006–1007, III:1008–1009
    distinguishing features of, III:999
    dual intracranial (DAVM), extraaxial, III:795–802
        neuroimaging of, III:796–798, III:801
        therapeutic approaches to, III:801–802
    extremity lesions in, III:1018–1022
        complications of, III:1003, III:1006
    femoral arteriography in, 1731–1733
    in hemangioma
        of metacarpal, 1805
        of upper arm, 1806
    of index finger, 1756
    inferior mesenteric arteriography in, 1609
    in kidney, 181
    in lung, 180, 181
    mechanical embolic agents for, III:71, III:74
    pelvic, 1654–1658, III:1016–1018, III:1019, III:1020
    pulmonary (PAVMs). *See* Pulmonary arteriovenous malformations (PAVMs)
    of shoulder, 1761
    sonography of, 216, color plate 5
    of thumb, 1757
    treatment of, III:1008–1016. *See also* specific agent or device
        absolute ethanol in, III:1013, III:1015
        acrylic adhesives in, III:1015–1016
        coils in, III:1011, III:1012
        detachable balloons in, III:1011, III:1012
        Gelfoam in, III:1010–1011

Arteriovenous malformations (AVMs)—
    Continued
    polyvinyl alcohol in, III:1011–1013,
        III:1014–1015
    upper extremity, 1756, 1757, 1759–
        1760, 1761
Arteritis
    cerebral, 304–307
        angiography technique in, 251
    giant-cell, in thoracic outlet syndrome,
        996, 998
    nonspecific, arteriosclerotic disease ver-
        sus, 1054
    pulmonary, 181
        Takayasu, 819
    as renal pseudotumor, 1228
    renovascular hypertension in, 1272–
        1273, 1274, 1275
    in splanchnic arteries, 1399
    in splenic artery, 1474
    Takayasu. *See* Takayasu arteritis
Arthritis
    of knee after thrombolytic therapy, 1043
    rheumatoid, III:173
Arthroplasty, hip, 1851
Artifacts
    in coronary arteriography related to flow
        patterns, 737–738
    in film, quality control and, 123
    image subtraction and, 150–151
    in peripheral vascular magnetic reso-
        nance angiography, 1828–1829,
        1830
    in vascular intervention angiography,
        141, 142
Artificial ventilation, 36–39, 47–48
As low as reasonably achievable (ALARA)
    standards, 137
Ascending aorta. *See* Aorta, ascending
Ascending frontal arteries, 270
Ascending pharyngeal artery, juvenile angio-
    fibromas and, 340
Ascites
    after transjugular intrahepatic portosys-
        temic shunt, III:536–537
    as gastrostomy tube contraindication,
        III:548
    leaking fluid from, after percutaneous
        gastrostomy, III:556
ASD. *See* Atrial septal defect (ASD)
ASPD (anterior superior pancreaticoduode-
    nal vein), 1426, 1427, 1429
Aspergillus, 1200
Aspiration
    abscess
        abdominal, III:927, III:928
        pelvic, III:947–948
    of paraprosthetic fluid after aortoiliac
        interventions, 1694, 1695
    percutaneous, for parathyroid hormone
        assay, 977
    of renal cyst, III:660–662
    of seminal vesicle fluid, III:640–642
    in transjugular liver biopsy, III:198
Aspiration pneumonia after percutaneous
    gastrostomy, III:557
Aspirin
    coronary angioplasty and, III:369, III:
        377
    infrapopliteal revascularization and, III:
        290

intraaxial embolotherapy for central ner-
    vous system and, III:765
oral hypoglycemics and, III:217
pulse-spray thrombolysis and, III:127,
    III:128, III:137
    for hemodialysis grafts, III:147
revascularization preparation and, III:
    230
in superior vena cava obstruction treat-
    ment, 927
in thrombolysis action, III:126
Asplenia, 1471–1472
Asymptomatic Carotid Artery Surgery
    (ACAS), III:340
Asymptomatic Carotid Atherosclerosis
    Study, 286–287
Asynchrony, ventricular, 640
Asyneresis, ventricular, 640
Asynergy, ventricular, 639–640
Atelectasis, 802, 816–818
Atherectomy
    in aortoiliac disease, III:234–240
        complications of, III:254
        results of, III:254
    atheroplasty versus, III:44
    catheters for, III:44–51
        Auth-Rotoblator, III:45, III:47, III:
            378, III:379–380
        in biopsy, III:49
        classification of, III:45
        niche applications of, III:47–49, III:
            50
        Pullback, III:47, III:379, III:380
        Simpson AtheroCath in. *See* Simpson
            AtheroCath catheter
        Trac-Wright, III:45, III:46–47
        transluminal extraction, III:47, III:
            378, III:379
    complications of, 1041–1042, III:44,
        III:47–49
    in coronary angioplasty, III:377–380
    in dialysis fistula stenoses, III:735, III:
        737, III:739
    femoral arteriography in, 1709
    in femoropopliteal revascularization, III:
        278–280
    in iatrogenic dissection, 1029
    in infrapopliteal revascularization, III:
        292–293
    lumen diameter after, III:7
    in restenosis after balloon angioplasty,
        III:14
    results of, III:254
    techniques for, III:234–240
    vascular sonography after, 226–227,
        228, color plates 1 & 2
AtheroCath. *See* Simpson AtheroCath cath-
    eter
Atheroma
    atherectomy catheter in removal of, III:
        44
    percutaneous suction thromboembolec-
        tomy removal of, III:160–165
Atheroplasty, atherectomy versus, III:44
Atherosclerosis. *See* Arteriosclerosis
Atherosclerosis obliterans
    combined lesions in, 1715, 1718
    femoral arteriography in, 1709, 1715–
        1722
        baseline evaluation and, 1715–1717,
            1718, 1719

bypass grafts in, 1709, 1717–1722
    revascularization in, 1709, 1717–1722
ATN (Acute tubular necrosis) from throm-
    bolysis complications, III:250
Atresia
    of aortic arch, coarctation of aorta and,
        446, 447
    of coronary arteries, congenital, 744,
        745–746
    of pulmonary artery, 789, 790, 791
    pulmonary valve
        anomalous origin of coronary arteries
            and, 833, 838
        hypoplasia of peripheral pulmonary
            arteries and, 842
        patent ductus arteriosus and, 838
        pulmonary artery aneurysm and, 843
        tricuspid valve, pulmonary valve stenosis
            in, 826
Atrial arteries, 615–619, 620, 621
    anterior, 589
    intermediate
        left, 589
        right, 616
Atrial collaterals, 709, 710–711
Atrial fibrillation, 43, 44
    from embolism in peripheral occlusion,
        1725
Atrial flutter, 43, 44
Atrial septal defect (ASD)
    central pulmonary artery stenosis and,
        831
    closure of, in patent ductus arteriosus,
        428
    partial anomalous pulmonary venous con-
        nection in, 880–887
    pulmonary arteriography in, 786–787
Atrioventricular (AV) nodal block, 43, 44
    in coronary artery catheterization compli-
        cations, 577
Atrioventricular (AV) node, 617, 618
Atrioventricular (AV) node artery, 617,
    618
    anatomic variations of, 750
    collaterals and, 711
Atrioventricular (AV) sulcus
    collaterals of, 710–711
    connections in, 704–708
Atrium
    arteries of. *See* Atrial arteries
    left
        anomalous drainage of hemiazygos
            vein into, 900, 910
        anomalous entrance of superior vena
            cava into, 900, 909
Atrophic pyelonephritis, chronic, 1197–
    1198
Atropine, 46
    in coronary arteriography, 569
        complications of, 577
    in heart block, 43, 44
    in interventional radiology, III:215, III:
        216
    before percutaneous cholecystomy, III:
        484
    before pulmonary arteriography, 771
    in pulmonary arteriovenous malforma-
        tion embolotherapy complications,
        III:850
    recommended intravenous dosages for,
        46

in renal angiography, 1101
in sinus bradycardia, 43
   from selective coronary artery catheter-
      ization, 568
strengths and volumes of, 48
in thoracic aortography, 391, 398
for vasovagal reactions to contrast
   agents, 30
Attenuation, temporal subtraction and,
   149
AUA (American Urological Association)
   Guidelines Panel Review of, III:595
   symptom score evaluation of, III:626
Auth-Rotoblator atherectomy catheter. *See*
   Rotoblator atherectomy catheter
Autocorrelator, 210
Autoimmune diseases, 692
Autologous blood clot in pelvic hemor-
   rhage, 1651, 1652
Autologous vein grafts, sonography of,
   223–225, 226, color plates 10 and
   11
Automatic cine film processors, 112, 113
Automatic exposure control in cardiac cath-
   eterization, 93–94
   calibration of, 123
Automatic guns with needles for biopsy,
   III:174
Automatic injectors, 172–173
Autonomic hyperreflexia, 1036
Auxiliary personnel, preintervention assess-
   ment and, III:205
AV (atrioventricular) nodal block, 43, 44
   in coronary artery catheterization compli-
      cations, 577
AV (atrioventricular) node, 617, 618
AV (atrioventricular) sulcus
   collaterals of, 710–711
   connections in, 704–708
AV node artery. *See* Atrioventricular (AV)
   node artery
Avitene, III:53
AVMs (arteriovenous malformations). *See*
   Arteriovenous malformations
   (AVMs)
Axen O, 9
Axial angiography in peripheral vascular disease, 1824–1825
Axial skeleton sarcomas, intraarterial chemotherapy for, III:1034–1035
Axillary approach in renal angioplasty, III:
   301–302
Axillary arteries, 995
   in abdominal aortography, 158
   arteriovenous fistulas of, III:1004
   catheterization of, 1016
   in cerebral angiography, 248–249
      emboli as complication of, 1029
   compression of, 1008
   displacement of, by hematoma, 1008
   embolization of, in venous malforma-
      tions, III:1005
   in extremity angiography after aortoiliac
      interventions, 1682–1683
   in femoral arteriography, 1705, 1709
   gun wound of, 1757
   sonography of, 212
   in thoracic aortography, 394
      of traumatic aneurysms, 479, 481
Axillary lymph nodes, 1882–1883, 1888,
   1889

Axillary region, cavernous lymphangioma
   in, 1921
Axillary veins
   catheterization of, 1016
   in dialysis shunts, 1767
      occlusion of, 1777
   for inferior vena cava collateral circula-
      tion, 954, 956
   neoplasm compression of, 1008
   sonography of, 212
   thrombolysis in, III:150, III:152
   venous access catheters and, III:969–
      971
Axillofemoral bypass
   in arteriosclerotic disease, 1053
   femoral arteriography after, 1717–1718
Azotemia, 1025–1026
Azygos lobe, 896
Azygos veins, 891–914, 1295, 1299. *See
   also* Vertebral and azygos veins
   continuation of inferior vena cava in,
      in polysplenia syndrome, 949
   dilatation of, 911
   embryology of, 869, 870
   esophageal location of, 898
   in inferior vena cava collateral circula-
      tion, 900, 905, 951–953, 955–957
   partial anomalous pulmonary venous con-
      nection to, 884
   in portal hypertension, 911
   rupture of, 911
Azygos-hemiazygos complex for inferior
   vena cava collateral circulation, 951,
   952

Bachmann bundle, 616
Bacille Calmette-Guérin vaccine, III:437
Bacillus proteus, 1183, 1193
Background suppression in magnetic resonance imaging, 195–197
Bacteremia, III:209
Bacterial infection
   after nephrostomy, 1036
   in bacteremia, III:209
   in endocarditis, 1077
   intracranial changes in, 303
   mycotic aneurysms and, 1077, 1080
   in nephritis, 1178–1182, 1183
   in renal abscess, 1182, 1183
   thoracic aneurysms and, 484
Baffles in embolization, III:62
Bag-valve-mask units, 38
Bailey CP, 635
Balanced coronary distribution, 589, 625
Balloon. *See also* Balloon catheter
   calibrated leak, III:65
   complications of nondetachable occlu-
      sion, III:64
   detachable. *See* Detachable balloons in
      embolization
   as mechanical embolic agent, III:55, III:
      63–70
      detachable. *See* Detachable balloons in
         embolization
      embolization coils compared to, III:
         72
      imaging of, III:70
      nondetachable occlusion, III:63–65
      potential complications of, III:64
      thrombogenic, III:70
   migration of, after embolization, III:68

paradoxical embolization of, in pulmonary arteriovenous malformations,
   III:845, III:850
Balloon angioplasty. *See also* Balloon catheter
   in aortoiliac disease, III:230–232, III:
      233
   in benign biliary obstructions, III:468
   catheter in. *See* Balloon catheter
   in coronary disease, III:368–374
      complications of, III:372–373, III:
         374
      deficiencies of, III:374
      instrumentation for, III:368–369
      in multivessel disease, III:373–374
      myocardial infarction in, III:373
      results of, III:372–373
      technique for, III:369–372
      unstable angina in, III:373
   in dialysis fistula thrombolysis, III:732–
      735
   history of, III:3–4
   laser. *See* Laser angioplasty
   lumen diameter after, III:7
   mechanisms of, III:1–23
      disproved compression hypothesis in,
         III:4
      documentation of, III:4–5, III:6
      pathophysiologic, III:3–5, III:6
   radiofrequency, III:14
   renal angioplasty mechanism and, III:
      296. *See also* Renal angioplasty
   restenosis after, III:5–19
      angiographic diagnosis of, III:6–8,
         III:9–11
      clinical diagnosis of, III:6, III:8
      combined maneuvers and, III:16, III:
         17
      histopathologic diagnosis of, III:6,
         III:8–11
      infection and, III:17
      loss index and, III:8
      molecular genetics and, III:16–17
      newer concepts and potential therapeu-
         tic implications in, III:17–19
      pathogenesis of, III:11–14
      pharmacologic maneuvers and, III:
         15–16
      strategies for prevention of, III:14–
         17
      target vessel revascularization and, III:
         8
      technical approach and, III:14–15
      thrombus replacement theory of, III:
         17, III:18
      vascular remodeling theory of, III:17–
         19
   thermal, III:14
Balloon catheter, III:24–43. *See also* Balloon; Balloon angioplasty; Embolization
   arterial access sheath for, III:27
   in balloon-on-a-wire system in renal
      angioplasty, III:303, III:304
   beginnings of modern, III:24–25
   in bile duct dilations, III:459–462, III:
      468, III:496
   caged, III:24, III:26
   in chronic mesenteric ischemia interven-
      tions, III:329
   compliance of, III:25–26, III:27

Balloon catheter—*Continued*
in dialysis fistula thrombolysis, III:732–735
in dilatation
in central pulmonary artery stenosis, 834–835
in coarctation of aorta repair, 457–460
complications from, 1029, 1030
in occlusion angiography, 84, 1492
in patent ductus arteriosus, 426, 427
in pelvic arteriosclerotic disease, 1638–1640
in pulmonary arteriography, 772, 777
in splenic artery embolization, 1492
of stenotic pulmonary valve, 826–828
in thoracic aortography, 393
in dilatation of ureteroileal anastomotic strictures, III:650–652
dilating force of, III:25–26, III:27
drug-delivery systems in, III:39–42
in embolectomy, femoral arteriography and, 1723
in fallopian tubal recanalization, III:676
femoral, in renal angioplasty, III:300–302
in femoropopliteal revascularization, III:263
Fogarty
in complicated biliary calculi removal, III:497
in iatrogenic dissection from catheter, 1029
in foreign body removal, III:963
history of, III:24–25, III:26
hoop strength of, III:26–27
in iliac angioplasty, III:231–232
inflation and deflation times of, III:39
in infrapopliteal revascularization, III:285–286
selection of, III:286
for intracranial angioplasty, III:755–756
kink resistance of, III:31–37
laser angioplasty, in complicated biliary calculi removal, III:497
lesion crossability for, III:27
liquid polymers for paving vessels in, III:42
in liver transplantation biliary tract strictures, III:518, III:519
nomenclature in, III:42–43
in pediatric angioplasty, III:910–916
in pediatric embolization, III:906
in pelvic fracture hemorrhage, III:879
in penile transluminal angioplasty, III:722
in percutaneous biliary calculi removal complications, III:497
in percutaneous revision of surgical portosystemic shunts, III:528–530
profile of, III:27–29, III:30–31
in prostatic urethroplasty, III:629–630
in pulmonary arteriovenous malformation embolotherapy, III:846–847, III:848–850
pushability of, III:37, III:38
radiofrequency-delivery systems in, III:42
in renal angioplasty
diameter of, III:297–298

material and inflation pressures of, III:298–300
restenosis and, III:39–42
rupture of, in peripheral angioplasty, 1040
shaft of, III:27–28
small-vessel, III:28–29, III:30
stent compatibility of, III:39, III:40–42
in subclavian, innominate, and vertebral artery angioplasty, III:762
for superselective catheterization, 159–161
tip of, III:37
trackability of, III:29–31, III:32–36
in transjugular intrahepatic portosystemic shunt, III:532, III:534
in ureteral strictures, III:578–580
in urethral strictures, III:619
wing of, III:29, III:30, III:31
Balloon tonometers in intestinal intramural pressure measurements, 1632
Balloon-expandable stents, III:86–89
current use of, III:85
titanium intraurethral, III:633, III:634
Balloon-on-a-wire system in renal angioplasty, III:303, III:304
Balt microcatheters, 165
for superselective catheterization, 163
Baltaxe HA, 605
Bamboo pattern in arteriography, 1733
Banchi A, 583
Bancroft filariasis, 1925
Banding artifact, 1828, 1829
Barbed coils, III:61
Barbiturates in premedication
for bronchial artery embolization, III:825
for femoral arteriography, 1713
Bard catheter, III:285
Bard gastric button, III:555
BARI (Bypass Angioplasty Revascularization Investigation), III:382
Barium studies in gastrointestinal bleeding, III:391
Baroldi G, 589, 701, 711
Barwell R, III:678
Basal ganglia, gliomas in, 340
Basal occlusive disease
with telangiectasia, 307, 310
of unknown etiology, 312, 313
Base wires in metal-based mechanical embolic agents, III:62
Basic life support, 35–36
Basilar artery
aneurysms of, 318, 320, III:772–775
bifurcation of, 271, 272
occlusion of
with telangiectasia, 307, 310
of unknown etiology, 312, 313
in posterior fossa, 272, 278
stroke and occlusion of, 300–301
in subclavian steal syndrome, 1765
vertebral flow reversal syndrome and, 553
Basilic lymph nodes, 1881–1882
Basilic vein, medial, 771
Basivertebral veins, 893, 894
Basket retrieval
in biliary calculi removal, III:492, III:493

in foreign body removal, III:961, III:962, III:966
Batson OV, 891, 892
Batson plexus of prostate, III:622
Beading pattern, 1733
in thoracic duct, 1884, 1896, 1897
Beam limitation in radiation protection, 124–125
Beam-shaping system of iris-type collimators, 97, 98
Becher W, 3
Behçet disease, 819
Bellman S, 635
Benadryl. *See* Diphenhydramine
Benign biliary obstruction, III:455–471. *See also* Biliary obstruction, benign
Benign hyperplasia of prostate (BPH), III:625–634, III:635
prostatic hyperthermia in, III:635
Benign lymph node disease
in inflammatory disease, 1923–1925, 1926
in involutive changes, 1923, 1924
lymphangiography in, 1923–1926
in reactive hyperplasia, 1923, 1924, 1925
Benign prostatic hyperplasia (BPH), III:625–634, III:635
prostatic hyperthermia in, III:635
Benign renal parenchymal disease, 1315–1320
Benign tubular ectasia, 1226
Benign tumors
in bone. *See* Bone tumors, benign
hepatic, hepatic arteriography in, 1439–1445
in spleen, 1482–1483
Bennett W, III:678
Bentec biliary stent, III:477
Bentson wire, III:31, III:34–35
in femoropopliteal revascularization, III:263
in infrapopliteal revascularization, III:286
in mesenteric angioplasty, III:327
in pulmonary arteriovenous malformation embolotherapy, III:846
in renal angioplasty, III:296, III:300
Bentson-Hanafee-Wilson (JB) catheters, 244, 245
Benzodiazepines in premedication, 1713, III:212, III:213
Benzyl alcohol in varicocele percutaneous embolization, III:696
Berberich J, 5, 6, 13
Berman balloon catheter, 84
Bernstein catheter, 245, III:694
Berry aneurysms, 312, 314–316
mycotic, 319
Bertin columns, prominent, 1166, 1167, 1168
Beta-adrenergic blockers
in autonomic hyperreflexia, 1036
in esophageal varices, III:397
in portal hypertension, III:397, III:525
Beta-adrenergic receptors
catecholamines and, 52–53
dopamine and, 61
isoproterenol and, 59
vascular response to, 51

Beta-adrenergic stimulators in pancreatic angiography, 1394
Betadine, III:663, III:665
Beta-galactosidase synthesis, III:16
Bicarbonate sodium, III:216
 in cardiac standstill, 45
 intravenous infusion of, in emergency treatment, 39, 41, 45
 recommended intravenous dosages for, 46
 strengths and volumes of, 48
 in ventricular fibrillation, 45
Bicuspid aortic valve
 with coarctation of aorta, 434, 435, 447
 dissecting aortic aneurysms and, 493
Bicuspid valves in thoracic duct, 1896, 1897
Bierman HR, 1383, 1433
Bifurcation
 of aorta, balloon angioplasty and, III:37
 of left main coronary artery, 751–752
  absent or early, 726–727
Bile
 drainage of. *See* Biliary drainage
 leakage of, 1037
  in liver transplantation, III:520–522
  in peritonitis, III:489
 sampling of, percutaneous cholecystomy and, III:485
Bile duct
 carcinoma of, III:472–482
  primary, 1450, 1451
 fistula of, to transjugular intrahepatic portosystemic shunt, III:542
 injuries to, III:455, III:456, III:457
 liver transplantation complications and, III:517–520
 obstructions in
  benign, III:455–471. *See also* Biliary obstruction, benign
  malignant, III:472–482
 pseudocalculus in, III:500
 strictures of
  atherectomy catheter for, III:49
  obstructions in. *See* Biliary obstruction, benign
Biliary calculi
 in liver transplantation biliary tract complications, III:520
 percutaneous removal of, III:491–508. *See also* Percutaneous biliary calculi removal
Biliary catheters in pelvic abscess drainage, III:952
Biliary colic, III:491
Biliary drainage. *See also* Bile
 complications of, 1038
 in malignant hepatobiliary obstruction, III:473–476
Biliary obstruction
 after drainage procedures, 1038
 benign, III:455–471
  AIDS-related cholangiopathy in, III:470
  causes of, III:455, III:456
  imaging procedures for, III:457, III:458–459
  primary sclerosing cholangitis in, III:465–470
  treatment of, III:456, III:459–465, III:466

 in liver transplantation, III:517–520
 malignant, III:472–482. *See also* Hepatobiliary obstruction, malignant
Biliary sepsis, electrocorporeal shock wave lithotripsy and, III:500
Biliary tract
 in liver transplantation
  complications and interventions of, III:517–522
  reconstruction of, III:516–517
  postintervention care in procedures of, III:219–221
Biliary tree procedures, complications of, 1030, 1037–1039
Biloma, 1037, III:521, III:522
Binz A, 7, 13, 14
Biology, cell, 50–52
Biopsy
 abdominal, complications of, 1035
 atherectomy catheter for, III:49
 breast. *See* Breast, biopsy of
 intravascular, III:195–200
  transvenous liver and kidney, III:195, III:197–199
  of vessel material, III:195–197
 lung, complications of percutaneous, 1033–1035
 mechanical embolic agents for tracks from, III:76
 percutaneous image-guided. *See* Percutaneous image-guided biopsy
 of prostate, III:636–639
 quick-stain technique for tissue specimens from, III:170
 regional considerations for, III:184–192
 renal, III:188–189
 vascular injuries from, 1231, 1237
 thyroid, complications of, 1033
Biopsy brushes in intravascular biopsy, III:197
Biopsys Mammotome, III:1042–1043, III:1044
Biplane radiography
 in abdominal aorta arteriosclerosis and other diseases, 1057–1058, 1086
 in determining operability of coronary disease, 689
 exposure factors and, 70
 in serial radiography
  in aortic arch anomalies, 547
  generators for, 91–92
  for ventricular study, 121
Bipolar gradient, magnetic resonance signal and, 200
Bird's Nest filter, 970, III:987, III:989–990
 complications with, 1044
 magnetic resonance venography and, 1852
 thrombus trapped in, 940
Birtcher cine viewer, 115
Bismuth
 first use of, 4
 in renal cyst sclerosis, III:663, III:665
 as sclerosant after lymphocele percutaneous drainage, III:946
Bismuth portosystemic shunt, III:526
Bjure A, 849
Bladder, urinary, 614–615
 calculi in, III:618

 diagnostic algorithm for outflow from, III:627
 hemorrhage from, 1651
 interventional procedures for, III:614–615
 pelvic arteriography and, 1636–1668. *See also* Pelvic angiography
 trabeculation or hypertrophy of, III:618
 tumors of
  chemotherapy in, III:82
  malignant metastatic spread of, 1933, 1936
  percutaneous nephrostomy for, III:561, III:563
  in wall, 1649, 1658, 1659
Blakemore AH, 1527
Blalock-Taussig procedure
 arteriovenous fistulas after, III:74
 embolization in, III:908
 pediatric thrombolysis in, III:917
 stenoses of shunts for, angioplasty in, III:916
 for tetralogy of Fallot, evaluation of status of, 549–551
 thoracic aortography in, 396
Bleeding. *See also* Hemorrhage
 in biopsy, III:180–183
 from colon
  angiographic detection rates in, 1611
  inferior mesenteric angiography in, 1608–1611, 1612–1613
  of undetermined artery, 1590
 as complication of thrombolysis, III:154–155
 as contraindication to thrombolysis, III:133
 from duodenum. *See* Duodenum, bleeding from
 in extremity trauma, arteriography and, III:860
 of false aneurysm of hepatic artery, 1453–1454
 gastrointestinal, III:389–421. *See also* Gastrointestinal system, arteriography in; Gastrointestinal system, bleeding in
 in percutaneous gastrostomy, III:556–557
 in percutaneous renal stone removal, III:602
 renal transplant obstruction from, III:581
 in small bowel, localization of, III:394
 variceal. *See* Varices
Bleeding diathesis as percutaneous stone removal contraindication, III:601
Bleeding time (BT), III:208
Bleomycin, III:81
 in hepatic malignancy, III:437
 as sclerosant after lymphocele percutaneous drainage, III:946
Block, heart. *See* Heart block
Blood containment systems in arterial puncture, 156–157
Blood cysts in pancreatitis, 1413
Blood flow. *See also* Doppler imaging
 biopsy complications and, III:181–182
 cerebral, in intracranial, extraaxial lesions, III:791–795
 in coronary arteries, measurements of, 623–626

Blood flow—*Continued*
  to cranial nerves, III:814
  dural, III:792
  redistribution of, 859
    mechanical embolic agents for, III:76
  renal, 1125–1126
    magnification angiography of, 181
  signal in magnetic resonance angiography and, 188–191, 192
Blood group incompatibility in liver transplantation, III:518
Blood pressure
  in cardiac catheterization, 114–116, 117
  complications in elevations of, III:214–217
  contrast agent toxicity and, 28
Blood sugar, III:214–217
Blood supply. *See* Blood flow
Blood vessels. *See* Vessels
Blood viscosity
  contrast agent effects on, 27
  pulmonary blood flow and, 857
Blue rubber bleb nevus, 1573
Blue toe syndrome
  angioplasty and, III:242
  in aortoiliac disease, III:227
  atherectomy in, III:44, III:49
Blue-violet dye in lymphangiography, 1866
  allergy to, 1868
Blumgart HL, 700
Blunt trauma
  to aorta and brachiocephalic arteries, 521–539
    angiography in, 523, 524–527
    broadside impact injuries in, 522, 529–532
    car occupants and, 522, 528–529
    crushing injuries in, 533, 534, 535
    fractured sternum in, 532, 533
    frontal collisions in, 522–523, 528–529
    initial assessment of, 521–524
    mechanisms of injury in, 521, 523
    motorcycle riders in, 522, 528–529
    review of injuries in, 527–537
    seat belts and, 528, 532–533
    spontaneous healing in, 537
    thoracic aortic aneurysm and, 477–483
    untreated injuries in, 535–537
    violent trauma in, 533–535
  of extremity, III:858–859
  to spleen, 1485
Bock AC, 891
Body habitat, abnormal, percutaneous stone removal and, III:597, III:598
Boerhaave syndrome, III:832
Boijsen E, 1587
Bone, 1779–1821
  anatomy of, 1779–1780
  aneurysmal cysts of, 1797–1798
    embolization in, III:905
  angiography of, 1779–1783. *See also* Bone tumors
    technique for, 1780–1781
  lymphangiomatosis of, 1908, 1912–1913
  sarcomas of, III:1031
  tumors of. *See* Bone tumors
Bone grafts, femoral arteriography in, 1730–1730

Bone scan in renal cell carcinoma, 1154
Bone tumors
  anatomy and, 1779–1780
  angiographic appearance of, 1781–1782
  appearance of, 1781–1782
  benign
    angiographic characteristics of, 1782
    of fibrous origin, 1798, 1799
    of osteoblastic origin, 1787–1788, 1789–1791
    of vascular origin, 1801–1804, 1805, 1806
  biopsy of, III:191–192
  embolization of, 1813–1819
  femoral arteriography in, 1711
  inflammatory lesions and, 1782–1783
  malignant
    aneurysmal bone cysts in, 1797–1798
    angiographic characteristics of, 1781–1782
    Ewing sarcomas in, 1794–1797
    of fibrous origin, 1798–1801, 1802
    giant-cell tumors in, 1797, 1798
    of marrow origin, 1793–1794
    metastatic, 1807–1808, 1809
    of osteoblastic origin, 1788–1791, 1793–1795
    plasma cell myelomas in, 1793–1794
    reticulum cell sarcomas in, 1797
    of uncertain origin, 1797–1798
    of vascular origin, 1806
  origin of
    cartilaginous, 1783–1786, 1787, 1788
    fibrous, 1798–1801, 1802
    marrow, 1793–1797
    osteoblastic, 1787–1792, 1793–1795
    uncertain, 1797–1798
    vascular, 1801–1806
Bookbinder stents, III:89–90
Bookstein JJ, 702, 768
Botallooccluder, III:70
Boulvin R, 1497
Bourassa technique for coronary arteriography, 570–571
Bowditch HP, 3
Bowel
  biliary calculi removal into, III:493–495
  ischemia of. *See* Mesenteric ischemia
  magnification angiography of, 181–182, 183
  resection of, ureteral strictures after, III:578
  segment of, for esophageal transplantation, 1590
BPH (benign hyperplasia of prostate), III:625–634, III:635
  prostatic hyperthermia in, III:635
Brachial aortography, retrograde, 392
  historical notes on, 8, 11
Brachial artery, 995
  in abdominal aortography, 158
  in Brescia-Ciminno shunts, 1767, 1768, 1769
  for cerebral angiography, 248, 1029
  coronary artery catheterization technique and, 570
  in dialysis shunts, 1767, 1768, 1769
    stenosis of, 1778
  in extremity arteriography, 1755, 1756, 1758

  after aortoiliac interventions, 1682–1683
  lytic therapy and, 1762, 1763
  reconstruction of artery and, 1762
  in femoral arteriography, 1705
  in mesenteric angioplasty, III:326–327
  occlusion of, after supracondylar fracture, III:917, III:919
  pseudoaneurysm of, in puncture site complications, 1028
  pulse-spray thrombolysis for, III:150
  in renal angiography, 1102
  in thoracic aortography, 394
  thrombosis of, after transbrachial arteriography, 1030
Brachial fascial compartment compression after transaxillary arteriography, 1031
Brachial plexus
  anatomy of, 996
  injuries to, after transaxillary arteriography, 1031
Brachial vein
  in dialysis shunts, 1767
  in intravascular biopsy, III:197
Brachiocephalic arteries, 552, 553
  angioplasty of
    for cerebral ischemia, III:757–763
    extracranial, III:339–355. *See also* Extracranial brachiocephalic arterioplasty
  blunt trauma to, 521–539. *See also* Blunt trauma, to aorta and brachiocephalic arteries
  buckling of, thoracic aortography in, 397
  ductus arising from, 416, 417
  extracranial. *See* Extracranial brachiocephalic arterioplasty
  stenosis of
    angiography in, 543
    stents for, III:1049, III:1050
  thoracic aortography of, 552, 553
Brachiocephalic veins, 552, 553
  angioplasty of
    for cerebral ischemia, III:757–763
    complications of, 1041
    extracranial, III:339–355. *See also* Extracranial brachiocephalic arterioplasty
  magnetic resonance venography of, 1856
  sonography of, 219
  stenosis of
    angiography in, 543
    stents for, III:1049, III:1050
  thoracic aortography of, 552, 553
Bradycardia, III:215, III:216
  in coronary arteriography complications, 577, 579–580
  sinus, 43, 44
    in selective coronary artery catheterization, 568
Bradykinin, 62
  metabolism of, 49
  in pancreatic angiography, 62, 1392, 1394
  in superior mesenteric angiography, 62, 1557
Brahme F, 1587
Brain
  historical notes on study of, 6, 8, 13

metastases to, cerebral vascular malformations in, 342
Brainstem, gliomas in, 340
Branchial arch, aortic arch development from, 435
Branham-Nicoladoni sign, III:1002
Breast
  biopsy of, III:191, III:1037–1046
    comparison of cytology from fine-needle versus core, III:1038, III:1039
    diagnosis in, III:1038–1041
    equipment in, III:1037–1039
    techniques in, III:1041–1044, III:1041–1045
    ultrasonography in, III:1037–1038, III:1040–1041
  calcifications in, III:1040
  carcinoma of
    definitive diagnosis in, III:1038, III:1049
    lymphangiography in, 1938
    percutaneous biopsy in, III:191, III:1037–1046
    regional chemotherapy in, III:82
  fibroadenoma of, III:1038, III:1040
  sonography of, 233
Brescia MJ, 1767
Brescia-Cimino shunt, 226
  modified, 1767, 1768, 1769
  reduced outflow from, 1777
Brewster classification of iliac artery disease, III:107
Bricker loop, III:645, III:646–647
Bridging, myocardial. *See* Myocardial bridging
Brigham and Women's Hospital classification of dissecting aortic aneurysms, 495, 504
Brightness
  automatic stabilization system for, in cineradiography, 93–94
  calibration of, 123
  image display in digital angiography and, 146
Bristle brushes in mechanical embolization, III:55, III:71
Broadside impacts in blunt aortic and brachiocephalic artery trauma, 522, 529–532
Brodén B, 391
Brodie abscess, 1783
Bronchial arteries
  anatomy of, III:820–822
  aneurysms of, 489
  collateral circulation and, 719
  embolization of, III:819–828
    anatomy and, III:820–822
    angiography in, III:820–824
    clinical considerations in, III:819–820
    complications of, 1033, III:826–827
    procedure for, III:821, III:824, III:825–826, III:827
    results of, III:824, III:827
    technique for, III:820–827
    truncus arteriosus of, 549
Bronchial infarction after embolization, III:827
Bronchiectasis, hemoptysis in, III:819
Bronchoesophageal fistulas after embolization, III:827

Bronchopleural fistulas, mechanical embolic agents for, III:76
Bronchoscopy in hemoptysis, III:819
Bronchospasm, III:217
  in systemic reactions to contrast agents, 29
Brooks B, 5, 7
Brown fat tumors, 1373
Bruit
  in extremity trauma, III:857
  spinal dural arteriovenous fistulas and, 377
Brushes, bristle, in mechanical embolization, III:55, III:71
Brushite renal calculi, III:606
BT (bleeding time), III:208
Bubble echocardiography in pulmonary arteriovenous malformations, III:838
Buckling of great vessels, 397, 551
Bucky diaphragm, 78
Bucrylate
  in selective embolization in gastrointestinal bleeding, III:403
  in transhepatic variceal embolization, III:526
Budd-Chiari syndrome
  liver transplantation complications and, III:515
  in pediatric angioplasty, III:913
  stents for benign obstructions in, III:1052–1053
  transjugular intrahepatic portosystemic shunt in, III:539
Buerger disease, III:151
  femoral arteriography in, 1726, 1727
  upper extremity angiography of, 1759, 1760
Buhler, artery of, 1458, 1459
Bulbomembranous urethral rupture, III:617
Bulbourethral glands of Cowper, III:616
Bullet wounds. *See* Gunshot wounds
Bullous emphysema, 801, 802, 803
Bundles of conducting system, 615, 616, 621
Bupivacaine, III:201, III:214
Burford TH, 392
Busulfan, III:81
Button, gastrostomy, III:555–556
Buttoned double-disk occluder, III:70
N-Butylcyanoacrylate embolization (NBCA), III:791, III:802
  in spinal dural fistulas, 376
Bypass Angioplasty Revascularization Investigation (BARI), III:382
Bypass grafts. *See* Grafts

CABG, arteriography after. *See* Coronary artery bypass grafts (CABG), arteriography after
Cables in cardiac catheterization laboratory, 88, 117
Caged balloon catheter, III:24, III:26
Calcarine artery, 274
Calcifications
  in arteriosclerosis
    of abdominal aorta, 1056, 1057, 1062
    of splenic artery, 1473
  biliary. *See* Biliary calculi

in breast, III:1040
in coronary arteriography, 645, 655
in dialysis shunt complications, 1769
in dissecting aortic aneurysms, 498–499, 501–502, 503
in hepatomas, 1447
hydronephrosis and, 1212, 1213
in ileal conduits, III:654, III:655
in Kock pouch urinary diversions, III:654–655
of ligamentum arteriosum, 423
in pancreatitis, 1411
in patent ductus arteriosus, 423, 838
renal. *See* Renal calculi
in renal artery aneurysm, 1265
in renal cell carcinoma, 1139
in renal hamartoma, 1163
in sonographic terminology, 217
in splenic artery
  with aneurysms, 1474–1475, 1476
  with arteriosclerosis, 1473
in splenic cyst, 1482
in thoracic aorta computerized tomography, 469
in urinary bladder, III:618
in vascular wall after balloon angioplasty, III:5, III:6
Calcium, vascular smooth muscles and, 51, 60
Calcium binding, contrast agent toxicity and, 27
Calcium channel blockers, 60
  alpha receptors and, 53
  in cerebral vessel vasospasm, III:755
  coronary artery catheterization complications and, 577
  in extremity trauma, III:861
  in femoropopliteal revascularization, III:263, III:267
  intraaxial embolotherapy for central nervous system and, III:767
  in restenosis after balloon angioplasty, III:15
  revascularization and, III:230
  in spasm after renal angioplasty, III:305–306
Calcium chloride, 46–47
  in cardiac standstill, 45
  recommended intravenous dosages for, 46
  strengths and volumes of, 48
Calcium gluconate, 48
Calcium oxalate renal calculi, III:597
  extracorporeal shock wave lithotripsy for, III:606
Calculated vascular signal as function of flip angle, 195
Calculi. *See* Calcifications
Caldas J, 66–67
Calf, disorders of
  vascular sonography in, 218, 219
  venography in, 1743–1754. *See also* Magnetic resonance venography magnetic resonance, 1842
Calibrated leak balloon, III:65
Calices
  diverticula of
    infected, 1199
    obstruction of, III:590–595
  renal stones in, III:590–595
Callosomarginal artery, 267

Camera
  aperture size of, x-ray exposure versus, 139, 140
  cine
    in cardiac catheterization laboratory, 99–100
    silicone on runners of, 123
    spot-film, for fluorography, 101
  video, for digital angiography
    aperture of, 139–140
    for vascular intervention, 134–135
Camera control unit (CCU), sweep generator of, 141
Cameron R, 1426
cAMP (cyclic adenosine monophosphate), 51
Campbell JS, 584
Campi L, 1497, 1527
Candelabra group of frontal arteries, 270–271
Candida, 1200, 1344
  in hepatic abscess, III:929
  in percutaneous stone removal complications, III:602
Cannon WB, 3
Cannulation
  of cisterna chyli, percutaneous, 1901–1902
  thoracic duct, 1904
Capillary network in heart, 589
Capitate, osteoid osteomas of, 1790
Capnocavography, 936–937
Capsular arteries
  adrenal, 1124
  perforating, 1122
  in renal angiography, 1114, 1118, 1119, 1120–1122, 1124
  ruptured, 1106, 1108
Capsular vein, 1292, 1295, 1299
Captopril
  for renal angioplasty patient, III:305
  in renal scintigraphy, 1245
  in stimulated peripheral renin analysis, III:295
Car occupants, blunt trauma to, 522, 528–529
Carbon dioxide in renal transplantation angiography, 1329
Carbon fiber-reinforced plastic (CFRP), 75
Carboplatinum, III:437
Carcinoid
  hepatic, III:451–452
    after biopsy metastasis, 1035
    after embolization, 1037
  ileal, 1576, 1577
    metastatic to liver, 1451
  pancreatic, 1402, 1405, 1406
  superior mesenteric angiography in, 1576, 1577
Carcinoma. *See also* Malignancy; Neoplasms
  of adrenal glands. *See* Adrenal glands, carcinomas of
  bile duct, primary, 1450, 1451
  of bladder, III:82
  breast
    biopsy in, III:191, III:1039, III:1045
    lymphangiography in, 1938
    regional chemotherapy in, III:82
  of cecum, superior mesenteric angiography in, 1574

of cervix. *See* Cervix, carcinoma of
of colon. *See* Colon, adenocarcinoma of
endometrial, III:82
gastric, III:548
of head and neck, III:82
hepatocellular, 1446–1450, 1451. *See also* Hepatic malignancy
ileocecal, 1568
of kidney. *See* Kidney, carcinoma of
lung. *See* Lung cancer
mesenteric, 1568, 1570
ovarian, 1485
pancreatic. *See* Pancreatic carcinoma
of penis, 1933, 1935
of prostate, 1664, 1933, 1936, III:568
of rectum, 1936–1938
  metastatic to liver, III:450–451
renal cell, renal cyst versus, III:660
retroperitoneal, undifferentiated, 1669
thyroid, 917
of tongue, III:82, III:83
transitional cell
  fluid collections in, III:944, III:945
  percutaneous nephrostomy and, III:563, III:564
  of urethra, III:617
urothelial, III:561, III:563, III:564, III:567, III:568
of uterus
  lymphatic spread of, 1931, 1932
  radiation fibrosis after therapy for, 1916
of vagina, 1932–1933
of vulva, 1932–1933
Cardiac angiography. *See also* Cardiac catheterization laboratory
  electrocardiography during, 116
  measurements during, 116–117
    equipment for, 117–118
  nonsubtraction imaging in, 152
  in total anomalous pulmonary venous connection, 878
Cardiac arrest, evidence of, 36–37
Cardiac arrhythmias in pulmonary arteriography, 783
Cardiac catheterization laboratory, 86–133. *See also* Cardiac angiography
  automatic exposure control and, 93–94
  cardiac serial radiography in, 101–102
  cine camera in, 99–100
  cine framing in, 100–101
  cine processing in, 106–111, 112, 113
  cine pulsing systems in, 92–93
  cine viewers in, 111–114, 115
  clean supply room for, 89
  collimation in, 97–98
  components of, 89, 90
  control room for, 87–88
  electrical power in, 94, 95
  electrical safety in, 130
  emergency equipment in, 118–119
  equipment room for, 88–89
  exposure reduction in, 128–130
  generators in, 89–92
  grids in, 103
  image intensifiers in, 98–99
    optics for, 99
  overhead supports in, 105
  patient and equipment supports in, 103–105
  personnel for, 130–133

physicians in, 131
physiologic studies and equipment in, 114–119
procedure room for, 87
quality control in, 122–124
radiation protection in, 124–128
radiographic film for, 105, 106, 107, 108
radiographic tubes in, 94–97
radiologic technologist in, 132
space requirements for, 87–89
specific requirements for, 119–122
spot-film cameras for fluorography in, 101
staffing patterns in, 132–133
support personnel in, 131–132
table in, 105
technician in, 132
video systems in, 102–103
workroom for, 89
Cardiac complications in extracorporeal shock wave lithotripsy, III:608
Cardiac compression, external, 39, 40
Cardiac contour collimators, 97, 98
  Siemens, 98
Cardiac death, 41
Cardiac disease. *See* Heart disease
Cardiac effects of contrast agents, 26–29
Cardiac malformations, aorticopulmonary window and, 464, 465, 796, 798
Cardiac massage, open chest, 40
Cardiac motion in magnetic resonance angiography, 198
Cardiac output
  monitoring of, during cardiac catheterization, 117
  splanchnic circulation and, 1615
Cardiac rhythm abnormalities in preintervention assessment, III:209
Cardiac serial radiography, 101–102
Cardiac standstill, 45
Cardiac tip pressure, monitoring of, 114–116
Cardiac topography, 586–590
Cardiac venous system, 590
  great vein in, 590, 591
  inferior vena cava anomalies and, 945–947
Cardio Diagnost support unit, 104
Cardioangiography, magnification tubes for, 97
Cardiografin, 170
Cardiomegaly
  in dissecting aortic aneurysms, 500, 502, 503
  in infant with coarctation of aorta, 441, 442
  laboratory for study of, 121–122
Cardiopulmonary resuscitation, 37, 39–40
  apparent needs for, 35
  care after, 41
  criteria of effective, 40–41
  discontinuance of, 41
  one-rescuer, 37
  pupillary response to, 41
  standards for, 34
  two-rescuer, 37
Cardiopulmonary technician, 132
Cardiorespiratory arrest from contrast media reactions, 29, 30. *See also* Cardiopulmonary resuscitation

Cardiovascular foreign body removal, III:
959–960
Cardiovascular reactions
cardiorespiratory arrest in, 29, 30
in ESWL complications, III:608
in interventional radiology procedures,
III:212
to lymphangiography, 1870
to thoracic aortography, 399
Carel's vascular anastomosis, III:1000
Carey-Alzate-Coons Gastrostomy Set, III:
553
Carey-Coons endoprosthesis in malignant
hepatobiliary obstructions, III:479
C-arm equipment
in craniocaudal and caudocranial
imaging, 103–105
in intraoperative angiography, 253
in percutaneous gastrostomy, III:553
in prostatic urethroplasty, III:628
radiation safety and, 88, 124, 125, 126,
127
in thoracic aortic aneurysm grafting guidance, III:360
for vascular intervention angiography,
134, 136
Carnett JB, 5
Carotid aortography, retrograde, 392–393
Carotid arteries
angioplasty of, III:760–761
arteritis of, 307
catheterization technique for, 250
cavernous. *See* Carotid-cavernous artery
collateral flow to, 292–296
common, 254–261, 262, 263
anatomy of, 254–261, 262, 263
aneurysms of, 489
blunt trauma to, 527
ductus arteriosus and, 416
gray scale image of, 206, 207
sonography of, 213
stenosis of, magnetic resonance angiography of, 194
thrombus in, 298
duplex ultrasonography of, 252
endarterectomy of, 252–253, 286, 287
external, 254–257
branches of, 254–257
collateral flow to, 292–296
lateral origin of, 254, 255
sonography of, 212, 213
in trauma, 344
vasospasm of, 344
external (ECA)
cranial nerve supply from, III:814
in intracranial, extraaxial lesion embolization, III:790, III:799–800
in extracranial brachiocephalic arterioplasty, III:339–347
examinations before, III:340–344, III:
345, III:346
management of complications in, III:
344–345
in gunshot wound, 344
hemodynamically significant stenoses in,
220–221
historical notes on study of, 6, 8
iatrogenic dissection of, 348, 351
internal (ICA), 257–261, 262, 263
anatomy of, 257–261, 262, 263
blunt trauma to, 347–348, 350

cerebral aneurysms in, 314, 316, 319,
III:768
collateral flow to, 292–296
cranial nerve supply from, III:814
in intracranial, extraaxial lesion embolization, III:790–791, III:799–800,
III:803–808
occlusion of, 297–298, 299, 350
retrograde opacification of, 259
sonography of, 212, 213
stenosis of, 296–297
stroke and, 297–298, 299
supraclinoid segment of, 257–263,
273
trauma to, 347–348, 350
ulcerated plaques at origins of, 288
main (MCA), bifurcation of
cerebral aneurysms in, 314, 316
gunshot wound and, 345
peak velocity in, 220
petrous, aneurysm of, III:768–769
pseudoaneurysm of, in trauma, 350, 354
stenosis of
angioplasty in, III:339–347
common sites of, 287, 288–289
efficacy of surgical repair in, 286–287
magnetic resonance angiography of,
194
progressive, 285, 286, 287, 288–289
tandem lesions in, 285, 286
tumor encasement of, 329
Carotid body tumors, 337–339
Carotid endarterectomy
intraoperative studies in, 252–253
studies of effectiveness of, 286, 287
Carotid pulse in cardiopulmonary resuscitation, 41
Carotid-cavernous artery
aneurysm of, 320–322, III:769–772,
III:773
fistulas in, III:802
fistulas of (CCFs). *See* Carotid-cavernous
fistulas (CCFs)
Carotid-cavernous fistulas (CCFs), 347,
353, III:802–808, III:1002, III:
1003
arteriovenous, 347
detachable balloons for, III:1011
complications of embolization of, 1032
neurointerventional management of, III:
807–808
sonography of, 233
therapeutic approaches to, III:807
Carotid-jugular compression in dural arteriovenous malformations, III:801
Carrel patch
of aorta, 1325, 1326
renal artery stenosis after, 1342
in donor liver preparation, III:509
Carson MJ, 392
Cartilaginous tumors
anatomy and, 1779–1780
appearance of, 1781–1782
benign, 1783, 1784, 1785
angiographic characteristics of, 1782
malignant, 1783–1786, 1787, 1788
angiographic characteristics of, 1781–
1782
CASS. *See* Coronary Artery Surgery Study
(CASS)
Cassarella WJ, 1443

Cassette changers
for cerebral angiography, 67
history of, 67–68
Picker-Amplatz vacuum contact system
for, 71
principles of, 69
Sanchez-Perez, 70, 71
types of, 70–71
Castellanos A, 7, 8, 11, 391, 392
Casting technique in coronary collateral circulation study, 701–702
Catecholamines, 52–54
assay of, 1373
clinical indications for, 54
contraindications to, 54
reserpine and, 59
Catechol-O-methyltransferase (COMT), 54
Catheter. *See also* Catheterization
in adrenal angiography, 1354
Amplatz, 556–558
angioplasty. *See* Balloon angioplasty; Balloon catheter
in arterial portography, 1529
atherectomy, III:44–51
Auth-Rotoblator, III:45, III:47, III:
378, III:379–380
classification of, III:45
Fogarty, introduction of, III:160–161
in iatrogenic dissection, 1029
niche applications of, III:47–49, III:
50
Pullback, III:47, III:379, III:380
Simpson AtheroCath in. *See* Simpson
AtheroCath catheter
Trac-Wright, III:45, III:46–47, III:
378, III:379
transluminal extraction, III:47, III:
378, III:379
balloon. *See* Balloon catheter
in bronchial artery embolization, III:
822, III:825
in carotid-cavernous fistula embolization,
III:807
in central nervous system interaxial
embolotherapy, III:766
central venous, III:970
broken fragment of, III:964, III:965
postintervention care for, III:219–221
for cerebral angiography, 242–245, 246
coaxial. *See* Coaxial catheters
complications of, 1028–1029
in coronary arteriography, 685, 731–
733
in renal angiography, 1103–1110
in coronary angioplasty, III:369, III:370
in coronary arteriography, 556–558,
562–565, 627
after coronary artery bypass graft, 760,
761
electrode, 107
vasospasm and, 685, 731–733
dialysis, III:977–978
dual-lumen, III:970, III:978
in fistula thrombolysis, III:729, III:
730
in embolization
of pelvic organs, 1661, 1664
of penile artery, 1661
in extremity arteriography, 1697, 1703–
1706
after aortoiliac interventions, 1681–
1682, 1683

Catheter.—*Continued*
in femoral arteriography, 1697, 1703–1706
in femoropopliteal atherectomy, III:278–280
in femoropopliteal revascularization, III:263–264
Foley
in percutaneous cholecystolithotomy, III:504
in percutaneous nephrostomy, III:566
in foreign body removal
balloon, III:963
basket retriever, III:961, III:962, III:966
grasping, III:961, III:963
hook-tip, III:961, III:962
loops-snare, III:960–961, III:962–965
French. *See* French catheters
in gastrointestinal arteriography, problems related to, III:417
Grollman, 773, 774
Groshong, III:975, III:976, III:978
heparin-bonded, III:1034
hepatic
in abscess drainage, III:929–930
in arteriography, 1433–1434, III:431
Hickman, III:970, III:975, III:978
Hohn, III:970, III:978
in hysterosalpingography, III:673, III:676
in infrapopliteal revascularization, III:285
in internal iliac artery angiography, III:871, III:876, III:879
in intraarterial chemotherapy, III:1034–1035
in intracranial, extraaxial lesion embolization, III:789–790
introducer sets for, 157–158
jamming of holes in, in coil embolization, III:59
Judkins. *See* Judkins catheters
long-term, III:219–221
in mediastinal abscess drainage, III:835
in mesenteric angioplasty, III:327–330
in pancreatic abscess drainage, III:936
in pancreatic pseudocyst drainage, III:933
in patent ductus arteriosus aortography, 422–426
in pediatric angiography, 244
in pelvic abscess percutaneous drainage
insertion of, III:952
lavage and irrigation of, III:952
management of, III:952–953
selection of, III:951–952
withdrawal of, III:952–953
in pelvic digital angiography, 1638
in penile transluminal therapy, III:722
in penile vascularization, III:709
in percutaneous abdominal abscess drainage, III:930
in percutaneous biliary calculi removal
complications, III:497, III:498–499
in percutaneous gastrostomy, III:548–549, III:551
in percutaneous nephrostomy, III:566, III:570–572

in percutaneous suction thromboembolectomy, III:161, III:164
pigtail. *See* Pigtail catheter
postintervention care for, III:219–221
in pulmonary arteriography, 772
in pulmonary arteriovenous malformation embolotherapy, III:846–847, III:848–850
in renal angiography, 1102–1110, 1114, 1115, 1117
hazards of, 1103–1110
transplants and, 1327, 1328
in renal angioplasty, III:296–300
in femoral balloon catheter system, III:300–303
in renal venography, 1290, 1291
in renin determination, 1306
reproductive organ dose and, 129
shepherd's crook. *See* Shepherd's crook catheter
sidewinder, 1016
in iliac artery obstruction, III:38
in renal angioplasty, III:302
for thoracic abscess drainage, III:830
in thoracic aortography in aneurysms, 472–473
in thoracic empyema drainage, III:832
in transaxillary catheterization, 1016
in transfemoral catheterization, 1014–1015
in transjejunal choledocholithotomy, III:496
for upper extremity angiography, 1755
in ureteral stenting, III:575, III:576
in ureteroenteral anastomotic strictures, III:653
in urethral procedures, III:619, III:620, III:621
in varicocele embolization, III:694–699
venous access. *See* Venous access catheters
in vertebral and azygos vein study, 911
Catheter aortography. *See also* Angiography; specific procedure
abdominal. *See* Abdominal aortography
historical notes on, 8, 11
technique for, 249–250
thoracic, 393–394. *See also* Thoracic aortography
Catheterization. *See also* Catheter
in arterial portography, 1529
cystic duct, III:487–489
in femoral arteriography
approaches in, 1703–1706
pseudoaneurysms after, 1693, 1694, 1695
technique for, 1013–1016, 1703–1706
of femoral veins. *See* Femoral veins
of left ventricle in coronary arteriography, 558–560
of pancreatic veins
complications of, 1428–1429
in endocrine tumors, 1429–1431
indications for, 1428
technique of, 1428
penile vascular, III:705–725. *See also* Penile vascular catheterization in erectile dysfunction
in pulmonary arteriography, 773–774, 775

in renal angiography, 1102–1110, 1114, 1115, 1117
hazards of, 1103–1110
superselective, 155–175
for abdominal aortography, 158
for aortic catheterization, 156–158
for arterial puncture, 156–158
balloon in, 159–161, III:65
for chemotherapy and chemoembolization in pelvic angiography, 1661–1665
clinical usefulness of, 167–169, 170
with coaxial technique, 161–165
flow-sensitive microcatheters in, 164–165, 166
fragility of, 166
guidewires in, 161–164
introduction sheaths in, 157, 158
microinjectors in, 170–171
in pancreatic angiography, 1388–1389, 1394–1395
perforation, rupture, and separation in, 166
preshaped catheters in, 159, 160
pressure injectors in, 171–173
problems with, 165–166
radiopacity in, 166
reflux and whipping in, 166
simple catheters in, 159–161
standard catheters in, 155–156
superselective catheters in, 155–156, 166
toposcopic, 159, 160
transaxillary, technique of, 1016
umbilical artery, hypertension and, 1276
ureteral, strictures after, III:578
of ureteroileal anastomoses, III:650
Cat's eye syndrome, 868
Cat-scratch disease, 1925
Caval obstruction, effects of, 910
CAVEAT (Coronary Angioplasty Versus Excisional Atherectomy Trial), III:378–379
Cavernosal arteries, 1644, 1645
anatomy of, III:711–712
obstruction of, III:712, III:713
in penile vascularization, III:709
Cavernosal pulse amplitude (CPA), III:710, III:717, III:718
Cavernosography, 1643–1645, III:708, III:715–721
Cavernosometry, 1643–1645, III:710, III:716–717
Cavernous angiomas, 385
Cavernous carotid arteries
aneurysms of, 320–322, III:769–772, III:773
fistulas in, III:802
fistulas of, after head wound, 347, 353
Cavernous hemangiomas
femoral arteriography in, 1731–1733
hepatic arteriography in, 1439–1441, 1442, 1443
hepatic biopsy in, III:176
bleeding in, III:180, III:181
venous malformations and, III:1022–1026, III:1027
Cavernous lymphangioma in axillary region, 1921
Cavernous sinus, 276
approaches to, 253

intracranial, extraaxial lesions of, III:794, III:798–800
Cavernous venous malformations, III: 1022–1026, III:1027
of brain, 323
Cavography, inferior vena. *See* Inferior vena cavography
Cavro-pump, III:709
CCD (charged coupled devices) technology, 135, 141
CCFs (carotid-cavernous fistulas), intracranial, extraaxial, III:802–808
diagnostic imaging in, III:802–807
neurointerventional management of, III: 807–808
therapeutic approaches to, III:807
CCU (camera control unit), 141
Cecum
angiodysplasia of, 184, III:414–417, III: 418
angiomas of, 1550–1551
carcinoma of, 1574
Cefazolin, III:532
Cefoperazone sodium, III:209
Cefotetan, III:209
Ceftriaxone sodium, III:209
Ceiling suspension of tubes, intensifiers, and ancillary equipment, 105
Celiac angiography. *See also* Celiac arteries
bradykinin and, 62
in hepatic arteriography, 1433–1434. *See also* Hepatic arteriography
in nonocclusive mesenteric ischemia, 1619
in splenic artery embolus, 1617
superior mesenteric angiography with, 1556
Celiac arteries. *See also* Celiac angiography
in adrenal angiography, 1354
anatomy of, 1015, 1017–1018, 1020
aneurysms of, 1631
branches of, 1462
chronic intestinal ischemia and, 1354, 1631
configurations of, 1462
magnification angiography of, 181–182, 183
occlusion of
balloon catheter in, III:32–33
inferior mesenteric arteriography in, 1597
interventional radiology and, III:327, III:331–336
intestinal collateral circulation in, 1595
superior mesenteric artery thrombosis and, 1623
in pancreatic angiography, 1384, 1390
technique and, 1391
in portography, 1527–1528. *See also* Arterial portography
renal artery arteritis and, 1275
splenic arterial branches and, 1458
in splenic arteriography, 1462
with splenic artery aneurysms, 1476
splenic renal artery anastomoses and, 1285
Celiac axis
in donor liver, III:509
in hepatic arteriography, 1433, 1434–1436

in hepatic embolization, III:440, III: 443–444
occlusion of, in superior mesenteric angiography, 1553
in pancreatic vasculature, 1384, 1390
stenosis of, in pancreatitis, 1411, 1413
vasopressin infusion in, III:396
Celiac ganglion, 958
Celiac ganglion block, III:201
Celiac vessels. *See also* Celiac arteries
arteritis of renal arteries and, 1275
magnification angiography of, 181–182, 183
splenic arterial branches and, 1458
splenic renal artery anastomoses and, 1285
Cell biology and physiology of blood vessels, 50–52
Cellule formation in urinary bladder, III: 618
Central anastomotic artery, 1067
Central nervous system, 239–388
aneurysm of. *See* Cerebral aneurysm
arteriovenous malformations of, III:1006
direct arteriovenous fistulas in, III:781
interaxial embolotherapy in, III:775–784
nidus, III:775–779
postembolization care in, III:782–784
radiosurgery for, III:779–781
vein of Galen, III:782, III:783, III: 784
cerebral vascular angiography of, 241–355
history of, 241
indications for, 241
intraoperative, 252–253
materials for, 242–245, 246
noninvasive methods for neck and head imaging and, 252
normal anatomy in, 254–281. *See also* Cerebral vascular anatomy
technique for, 245–252
venography and, 253–254
cerebral vessel abnormalities in, 284–355. *See also* Cerebral vascular anatomy, abnormalities and
interaxial embolotherapy in, III:765–788
for aneurysms, III:767–775. *See also* Cerebral aneurysm
for arteriovenous malformations, III: 775–784. *See also* Arteriovenous malformations (AVMs), cerebral
catheter systems for, III:766
complications of, III:767
embolic agents for, III:766–767
equipment and materials in, III:766–767
patient management in, III:765–766
interventional radiology for, III:743–816
interaxial embolotherapy in, III:765–788. *See also* Central nervous system, interaxial embolotherapy in
in intracranial, extraaxial lesions, III: 789–816. *See also* Intracranial, extraaxial lesions
revascularization in, III:745–764. *See also* Central nervous system, revascularization in

intracranial, extraaxial lesions in, III: 789–816. *See also* Intracranial, extraaxial lesions
revascularization in, III:745–764
acute intraarterial thrombolytic therapy in, III:745–751, III:752, III: 753
angioplasty of brachiocephalic vessels for cerebral ischemia in, III:757–763
carotid artery angioplasty in, III:760–761
innominate artery angioplasty in, III: 761–763
intracranial angioplasty and pharmacologic dilation in post-subarachnoid hemorrhage vasospasm in, III:753–757, III:758
subclavian artery angioplasty in, III: 761–763
vertebral artery occlusive disease in, III:761–763
spinal angiography in, 356–388. *See also* Spinal angiography
thrombolytic therapy in, acute intraarterial, III:745–751, III:752, III:753
vasculitis of, isolated, 307, 308–309
Central pulmonary arteries
developmental anomalies in, 822–838, 839
absence of pulmonary valve in, 828–829
anomalous origin of coronary arteries in, 833, 837, 838
anomalous origin of pulmonary arteries in, 832–833, 836
aorticopulmonary window in, 829
central pulmonary artery stenosis in, 831–832, 833–835
embryology and, 822, 823–824
hypoplastic central pulmonary arteries in, 831, 832
idiopathic pulmonary artery dilatation in, 829, 830
normal anatomy and, 824
patent ductus arteriosus in, 833, 838, 839
pulmonary valve atresia in, 828
pulmonary valve stenosis in, 826–828
truncus arteriosus, 822, 824–827
varying degrees of distention of, 860
Central sulcus, artery of, 270, 271
Central venous catheters, III:970
broken fragment of, III:964, III:965
postintervention care for, III:219–221
Central venous pressure in blunt trauma, 522
Central venous stenoses in dialysis fistula, III:735, III:737
Cephalic lymph nodes, 1881–1882
Cephalic veins, 771
Cephalosporins, 1492
prostatic urethroplasty and, III:628
Ceramic tube for cooling of radiographic tube, 95
Cerebellar arteries
anterior inferior (AICAs), 278
posterior inferior (PICAs), 277–278
aneurysms of, 318
emboli in, 298
superior, 272, 274, 278

Cerebellar vein, precentral (PCV), 278, 279
Cerebral aneurysm, 312–323. *See also* Aneurysm, intracranial
  angiography for diagnosis of, 250–251
  arterial, 312–323
  carotid-cavernous artery, III:769–772, III:773
  criteria for embolotherapy in, III:767
  frequency of, at common sites, 316, 317
  interaxial embolotherapy in, III:767–775
  intraoperative studies in, 252–253
  multiple, 316–319
  pediatric, 316
  petrous carotid artery, III:768–769
  of posterior communicating artery, 260–261, 323
  rupture of, III:753–757, III:758
  types of endovascular therapy for, III:768
  with vascular malformations, 323, 325–326
  vertebral and basilar artery, III:772–775
Cerebral angiography, 241–355
  anatomy in, 254–281. *See also* Cerebral vascular anatomy
  complications of, 245–246
    emboli as, 1029
  film changers for, 68
  history of, 241, 284
  indications for, 241, 284
  intraoperative, 252–253, 284
    in aneurysms, 322–323
  magnification angiography in, 185, 186
  materials for, 242–245, 246
  Moniz cassette changer for, 67
  noninvasive methods for neck and head imaging and, 252
  postprocedural care for, 252
  puncture for, 247–249
  sedation for, 246
  supplies for, 242
  technique for, 245–252
  venography and, 253–254
Cerebral arteries
  aneurysms of, 312–323
  anterior, 261–267
    cortical branches of, 266–267
    horizontal segment of, 261–264
    major variations of, 263
    pericallosal segment of, 264–266
  arteriovenous malformations of. *See* Arteriovenous malformations (AVMs), cerebral
  collateral, 259, 279–281, 287–296
  dissection of, 297–298, 299
  embolism or thrombosis in, 297, 298. *See also* Stroke
  middle, 267–271
    branches of, 266, 269, 270–274
    horizontal segment of, 259, 260–261, 262, 267–268
    insular segment of, 265, 268–269, 270
    stroke and occlusion of, 297–298, 299–302
  posterior, 271–274
    fetal, 260
  shifts of, 329–334

  tumors displacement of, 329–334
  vasospasm of, angioplasty and pharmacologic vasodilation in, III:753–757, III:758
Cerebral fossa. *See* Fossa, cerebral
Cerebral hemorrhage or edema, intraparenchymal, 342
Cerebral infarction, subacute, 302. *See also* Stroke
Cerebral ischemia, angioplasty of brachiocephalic vessels for, III:757–763
Cerebral oil embolism, 1870
Cerebral reactions to thoracic aortography, 399
Cerebral tumors, 328–342
  metastatic, vascular malformations in, 342
Cerebral vascular anatomy, 254–281
  abnormalities and, 284–355
    aneurysms in, 312–323
    atherosclerotic disease in, 285–297
    malformations and fistulas in, 323–328
    stroke in, 297–303
    trauma in, 342–353
    tumor mass effects in, 328–342
    vasculitis and similar disorders in, 303–312, 313
  anterior, 261–267
  carotid artery in
    common, 254–261, 262, 263
    external, 254–257
    internal, 257–261, 262, 263
  collateral circulation in, 259, 279–281, 287–296
  fossa in, 272, 277–279, 280
    basilar artery in, 278
    veins in, 278–279, 280
    vertebral artery in, 277–278
  historical notes on study of, 6, 8, 13
  middle, 267–271
    anterior, 259–262, 266
    cortical branches of, 266, 269, 270–271
    horizontal segment of, 259, 260–261, 262, 267–268
    insular segment of, 265, 268–269, 270
  posterior, 271–274
  supratentorial venous system in, 274–277, 279
Cerebral veins
  circulation time in, 276–277
  collateral, 259, 279–281, 287–296
  dural sinuses in, 274, 276
  sequence of drainage of, 276
  supratentorial, 274–277, 279
    deep, 274, 275–276, 279
    superficial, 274–275
Cerebrovascular ischemia
  pathophysiology of, III:746–747
  revascularization procedures in, III:745–764. *See also* Central nervous system, revascularization in
Cervical carcinoma. *See* Cervix, carcinoma of
Cervical ribs, 996
Cervical spinal cord, 360, 361
Cervical spine
  obscuring parathyroid adenomas, 986
  osteoblastomas of, 1791

Cervical vacuum cup device for hysterosalpingography, III:673, III:674, III:676
Cervical vertebral stenoses, nonorifice, angioplasty of, III:350
Cervicothoracic region
  angiography technique for, 367–368
  spinal artery in, 360, 361
Cervix, carcinoma of, 1645, 1646, 1658
  lymphatic malignant metastases from, 1932
  lymphocyst after lymphadenectomy in, 1920
  regional chemotherapy in, III:82
  ureteral strictures after, III:580
Cesarean section, ureteral strictures after, III:578
Cesium iodide image intensifiers, 98–99, 121
C-Flex ureteral stents, III:573
CFRP (carbon fiber-reinforced plastic), 75
cGMP (cyclic guanosine monophosphate), 51
  nitrates and, 58
CGR roll-film changers, 78–80
cGTP (cyclic guanosine triphosphate), 51
Chamberlain WE, 9, 66
Changer design in cardiac serial radiography, 102
Chapman CB, 9
Charbonnel, 6
Charged coupled devices (CCD) technology, 135, 141
Charny C, III:678
Chávez I, 8
Chemical pneumonia after lymphangiography, 1868–1869
Chemoembolization
  cyanoacrylate in, 1646, 1648
  doxorubicin and ethiodol in, 1646, 1648
  of hepatoma omental metastases, 167
  pain after, III:201
  pelvic angiography in, 1661–1665
  in sarcomas, III:1031–1036
  superselective catheterization in
    hepatic artery, 160–161
    problems during, 165
Chemoprophylaxis in patent ductus arteriosus, 421
Chemotherapy
  intraarterial, for sarcomas, III:1031–1036
  regional, III:80–84
    clinical applications of, III:82, III:83
    complications of, III:82–84
    drug classes and mechanisms of action of, III:80–82
    in hepatic malignancy, III:437–438
    pharmacokinetics of, III:80
    superselective, 1661–1665
Chest compression in blunt trauma, 528
Chest pain
  after bronchial artery embolization, III:827
  atypical, coronary arteriography in diagnosis of, 638
  dissecting aortic aneurysms with, 496, 497
Chest tube in thoracic empyema drainage, III:832, III:833, III:834

Chest x-ray
  admission, in blunt trauma, 524
  in coarctation of aorta, 441, 442, 443
  in dissecting aortic aneurysms, 497–503
  in patent ductus arteriosus, 421–422, 423
  in pulmonary arteriovenous malformations, III:838, III:839
  in renal cell carcinoma, 1154
  in thoracic aortic aneurysms, 468
Chiba needle
  in percutaneous transhepatic cholangiography, III:474
  in venous access catheter placement, III:975
Child. *See* Pediatrics, interventional angiography in
Child classification of cirrhosis, III:536
Chloral hydrate, III:213
Chlorambucil, III:81
Chloroprocaine, III:214
Cholangiocarcinoma, extrahepatic
  biopsy in, III:176
  obstruction in, III:472–482
Cholangiography, percutaneous transhepatic. *See* Percutaneous transhepatic cholangiography (PTC)
Cholangiopathy, AIDS-related, III:470
Cholangitis
  hepatic arteriography in, 1438
  primary sclerosing, III:465–470
Cholecystectomy, laparoscopic, percutaneous cholecystolithotomy versus, III:505–506
Cholecystitis
  acalculous, percutaneous cholecystomy in, III:485
  acute
    calculous, percutaneous cholecystolithotomy in, III:505
    percutaneous cholecystomy in, III:485, III:486–487, III:488
Cholecystocholangiography, III:485–486
Cholecystokinin
  in pancreatic angiography, 1392
  in superior mesenteric angiography, 1557
Cholecystolithotomy, percutaneous (PCCL), III:487–489, III:501–507
  complications of, III:500
  extracorporeal shock wave lithotripsy in, III:505
  gallstone dissolution therapy and, III:504–505
  laparoscopic cholecystectomy versus, III:505–506
  morbidity in, III:500
  preferred methods for, III:502–504
  in removal of biliary calculi, III:501–507
  results of, III:505–507
  techniques for, III:501–502
Cholecystostomy, percutaneous, III:483–490
  complications of, III:489
  diagnostic indications for, III:485–486
  history of, III:483
  interventional indications for, III:485, III:486–487, III:488
  percutaneous cholecystolithotomy in, III:487–489
  technical considerations in, III:483–485

Choledochoenterostomy, III:477
Choledochojejunostomy
  in liver transplantation biliary tract reconstruction, III:516–517
  transjejunal removal of biliary calculi after, III:496
Choledocholithotomy in percutaneous stone removal
  transhepatic, III:495–496
  transjejunal, III:496
Cholesterol
  aneurysms and, 1073
  restenosis after balloon angioplasty and, III:8, III:14, III:15–16
Cholesterol embolism syndrome, 1060, 1110, 1111
  multiple, 1029
Cholinergic receptors, 51
Chondroblastoma, 1783, 1784
Chondromas of spleen, 1482
Chondrosarcomas
  of extremities, 1735, 1783–1786, 1787, 1788
  of pelvis, 1814
  retroperitoneal, 1669
Chorioadenoma, 1646
Choriocarcinoma, testicular, 1933, 1935
Chorioepithelioma, 1646, 1647
Choroidal arteries
  anterior, 260–261, 262, 263, 273
    arteritis of, 307
  lateral, 271, 273
  medial, 271–274
Chrondromyxoid fibromas, 1783
Chronic obstructive pulmonary diseases, percutaneous biopsy complications in, III:178, III:187
Chung catheter, III:433
Churton T, III:837
Chyloderma, 1908
Chyloperitoneum, 1900, 1918–1919
Chyloretroperitoneum, 1918, 1919
Chylorrhea, 1908
Chylothorax, 1900–1901, 1918–1919, 1920
  congenital, 1901
Chylous edema, 1907–1908, 1910–1911
Chylous reflux, 1907
Chyluria, 1920
Cigarette smoking
  aneurysm and, 1073
  in aortoiliac disease, III:227
  arteriosclerosis and, 1052
  restenosis after balloon angioplasty and, III:8, III:14
Cilazapril, III:15
Cimino JE, 1767
Cine camera
  in cardiac catheterization laboratory, 99–100
  silicone on runners of, 123
Cine framing in cardiac catheterization laboratory, 100–101
Cine magazines, cleaning of, 123
Cine processing
  in cardiac catheterization, 106–111, 112, 113
  equipment for, 109–111, 112, 113
  quality control for, 123–124
Cine pulsing systems in cardiac catheterization, 92–93

Cine viewers
  in cardiac catheterization, 111–114, 115
  film transport in, 113–114, 115
  image optics in, 111–113
Cineangiography
  in aortic arch anomalies, 547
  beam limitation in, 124–125
  in cardiac catheterization, 87. *See also* Cardiac catheterization laboratory
  collimators for, 97
  in evaluation of aortic grafts, 549
  generators for, 91
  historical notes on, 8, 9
  image intensifiers for, 99
  for ischemic heart disease study, 121
  in left ventriculography, 561
  in pulmonary arteriography, 777
  in thoracic aortography, 410
  transformer for, 94, 95
  tubes for, 96–97
Cinedensitometry, renal function and, 1125
Cine-fill technique in nonsubtraction cardiac angiography, 152
Cineless laboratories, archiving for, 149
Cipro 35 cine viewer, 115
Ciprostene, III:15
Circle of Willis, 261, 280
  collateral circulation in, 287, 290–291, 293
  in magnetic resonance angiography, 196
Circulation
  collateral. *See* Collateral circulation
  in coronary arteries. *See* Coronary arteries
  equipment for emergency treatment of, 48
  pulmonary, drug effects on, magnification angiography in, 181
  satellite anastomotic, 701
Circulation time in cerebral veins, 276–277
Circulatory equipment for emergency treatment, 48
Circumaortic venous ring, 1315, 1317
  persistent, 947, 950
Circumcaval ureter, 945, 946
Circumflex arteries
  as branches of profunda femoris artery, 1698
  coronary. *See* Coronary arteries, circumflex
  deep iliac, 1067
  humeral, compression of, 1008
  left atrial, 589, 619
  medial femoral, pseudoaneurysm of, 1652
Circumflex iliac veins, 954, 956
Cirrhosis
  arterial–portal venous shunts in, 1436, 1437
  biopsy and, III:180, III:186
  computerized tomography during portography of, 1545
  hepatic arteriography in, 1436–1438, 1439
    computerized tomography during, 1545
  in inferior vena cava obstruction, 959
  portosystemic shunt surgery in, III:526

Cirrhosis—*Continued*
splenic arteriography in
aneurysms and, 1477
splenomegaly and, 1467
splenomegaly in, 1467
splenoportography in, 1508, 1512–1521
transhepatic portal venography in, 1423
Cisplatin, III:81
in axial skeleton sarcomas, III:1035
in cervical carcinoma, III:82
in endometrial carcinoma, III:82
in extremity sarcomas, III:1032
in gastrointestinal sarcomas, III:1035
in head and neck carcinoma, III:82, III:
83
in hepatic malignancy, III:437
in osteosarcomas, III:1032–1033
postembolization syndrome and, III:202
in soft tissue sarcomas, III:1034
Cisterna chyli, 1891, 1892, 1893
absence of, 1898, 1899
ampullaceous, 1885, 1888
conical, 1885
fusiform, 1884, 1885
magnetic resonance lymphangiography
of, 1902
percutaneous cannulation of, 1901–
1902
various shapes of, 1892–1893, 1894
CK1 (Kerber) catheter, 244, 245
Clam shell device in atrial septal defect closure, 428
Claudication
in aortoiliac disease
angioplasty in, III:231, III:232, III:
245–250
atherectomy and, III:238–239
in blue toe syndrome, III:227
stents and, III:236–238, III:251–253,
III:255
thrombolysis and, III:233, III:234–
235, III:251–253
in treatment indications, III:240, III:
241, III:243–244
attempted stent deployment in, III:40–
42
in coronary artery catheterization complications, 579
femoropopliteal revascularization and,
III:266–271, III:273
infrapopliteal revascularization and, III:
284
recurrent, after aortobilateral common
iliac graft, 1682
test for, 999
in vertebrobasilar artery vasospasm, III:
761–763
Clavicle
congenital or acquired lesions of, in thoracic outlet syndrome, 996, 997
fracture of, 997
Clean supply room for cardiac catheterization, 89
Clips for partial interruption of inferior
vena cava, III:982–983
Clival lesions, intracranial, extraaxial, III:
794–795
Clonidine, 1306
Clot
renal transplant obstruction from, III:
581

surface characteristics of, III:124–125
Clot retraction, III:124
Clothing of personnel for cerebral angiography, 247
CMV (cytomegalovirus), III:17, III:518
c-myc protooncogene, III:16
Coagulation
disorders of. *See* Coagulation disorders
monitoring of, in angioplasty, III:368
in pediatric interventional angiography,
III:903
Coagulation cascade, 25
Coagulation disorders
in bleeding with biopsy, III:180, III:183
as gastrostomy tube contraindication,
III:548
preintervention assessment and, III:207–
208
Coagulative necrosis in prostatic hyperthermia, III:635–636
Coarctation
of aorta. *See* Aorta, coarctation of
of central pulmonary artery, 796–798
Coaxial catheters
in biopsy, III:175
in chronic obstructive pulmonary diseases, III:178, III:179
in bronchial artery embolization, III:
825, III:826
in detachable balloon embolization, III:
67
in hepatic embolization, III:440, III:
443–444
history of use of, III:24
in hysterosalpingography, III:673, III:
676
in intraaxial embolotherapy for central
nervous system, III:766
pelvic arteriography with, 1652
digital, 1637–1638
in renal angioplasty, III:302–303
in splenic trauma, III:890
for superselective catheterization, 161–
165
in urethral lesions, III:618
Cobb syndrome, 369
Cobblestone appearance after extracorporeal shock wave lithotripsy, III:608
Cobra catheter. *See* French Cobra catheters
Cockpit-type control room, 87–88
Codominant coronary distribution of coronary arteries, 589, 749–750
Coil baffles in embolization, III:62
Coils. *See also* Embolization; Metal-based
mechanical embolic agents
Amplatz positioner for, III:60, III:61
in arteriovenous malformations, III:
1011, III:1012
in fistulas, III:1002
pulmonary, in embolotherapy, III:
846, III:847, III:848, III:851
barbed, III:61
in bronchial artery embolization, III:
825, III:826
detachable balloon compared to, III:72
diameter of, III:59–60
in extremity trauma, III:863–867
Gianturco. *See* Gianturco coils
in intraaxial embolotherapy for central
nervous system, III:766

in intracranial, extraaxial lesion embolization, III:791
in carotid-cavernous fistula, III:808
in dural arteriovenous malformations,
III:802
magnetic resonance venography and,
1852
malpositioned, III:60
materials for, III:56–57
migrated, III:60
paradoxical embolization of, in pulmonary arteriovenous malformations,
III:845, III:850
in patent ductus arteriosus, 427
in pediatric embolization, III:906–908,
III:909, III:910
in pelvic arteriography, 1652, 1655,
1657
in pelvic chondrosarcoma, 1814
in pelvic fracture hemorrhage embolization, III:878–879
in penile transluminal angioplasty, III:
723
placement of, before embolization, III:
60
in pulmonary arteriovenous malformation embolotherapy, III:846, III:
848
oversized, III:847, III:851
in renal trauma embolization, III:897–
898
soaked in thrombin, III:61
technique in use of, III:57–59
in varicocele embolization, III:694, III:
696, III:697
in vein of Galen malformation embolotherapy, III:782, III:783, III:784
wool, III:55, III:56
Colapinto RF, III:199
Colapinto needle, III:531, III:532
for intravascular biopsy, III:198, III:199
Colapinto transjugular intrahepatic portosystemic shunt, III:530. *See also*
Transjugular intrahepatic portosystemic shunt (TIPS)
Colchicine, III:15
Colic arteries
anatomy of, 1019–1020, 1021
left, 1588, 1589, 1596–1597, 1598
retrograde filling of, in superior mesenteric angiography, 1591, 1592
middle
retrograde filling of, in inferior mesenteric angiography, 1591
in superior mesenteric angiography,
1552
variant of, 1460
right, in superior mesenteric angiography, 1552
Colitis
cytomegalovirus, 1607
granulomatous, 1607, 1608
mesenteric angiography in, III:327
inferior, 1605–1607, 1608, 1611,
1612–1613
superior, 1565–1566, 1568
ulcerative, 1606–1607, 1608
bleeding from, III:414–415
Collagen in small-vessel or tissue embolization, III:52–53
in hepatic malignancy, III:437

Collagen vascular diseases, cerebral arteries in, 307
Collateral circulation
in abdominal aorta arteriosclerosis and other diseases, 1056, 1060, 1061–1063, 1064–1069
parietal, 1063, 1065, 1067–1069
systemic-systemic, 1063, 1065, 1067–1069
visceral-systemic, 1056, 1061, 1062–1063, 1066–1067
after lymphadenectomy, 1909
in aortoiliac occlusion, 1063–1069
arteriovenous fistulas and, III:1001
cerebral, 259, 279–281, 287–296
coarctation of aorta and, 437–438, 447, 449, 450
coil blockade of, in hepatic embolization, III:440, III:447, III:448–449
coronary. *See* Coronary collateral circulation
femoral artery and, 1699, 1700–1703
of inferior vena cava, 949–958
central channels of, 951, 952
intermediate channels of, 951–954
intrarenal obstruction and, 951–957
middle obstruction and, 952–955, 957
portal system and, 953–957
potential routes for, 955–957
practical routes for, 951–955
superficial routes of, 954–955
upper obstruction and, 952–953, 955–956, 957–958
in intrahepatic obstruction, III:439, III:440, III:445–446, III:447, III:452
arterial portography of, 1532–1535
hepatofugal or hepatopetal, 1506
to left colon, inferior mesenteric angiography in, 1591–1593, 1594–1597
in lymphatic obstruction from malignancy, 1931
of mesenteric vessels
inferior mesenteric angiography in, 1591–1593, 1594–1597
ischemia and, 1615
superior mesenteric angiography in, 1552, 1553–1555
in moderator band, 703
to penis and corpus cavernosa, III:712, III:714–715
portosystemic, 1422, 1424
principles of availability of pathways in, 951
in pulmonary valve atresia, 828
of pulmonary vessels, III:822, III:823
in renal ischemia, hypertension and, 1276–1284
in renovascular hypertension, 1249
schematic diagram of major potential, 1064
spermatic vein, III:681–686, III:687
in varicocele recurrence after surgery, III:692, III:693
in subclavian artery stenoses, 996–998
superior vena cava and
obstructed, 915–916
route to, 1511
in thromboangiitis obliterans, 1726, 1727
venous access catheters and, III:975

Collateral steal, 722
Collecting system
duplicated, hydronephrosis and, 1210–1211
extension of renal abscess into, 1184–1185, 1189, 1199
Collett and Edwards classification of truncus arteriosus, 825
Collimation
in cardiac catheterization laboratory, 97–98
in vascular intervention angiography, 134
Collisions, blunt trauma from
broadside, 522, 529–532
frontal, 522–523, 528–529
Colon
adenocarcinoma of
arterial portography in, 1542, 1543
biopsy in, III:167, III:187
inferior mesenteric angiography in, 1603–1605
inferior vena cavogram in retroperitoneal metastases from, 936
magnification angiography of, 183
metastatic to liver, 183, 1453, 1542, 1543, III:167, III:436, III:450–451, III:472–474
polyps and, 1604, 1605
angiodysplasia of ascending, 184, III:414–417, III:418
bleeding from
angiographic detection rates in, 1611
diverticular, 1608, 1609, III:390, III:392, III:411–414
duodenal bleeding versus, III:394, III:396
inferior mesenteric angiography in, 1608–1611, 1612–1613
polyp removal and, III:411, III:412
of undetermined artery, 1590
inferior mesenteric artery and, 1590
inflammatory disease of, 1605–1607, 1608
injury to
in extracorporeal shock wave lithotripsy complication, III:607
as percutaneous stone removal complication, III:602
left
bleeding from, 1608–1611, 1612–1613
collateral circulation to, 1591–1593, 1594–1597
polyps of, malignant, 1604, 1605
transverse, in inferior vena cava obstruction, 958
villous adenoma of, 1604
Color Doppler sonography. *See* Color flow imaging
Color flow imaging. *See also* Doppler imaging
of inferior vena cava, 938, 939
physics of, 210–211, color plates 1 and 2
in postoperative vein surveillance, 224, 226, color plate 11
in thoracic outlet syndrome, 999–1001
in varicocele, 232, III:689
Color response of film, 105

Colorectal carcinoma metastatic to liver, III:450–451
Coltman JW, 9
Columns of Bertin, prominent, 1166, 1167, 1168
Coman DR, 892
Combilabor film processor, 112
Combination systems for exposure control, 94
Communicating arteries
anterior (ACOM), cerebral aneurysms in, 314, 315
posterior (PCOM)
anatomy of, 260
arteritis of, 307
infundibulum or aneurysm of, 260–261, 323
Compartment compression, brachial, 1031
Compartment syndrome as complication of transgraft thrombolysis, III:155
Compliance
in balloon catheter, III:25–26, III:27
lung, 865
Complications
of arterial portography, 1530
of contrast agents. *See* Contrast media
of dialysis shunt, 1768, 1769–1778
of inferior vena cavography, 971–972
of lumbar aortography, 1024–1051. *See also* Lumbar aortography, complications of
of lymphangiography, 1867–1870
of pancreatic vein catheterization, 1428–1429
of parathyroid angiography, 984
of pelvic intraarterial fibrinolytic therapy, 1640
of portal venography
with transhepatic approach, 1425
with transjugular approach, 1426
postoperative. *See* Postoperative complications
of splenoportography, 1500
of umbilical vein approach to portal vein, 1426
Compression. *See also* Displacement
balloon angioplasty and, III:4
of brachial plexus after transaxillary arteriography, 1031
of circumflex humeral artery, 1008
in liver injury, III:422, III:423
of lung
after empyema, 817
pulmonary hypovascularity in, 816
of portal veins, 1397, 1402
of renal artery, hypertension and, 1269–1270
of septal branches during ventricular systole, 686
of splenic veins, 1397, 1399–1400, 1410
of superior mesenteric veins, 1394, 1397
Computed phase differences in phase contrast angiography, 200, 201
Computed vascular signal as function of flip angle, 195
Computer programmer with Picker cassette changer, 71, 72
Computerized tomography (CT)
in abdominal abscesses, III:925–928
of liver, III:929, III:930

Computerized tomography (CT)—
  Continued
 in abdominal abscesses—*Continued*
  of pancreas, III:934–935
  of perirenal area, III:936
  in psoas infection, III:937
  of spleen, III:931–932
 in abdominal aorta aneurysms, 1074–
  1075, 1076, 1081, 1082–1086
  spiral volumetric, 1091, 1093, 1094
 in acute mesenteric venous thrombosis,
  1624
 in acute pyelonephritis, 1179
 of adrenal glands, 1357–1358
  in adrenal hemorrhage, 1379
  in pheochromocytoma, 1370
 after aortoiliac interventions, progression
  of disease and, 1682, 1685, 1687–
  1689, 1690–1695
 after renal transplantation, 1335
 in arterial portography, 1541–1545
 in arteriovenous malformations, III:1006
 in aspiration of paraprosthetic fluid after
  aortoiliac interventions, 1694, 1695
 in benign biliary obstructions, III:458
 in bilateral adrenal masses, 1362–1364
 in biopsy, III:174–177, III:185–186
  of musculoskeletal system, III:191
  pneumothorax and, III:179
 in blunt trauma to aorta and brachiocephalic arteries, 524
 in carotid angioplasty, III:340
 in cerebral artery vasospasm, III:754
 in cerebral studies, 252
 in chronic atrophic pyelonephritis, 1197
 in Crohn disease fistulas and abscesses,
  III:943
 in dissecting aortic aneurysms, 514–516
 in dural arteriovenous malformations,
  III:801
 in hepatic malignancy, III:438
 in hepatobiliary malignant obstructions,
  III:473, III:476
 in hydronephrosis, 1202, 1203, 1213
 in infected caliceal diverticulum, 1199
 of inferior vena cava, 940, 941, 942
 of intracranial, extraaxial lesions, III:789,
  III:812–813
 in islet-cell tumors, 1403
 in liver transplantation bile leakage complications, III:521
 in lymphoma diagnostic accuracy, 1951
 in pancreatic carcinoma, 1398
 in patent ductus arteriosus, 423
 in pelvic abscesses, III:943, III:946–
  947
 in pelvic interventional radiology, III:
  870–871
 in percutaneous cholecystomy, III:484
 in percutaneous nephrostomy, III:565
 in periappendiceal abscesses, III:941
 in preinterventional assessment, III:206
 in pulmonary arteriovenous malformations, III:838
 in pulmonary embolism, 812
 in regional chemotherapy artery selection, III:82
 in renal abscess, 1184
 in renal calculi, III:594, III:598, III:599
 in renal cell carcinoma, 1140, 1142,
  1143

 in renal cysts, 1171, 1173
  after marsupialization, III:666
  interventional therapy and, III:658,
   III:660, III:662, III:664–666
 in renal pelvic tumors, 1159–1160
 in renal trauma, 1230, III:894–895
 in renal tuberculosis, 1196
 in renal vein thrombosis, 1309
 of retroperitoneal space, 1670, 1676
 in sarcomas, III:1031
 in spinal dural arteriovenous fistulas of
  type I, 373–374
 in splenic trauma, III:885–886, III:888,
  III:890
 in stroke, III:747, III:748–749, III:
  752–753
 of superior mesenteric arteries, 1549
 in thoracic abscesses, III:829–836
 in thoracic aortic aneurysms, 469–471
 in thoracic duct studies, 1892, 1893
 in transjejunal choledocholithotomy, III:
  496
 in venous malformations, III:1023
 in xanthogranulomatous pyelonephritis,
  1193
COMT (catechol-O-methyltransferase), 54
Concurrent rethrombosis, III:125–127
Conducting system, 615–619, 620, 621
Conduit, ileal or urinary, complications
  related to, III:654–655, III:656
Confidence profile method for measuring
  femoropopliteal revascularization
  results, III:266
Congenital abnormalities. *See also* Anomalies and malformations
  arteriovenous malformations and, III:
   1003, III:1006
  in atresia of coronary arteries, 744, 745–
   746
  in chylothorax, 1901
  in clavicular lesions, 996
  coronary artery stenosis in, 744, 745–746
  of heart. *See* Congenital heart disease
  inferior vena cava obstruction and, 964
  of kidney, renal stones in, III:591, III:
   596
  in lobar emphysema, 799
  in lobulation of kidney, 1166
  lymphedema as, 1907
  pulmonary, 822–848. *See also* Congenital abnormalities, pulmonary arteriography in; Pulmonary
   developmental anomalies
   venous. *See* Anomalous pulmonary
    venous connection
  pulmonary arteriography in, 786–799,
   800. *See also* Pulmonary developmental anomalies
   anomalous origin of coronary artery
    in, 799, 800
   aorticopulmonary window in, 796,
    798
   arteriovenous fistula in, 794–795,
    796, 797
   atresia and coarctation in, 796–798,
    799
   coronary artery–pulmonary artery fis-
    tula in, 799
   idiopathic dilatation in, 796
   lobar emphysema in, 799
   multiple stenoses in, 792, 793

  patent ductus arteriosus in, 796, 798
  pathophysiologic considerations in,
   786–788, 789–791
  sequestration in, 798–799
  sling in, 794
  stenosis and poststenotic dilatation in,
   788–793
  of radial artery, 1755, 1756
  of renal pelvis, 1228
  renovascular hypertension and, 1258
  of spleen, 1459, 1461, 1468–1472
   accessory spleen and, 1471
   anomalies of number in, 1471–1472
   anomalies of position in, 1459, 1461,
    1468–1471
   asplenia and, 1471–1472
   polysplenia and, 1472
   variants of normal in, 1459, 1461,
    1468
   wandering spleen in, 1468–1471
  in thoracic duct, 396, 1898, 1899, 1901
  urethral strictures and, III:617
  in vascular hamartomas of spinal cord,
   386
Congenital aneurysms
  arteriovenous
   femoral arteriography in, 1731–1733
   pelvic, 1654–1658
  of thoracic aorta, 487–488
Congenital heart disease, 637–638
  aortic stenosis in, 540
  cardiac catheterization laboratory for,
   122
  devices for occluding defects and shunts
   in, III:55, III:70
  laboratory for study of, 122
  patent ductus arteriosus in. *See* Patent
   ductus arteriosus (PDA)
  pulmonary arteriography in. *See* Congenital abnormalities, pulmonary arteriography in
Congestive heart failure
  in congenital aortic stenosis, 541
  in coronary arteriography complications,
   575, 578
  dissecting aortic aneurysms with, 496–
   497
  hemangioma and, III:998
  in infant with coarctation of aorta, 438,
   441, 442
  nephrotoxicity of contrast agents and,
   23, 24
  portal venous hypertension and, 231
  pulmonary arteriography in, 786, 818–
   819
  pulmonary hypervascularity in, 815–816
Conical cisterna chyli, 1885
Coning, exposure factors and, 70
Connective tissue in arteriosclerosis, 1052
Connheim J, 700
Conray. *See* Iothalamate
Conray 43, cardiac toxicity of, 29
Conray 60%, 170
Conray 400, 170
Consent
  for pediatric interventional angiography,
   III:903
  in preinterventional assessment, III:206
Consoles, 135
Constant-potential generators, 91

Consultations in preintervention assessment, III:205–206

Contamination in arterial puncture, 156–157

Continuing filtration, cine film processing and, 109

Continuous flush systems, 1029

Continuous quality improvement (CQI). *See* Quality improvement

Continuous-wave argon laser systems, III:380, III:381

Contraceptives, oral
  hepatic adenomas and, 1444
  hypertension and, 1276
  pulmonary embolism and, 809

Contractility of vessels, contrast agents and, 27

Contrast
  image display in digital angiography and, 146, 150
  kilovoltage and, 105, 106
  latitude and, 105, 106, 108
  temporal subtraction and, 149–150

Contrast media
  advantages and disadvantages of, 20
  allergic reaction to, 29, 30, 49. *See also* Contrast media, complications of
    lymphangiography and, 1868
    in pulmonary arteriography, 783
    symptoms and treatment of, 35
  in angiography of extremities for aorto-iliac intervention problems, 1688
  in aortic stenosis, 541
  in arterial portography, 1529
  in blunt trauma to aorta and brachiocephalic arteries, 523, 526
  in cerebral angiography, 242
    injection of, 249
  chemistry of, 13–21
  column of
    eccentric changes of density in, 1056, 1057–1058
    filling defects in, 1056, 1057
  complications of, 23–30, 1024–1025, 1026. *See also* Contrast media, allergic reaction to
    cardiac effects in, 26–29
    in coronary arteriography, 568, 576–579
    emergency treatment for, 34–48. *See also* Emergency treatment
    immune-mediated systemic reactions in, 29
    layering of, in coronary angiography, 626, 627
    in lymphangiography, 1866–1867
    osmolality and, 24, 26–31
    in renal angiography, 1110–1113
    in thoracic aortography, 397–398
    vascular effects in, 24–26
  in coronary arteriography artifacts, 737–738
  delivery rate for, 70
  dilution of, in vascular system, 170
  dose-related toxicity of, 49
  extravasation of
    in extremity, 1752–1753
    intraadrenal, 1356
    renal, 1106–1107, 1108
  in extremity venography, 1743, 1746
    extravasation of, 1752–1753

factors affecting use of, 22
  in femoral arteriography, 1713–1714
  history of, 13–21
  iodinated, hot, in varicocele embolization, III:698
  osmolality of, 26–31
    cardiac complications and, 26–27, 28, 29
    for cerebral studies, 242
    renal toxicity and, 24
    vascular and hematologic effects of, 24–26
  in pancreatic angiography, 1395–1396
  in pelvic digital angiography, 1638
  in penile vascularization, III:709, III:710
    in cavernosography, III:717–719
  percent of, in superselective catheterization, 166
  physiologic effects and systemic reactions to, 22–33
    emergency treatment of, 34–48. *See also* Emergency treatment
  pooling or laking of, in tumor, 1781
  protracted injection of, 83
  in pulmonary arteriography, 776
  reflux of, into sinus of Valsalva, 726–727, 729
  for renal angiography, 1110–1113
    renal function and, 1125–1126
    techniques of, 1110
    toxicity of, 1110–1113
  renal effects in, 23–24, III:217
  renal failure in, 1025–1026
  in renal venography, 1290
  risk factors in, 1026
  in superior mesenteric angiography, 1555, 1556, 1557
  systemic effects in, 29–30
  in thoracic aortography, 395
    death from, 397–398
    site of injection of, in complications, 398
    volume of, 395, 396
  in transfemoral catheterization, 1015
  in upper extremity arteriography, 1755–1756
  varieties of, 13–21
  vascular and hematologic effects in, 24–26
  for vascular intervention angiography, 135
  viscosities of, 170

Contrast ratio
  of image intensifiers, 99
  of optical system, 99

Control console, 135

Control room
  in cardiac catheterization laboratory, 87–88
  in vascular intervention angiography laboratory, 136

Control venous access catheters, postintervention care for, III:219–221

Contusions of liver, 1455

Conus, pulmonary, collaterals of, 703–704, 706–708

Conus artery, 361
  in coronary artery catheterization, 565
  origin of
    separate, as arteriography pitfall, 729–731
    variation in, 750

Conversion
  analog-to-digital, 142–143
  progressive acquisition-to-interlaced-display scan, 146

Convexity, intracranial, extraaxial lesions of, III:791–793

Convolution, spatial, 144–146

Convulsions in thoracic aortography complications, 399

Cook anchor
  in percutaneous cholecystolithotomy, III:504
  in transjejunal choledocholithotomy, III:496

Cook catheter
  in bronchial artery embolization, III:825
  in dialysis fistula thrombolysis, III:729

Cook coils for embolization, III:56–57

Cook deflector wire
  in dialysis fistula thrombolysis, III:729
  in penile vascularization, III:709

Cook introducer sheath in percutaneous cholecystolithotomy, III:504

Cook micropuncture introducing set, 157, III:694

Cook needle
  in dialysis fistula thrombolysis, III:729, III:730
  in venous access catheter placement, III:973

Cooley Veri-Soft graft, III:359

Cooling device for radiographic tube, 95

Cope guidewire, 162
  in percutaneous cholecystostomy, III:484
  in percutaneous transhepatic cholangiography, III:474, III:475

Cope loop catheter
  in pelvic abscess drainage, III:952
  in percutaneous gastrostomy, III:550, III:552
  in percutaneous nephrostomy, III:566, III:568, III:570

Cope minivascular set, 1327

Cope suture anchor in percutaneous gastrostomy, III:554

Cor bovinum, 543

Cor pulmonale
  in obliterative pulmonary diseases, 803
  pulmonary arteriography and, 783, 799

Cordis catheter, III:329–330
  in penile vascularization, III:709, III:722

Cordis injector, 172

Cordis stent, III:89

Corkscrew appearance of collateral circulation, 1726, 1727

Coronary angioplasty, III:366–385
  angioplasty of other vessels versus, III:367–368
  atherectomy in, III:377–380
    lumen diameter after, III:7
  balloon, conventional, III:368–374. *See also* Balloon angioplasty, in coronary disease
  bypass surgery versus, in multivessel disease, III:382–383
  complications of, III:255–256, III:257, III:372–373
  efficacy of, III:381–382
  history of, III:366
  laser ablation techniques in, III:380–381

Coronary angioplasty—*Continued*
  monitoring requirements for, III:367–
    368
  new devices in, III:382
  radiologic equipment for, III:368
  radiologic projections in, III:369–370
  safety of, III:381–382
  stenting in, III:374–377
  surgical backup in, III:368
Coronary Angioplasty Versus Excisional
  Atherectomy Trial (CAVEAT), III:
  378–379
Coronary arteries, 583–634
  accessibility of, III:367
  acute marginal branch in, 587
  after coronary artery bypass graft, 760–
    762
  anatomic variations of, 749–755
  angioplasty of. *See* Coronary angioplasty
  anomalies of, 740–749
    altered myocardial perfusion from,
      740–745
    aorticopulmonary window and, 464,
      796, 798
    as arteriographic pitfalls, 738
    congenital stenosis or atresia in, 744,
      745–746
    fistulas in, 740–741, 742, 800
    of origin. *See* Coronary arteries, anom-
      alous origin of
    single coronary artery in, 747–748
    unaltered myocardial perfusion from,
      746–748
  anomalous origin of, 833, 837, 838
    all from either right or left sinus of
      Valsalva via two or three separate
      ostia, 748, 749
    circumflex, 602, 603, 746, 747, 750
    high, 748
    left, from pulmonary artery, 741–744
    left, from right sinus of Valsalva, 744,
      746
    left anterior descending, from right
      sinus of Valsalva, 746–747
    from pulmonary artery, 741–744,
      799, 800
    from right anterior aortic sinus, 599–
      602
    from right sinus of Valsalva, 744,
      746–747
    sinoatrial node artery and, 750
  anterior atrial branch in, 587
  anterior descending, 587–588, 602
  aortic root in, 591–603
  aplasia of, 596, 598
  arteriosclerosis of
    multivessel, 680–681, 682–683
    in obtuse marginal arteries, 674, 675,
      676–677, 682
    in right coronary arteries, 677–680,
      681
  atrial arteries in, 615–619, 620, 621
  atrioventricular node artery and, 750
  balanced distribution of, 589, 625
  cardiac topography and, 586–590
  catheterization of. *See* Coronary arteriog-
    raphy
  circulation in, 586–589
  circumflex
    branches of, to ventricular wall, 604,
      605, 606

  coronary artery catheterization and,
    564, 574
  left (LCX). *See* Coronary arteries, left
    circumflex (LCX)
  length and size of, 755
  origin of. *See* Coronary arteries, anom-
    alous origin of
  right, 586, 750
  sinoatrial node artery origin and, 750
codominant distribution of, 589
conducting system in, 615–619, 620,
  621
congenital stenosis or atresia of, 744,
  745–746
contractility of, contrast agents and, 27,
  28, 29
conus artery origin in, 750
coronary ostia in, 591–603
coronary veins in, 590, 591
diagnostic value of normal coronary
  angiogram and, 626–631
diagonal, 611
  in anatomic variations of coronary
    arteries, 753, 754
  arteriosclerosis of, 670–673, 674
  superimposed in arteriography over
    obstructions, 733
dilated and tortuous, with supravalvular
  aortic stenosis, 542
dimensions of, III:367
disease of. *See* Coronary disease
dominance variation in, 749–750, 751
ectopia of, 596
epicardial, vasospasm in, 731–733
fistulas in, 740–741, 742
general description of circulation and cardiac topography in, 586–590
intermediate atrial branch of, 587
intramural circulation in, 589–590,
  619–623, 630
ischemic heart disease angiography and,
  119–120
left (LCA), 587–588, 607–614
  Amplatz catheter and, 570
  anomalous origin of, from right ante-
    rior aortic sinus, 599, 600
  anterior descending branch of. *See* Cor-
    onary arteries, left anterior descend-
    ing (LAD)
  arteriosclerosis in, 662–677, 682–683
  branches of, to ventricle, 611–613
  catheterization and, 562–564
  circumflex. *See* Coronary arteries, left
    circumflex (LCX)
  intermediate, 589
  during isovolumetric contraction, 686
  obtuse marginal, arteriosclerosis in,
    674, 675, 676–677, 682
  RAO and LAO views of, 561, 566–
    568, 588, 593
  single, 748
left anterior descending (LAD)
  anatomy of, 587–588, 607–614
  arteriosclerosis of, 665–670, 671–674
  branches of, to ventricle, 611
  collaterals of, 712, 715, 721
  coronary artery catheterization and,
    564, 565, 566, 574
  diagonal branches of, 753, 754
  fistulas of, to pulmonary artery, 741
  intermediate branches of, 611

  length of, 753–755
  marginal branches of, 611
  origin of, from pulmonary artery,
    741–744
  origin of, from right sinus of Valsalva,
    744, 746–747
  right septal branch of, 611
  single coronary artery anomalies and,
    748
  termination point of, 609
  variations of, 602, 609–611
left circumflex (LCX)
  abnormal origin of, 602, 603
  anatomy of, 587–588, 589, 607–614
  arteriosclerosis in, 672, 673–676
  atrial, 589, 619
  collaterals of, 712, 715
  coronary artery catheterization compli-
    cations in, 574
  fistulas of, 741
  obtuse marginal branch of, 589, 614
  posterior left ventricular branch of,
    614, 748
  in single coronary artery anomalies,
    748
  sinoatrial node artery origin and, 750
left intermediate, 589
left main (LMCA)
  absence or early bifurcation of, 751–
    752
  absent, short, or early bifurcation of,
    564–565, 726–727, 751–752
  with angina pectoris, 636–637
  arteriosclerosis in, 662–665, 666
  coronary artery catheterization and,
    564–565
  disease of, coronary arteriography com-
    plications and, 574
  stenosis of, as coronary arteriography
    pitfall, 727–729
left posterior descending artery (LPDA),
  614
magnetic resonance angiography of,
  physiologic motion and, 198
myocardial bridging and, 751, 755
obstructive disease of small branches of,
  as arteriography pitfall, 736–737
obtuse marginal, 589, 614
  arteriosclerosis of, 674, 675, 676–
    677, 682
posterior atrial branch of, 587, 619
posterior descending (PDA), 587
  anatomic variations of, 750–751, 752,
    753
  left, 614
  in single coronary artery anomalies,
    748
posterior right, in single coronary artery
  anomalies, 748
posterior septal branches of, 587, 589
postmortem studies of, 583–585
quantitation of distribution of, 623–626
ramus medianus in, 752–753, 754
right (RCA), 603–607
  Amplatz catheter and, 570
  anatomy of, 586, 603–607
  arteriosclerosis of, 677–680, 681
  collateral circulation of, 703, 704,
    719, 720
  coronary artery catheterization and,
    564, 565, 570

fistulas of, to right ventricle, 741
preponderance of, 625
pulmonary arteriovenous malformation embolotherapy complications
and, III:850
RAO and LAO views of, 587, 593,
603
separate origin of conus artery and,
729–731
single, 747, 748
right circumflex
anatomy of, general description of,
586
branches to ventricle from, 605, 606
serial radiography of, in cardiac catheterization laboratory, 87, 101–102. *See
also* Cardiac catheterization laboratory
single, 596–598, 599, 747–748
sinoatrial node artery origin and, 750
size of
area supplied compared to, 627
difficulty in catheterization and, 627–
628
small vessel occlusion in, 736–737
subintimal dissection of, in catheterization complications, 575
supernumerary, 599–602
third, 601
in thoracic aortography, 406
thrombotic occlusion of, in catheterization complications, 575
variations in ostia and, 595–603
Coronary arteriography, 556–767. *See also*
Angiocardiography
after bypass surgery, 756–767. *See also*
Coronary artery bypass grafts
(CABG)
anatomy in, 583–634. *See also* Coronary
arteries
aneurysm in, 645, 653
angiographic-pathologic correlation in,
650–658
explanation of discrepancies in, 656–
657
false negatives in, 656
limitations of visual interpretation and,
657–658
underprediction in, 650
in anomalies and anatomic variations of
coronary arteries, 740–755. *See also*
Coronary arteries
arterial orifice in, 641, 642–643
arterial puncture and catheterization of
left ventricle in, 558–560
arterial sheath in, 558, 559
in arteriosclerosis, 662–681
of diagonal arteries, 670–673, 674
of left anterior descending branch,
665–670, 671–674
of left circumflex branch, 672, 673–
676
of left coronary arteries, 662–677,
682–683
of left main artery, 662–665, 666
multivessel, 680–681, 682–683
of obtuse marginal arteries, 674, 675,
676–677, 682
of right coronary arteries, 677–680,
681
atropine in, 569

in autoimmune and metabolic diseases,
692
calcification in, 645, 655
catheter placement in, 627
classification of results of, 658
relationship of lesions and clinical syndromes to, 661–662
collateral vessels in, 650, 660, 700–725.
See also Coronary collateral circulation
pitfalls in, 723
complications of, 572–582
continuous quality improvement and
total quality management for, 580
morbidity in, 573, 575–578
mortality and, 572–575
in pediatric and neonatal age group,
579–580
in coronary arteriosclerosis, 662–681.
See also Coronary arteriography, in
arteriosclerosis
coronary artery catheterization in, 562–
565
inadvertent superselective injection in,
564–565
selective, sinus bradycardia and, 568
in coronary disease, 635–699. *See also*
Coronary disease
abbreviations in, 635–636
in angina pectoris, 662, 689–690
angiographic-pathologic correlation in,
650–658
appraisal of significant, 657, 659–660
in arteriosclerosis, 662–681. *See also*
Coronary arteriography, in arteriosclerosis
determinants of operability and, 688–
689
grading of arteriogram in, 658–659,
680, 682–683
indications for, 636–639
in myocardial infarction with angiographically normal coronary arteries,
662
in positive exercise test, 690
in presence of hemodynamically significant stenosis or occlusion, 688
quantitative arteriography in, 659
relationship of morphology of lesions
to clinical syndromes in, 661–662
roentgen pathology in, 640–650,
651–655, 657
special problems in, 684–687. *See also*
Coronary arteriography, special
problems in
therapeutic alternatives and, 681–684
ventriculography indications and role
and, 639–640
in determinants of operability, 688–689
development of, 9
diffuse narrowing in, 641–643, 648
degree of, 657, 659–660
dilation and tortuosity in, 643, 652
in dissecting aortic aneurysms with coronary involvement, 691
drugs in, 568–569
electrocardiographic and hemodynamic
changes with, 568
embolus in, 643, 651
emerging methods for evaluation and,
692–693

ergonovine maleate in, 569
filling defects in, 641, 644–645
grading of arteriogram in, 658–659,
680, 682–683
guidewires and catheters in, 556–558
heparin in, 568–569
image intensifiers for, 98
indications for, 636–639
diagnostic, 638–639
therapeutic, 636–638
ventriculography and, 639–640
in intimal or medial fibroplasia, 692
layering of contrast agents in, 626, 627
limitations of visual interpretation in,
657–658
manifold in, 558
marginal irregularity in, 641, 642–643
morbidity in, 573, 575–578
mortality implications and, 690–691
in neonatal patients, 579
nitrates in, 58
nitroglycerin in, 569
normal
anatomy in, 583–634. *See also* Coronary arteries
diagnostic value of, 590–614, 626–
631. *See also* Coronary arteries
obstruction in, degree of, 657, 659–
660
occlusion in, 643, 649–650
determinants of operability and, 688
pediatric, vascular complications in,
579
pitfalls in, 726–739
absence or early bifurcation of main
left artery and, 726–727
anomalous origins or anatomic variations in, 738
artifacts related to flow and pressure
changes induced by contrast injections in, 737–738
eccentric stenoses and, 731
failure to detect obstructions due to
superimposition of other branches
in, 733–734, 735
myocardial bridging in, 735, 736
obstructive disease of small branches
in, 736–737
recanalization of occluding thrombi
in, 735–736
separate origin of conus artery and,
729–731
stenosis of main left artery and, 727–
729
vascular spasm in, 731–733
premedication in, 568
prognostic implications of, 690–692
projections for, 566–568, 629–631
quantitative, 659
radionuclide studies in, 660
schematic presentation of interarterial
connections in, 703
special problems in, 684–687
coronary artery spasm as, 684–686,
687, 731–733
myocardial bridging and, 686–687,
688, 689
Prinzmetal variant angina and, 685–
686, 687
spontaneously occurring vasospasm as,
685–686

Coronary arteriography—*Continued*
in stenosis, 641, 646–647, 657
in arteriosclerosis, 662–681. *See also*
Coronary arteriography, in arteriosclerosis
determinants of operability and, 688
eccentric, as arteriography pitfall, 731
surgical aspects of, 690
in syphilis, 691–692
technique of, 556–571
Amplatz, 557, 570
arterial puncture and catheterization
of left ventricle in, 558–560
arterial sheath in, 558, 559
Bourassa, 570–571
catheterizing coronary arteries in,
562–565
drugs and, 568–569
electrocardiographic and hemodynamic changes with, 568
guidewires and catheters in, 556–558
left ventriculography in, 560–562
manifold in, 558
projections and, 566–568
Schoonmaker-King, 571
Sones, 557, 570
in trauma, 692
ulceration in, 645, 654
velocity of flow in, 660
ventriculography in, 660
indications for, 639–640
left, 560–562
vessel caliber in, 641
Coronary artery bypass grafts (CABG), arteriography after, 756–767
anastomosis in
distal, 757, 759, 763
end-to-side, 757, 758
proximal, 762
pseudoaneurysm at site of, 759
side-to-side, 758, 759
anatomic considerations in, 757, 758,
759
bypassed vessels in, 763
catheter selection and use in, 760, 761
choice of, 684
clinical significance of, 764–765
collateral circulation in, 761–762
coronary circulation in, 760–762
end-to-side insertion in, 757, 758
graft in, 760, 761
anterior to pulmonary artery, 756,
757
body of, 763
course of, 756–758
injection of, 760
internal mammary artery, 758–759,
764
jump, insertion of, 758, 759
posterior to pulmonary artery, 756,
758
sites of origin of, from aorta, 756,
757
types of insertion of, 757, 758, 759
Y-, 758
left ventriculography in, 760
nonbypassed vessels in, 763, 764
objectives of, 760
progression of disease in native vessels
in, 763, 764
pseudoocclusion in, 761

side-to-side insertion in, 758, 759
status of native circulation in, 761–762
techniques for, 756–759
Coronary artery prevalence, term of, 624
Coronary Artery Surgery Study (CASS)
complications in, 572, 574, 575
morphology and, 661
reproducibility of results and, 657
Coronary artery–pulmonary artery fistula,
799
Coronary atherectomy, III:377–380
lumen diameter after, III:7
Coronary collateral circulation, 650, 660,
700–725
angiographic assessment of, 120, 650,
660, 721–723
pitfalls in, 723
reciprocating pattern in, 722
in coronary artery bypass graft, 760–762
extracoronary, 712–713
history of study of, 700–701
intercoronary, 703–711
intracoronary, 711–712
variability in, 713, 714–721
Coronary cusps, 593
Coronary disease, 635–699
abbreviations in, 635–636
in angina. *See* Angina pectoris
angioplasty in. *See* Coronary angioplasty
appraisal of significant, 657, 659–660
arteriography in, 635–699. *See also* Coronary arteriography
grading of, 658–659, 680, 682–683
indications for, 636–639
prognostic implications of, 690–692
quantitative, 659
ventriculography and, 639–640, 660
arteriosclerosis in, 662–681. *See also*
Arteriosclerosis; Coronary arteriography, in arteriosclerosis
causes of, other than arteriosclerosis,
691–692
collateral vessels in, 650, 660, 700–725.
See also Coronary collateral circulation
complications of, as indication for angiography, 635–636
determinants of operability in, 688–689
diagnostic, 638–639
emerging methods for, 692–693
diffuse narrowing in, 641–643, 648
degree of, 657, 659–660
functional class of, arteriography complications and, 575
grading of, 658–659, 680, 682–683
indications for, 636–639
with intractable heart failure as indication for angiography, 637
medical therapy for, angiography in evaluation of, 638
myocardial infarction in
with angiographically normal coronary
arteries, 662
multiple, as indication for angiography, 635–636
pathology in, 640–650, 651–655, 657
aneurysm as, 645, 653
angiographic correlation of, 650–658
arterial orifice, 641, 642–643
calcification as, 645, 655
in collateral vessels, 650

degree of obstruction in, 657, 659–
660
diffuse narrowing as, 641–643, 648,
657, 659–660
dilation and tortuosity as, 643, 652
embolus as, 643, 651
explanation of angiographic discrepancies with, 656–657
filling defects as, 641, 644–645
limitations of visual interpretation in,
657–658
marginal irregularity, 641, 642–643
occlusion as, 643, 649–650, 688
relationship of morphology of lesions
to clinical syndromes and, 661–662
stenosis as, 641, 646–647, 657, 688
ulceration as, 645, 654
vessel caliber in, 641
quantitative, 659
radionuclide studies in, 660
severe, arteriography complications and,
574
special angiography problems in, 684–
690
angina pectoris and, 689–690
coronary artery spasm as, 684–686,
687
determinants of operability as, 688–
689
myocardial bridging as, 686–687,
688, 689
positive exercise test and, 690
surgical aspects of, 690
surgery for
operability and, 635–636, 637
postprocedural evaluation of, 637
therapeutic alternatives in, 681–684
therapeutic indications for, 636–638
velocity of flow in, 660
ventriculography in
appraisal of, 660
indications for, 639–640
role of, 639–640
Coronary flow reserve, 659
Coronary ostia
anatomy of, 591–603
cranial displacement of, 595–596, 597
right, coronary artery catheterization
and, 564, 565
variations in, 595–603
Coronary sinus, 590
partial anomalous pulmonary venous connection to, 884
venous, 623
Coronary veins, 590, 591
after coronary artery bypass graft, 760–762
in arterial portography, 1532
left posterior, 590
middle, 590
Corpus callosum, pelvic arteriography and,
1642–1645
Corpus cavernosa
collateral circulation to, III:712, III:
714–715
lacunae of, III:705
relaxation of, with muscle relaxants, III:
708
Corrosion techniques in postmortem studies of coronary arteries, 585
Cortical arteries, 1114, 1115, 1120
spasm of, 1112–1113

Cortical hyperplasia, focal renal, 1166, 1167, 1168
Cortical nephrogram, 1122–1124
Cortical renal cyst, simple, III:658
Corticosteroids. *See* Steroids
Corticotropin. *See* Adrenocorticotropic hormone (ACTH)
Coumadin
  contraindicated in pregnancy, III:986
  interventional radiology and, III:208
  oral hypoglycemics and, III:217
Councill catheters and stiffening rods
  in bladder procedures, III:614, III:619
  in prostatic urethroplasty, III:629–631
Countershock
  during cardiac catheterization, 118–119
  direct current
    in atrial fibrillation, 43
    in atrial flutter, 43
    in ventricular fibrillation, 45
    in ventricular tachycardia, 45
CPA (cavernosal pulse amplitude), III:710, III:717, III:718
CPT (common pulmonary trunk), 871, 872
CQI (Continuous quality improvement). *See* Quality improvement
Crafoord C, III:525
Cragg infusion wire, III:57, III:72
  in bronchial artery embolization, III:825
Cragg vascular stent, III:85
Cranial base, anterior, intracranial, extraaxial lesions of, III:793, III:800
Cranial nerves, blood supply to, III:814
Creatinine, serum, 23–24, III:207
Crenation pattern in arteriography, 1733
Cricothyreotomy, 39
Crista supraventricularis, 611, 612
  collaterals in, 711
Crohn disease, 1560, 1568, 1575
  percutaneous drainage of abscess in, III:942–943
    efficacy and rationale of, III:940
Cross-linking in fibrinogen conversion to fibrin, III:120
Cross-training of radiation technologists, 133
Crushing injuries in blunt trauma, 533, 534, 535
Crystalloids, III:214, III:215
CT. *See* Computerized tomography (CT)
Culprit vessel in hepatic embolization, III:440, III:447
Curved catheter without pigtail in pulmonary arteriography, 772
Cushing syndrome, 1364–1368
Cut-film angiography of abdominal aorta, 22–23
Cut-film changers
  Puck, 74–75, 76
  roll-film changers versus, 68–69
  Schönander, 73–74, 75
Cutaneous angioma, spinal fistulas and, 377
Cutaneous T-cell lymphoma, 1950
Cutis laxa, 831
Cyanoacrylates
  in arteriovenous malformation embolization, III:1015–1016

in chemoembolization, 1646, 1648, 1656, 1657
Cyanosis, unexplained, 911
Cyclic adenosine monophosphate (cAMP), 51
Cyclic guanosine monophosphate (cGMP), 51
  nitrates and, 58
Cyclic guanosine triphosphate (cGTP), 51
Cyclophosphamide, III:81
  in hepatic malignancy, III:437
  in osteosarcomas, III:1033
Cyclosporin, 1338, 1339
Cyst
  adrenal, 1375–1376, 1377
  aneurysmal bone, 1797–1798
    embolization in, III:905
  blood, in pancreatitis, 1413
  breast, aspiration of, III:1041
  echinococcus, 1440–1441
  pancreatic, vascular displacement in, 1465
  parapelvic, III:658, III:665
  peripelvic, III:658
  renal. *See* Renal cysts
  splenic, 1480–1482, 1483
    false, 1481
  of thoracic duct, 1901
Cystadenocarcinoma of pancreas, 1407, 1408
Cystadenoma of pancreas, 1405, 1407
Cystic disease of kidney. *See* Polycystic disease
Cystic duct catheterization, III:487–489
Cystic fibrosis
  embolization in, III:826, III:827, III:905
  hemoptysis in, III:819, III:820
Cystic hygroma, 1921
Cystic medionecrosis, 493–494
Cystic neoplasms, pancreatic, 1393, 1405–1406, 1407, 1408
Cystine renal calculi, III:596–597
  extracorporeal shock wave lithotripsy for, III:606
Cystogram after renal cyst aspiration, III:660–661, III:663
Cystoscopy of renal pelvic tumors, 1160
Cytologic examination
  in biopsy, III:166–171
  quick-stain technique for, III:170
  of urine, 1160
Cytomegalovirus (CMV), III:17, III:518
  in colitis, 1607

DAC (digital-to-analog) conversion of image display, 146
Dacron grafts, femoral arteriography after, 1717
Dake endovascular stent-graft placement in thoracic aortic aneurysms, III:357–358
Dale WA, III:160
Darkroom technician, 132
Dasher 10 guidewire with flow-sensitive microcatheter, 164
Data compression algorithms, 148
Data points, sufficient, 89
Data storage
  in digital angiography, 146–149

for vascular intervention angiography, 135
Davis catheter, 245
DAVM. *See* Dual arteriovenous malformations (DAVM), intracranial, extraaxial
Dawson-Mueller catheter in abscess drainage
  from abdomen, III:930
  from pelvis, III:952
DCA (direct coronary atherectomy), III:377
dDAVP (desmopressin), 55
Death. *See also* Mortality
  from abdominal aorta aneurysms, 1073
  after biliary drainage procedures, 1038
  in arteriosclerotic disease, 1053
  cardiac, 41
  from dissecting aortic aneurysms, 493
  in peripheral angioplasty, 1041
  pulmonary angiography and, 1031
  from renal tumors, 1132
  from thoracic aorta aneurysms, 467–468
  in thoracic aortography, 397–398
DeBakey ME, III:982
DeBakey's classification of dissecting aortic aneurysms, 494, 495, 497
Debrun tie-on latex balloons, III:65, III:69
Debulking for staghorn calculi, III:588
Decadron. *See* Dextromethasone sodium phosphate
Deceleration injuries to liver, III:422, III:423
Decompression, intestinal, percutaneous gastrostomy in, III:547
Decubitus position, lung biopsy complication and, 1035
Deep vein thrombosis (DVT), 1743, 1747
  magnetic resonance venography in, 1837, 1838. *See also* Magnetic resonance venography
  sonography of, 218, 219
Defibrillation, electrical, 41. *See also* Direct current countershock
Deflation times of balloon catheter, III:39
Deflector wire
  in penile vascularization, III:709
  in pulmonary arteriography, 773, 775
Delay washout, 1335
Delayed rethrombosis, III:126–127
Delayed scanning in arterial portography, 1545
Delivery rate of contrast medium, 70
DeLong RP, 892
Delta sign, 303
Demerol. *See* Meperidine
Densitometers in quality control, 124
Density in sonographic terminology, 217
Derek Harwood-Nash (DHN) catheters, 244, 245
Descending aorta. *See* Aorta, descending
Desmoid tumors, 1798, 1799
Desmopressin (dDAVP), 55
Detachable balloons in embolization, III:65–70
  of arteriovenous fistulas, III:807–808, III:1002
  of arteriovenous malformations, III:1011, III:1012
  in dura, III:802

Detachable balloons in embolization—
  Continued
  of arteriovenous malformations—
    Continued
    in fistulas, III:1002
    in pulmonary disorders, III:848–850
  of carotid-cavernous fistula, III:807–
      808
  of cerebral aneurysms, III:769–774
  intraaxial, for central nervous system,
      III:766, III:769–774
  of intracranial, extraaxial lesions, III:802,
      III:807–808
  in pelvic arteriography, 1652
  pitfalls of, III:67–68
  two-valved, III:70
  of varicoceles, III:696–698
Detumescent phase of erection, III:706
Development time, cine film processing
    and, 107–109
Developmental anomalies, pulmonary,
    822–848. *See also* Pulmonary devel-
    opmental anomalies
Dexamethasone suppression test, 1357,
    1364
Dextran 40 in pulse-spray thrombolysis,
    III:137
Dextromethasone sodium phosphate, 48
Dextrose
  in insulin reactions, III:217
  strengths and volumes of, 48
  in water
    for acrylic adhesive embolization, III:
      1016
    in bronchial artery embolization, III:
      826
    in premature ventricular contractions,
      45
    in ventricular tachycardia, 45
DHN (Derek Harwood-Nash) catheters,
    244, 245
Diabetes mellitus
  atherosclerosis in, 1715, 1717
    upper extremity arteriography and,
      1759
  contrast media reactions and, 1026
  interventional radiology and, III:207
  nephrotoxicity of contrast agents and,
      23, 24
  renal abscess and, 1186
  restenosis after balloon angioplasty and,
      III:8, III:14
Diagnostic angiography
  complications of, 1024–1032, 1039–
      1044
  standards for, 1024, 1025
  value of normal coronary, 626–631. *See
      also* Coronary arteriography
Diagnostic decision tree in renal tumors,
    1173
Diagnostic peritoneal lavage (DPL), III:
    885, III:888, III:889
Diagnostic pharmacoangiography, 49–65.
    See also Pharmacoangiography
Diagonal branches of left coronary arteries.
    See Coronary arteries, diagonal
Dialysis
  fistula for. *See* Dialysis fistula
  frequency of use of, III:726
  peritoneal, thrombus in, 1850
  placement of access for, III:726

shunt complications of
  angiography in. *See* Dialysis shunt angi-
      ography
  atherectomy for, III:44, III:47–49
  vascular sonography in, 226
Dialysis catheter, III:977–978
  dual-lumen, III:970, III:978
  in fistula thrombolysis, III:729, III:730
Dialysis fistula
  approach to poorly functioning graft in,
      III:738–740
  blood flow adequacy in, III:726–727.
      See also Dialysis shunt angiography
  checking of, III:738
  causes and treatment of dysfunction of,
      III:727–728
  complications of, 1771, 1772, 1773,
      1776–1778
  distal extremity, 1776–1778
  endogenous arteriovenous or graft cre-
      ation of, III:726
  longevity of, III:727
  revascularization of, III:726–742
    arterial inflow stenoses in, III:734–
      735
    central venous stenoses in, III:735,
      III:737
    complications of, III:736–737
    intragraft stenoses in, III:735, III:737
    patient selection for, III:728
    percutaneous suction thromboembo-
        lectomy for thrombosed, III:163
    postprocedural patency rates and, III:
      739
    pulse-spray thrombolysis in, III:728–
      733, III:734, III:735
    results of, III:737–738
    venous anastomotic stenoses in, III:
      733–734, III:736
  stenoses in, III:727, III:733–737
    arterial inflow, III:734–735
    central venous, III:735, III:737
    intragraft, III:735, III:737
    thrombectomy for, III:727
    venous anastomoses for, III:733–734,
      III:736
  thrombolysis in, III:727
    pediatric, III:917
    pulse-spray, III:728–733, III:734, III:
      735
Dialysis graft
  complications of, atherectomy in, III:44,
      III:47–49
  lysis-resistant arterial plug after, III:138,
      III:139
  materials for, III:726
  percutaneous suction thromboembolec-
      tomy for, III:163
  stenoses in, III:735, III:737
  thrombolysis of, III:146–147, III:148,
      III:149
    pediatric, III:917
    pulse-spray, III:728–733, III:734, III:
      735
  technical modifications in, III:138,
      III:139
Dialysis shunt angiography, 1767–1778
  complications of, 1768, 1769–1778
    arterial anastomosis, 1768–1770,
      1771
    arterial steals and, 1776–1778

in body of fistula, 1771, 1772,
      1773
    in extremity distal to fistula, 1776–
      1778
    feeding artery, 1768, 1769
    occlusion of arterial outflow and,
      1776–1778
    outflow arterial occlusion in, 1776–
      1778
    outflow vein, 1770, 1773–1776,
      1777
    venous anastomosis, 1773, 1774
  technique for, 1767–1769, 1770
Diaphragm
  in inferior vena cava obstruction, 958
  musculotendinous fibers of, in extrinsic
      compression of renal artery, 1269–
      1270
  thoracic duct entering, 1891
Diathermy in metal-based mechanical
    embolization, III:63
Diatrizoate. *See* Sodium diatrizoate
Diazepam, III:213, III:216
  in femoral arteriography, 1714
  in neurologic deficits from spinal cord
      angiography, 357
  before thoracic aortography, 391
Diazoxide, renin determination and, 1306
Dibenzyline. *See* Phenoxybenzamine
Diet in pediatric interventional angiogra-
    phy, III:904
Differential growth theory of aortic arch
    development, 437
Diffuse angiomatous lesions, 1573
Diffuse hyperplasia in pancreatic islet-cell
    tumors, 1403
Diffuse intimal thickening (DIT) of aorta,
    412
Diffuse lymph node patterns in malignant
    lymphoma, 1940, 1942
Diffuse narrowing in coronary arteriogra-
    phy, 641–643, 648
Diffuse pulmonary parenchymal disease,
    biopsy and, III:185
Diffusely dilated vessels in abdominal aorta
    arteriosclerosis, 1058, 1059
Digit, ischemia of, 1762, 1763
Digital angiography, 138–152
  advantages of, for vascular intervention,
    135, 138
  digital systems for, 142–149
    archival storage in, 148–149
    digitization in, 142–143
    image display in, 146
    image processing hardware and, 144–
      146
    on-line disk storage and, 146–148
    pixel matrix in, 143–144
  disadvantages of, for vascular interven-
    tion, 138–139
  future developments of, 137–138
  image-processing algorithms in, 149–
    152
  imaging modalities in, 135
  intraarterial contrast in, 139
  intravenous contrast in, 139
  nonsubtracted, in pulmonary arteriogra-
    phy, 777
  of pancreas, 1394–1395
  pelvic, 1636–1638
  quality improvement and, 137

radiographic environment and, 134–135

space considerations for, 136

staffing for, 135–136

subtraction. *See* Digital subtraction angiography (DSA)

video systems for, 139–142, 143

Digital archives, 148–149

Digital road-mapping. *See* Road-mapping technique

Digital subtraction angiography (DSA). *See also* Digital angiography

of abdominal aorta, iodine content in, 22

advantages of, for vascular intervention, 135, 138

in blunt trauma to aorta and brachiocephalic arteries, 525, 526

in bronchial artery embolization, III:823

in carotid-cavernous fistulas, III:803–807

in cerebral studies, 138

in donor angiography before renal transplantation, 1326

for extremities

in aortoiliac intervention problems, 1686

in trauma, III:860

in femoral arteriography, 1707

glucagon and, 61

of iliac and pudendal arteries, 1643–1644

intraarterial, 1707, 1832

of intracranial, extraaxial lesions, III:789, III:796–797, III:804–806, III:809–813

in intraoperative angiography, 253

intravenous, 1686–1688, 1690

of pancreas, 1394–1395

in parathyroid arteriography, 977–978

in pelvic fractures, III:871, III:877–879

in pulmonary arteriography, 776–777

in renal angiography, 1110

in splenoportography, 1500

in superior vena cava obstruction, 916

in thoracic aortic aneurysms, 473, 484

Digital subtraction venography in renal vein thrombosis, 1309

Digital systems, 142–149

Digitalis, 56, III:216

in atrial fibrillation, 43

in atrial flutter, 43

mesenteric ischemia and, 1626

in premature atrial contractions, 43

in premature ventricular contractions, 45

Digital-to-analog (DAC) conversion of image display, 146

Digitization in digital angiography, 142–143

Digitoxin, 56

Digoxin, 48, 56

DiGuglielmo L, 635

Dihydroergotamine, 56

Dihydrotestosterone, III:627

Dilatation

in abdominal aorta arteriosclerosis, 1058, 1059

of azygos vein, 911

balloon. *See* Balloon catheter

in benign biliary obstruction, III:459–462

coronary arteriography and, 560, 643, 652

of pulmonary artery

idiopathic, 796, 829, 830

poststenotic, 788–793

of splanchnic arteries, 1633–1634

of subclavian artery, poststenotic, 1002, 1005

transluminal balloon, in pelvic arteries, 1638–1640

of ureteral strictures, III:576, III:578–581

of ureteroileal anastomotic strictures, III:650–652

Dilator, French Teflon, 560

Diodrast. *See* Iodopyracet

Diphenhydramine, III:212, III:213, III:217

in contrast media reactions, 1025

before coronary artery catheterization, 568

strengths and volumes of, 48

Dipyridamole, 627

angioplasty and

coronary, III:369

pediatric, III:911

renal, III:306

Direct arteriovenous fistulas of central nervous system, III:781

Direct bypass collaterals, 711–712

Direct coronary atherectomy (DCA), III:377–379

Direct current countershock, 41

in atrial fibrillation, 43

in atrial flutter, 43

during cardiac catheterization, 118–119

in ventricular fibrillation, 45

in ventricular tachycardia, 45

Direct geometric magnification in angiography, 177–186

Direct portal venography, 1422–1426

Direct puncture thoracic aortography, 392

Director

of cardiac catheterization laboratory, 130

of vascular intervention angiography laboratory, 135

Discharge instructions after interventional radiology, III:220–221

Disk storage, on-line, 146–148

Displacement. *See also* Compression

of axillary artery by hematoma, 1008

of vessels in tumor, 1781

Display and recording system for cardiac catheterization monitoring, 118

Dissecting aneurysms

of aorta, 493–520

age and, 496

aortography in, 500, 503–509, 510–515

ascending, in arteriography complications, 578

bicuspid aortic valve and, 493

classification and course of, 494–496

clinical findings in, 496–497

coarctation of aorta and, 493

computed tomography in, 514–516

computerized tomography in, 514–516

congestive heart failure with, 496–497

coronary arteriography in, 691

with coronary involvement, 691

cystic medionecrosis and, 493–494

death from, 493

direct intraaortic injection in, 503

gender and, 496

intimal flap in, 508–512

intravenous aortography in, 500, 503

magnetic resonance imaging in, 516–518

management and prognosis in, 518–519

in Marfan syndrome, 493, 494, 496, 498, 499

mediastinal widening or rupture in, 500, 502, 503

pathology and etiology of, 493–494

problems in establishing diagnosis of, 509

radiographic findings in, 497–503

repair of, hypertension and, 1276

thoracic aortography in, 397

transesophageal echocardiography in, 516, 518

transthoracic echocardiography in, 516, 518

of renal artery, hypertension in, 1251–1253, 1270–1271

Dissection

aortic. *See* Dissecting aneurysms, of aorta

in cerebral arteries, 297–298, 299

iatrogenic

atherectomy for, 1029

of carotid arteries, 348, 351

from catheter, intimal flap from, 1029

from catheter, Fogarty balloon in, 1029

in catheter or guidewire complications, 1029, 1030

of common hepatic arteries in superselective catheterization, 165

in coronary artery catheterization, 575

of iliac arteries, 1029

in lymphangiography, surgical, 1864–1865, 1866

in peripheral angioplasty, 1040

popliteal, 1825

in postmortem studies of coronary artery anatomy, 583, 584

postoperative, sonography of, 227

in renal angioplasty, 1041

of renal arteries

medial, 1252–1253

subintimal, 1103–1107, 1108

of superficial femoral artery, 1040

of veins after dialysis fistula thrombolysis, III:736

Distal as term in balloon catheter angioplasty, III:42

Distal embolization as complication of transgraft thrombolysis, III:155

Distance to radiation, dose and, 137

DIT (diffuse intimal thickening) of aorta, 412

Diuretics

in emergency treatment, 47

interventional radiology and, III:207

lymphocele formation and, III:944

renin determination and, 1306

Diversions, urinary, III:645–657. *See also* Urinary diversions

Diverticula
  abscesses and
    classification of, III:941
    drainage of sigmoid, III:941
    efficacy and rationale for drainage of,
      III:940
  caliceal, urinary obstruction in, III:590–
    595
  colonic
    abscess drainage near sigmoid, III:941
    bleeding from, 1608, 1609, III:390,
      III:392, III:411–414
  ductal
    residual, 418, 419
    in thoracic aortography for traumatic
      aneurysms, 481, 482–483
  infected caliceal, 1199
  of Kommerell, 416
  Meckel, 1579
  retroesophageal aortic, 548
  of urethra, III:618
Diverticulosis, 1608, 1609
Dog bites, arteriography in, III:858–859
Dominance
  coronary artery, 749–750, 751
  as term, 749
Donor angiography in renal transplantation, 1325–1327
Dopamine, 47, 61, III:215, III:216
  action of, 52–53
  in contrast media reactions, 1026
  recommended intravenous dosages for,
    46
  strengths and volumes of, 48
Dopaminergic receptors
  catecholamines and, 52–53
  dopamine and, 61
  vascular response to, 52
Doppler equation, 209
Doppler frequency shift, 208–209
Doppler gate location, 207–208
Doppler imaging. *See also* Color flow
    imaging
  after vascular intervention, 226–227,
    228, color plates 1 and 2
  in aorticopulmonary window, 466
  in aortoiliac disease, III:228
  of breast disorders, 233
  of extracranial neck arteries, 220–221
  imaging physics in, 206–211
  before percutaneous angioplasty and ath-
    erectomy, 226
  physics of, 206–211
  in postoperative vein surveillance, 224,
    226, color plate 11
  in thoracic aortography, 410
  transcerebral, III:754
  in varicocele diagnosis, III:689, III:690
Doppler velocity ratio, diagram of, 223
Doppler-derived ankle-brachial index, III:
    858
Dormia basket, III:504
Dornier HM-3 lithotriptor, III:604
Dorsalis pedis arteries, 1698
  arteriovenous fistulas and, III:1005
  2D-TOF magnetic resonance imaging
    of, 1827, 1828
dos Santos R, 6, 8, 393, 932, 1016, 1705
Dose of radiation, variables in reducing,
    137
Dose-related toxicity of contrast agents, 49

Dotter CT, 9, 635, 773, III:3, III:24
  femoropopliteal angioplasty description
    of, III:262
  vascular stent use by, III:85
Dotter coaxial dilating catheter, III:24, III:
    25
Dotter computerized tomography (CT), 768
Dotter intravascular biopsy technique, III:
    195
Dotter reinforced balloon dilator catheter,
    III:24, III:25
Dotter selective transcatheter parathrombic
    infusion of thrombolytic agents, III:
    127
Double aortic arch, 548
  Edwards' hypothetical, 415, 416
Double Malecot plastic urethral stent, III:
    633–634
Double postrenal vena cava, 945, 947
Double wall arterial puncture, 248
Double-barrel anastomoses in renal trans-
    plantation, 1325
Double-disk occluder
  buttoned, III:70
  in pediatric embolization, III:906
Double-helix stent in urethra, III:632–633
Double-outlet right ventricle, 826
Doubling of thoracic duct, 1898, 1899
Down syndrome, 1901
Doxorubicin, III:81, 1648
  in carcinoma
    of bladder, III:82
    of breast, III:82
    of endometrium, III:82
  complications from intraarterial chemo-
    therapy with, III:1035
  in hepatic malignancy, III:437, III:438
  in sarcomas
    of bone, III:1032–1033
    of extremity, III:1032
    of soft tissue, III:1033–1034
D-Phe-Pro-Arg chloromethyl ketone
    (PPACK) in restenosis after balloon
    angioplasty, III:15
DPL (diagnostic peritoneal lavage), III:
    885, III:888, III:889
Drainage
  abdominal abscess, 1035–1036, III:
    925–938. *See also* Abdominal
    abscess, percutaneous drainage of
  biliary. *See also* Bile
    complications of, 1038
    in malignant hepatobiliary obstruction,
      III:473–476
  pelvic, III:939–955. *See also* Pelvic
    abscess percutaneous drainage
    (PAD)
  preintervention assessment and, III:209–
    210
  thoracic abscess, III:829–836
Droperidol, 246, III:214
  in transjugular intrahepatic portosystemic
    shunt, III:532
Drug cart for emergency treatment, 47–48
Drug classes and mechanisms of action,
    III:80–82
Drugs, 49–65. *See also* Pharmacoangiog-
    raphy
  in coronary arteriography, 568–569
  in dysrhythmias, 43–45
  effects of, on pulmonary circulation, 181

  in emergency treatment, 45–47. *See also*
    Emergency treatment
    strengths and volumes of, 48
  in femoral arteriography, 1714
  in pediatric interventional angiography,
    III:904
  in preintervention assessment, III:207
Drummond H, 1588
DSA. *See* Digital subtraction angiography
    (DSA)
DSAA (transarterial digital subtraction angi-
    ography), 525, 526
DSAV (transvenous digital subtraction angi-
    ography), 525
Dual arteriovenous malformations
    (DAVM), intracranial, extraaxial,
    III:795–802
  neuroimaging of, III:796–798, III:801
  therapeutic approaches to, III:801–802
Dual-lumen dialysis catheters, III:970, III:
    978
Dual-mode image intensifiers in left ventric-
    ulography, 561
Dual-shaped collimators, 97
Ductal diverticulum, residual, 418, 419
Ductal theory of aortic arch development,
    437
Ductus arteriosus
  absent or bilateral, 416
  anatomic variability of, 415, 416
  aneurysms of, 420–421
  closure of, 417–418, 419
  contralateral, 416
  embryology of, 415–416, 435–436
  ipsilateral, 416
  meeting aorta, angle of, 417
  patent. *See* Patent ductus arteriosus
    (PDA)
  prostaglandins and, 61
Ductus arteriosus sling, 416
Ductus bump, 483
Ductus deferens, III:679
Ductus diverticulum
  endovascular treatment of, III:361
  in infant, 402, 403, 404, 405
  in thoracic aortography in traumatic
    aneurysms, 481, 482–483
Duodenography, hypertonic, 61
Duodenum
  biliary calculi removal into, III:493, III:
    494–495
  bleeding from
    colonic bleeding versus, III:394, III:
      396
    gastritis and, III:393, III:395
    superselective catheterization in, 160,
      III:400, III:402
    ulcers in, III:405, III:408, III:409,
      III:410
  in inferior vena cava obstruction, 958
  injury to, as percutaneous stone removal
    complication, III:602
Duplex ultrasonography, 207. *See also*
    Ultrasonography
  in deep venous thrombosis, 1839
  of inferior vena cava, 938, 939
  in penile visualization, III:719–721
  in varicocele diagnosis, III:689, III:690
Duplications
  of popliteal veins, 218
  renal, 1210–1211, 1228

Dura, spinal, arteriovenous fistulas of. *See* Spinal dural arteriovenous fistulas
Dural blood supply, III:792
Dural sinuses, 274, 276
Dural vascular malformations, 323, 327
Duralyn balloons, scratch-resistance of, III:39
DVT. *See* Deep vein thrombosis (DVT)
Dyes
in cardiac output measurement, 117
in lymphangiography, 1866
interdigital injections of, 1864, 1865
in postmortem studies of coronary arteries, 583–584, 585
Dyskinesia, ventricular, 561, 640
Dysphagia after bronchial artery embolization, III:827
Dysplasia
fibromuscular, renal angioplasty results in, III:311–316
inferior mesenteric arteriography in vascular, 1609
of kidney, 1222–1224
cysts in, III:658, III:664
renal artery
in renovascular hypertension, 1250–1257
without hypertension, 1257
of splenic artery, 1474
Dysrhythmias
contrast agent toxicity and, 29
coronary arteriography and, 577
for pediatric and neonatal patients, 579–580
emergency treatment for, 41, 43–45
in interventional radiology, III:216
intractable ventricular, 638. *See also* Ventricular fibrillation
pulmonary angiography and, 783, 1031
Dystopic kidney, 1217

Early bifurcation of main left coronary artery, 726–727
EAST (Emory Angioplasty Versus Surgery Trial), III:374, III:383
ECAP (aminocaproic acid), 1651, III:403, III:826
Eccentric plaque in common iliac artery, 1637
Eccentric stenoses of coronary arteries, 731
ECG. *See* Electrocardiography (ECG)
Echinococcal cyst or abscess, 1440–1441, III:930–931
Echocardiography (ECG)
in aorticopulmonary window, 466
bubble, in pulmonary arteriovenous malformations, III:838
in coarctation of aorta, 441–444
in patent ductus arteriosus, 422, 423
in thoracic aortic aneurysm diagnosis, 469, 479, 488
transesophageal, 469, 479
Echogenicity in sonographic terminology, 217
Eck's fistula, III:526
Eclampsia, 310, 312
ECs (endothelial cells), 50–52
ECST (European Carotid Surgery Trial), III:340
Ectasia, vascular. *See also* Angiodysplasia
in arteriosclerosis, 1716

benign tubular, 1226
inferior mesenteric arteriography in, 1609
Ectopic coronary artery, 596
Ectopic kidney, 1221, 1222–1224
renal stones in, III:590
Ectopic spleen, 1468–1471
Ectopic superior parathyroids, 988
Edema
alveolar, in pulmonary venous hypertension, 863–864
angioneurotic, III:217
cerebral intraparenchymal, 342
chylous, 1907–1908, 1910–1911
laryngeal, 29
lymphedema as. *See* Lymphedema
pulmonary, 864, 865
in coronary arteriography complications, 578
septal interstitial, in hypertension, 863
Edge enhancement, 144, 145
Edison TA, 3
EDRF (endothelial-derived relaxation factor), III:705, III:707, III:709
Edwards' hypothetical double aortic arch, 415, 416
Effusion, pleural, 865
EHL (electrohydraulic lithotripsy), III:497, III:499
Ehlers-Danlos syndrome, III:802
central pulmonary artery stenosis and, 831
cerebral vessels in, 310, 311
Eisenberg coaxial set, 161–162
Eisenmenger complex, 422
Ejaculatory ducts, III:639–641
Ejection fraction, left ventricular. *See* Ventricular ejection fraction, left (LVEF)
Elastic pulmonary arteries, 769
Elastic recoil after renal angioplasty, III:321
Elastin, 1723
Electrical defibrillation, 41
Electrical energy conversion to roentgen rays, 94
Electrical power in cardiac catheterization laboratory, 94, 95
Electrical safety in cardiac catheterization laboratory, 130
Electrical wiring and fittings, 130
Electrocardiography (ECG)
in angina pectoris with normal resting and exercise, 662
in angioplasty, III:367–368
atypical chest pain and, 638
during cardiac catheterization, 116
amplifiers for, 118
laboratory for, 114–116
leads for, 117
in coronary angioplasty, III:367–368
in coronary arteriography, 568
in dysrhythmias, 43, 44
thoracic aortography and, 395
magnetic resonance imaging with, 471
Electrode catheter in cardiac catheterization, 107
Electrohydraulic lithotripsy (EHL)
of ileal conduit calculi, III:654
with percutaneous stone removal, III:497, III:499, III:601

Electronic magnification in angiography, 186
Elema roll-film changers, 75–76, 77
closure time in, 72
Elema-Schönander apparatus, 68
Embolectomy, 1722–1723
after dialysis fistula thrombolysis, III:736–737
Embolic agents. *See also* Embolization; specific embolic agent
for central nervous system interaxial embolotherapy, III:766–767
for intracranial, extraaxial lesions, III:791
Embolism
after cardiac angioplasty, 1039
after carotid angioplasty, III:344
after dialysis fistula thrombolysis, III:736–737
after intraaxial embolotherapy for central nervous system, III:767
air
as lung biopsy complication, 1035, III:185
in pulmonary arteriovenous malformation embolotherapy, III:850–851
angioplasty results in, III:242–243
aortoiliac disease and, III:226–228
in blue toe syndrome. *See* Blue toe syndrome
in cerebral vessels, 297, 298. *See also* Stroke
cholesterol, 1060, 1110, 1111
coronary arteriography and, 578, 643, 651
digital ischemia from, 1762
femoral arteriography in, 1722–1723, 1725
in infrapopliteal revascularization complications, III:290–291
oil
cerebral, 1870
hepatic, 1869–1870
percutaneous suction thromboembolectomy removal of, III:160–165
pulmonary. *See* Pulmonary embolism
as renal angiography hazard, 1107–1109
in renal infarction, 1262–1264
in superior mesenteric artery, 1619–1620, 1621
venous access catheters and, III:979
Embolization. *See also* Balloon catheter, in dilatation; Embolotherapy; specific embolic agent
adrenal, 1380
after pelvic intraarterial fibrinolytic therapy, 1640
after renal angiography, 1110
after renal transplantation, 1338, 1339, 1345–1346, 1347
in angiography complications, 1025, 1028–1029
of arteriovenous malformations, III:1008–1016
pulmonary. *See* Pulmonary arteriovenous malformations (PAVMs), embolotherapy in
in upper extremity, 1760, 1762, 1763
of biopsy tracts, III:182–183
bronchial artery, III:819–828. *See also* Bronchial arteries, embolization of

Embolization—*Continued*
  chemical. *See* Chemoembolization
  common materials used for, III:53
  as complication of transgraft thrombolysis, III:155
  of congenital arteriovenous fistulas, 1732–1733
  detachable balloons in, III:62
  in dural arteriovenous malformations, III:796–800, III:801–802
  ethanol
    in spinal vascular metastatic lesions, 386
    in transcatheter adrenal ablation, 1380
  in extremity trauma, III:861–867
  in gastrointestinal bleeding, III:400–403
    problems related to, III:419
  in hemangioma, III:999–1000
  of hepatic arteries. *See* Hepatic arteries, embolization in
  hepatic tumor, 1037
  for high-flow priapism, 1661
  ideal agent for, III:55
  inadvertent, III:77
  intracranial, III:789
    agents for, III:791
    complications of, 1032–1033, III:814
    in neoplasms, III:808–814
  liquid agents for, for small-vessels or tissues, III:54
  mechanical. *See* Mechanical embolic agents
  modifications in, III:60–61
  pain medications in, III:201
  in parathyroid ablation, 990
  in patent ductus arteriosus, 427
  for pediatric interventional angiography, III:904–908, III:909, III:910
    complications of, III:908
    devices in, III:906–908, III:909, III:910
    liquids in, III:906, III:907–908
    particles in, III:904–906
  in pelvic fractures, III:872–873, III:875, III:877–881
  for pelvic intractable hemorrhage, 1650–1654
    from neoplastic disease, 1658–1661
  percutaneous transhepatic variceal, III:526–528, III:529
  placement of coil before, III:60
  of placenta, 1646
  polyvinyl alcohol
    in hemorrhage of pelvic organs, 1651
    in spinal vascular metastatic lesions, 386
  preintervention assessment and, III:204–210
  preoperative, stump of vessel and, III:60
  problems related to, III:419
  of pulmonary artery fistula, complications of, 1033
  with radiotherapy in central nervous system arteriovenous malformations, III:779–781
  in renal trauma, 1232, 1239–1243. *See also* Renal trauma
    classification of trauma and, 1231
    complications of, 1243
    indications for, 1232, 1239, 1240, 1241

  successes and failures of, 1237, 1243
  techniques for, 1232, 1239, 1240, 1242
  timing of, 1231, 1236–1238
  selective arterial transcatheter
    in bone and soft tissue tumors, 1813–1819
    in hepatic malignancy, III:437–438. *See also* Hepatic malignancy
    in renal cell carcinoma, 1154
  small-vessel, III:52–54
  in spinal dural arteriovenous fistulas, 376
    complications of, 1032
  splenic
    transcatheter, 1492
    in trauma, III:887–890
  tissue, III:52–54
  Tracker catheter in. *See* Tracker catheter
  transcatheter
    bronchial artery, III:819–828. *See also* Bronchial arteries, embolization of
    parathyroid angiography for, 990–992
    pulmonary arteriovenous malformation, III:837–854. *See also* Pulmonary arteriovenous malformations (PAVMs)
    renal, III:896–898
    selective arterial. *See* Embolization, selective arterial transcatheter
    splenic, 1492
  transshunt, in percutaneous revision of surgical portosystemic shunts, III:528–530
  tumor
    bone, 1813–1819
    hepatic, 1037
    intractable hemorrhage and, 1658–1661
    mechanical embolic agents for, III:76
    in renal cell carcinoma, 1154
    soft tissue, 1813–1819
    in spinal metastases, 386
    spinal metastatic, 386
  for uncontrollable hemorrhage from pelvic organs, 1650–1654
  upper extremity, angiography in, 1762, 1763
  wire baffles in, III:62
Embolization coils. *See* Coils
Embolotherapy. *See also* Embolization
  for central nervous system, interaxial, III:765–788. *See also* Central nervous system, interaxial embolotherapy in
  for hepatic arterial injuries, III:422–435. *See also* Hepatic arteries, injuries to
Embryology
  anomalous pulmonary venous connection
    partial, 881, 882
    total, 868–871
  coarctation of aorta, 435–437
  inferior vena cava, abnormal anatomy and, 941–943, 945
  patent ductus arteriosus, 415–416
  pulmonary, 869, 870
    developmental anomalies and, 822, 823–824, 868–871, 881, 882
  renal vein, 1291–1292
  spinal angiography and, 357
  thoracic duct, 1891

Emergency equipment, 118–119
Emergency treatment, 34–48
  actions needed in, 35
  airway adjuncts in, 38–39
  artificial ventilation in, 36–39
  cardiopulmonary resuscitation in, 37, 39–40
    criteria of effective, 40–41
    discontinuance of, 41
    for infant or child, 39–40
  cricothyreotomy in, 39
  equipment and drug cart for, 47–48
  essential drugs in, 45–47
  external cardiac compression in, 39, 40
  general precautions for, 34
  in interventional radiology, III:216
  intravenous infusion in, 39
  in major reaction, 35–41
  mechanical resuscitation in, 37
  in minor reaction, 35
  open chest cardiac massage in, 40
  quick reference for, 34
  tracheal intubation in, 39
  vital functions in, 36
Emissary veins of adrenal gland, 1353
Emory Angioplasty Versus Surgery Trial (EAST), III:374, III:383
Emphysema, pulmonary
  arteriography in, 799, 801, 802, 803
  congenital lobar, 799
  magnification angiography in, 181
Empyema, thoracic, III:831–832, III:833, III:834
  pulmonary compression after, 817
Empyema catheters, III:832
Enchondromas, 1783
  of inferior vena cava, 971
Endarterectomy
  abdominal aorta defects after, 1070
  aortoiliac, in arteriosclerotic disease, 1053
  carotid
    angioplasty after, III:339–347
    intraoperative studies in, 252–253
    studies of effectiveness of, 286, 287
    in chronic mesenteric ischemia, 1633–1634
    femoral arteriography after, 1717
    innominate artery, angioplasty after, III:352, III:354
    pseudoaneurysms after, 1693
    in stroke, III:752–753
Endocarditis
  mycotic aneurysms and, 1077
    cerebral, 319
    thoracic aortic, 484
  patent ductus arteriosus and, 421
Endocrine tumors, pancreatic venography in, 1429–1431
Endolarynx, 983
Endoluminal grafting with fluoroscopic guidance in abdominal aorta aneurysms, 1093–1095
Endoluminal paving with hydrogel polymers in restenosis after balloon angioplasty, III:16
Endometrial carcinoma, III:82
Endoprosthesis
  in benign biliary obstruction, III:462
  in malignant hepatobiliary obstructions, III:478–480

Endopyelotomy for ureteropelvic junction obstruction, III:561

Endoscopic retrograde cholangiopancreatography (ERCP), 1383, 1398
in benign biliary obstructions, III:458–459
in AIDS-related cholangiopathy, III:470
with primary sclerosing cholangitis, III:466–468
in pancreatic pseudocyst, III:933

Endoscopy
in aortoenteric and paraprosthetic fistula diagnosis, 1693
for electroincision in ureteroileal anastomotic strictures, III:652
in percutaneous biliary calculi removal complications, III:500–501
in percutaneous cholecystostomy, III:489
in portal hypertension, history of, III:525–526
in primary sclerosing cholangitis, III:467–468
in retrograde cholangiopancreatography. *See* Endoscopic retrograde cholangiopancreatography (ERCP)
in sclerotherapy of esophageal varices, 1422

Endothelial cells (ECs), 50–52

Endothelial-derived relaxation factor (EDRF), III:705, III:707, III:709

Endothelins, 51

Endotheliomas of inferior vena cava, 971

Endothelium, contrast agent toxicity and, 24–26

Endothelium-dependent substances, 50

Endovascular interventions
of diathermy in metal-based mechanical embolization, III:63
of grafts in mechanical embolization, III:55, III:71
for mesenteric vascular insufficiency, III:326–338
discussion of, III:336–337
etiologies and, III:326, III:328
results of, III:330–336
techniques for, III:326–330
for thoracic aortic aneurysms. *See* Thoracic aortic aneurysms, stent-grafts for

End-stage arteriolar nephrosclerosis, 1261

End-stage renal disease (ESRD), III:726

End-to-side anastomosis in coronary artery bypass grafts, 757, 758

Energy conversion from electrical to roentgen rays, 94

Enhancement
edge, 144, 145
fluoroscopic, 151–152

Entamoeba parasites in hepatic abscesses, III:931

Enteric communications, pelvic percutaneous abscess drainage and, III:953, III:954

Enteritis
granulomatous, 1560, 1568
radiation, 1579
regional
inferior mesenteric angiography in, 1605–1607, 1608

superior mesenteric angiography in, 1575

Strongyloides stercoralis, 1568

Enterocolitis, regional, 1605–1607, 1608

Enteroenteral fistulas after ureteroileostomy, III:648

Enteropathy, exudative, 1919

Environment, radiographic, for intervention angiography, 134–135

Enzymes, urinary excretion of, lithotripsy and, III:607

Ephedrine sulfate, 48

Epicardial collaterals
at apex, 704, 707
of right ventricular wall, 703, 706

Epicardial coronary arteries, spasm in, 731–733

Epidural hematoma, 352

Epigastric arteries
anatomy of, 1021
in arteriosclerotic disease, 1065
in collateral circulation, 1068

Epigastric veins, 954, 956

Epinephrine
action of, 52, 53
in arterial portography, 1530
in cardiac standstill, 45
clinical indications for, 54
in contrast media reactions, 35, 1025
of respiratory system, 30
dosage and preparation of, 52
in emergency treatment, 39, 41, 45–46
in erection reversal, III:706
in hepatic arteriography of hemangiomas, 1442
in implantation for subcutaneous port, III:976
in interventional radiology reactions, III:216, III:217
neoplastic response to
in renal cell carcinoma, 1146, 1147, 1148, 1149–1150
in renal pelvic tumors, 1161
in pancreatic angiography, 1392, 1394
in pelvic digital angiography, 1638
pheochromocytoma producing, 1369
in platelet activation, III:126
recommended intravenous dosages for, 46
strengths and volumes of, 48
in superior mesenteric angiography, 1557
in ventricular fibrillation, 39, 41

Epiploic veins, 955

Epirubicin, III:437

Epistaxis, 347, 348–349

Epithelioid cells, granulomatous inflammatory changes in, 1925, 1926

Epsilon aminocaproic acid (ECA), 1651, III:403, III:826

Equipment
angiographic, 86–154
cardiac catheterization, 86–133. *See also* Cardiac catheterization laboratory
in cerebral angiography, 242–245, 246
digital angiography and. *See* Digital angiography
future developments of, 137–138
imaging modalities in, 135

optimal, 133–138
quality improvement and, 137
radiation safety and, 136–137
radiographic environment and, 134–135
space considerations for, 136
staffing in, 135–136
for emergency treatment, 47–48

Equipment room for cardiac catheterization laboratory, 88–89

Equipment supports in cardiac catheterization laboratory, 103–105

ERCP (endoscopic retrograde cholangiopancreatography). *See* Endoscopic retrograde cholangiopancreatography (ERCP)

Erection
dysfunction of, 1641–1645, III:705–725. *See also* Penile vascular catheterization in erectile dysfunction
papaverine and, 56, III:706–707, III:708
phentolamine with, III:710
phases of, III:705–706
physiology of, III:705–707
venoocclusive mechanism in, III:705, III:706
failure of, III:707

Ergonovine, 52, 56
in coronary arteriography, 569

Ergot alkaloids, 55–56

Ergotamine, 55–56

Escamoteur, 67

Escherichia coli
in adrenal gland infection, 1379
bile peritonitis and, III:489
gene of, in preventing restenosis after balloon angioplasty, III:16
in pyelonephritis, 1178–1179
in renal abscess, 1183
in thoracic aortic mycotic aneurysms, 485
in xanthogranulomatous pyelonephritis, 1193

Esophageal airway, 38

Esophageal disorders
compression in, in patent ductus arteriosus, 421
somatostatin and, 56
varices in. *See* Varices

Esophageal prosthesis, bowel segment for, 1590

Esophageal varices. *See* Varices

Esophageal veins for inferior vena cava collateral circulation, 955

ESRD (end-stage renal disease), III:726

Essential drugs in emergency treatment, 45–47

Essential hypertension, 1259–1260

ESWL. *See* Extracorporeal shock wave lithotripsy (ESWL)

Ethanol embolization. *See also* Alcohol
after lymphocele percutaneous drainage, III:946
in arteriovenous malformations, III:1011–1013, III:1014–1015
in hepatic malignancy, III:437
in intracranial, extraaxial lesions, III:791, III:802
in pediatrics, III:906, III:907–908
in renal cyst sclerosis, III:663, III:665

Ethanol embolization—*Continued*
  in spinal vascular metastatic lesions, 386
  in transcatheter adrenal ablation, 1380
  transhepatic variceal, III:526
  in transjugular intrahepatic portosystemic
    shunt, III:533
Ethibloc, III:906
Ethiodol
  in embolization
    with alcohol in pediatrics, III:906
    with cyanoacrylates in arteriovenous
      malformations, III:1015
    superselective, 1646, 1648, 1664
  in lymphangiography, 1867
  pulmonary embolism from, 1868,
    1869
Ethylcellulose microspheres in hepatic
    malignancy embolization, III:437
Etidocaine, III:214
European Carotid Surgery Trial (ECST),
    III:340
Ewing sarcomas, 1794–1797
Exact framing in cinefluorography, 100
Excimer laser systems, III:380, III:381
Excretory urography, 1210–1211
Exercise, pulmonary artery blood flow and,
    857
Exercise test
  angina pectoris with normal, 662
  atypical chest pain and, 638
  positive, coronary arteriography and,
    690
Exposure
  automatic control of
    calibration of equipment for, 123
    in cardiac catheterization laboratory,
      93–94
  calculation of, 129
  cardiac catheterization laboratory
    automatic control of, 93–94
    patient, 129–130
    personnel, 128–129
    reduction of, 128–130
  common mistakes in, 69–70
  dose and, 137
  rate of, rapid film changers and, 72
  records of, 129
  reproductive organ, 129–130
  round field for, Bucky diaphragm and,
    78
  x-ray
    versus camera aperture size, 139, 140
    peak detected, 139, 140
    testing for, 140
External cardiac compression, 39, 40
External carotid artery. *See* Carotid arteries,
    external
External elastic lamina after balloon angio-
    plasty, III:18
External iliac arteries. *See* Iliac arteries,
    external
External iliac veins. *See* Iliac veins, external
Extraaxial, intracranial lesions in central ner-
    vous system, III:789–816. *See also*
    Intracranial, extraaxial lesions
Extracoronary coronary collateral circula-
    tion, 712–713
Extracorporeal shock wave lithotripsy
    (ESWL), III:603–608, III:609
  complications of, III:607–608, III:609
  contraindications to, III:606–607

  in percutaneous biliary calculi removal
    complications, III:497–500
  principles of, III:603–604
  results of, III:604–606
  in ureteral calculi, III:609–611
Extracranial arteries
  angioplasty of. *See* Extracranial brachio-
    cephalic arterioplasty
  normal vascular sonography flow pat-
    terns in, 212–213
Extracranial brachiocephalic arterioplasty,
    III:339–355
  carotid artery, III:339–347
    examinations before, III:340–344, III:
      345, III:346
    management of complications in, III:
      344–345
  in central nervous system ischemia, III:
    757–763
  future directions of, III:354
  innominate artery, III:352, III:354
  stents in, III:352–354
  subclavian artery, III:350–352, III:353
  vertebral artery, III:347–350
Extracranial embolization, complications
    of, 1033
Extracranial neck arteries, sonography of,
    220–222
Extrahepatic cholangiocarcinoma, biopsy
    in, III:176
Extrahepatic portal obstruction, 1535,
    1536, 1537
Extrahepatic vascular circulation, 1498,
    1501–1504, 1505–1506
  anatomic changes in, 1526
  obstruction of, 1499, 1508–1512,
    1513–1517
Extralobar sequestration, 798
Extraperitoneal hemorrhage, massive, 1648
Extraperitoneal injuries in blunt trauma,
    522
Extrarenal metastases of Wilms tumor,
    1133
Extrarenal neuroblastomas, retroperitoneal,
    1669
Extrarenal parts of renal veins, 1115,
    1118, 1125
Extravasation
  of contrast media in renal angiography,
    1106–1107, 1108
  in extremity trauma, arteriography and,
    III:860
  in pelvic fractures, III:871
  in percutaneous embolization in varico-
    cele, III:699
  in renal trauma, III:895
    arterial, 1231, 1233, 1234, 1239
  in splenic trauma, III:888–890
  in transgraft thrombolysis, III:155
Extravascular lung water, 864, 865
Extremities, 1679–1863
  angiography of
    bones in, 1779–1821. *See also* Bone
    dialysis shunt in, 1767–1778. *See also*
      Dialysis shunt angiography
    femoral arteriography in, 1697–1742.
      See also Femoral arteriography
    joints in, 1779–1821. *See also* Joints
    magnetic resonance, 1822–1863. *See
      also* Magnetic resonance venogra-

  phy; Peripheral vascular magnetic
    resonance angiography (PVMRA)
  previous aortoiliac interventions and,
    1681–1696. *See also* Aortoiliac dis-
    ease, angiography of extremities
    after interventions for
  soft tissue in. *See* Soft tissue
  upper extremity. *See* Upper extremities
    venography in, 1743–1754. *See also*
    Magnetic resonance venography
  arteriovenous fistula in, III:1001
  arteriovenous malformations in, III:
    1006, III:1018–1022
  bone tumors of. *See also* Bone tumors
    femoral arteriography in, 1711
    upper extremity arteriography in,
      1765–1766
  lower. *See* Lower extremities
  magnetic resonance venography of,
    1837–1863. *See also* Magnetic reso-
    nance venography
  sarcomas of
    intraarterial chemotherapy for, III:
      1034–1035
    limb-sparing resection in, III:1032–
      1034
  thrombosis in, sonography of, 217–220
  trauma to, III:857–868
    arteriography indications in, III:857–
      859
    arteriography technique in, III:860–
      861
    conservative management versus inter-
      ventional radiology for, III:859–
      860
    history of treatment of, III:857
    predictors of, III:859
    transcatheter management in, III:
      861–867
  upper. *See* Upper extremities
  venography of, 1743–1754. *See also*
    Magnetic resonance venography
Exudative enteropathy, 1919

Fabian stent, III:632–633
Factor XIII$_a$, III:120
Falconer A, 1426
Fallopian tube
  proximal obstruction of, III:672
  recanalization of, III:672–677
  tumor of, 1648
Fallot tetralogy. *See* Tetralogy of Fallot
False aneurysms. *See also* Pseudoaneurysms
  in blunt trauma to aorta and brachio-
    cephalic arteries, 529, 530, 531,
    535–537
  embolization in, 1239, 1241, 1242
  of extremities after aortoiliac interven-
    tions, 1686, 1691–1692
  hepatic artery, III:432, III:433
    bleeding, 1453–1454
  in renal arterial trauma, 1231, 1234,
    1235, 1237, 1238
    embolization in, 1239, 1241, 1242
  from stab wound of superficial femoral
    artery, 1726
  thoracic aortic, III:363
False cysts, splenic, 1481
False negatives or false positives
  in biopsy, III:167–168
  in coronary arteriography, 656

in gastrointestinal bleeding arteriography, III:393–394, III:395
in lymphography, 1943
Falx artery, anterior, 258, 259
Falx cerebri, intracranial, extraaxial lesions of, III:793
Famotidine, 1043
Fariñas PL, 8, 393, 394, 932
Fascial compartment compression after transaxillary arteriography, 1031
Fascicles of conducting system, 615
Fasciculus interauricularis anterior, 615
Fatty streaks in arteriosclerosis, 1052
Favaloro RG, 756
FDPs (fibrin degradation products), III:119
Feeding artery complications of dialysis shunt, 1768, 1769
Feeding tube, care of, III:555
Feedings after percutaneous gastrostomy, III:554–555
Female urethra, III:616–617
Feminizing disorders, 1368
Femoral arteries
  in aortography
    abdominal, 158
    historical notes on, 8–9
  arteriovenous fistula of, in puncture site complications, 1027
  atherectomy catheter for, III:44, III:46, III:49
  for cerebral angiography puncture, 247–248
  circumflex, pseudoaneurysm of, 1652
  common
    in abdominal aortography, 1013, 1014
    anatomy of, 1021
    in bronchial artery embolization, III:822
    in femoral arteriography approach, 1697–1698
    in pelvic magnetic resonance angiography, 1637
    regional chemotherapy in, III:82
    2D-TOF magnetic resonance imaging of, 1826, 1834
  Doppler waveform analysis in, 212
  in mesenteric angioplasty, III:326
  pediatric thrombolysis in, III:917
  positioning of percutaneous needle into, 1013, 1014
  profunda, in pelvic magnetic resonance angiography, 1637
  pseudoaneurysm of, 1652
  in renal angiography, 1102
  in renal angioplasty, III:300–301
  stenoses in
    eccentric, III:44, III:46
    sonography of, 222
  superficial (SFA)
    aneurysm of, 1725–1726
    bleeding point from, superselective catheterization in, 170
    collateral circulation of, 1700–1703
    dissection of, in peripheral angioplasty, 1040
    false aneurysm of, 1726
    obstruction of, in arteriosclerosis, 1065

in pelvic magnetic resonance angiography, 1637
2D-TOF magnetic resonance imaging of, 1826
wounds of, femoral arteriography in, 1700, 1728
2D-TOF magnetic resonance imaging of, 1824, 1826
Femoral arteriography, 1697–1742
  after angioplasty, 1713
  anatomy of, 1697–1703
    collateral circulation in, 1699, 1700–1703
    normal, 1697–1699, 1700
    variants in, 1698, 1699–1700, 1701
  antegrade approach for, 1705
  approaches in, 1703–1706
  axillary artery approach in, 1705, 1709
  in bone or soft tissue tumors of extremity, 1711
  brachial artery approach in, 1705
  contrast agents in, 1713–1714
  digital subtraction imaging equipment in, 1707
  filming equipment in, 1706–1707
    aortogram, 1706
    serial, 1706–1707
  first, 5, 7
  graft puncture approach in, 1705
  in grafts, projections for, 1709, 1710, 1711
  history of, 1697
  indications for, 1714–1737, 1738
    in aneurysms, 1723–1726
    in arteriovenous fistulas, 1729–1730
    in arteriovenous malformations, 1730–1733
    in atherosclerosis obliterans, 1709, 1715–1722
    in Buerger disease, 1726, 1727
    in hemorrhage, 1726–1727
    in occlusion and intimal injuries, 1700, 1727–1729
    in skin and bone grafts, 1730–1730
    in thromboangiitis obliterans, 1726, 1727
    in thromboembolism, 1722–1723, 1725
    in trauma, 1726–1730
    in tumors, 1733–1737, 1738
    in vasospasm, 1733
  intraarterial imaging equipment in, 1707
  long-leg film changers in, 81
  medications in, 1714
  monitoring in, 1714
  patient issues in, 1713–1714
  patient preparation in, 1713
  in percutaneous angioplasty, projections for, 1709
  in peripheral artery aneurysms, 1709–1711
  in peripheral artery arteriovenous fistulas, 1709–1711
  peripheral runoff in
    filming equipment for, 1706–1707
    positioning and, 1707
    visualizing distal, 1712, 1713
  popliteal artery approach in, 1706
  positioning in, 1707–1711
    for selected projections, 1707–1709, 1710, 1711

procedural advances in, 1697
projections in, 1707–1709, 1710, 1711
puncture and catheterization in, 1703–1706
special techniques in, 1711–1713
technical advances in, 1697
through graft in angiography of extremities after aortoiliac interventions, 1683, 1685
translumbar approach in, 1705–1706
transvenous approach in, 1706
transvenous imaging equipment in, 1707
vasodilatation in, 1711–1713
Femoral balloon catheter system in renal angioplasty, III:300–302
Femoral neuralgia syndrome, 1028
Femoral stents, complications of, 1042
Femoral triangle, frontal view of, 247
Femoral veins
  arteriovenous fistula of, in puncture site complications, 1027
  common
    in intravascular biopsy, III:196–197, III:198–199
    magnetic resonance venography of, 1851
    as vena cava filter insertion site, III:985
  Doppler waveform analysis in, 211
  hematoma of, after angioplasty, 1042
  in inferior vena cavography, 933
  insufficiency in, sonography of, 220
  magnetic resonance venography of, 1843
  in percutaneous revision of surgical portosystemic shunts, III:528–530
  profunda, 1843
  pseudoaneurysms of, 1693, 1694, 1695
  pulmonary arteriography approach and, 771, 773–774, 775
  puncture site of
    in coronary artery catheterization complications, 579
    neuralgia syndrome as complications of angiography and, 1028
    in percutaneous transluminal angioplasty (PTA), complications of, 459–460
  superficial, 1843, 1844, 1846
  in superior vena cava obstruction treatment, 928–929
  thrombosis of, after renal angiography, 1110
  2D-TOF magnetic resonance imaging of, 1824
  in venography of lumbar spinal plexus, 933
Femorofemoral bypass, 1690
Femorofemoral crossover grafts, 1710, 1717
  thrombolysis in, III:147
Femoroperoneal grafts, 1718, 1719
Femoropopliteal revascularization, III:108–110, III:262–283
  angioplasty in, III:262–278
    alternative methods to, III:278–281
    in asymptomatic patients, III:270
    confidence profile method for measuring results of, III:266
    criteria for assessing results of, III:265–266
    history of, III:262

Femoropopliteal revascularization—
  Continued
  angioplasty in—*Continued*
    indications for, III:270–278
    laser, III:280–281
    in occlusions, III:263–264, III:274,
      III:277
    patient care during, III:265
    results of, III:266–270
    in stenoses, III:262–263, III:272, III:
      274
    in symptomatic patients, III:270–272,
      III:273–277
    technique for, III:262–264
  atherectomy in, III:278–280
  frequency of lesions versus length in, III:
    262, III:263
  grafts in, 1709
    femoral arteriography after, 1718,
      1720, 1722
    stenosis of, 1709, III:284–293
    synthetic, thrombolysis in, III:146
  long-term patency after, III:265
  stents in, III:110–112, III:262
Femorotibial grafts, 1721
  femoral arteriography after, 1718, 1719
Femur
  chondroblastoma of, 1784
  lung cancer metastasis to, tumor emboli-
    zation in, 1817
  malignant fibrous histiocytomas of,
    1800–1801
  osteogenic sarcoma of, 1734
  osteosarcoma of, 1792, 1793, 1794
  renal cell carcinoma metastases to, 1808
Fentanyl, III:213
  in arterial portography preparation, 1528
  in cerebral angiography, 246
  in femoral arteriography, 1713, 1714
  in percutaneous pelvic abscess drainage,
    III:947
  in transjugular intrahepatic portosystemic
    shunt, III:532
  in varicocele embolization, III:694
Fetal posterior cerebral artery, 260
Fiberendoscopes in biliary calculi removal,
  III:500–501
Fibrillation
  atrial, 43, 44
    from embolism in peripheral occlu-
      sion, 1725
  ventricular, 44, 45
    contrast agent toxicity and, 27
    in coronary arteriography complica-
      tions, 577
    prevention of, in emergency treat-
      ment, 39
Fibrin, III:119–120
  contrast agent toxicity and, 25
  fibrils of, III:124
  in plasminogen, III:120–121
  tissue-type plasminogen activator and,
    III:121
Fibrin degradation products (FDPs), III:
  119
Fibrinogen, III:119–120
  metallic stent implantation and, III:93
  molecule of, III:120
Fibrinolysis, selective, single-chain urokinase plasminogen activator in, III:
  122

Fibrinolytic system, III:119–123
Fibrinolytic therapy. *See also* Thrombolytic
  agents
  agents in
    choice of, III:133–134
    endogenous and exogenous, III:119
  contraindications to, 1043
  intraarterial, pelvic angiography in,
    1640–1641, 1642
  pulmonary arteriography and, 808–809,
    810
Fibrinopeptides A and B, III:119, III:120
Fibroadenoma of breast, III:1038, III:
  1040
Fibrolipomatosis
  of inguinal lymph nodes, 1873
    in malignant metastatic lymph node
      disease, 1927–1929
  renal, 1166, 1317–1320, 1321
    renal cysts versus, 1173
Fibromas
  of extremities
    chondromyxoid, 1783
    nonossifying, 1798
  renal, 1165
  of spleen, 1482
Fibromatosis of lymph nodes
  in benign disease, 1923, 1924
  in metastatic disease, 1927–1930,
    1932–1934, 1936, 1937
Fibromuscular dysplasia (FMD), 307–310,
  311
  carotid-cavernous fistulas in, III:802
  endovascular interventions for chronic
    mesenteric ischemia in, III:326, III:
    336
  mesenteric ischemia and, III:336
  renal angioplasty results in, III:311–316
  renal artery stenosis in, III:294
Fibromuscular hyperplasia of renal arteries,
  1250–1257
Fibronectin, III:123, III:124
Fibroplasia
  intimal, coronary arteriography in, 692
  medial
    coronary arteriography in, 692
    of renal arteries with aneurysm, 1254,
      1255
    of renal arteries, 1250–1257
      with aneurysm, 1254, 1255
      periarterial, 1255–1256
      perimedial, 1255, 1256
Fibrosarcomas
  of extremities, 1798–1799, 1800–1801
    femoral arteriography in, 1735
  retroperitoneal, 1669, 1670, 1671
  of spleen, 1483, 1484
Fibrosing mediastinitis, 919, 921–922
Fibrosis
  irradiation, 1926
    lymphedema in, 1909, 1915, 1916
  retroperitoneal. *See* Retroperitoneum,
    fibrosis in
Fibrous histiocytomas, malignant
  of extremities, 1799–1801, 1802
    in differential diagnosis, 1811
  retroperitoneal, 1669
Fibrous plaques in arteriosclerosis, 1052
Filariasis, 1909
  Bancroft, 1925
  chyluria in, 1920

Filling defects
  in contrast column in abdominal aorta,
    1056, 1057
  in coronary arteriography, 641, 644–
    645
  in fibromatosis of lymph nodes
    in benign disease, 1923, 1924
    in malignant disease, 1927–1930,
      1932–1934, 1936, 1937
  washout effects simulating, 971
Filling phase of erection, III:705
Film
  in magnification angiography, 177–180
  in pancreatic angiography, 1395–1396
  radiographic
    for cardiac catheterization laboratory,
      105, 106, 107, 108
    color response of, 105
Film badge for radiation exposure, 128
Film changers
  avoiding air entrapment in, 69
  for cerebral angiography, 68
  common mistakes in use of, 69–70
  design of, in cardiac serial radiography,
    102
  large-field, 81–82
    Amplatz, 82
  long-leg, in large-field angiography, 81–
    82
    in diabetic patient, 84
  for pulmonary angiography, 68
  rapid, 66–68. *See also* Rapid film
    changers
  for renal angiography, 68
  timing cycle of, 72–80
    diagram of, 73
Film drying, cine film processing and,
  109
Film position in arterial portography,
  1529–1530
Film processing, quality control for, 123–
  124
Film transport in cine viewers, 113–114,
  115
Filming in arterial portography, 1529
Filming equipment in femoral arteriography, 1706–1707
Filter
  in vascular intervention angiography,
    134
  vena cava. *See* Vena cava filters
  of video system in vascular intervention
    angiography, 141
Filtering operation, 144–146
Filtration
  cine film processing and, 109
  spatial, in nonsubtraction imaging, 152
  temporal, in nonsubtraction imaging,
    152
Filum terminale, artery of, 359
Final resolving power in magnification angiography, 179
Fingers, arteriovenous malformation of,
  1756
First degree heart block, 43, 44
First moment of encoding gradient, 199
First septal perforator, 611, 612
  superimposed in arteriography over
    obstructions, 734, 735
Fischer Pullback atherectomy catheter, III:
  47, III:379, III:380

Fischgold H, 893
Fish oils in restenosis after balloon angioplasty, III:15
Fistula
aortocaval, 962
aortoenteric, 1069, 1070
after aneurysms repair, 1095–1096
after aortoiliac interventions, 1692–1693
arteriocaliceal, 1346–1347
arteriovenous. *See* Arteriovenous fistula
biliary-to-TIPS, III:542
bronchoesophageal, after embolization, III:827
bronchopleural, mechanical embolic agents for, III:76
carotid-cavernous. *See* Carotid-cavernous fistulas (CCFs)
cerebral, 323–328
complications of embolization in, 1032
coronary artery, 740–741, 742
coronary artery–pulmonary artery, pulmonary arteriography in, 799
enteroenteral, after ureteroileostomy, III:648
hepatic, III:425–426, III:428
techniques for, III:431–432
lymph, 1918, 1919–1920
lymphointestinal, 1919
mesenteric, 1568, 1573
pelvic, abscess with, III:953
pulmonary artery, complications of embolization for, 1033
urinary
after ureteral stenting, III:577
mechanical embolic agents for, III:76
percutaneous nephrostomy in, III:563
in vertebral and azygos vein variations, 911
Fixing solution, 109
Flail chest, 522
Flexible disk systems, on-line digital recording and, 148
Flexible fiberendoscopes in biliary calculi removal, III:500–501
Flexible ureteroscopy, percutaneous stone removal with, III:595
Flex-T guidewire, III:285
Flip angle, 195, 196, 197
Flooring in control and equipment room, 88
Floppy tip of microcatheter, 163, 165
Flow artifacts, in-plane, 1829, 1830
Flow image, creation of, 210
Flow-caliber relationship in pulmonary vessels, 856–858, 859
Flow-related enhancement, 189
Flow-sensitive catheters
in intraaxial embolotherapy, III:766
in superselective catheterization, 164–165, 166
Floxuridine. *See* Fluorodeoxyuridine (FUDR)
Fluid collections, pelvic. *See also* Pelvic abscess percutaneous drainage (PAD)
common sites and etiologies of, III:939
percutaneous drainage of, III:944, III:945. *See also* Pelvic abscess percutaneous drainage (PAD)

Fluids in interventional radiology, III:214
for child, III:904, III:920
Flumazenil, III:213, III:216
Fluorodeoxyuridine (FUDR), III:81, III:437, III:450, III:451
in cervical carcinoma, III:82
in osteosarcomas, III:1033
Fluorography, spot-film. *See* Spot-film fluorography
Fluoropyrimidine, III:80–81
Fluoroscopic timer, 126
Fluoroscopy
in biopsy, III:175
of musculoskeletal system, III:191
in digital angiography, 151–152
in endoluminal grafting guidance, 1093–1095
in fallopian tubal catheterization, III:676
in percutaneous gastrostomy, III:548–549, III:553, III:557
in percutaneous nephrostomy, III:564
pulsed-progressive, in nonsubtraction imaging, 151
in renal angioplasty, III:301
in renal calculi removal, III:599
in retrograde catheterization of ureteroileal anastomoses, III:650
in thoracic abscess drainage, III:830
in thoracic aortic aneurysm diagnosis, 468
in thoracic aortic aneurysm stent-grafts, III:360
in thoracic empyema drainage, III:832
in ureteral stenting, III:575
in urethral lesions, III:618
in venous access catheter placement, III:970–971
5-Fluorouracil, 1037, III:80–81
in extremity sarcomas, III:1032
in hepatic malignancy, III:436, III:437, III:450
Flush systems, continuous, 1029
Flutamide, III:627
Flutter, atrial, 43, 44
FMD (fibromuscular dysplasia), 307–310, 311
carotid-cavernous fistulas in, III:802
mesenteric ischemia and, III:326, III:336
renal angioplasty results in, III:311–316
renal artery stenosis in, III:294
Foam cells in arteriosclerosis, 1052
Focal cortical hyperplasia, renal, 1166, 1167, 1168
Focal nodular hyperplasia, hepatic, 1441–1443, 1444
Focal pyelonephritis, acute, terminology, 1179
Focal spot
blurred, in digitization, 143
shape and intensity distribution of, in tube, 96
size of
in magnification angiography, 177
in tube, 96
Focal-spot tube
in cardiac catheterization, 95
in vascular intervention angiography, 134
Fogarty TJ, III:160–161

Fogarty balloon
iatrogenic dissection from catheter and, 1029
in percutaneous biliary calculi removal, III:497
Fogarty thromboembolectomy, III:160–161
Foley catheter
in percutaneous cholecystolithotomy, III:504
in percutaneous nephrostomy, III:566
Follicular hyperplasia, reactive
malignant lymphoma versus, 1944–1947
repeat lymphography in, 1948, 1949, 1950
Follicular lymph node patterns in malignant lymphoma, 1940, 1942, 1944
Follow-up after interventional radiology, III:219–221
in percutaneous nephrostomy, III:570–572
for pulmonary arteriovenous malformations, III:852, III:853
Fontaine-Dake stent, III:89, III:90
Fontan operation, 868
Foot
cross section, 1828
lymphangiography of, 1866
magnetic resonance angiography of, 1824, 1825
runoff vessels in, PVMRA of, 1831
Foramen magnum, intracranial, extraaxial lesions of, III:794–795
Foramen of Monro, 275
Force, dilating, of balloon catheter, III:25–26, III:27
Forceps, grasping, in foreign body removal, III:963
Forearm
hemangioma of, tumor embolization in, 1814–1815
lymph nodes of, 1881–1882
Foreign body
in kidneys after renal angiography, 1110
percutaneous removal of, III:959–968
cardiovascular, III:959–960
catheters in, III:960–963, III:964–966
complications of, III:967
grasping forceps or catheters in, III:963
nonvascular foreign bodies in, III:963–967
pediatric, III:919
transluminal techniques in, III:960–963, III:964–966
reaction to, in lymphangiography, 1867–1868
in upper airway obstruction, 36
Forestier G, 4, 13
Formocath RPX 045 catheter, 1529
Forssmann W, 6, 14, 768
Forsyth C, 392
Fossa, cerebral, 272, 277–279, 280
basilar artery in, 278
posterior, lesions of, III:794–795
veins in, 278–279, 280
vertebral artery in, 277–278

Fowler percutaneous nephrostomy, III:561
Fracture
  of clavicle, 997
  of kidney, 1272
  pelvic, 523–524, III:869–883. *See also*
    Pelvic fractures, interventional radiol-
    ogy in
  of sternum, 522, 532, 533
  supracondylar, pediatric thrombolysis in
    brachial artery occlusion after, III:
    917, III:919
  of thoracic spine, 522–523
Frame integration, image acquisition using,
  142, 143
Frame rates
  acquisition, for vascular intervention angi-
    ography, 135
  of cine cameras, 100
  on-line digital recording and, 148
  reduction of, in nonsubtraction imaging,
    151
  for spot-film fluorography, 101
Framing, cine, 100–101
Franck O, 4
Franklin KJ, 891
Franklin roll-film changers, 76–77, 78
  closure time in, 72
Fredzell G, 67
Free wall, ventricular, collaterals at, 708–
    710, 711, 712
Freeman NE, 392
French catheter-introducing sheath, 158
  in biliary calculi removal, III:493
  for guidewire-controlled superselective
    catheterization, 162, 165
  in hysterosalpingography, III:673
  in percutaneous cholecystomy, III:484
  in percutaneous suction thromboembo-
    lectomy, III:161, III:164
  in pulmonary arteriovenous malforma-
    tion embolotherapy, III:846, III:
    849
  in varicocele embolization, III:694
French catheters, III:329–330
  in abdominal abscess drainage, III:930
  in adrenal angiography, 1354
  in arterial portography, 1529
  in arteriovenous malformations, III:
    1011, III:1012
  in balloon angioplasty, III:27–28, III:
    34, III:36
    scratch-resistance of, III:39
  in biliary calculi removal, III:492, III:
    493, III:495–496
  in biliary drainage procedures, III:475,
    III:477
  in bronchial artery embolization, III:
    822, III:825, III:826
  in carotid-cavernous fistula embolization,
    III:807
  in cerebral angiography, 243–245
  in cholecystolithotomy, III:504
  in cholecystomy, III:484, III:485
  in coronary angioplasty, III:368–369
  in coronary artery catheterization, 558,
    570
  in dialysis fistula thrombolysis, III:729
  in electrohydraulic lithotripsy, III:497,
    III:499
  in femoropopliteal revascularization, III:
    263, III:264

in gastrostomy, III:548–549, III:550–
    552, III:557
in hepatic embolization, III:440, III:
    441–442
in hysterosalpingography, III:673, III:
    675
in infrapopliteal revascularization, III:
    285
in internal iliac artery angiography, III:
    871, III:876, III:879
in intraaxial embolotherapy for central
    nervous system, III:766
in intravascular biopsy, III:197
in lower extremity arteriography, 1697,
    1703–1706
in mediastinal abscess drainage, III:835
in pancreatic venography, 1428
in pediatrics, III:904
  for angioplasty, III:910
  for embolization, III:908
in pelvic abscess drainage, III:951–952
in pelvic arteriography, 1652
in pelvic digital angiography, 1638
in penile transluminal therapy, III:722
in prostatic hyperthermia, III:635
in prostatic urethroplasty, III:629
in pulmonary arteriovenous malforma-
    tion embolotherapy, III:846, III:
    849
in renal angioplasty, III:296, III:300–
    303
in renal aortography, 1102, 1103
in renal arteriography in trauma, III:895
in renal transplant angiography, 1327,
    1328
in renin determination, 1306
shafts of, III:27–28
in suction thromboembolectomy, III:
    161
  modified, III:162
in superior mesenteric angiography,
    1555
in superselective catheterization, 161–
    162, 163
in thoracic abscess drainage, III:830
in thoracic aortic aneurysm stent-grafts,
    III:359–360
in thoracic empyema drainage, III:832
in transjugular intrahepatic portosystemic
    shunt, III:532
in upper extremity angiography, 1755
in ureteral stricture dilation, III:579
in urethral procedures, III:619, III:620,
    III:621
in varicocele embolization, III:694
in venous access procedures, III:978
French Cobra catheters
  in arterial portography, 1527, 1542
  in bronchial artery embolization, III:822
  in hepatic arteriography with hepatic
    artery injuries, III:431
  in internal iliac artery angiography, III:
    871, III:876
  in percutaneous cholecystolithotomy,
    III:488–489
  in renal arteriography in trauma, III:895
  in spinal angiography, 368
  in superselective catheterization, 159
  in urethral procedures, III:619
French Cope locking-loop catheters
  in biliary calculi removal, III:495–496

in percutaneous cholecystomy, III:484,
    III:485
French endoscopes in biliary calculi
    removal, III:500–501
French hemostatic sheath in transjugular
    intrahepatic portosystemic shunt,
    III:532
French Pursil catheter, 165
French Simmons catheters, 244, 245
  in arterial portography, 1529
  in spinal angiography, 369
  in superselective catheterization, 159,
    160
French Teflon dilator in coronary arteriog-
    raphy, 560
Frenckner P, III:525
Frequency limit, Nyquist, 209, 210
Frequency selection in gray scale imaging,
    physics of, 205–206, 207
Frequency shift, Doppler, 208–209
Fresh-frozen plasma in arterial portography
    preparation, 1528
Frische LH, 9
Frische LJ, 635
Frontal arteries, ascending, 270
Frontal collisions, blunt trauma to aorta
    and brachiocephalic arteries in,
    522–523, 528–529
Frontal veins, anterior, 276
Frontopolar artery, 266–267
Fryett AG, 583
5-FU. *See* 5-Fluorouracil
FUDR. *See* Fluorodeoxyuridine (FUDR)
Fulton WFM, 584
Functional class of coronary artery disease,
    coronary arteriography complica-
    tions and, 575
Fungal infections
  in aneurysms of thoracic aorta, 483–
    486
  intracranial changes in, 303, 305
  renal, 1200
    transplant obstruction from, III:581
Furosemide, 48, III:537
Fused kidney, 1221, 1222–1223, 1224
Fusiform aneurysms, 1601
Fusiform cisterna chyli, 1884, 1885

GABI (The German Angioplasty Bypass
    Investigation), III:382–383
Gadolinium in peripheral vascular magnetic
    resonance angiography, 1829–
    1831, 1852, 1853–1855, 1857
Galen, great vein of, 275, 276
  malformations of, III:782, III:783, III:
    784
Gallbladder
  colic and, III:491
  infarction of, 1037
    after hepatic arteriography, III:434
    percutaneous cholecystomy for, III:483–
      490
Gallium 67 scanning of pelvic abscesses
    and fluid collections, III:946
γ-mapping technique, 141
Ganciclovir, III:17
Ganglia, basal, gliomas in, 340
Ganglioneuromas
  adrenal, 1373, 1376, 1378
  retroperitoneal, 1669

Ganglionic blockers, renin determination and, 1306

Gangrene after thoracic aortography, 399–400, 401

Garcia A, 7

Gas pressures in alveoli, 854–855. *See also* Pressure

Gastric arteries, 1017–1018, 1434–1436
  hepatic branches from, superselective embolization of, 169
  left
    accessory, 1463
    as collateral vessel in splenic artery thrombosis, 1480
    vasopressin infusion in, III:396

Gastric carcinoma, III:548

Gastric emptying, gastrojejunostomy tube and, III:548

Gastric feedings after percutaneous gastrostomy, III:554–555

Gastric mucosa
  hemorrhage of, III:392, III:404–405, III:406, III:407
  injury to, in lithotripsy, III:607

Gastric varices, 1314
  in arterial portography, 1533–1535, 1536, 1537
  partial splenic ablation in, 1492

Gastrinoma
  blood sampling from veins in, 1431
  pancreatic, 1401, 1403–1405

Gastritis
  bleeding from duodenum in, III:393, III:395
  gastric mucosal hemorrhage in, III:404, III:407
  in Mallory-Weiss tears, III:393

Gastroduodenal artery
  anatomy of, 1018
  in arterial portography, 1532
  hemorrhage of, III:75
  in pancreatic vasculature, 1384
  splenic renal artery anastomoses and, 1285
  superselective catheterization in, 160

Gastroenteropancreatic peptides, somatostatin and, 56

Gastroepiploic artery
  anatomy of, 1018
  chemoembolization in, 167, III:910
  as collateral vessel in splenic artery thrombosis, 1480

Gastroepiploic veins, 1532

Gastroesophageal reflux, gastrojejunostomy tube in, III:548

Gastrointestinal sarcomas, intraarterial chemotherapy for, III:1035

Gastrointestinal system, III:387–558
  arteriography in
    for angiodysplasia, III:415–417, III:418
    appearance in, III:391, III:392, III:393
    catheter-related problems in, III:417
    complications of, III:417–419
    for diverticular bleeding, III:390, III:411–414
    embolization in, III:400–403
    for esophageal bleeding, III:397, III:403–404, III:405

    for gastric mucosal bleeding, III:392, III:404–405, III:406, III:407
    for inflammatory bowel disease, III:414–415
    pharmacologic infusion in, III:394–400
    pitfalls in, III:392–394, III:395, III:396
    for postoperative bleeding, III:411, III:412
    site localization in, III:389–391
    technique problems in, III:419
    techniques for, III:394–403
    vasopressin infusion problems and, III:417–419
  benign biliary obstruction in, III:455–471. *See also* Biliary obstruction, benign
  biliary calculi removal in, III:491–508. *See also* Percutaneous biliary calculi removal
  bleeding in, III:389–421
    anastomotic ulcers and, III:405, III:411
    angiodysplasia and, III:415–417, III:418
    angiography for control of, III:389–421. *See also* Gastrointestinal system, arteriography in
    arteriography of, III:389–421. *See also* Gastrointestinal system, arteriography in
    diverticular, III:390, III:411–414
    esophageal, III:397, III:398, III:403–404, III:405
    false-negative and false-positive examinations of, III:393–394, III:395, III:396
    gastric mucosal, III:392, III:404–405, III:406, III:407
    inflammatory bowel disease and, III:414–415
    mesenteric varices and, III:397–400
    neoplasms and, III:417
    peptic ulceration of stomach and duodenum and, III:405, III:408, III:409, III:410
    postoperative, III:411, III:412
    radioactive isotopes in scanning of, III:389–390
    small bowel, III:394
    in superior mesenteric vessels, 1573
    superselective catheterization in, 168
    vasopressin and, 55
  cholecystomy and, III:483–490. *See also* Percutaneous cholecystostomy
  gastrostomy and gastrojejunostomy in, III:547–558
  hepatic arterial injuries in. *See* Hepatic arteries, embolization in
  in inferior vena cava obstruction, 959
  injuries in
    hepatic arterial, III:422–435. *See also* Hepatic arteries, embolization in
    in lithotripsy, III:607
  liver transplantation and, III:509–524. *See also* Liver, transplantation of
  malignancy in
    hepatic, III:436–454. *See also* Hepatic malignancy
    hepatobiliary obstruction and, III:

    472–482. *See also* Hepatobiliary obstruction, malignant
  percutaneous biliary calculi removal in. *See* Percutaneous biliary calculi removal
  percutaneous cholecystomy and. *See* Percutaneous cholecystostomy
  portal hypertension and, III:525–546. *See also* Portal hypertension
  tumors of, lymphangiography in, 1936–1938

Gastrojejunostomy, percutaneous, III:547–558. *See also* Percutaneous gastrojejunostomy

Gastrostomy, percutaneous, 1038–1039, III:547–558. *See also* Percutaneous gastrostomy

Gastrostomy tube, care of, III:555

Gate location in Doppler imaging, 207–208

Gating in magnetic resonance angiography, 197, 198

Gelfoam embolization. *See also* Embolization
  in arteriovenous malformations, III:1010–1011
  in biopsy tracks, III:76, III:182–183
  in bronchial artery, III:825–826
  in gastrointestinal bleeding, III:400–403
  in hepatic artery, III:432
  in hepatic malignancy, III:437, III:438
  in hypogastric artery embolization, 1661
  in intracranial, extraaxial lesions, III:790, III:791
  in intracranial tumors, III:811–814
  in parathyroid ablation, 990
  in pediatrics, III:904
  in pelvic chondrosarcoma, 1814
  in pelvic fracture hemorrhage, III:872–873, III:878–880
  in pelvic organ hemorrhage, 1651, 1655
  problems related to, III:419
  in renal artery embolization, 1239, 1240
  in renal trauma, III:897–898
  in small-vessels or tissues, III:52–53
  in transhepatic varices, III:526
  in transjugular liver biopsy, III:199
  in ureter, III:76

General Electric L/U Cardio system, 104

Generators
  for biplane serial radiography, 91–92
  in cardiac catheterization laboratory, 89–92
  constant-potential, 91
  of modular design, 92
  power to, 94, 95
  silicon-controlled rectifier (SCR) contacting, 91
  for vascular intervention angiography, 134

Genetics, molecular, balloon angioplasty restenosis and, III:16–17

Genicular arteries, 1698, 1699
  collateral circulation of, 1700–1703

Genitourinary system, III:560–742
  dialysis fistula revascularization in, III:726–742. *See also* Dialysis fistula
  fallopian tube recanalization in, III:672–677
  lower tract in, III:614–644. *See also* Lower genitourinary tract

Genitourinary system—*Continued*
  nephroureteral obstruction in, III:561–586. *See also* Nephroureteral obstruction
  penile vascular catheterization in diagnosis and therapy of erectile dysfunction in, III:705–725. *See also* Penile vascular catheterization in erectile dysfunction
  renal calculus disease in, III:587–613. *See also* Renal calculi
  renal cysts and urinomas in, III:658–671. *See also* Renal cysts; Urinomas
  revascularization of dialysis fistula in, III:726–742
  selective salpingography in, III:672–677
  tumors of, lymphangiography in, 1933–1936
  urinary diversions in, III:645–657. *See also* Urinary diversions
  varicocele in, III:678–704. *See also* Varicocele
Gentamicin
  before biliary calculi removal, III:492
  interventional radiology and, III:209
  before partial splenic ablation, 1492
  percutaneous nephrostomy and, III:562
  in sepsis after biliary drainage procedures, 1038
Geometric magnification
  direct, 177–186
  focal-spot blur exceeding pixel matrix and, 143
The German Angioplasty Bypass Investigation (GABI), III:382–383
Gerota fascia, III:892
Gevimatic R10 film processor, 113
GFR (glomerular filtration rate), 54
Giant-cell arteritis, 304–305
  splenic artery and, 1474
  in thoracic outlet syndrome, 996, 998
Giant-cell tumors in bone, 1797, 1798
Gianturco coils, III:56
  in arteriovenous malformations, III:1011
  in extremity trauma, III:863–867
  in hepatic malignancy embolization, III:437
  magnetic resonance venography and, 1852
  in pelvic arteriography, 1652, 1655, 1657
  in pelvic chondrosarcoma, 1814
  in penile transluminal angioplasty, III:723
  thrombin and, III:61
  in transhepatic variceal embolization, III:526
  in varicocele embolization, III:694, III:696, III:697
Gianturco Z stents, III:92–93, III:94–95
  in benign biliary obstruction, III:462–464, III:468
    multiple stents in, III:469
  in Budd-Chiari syndrome, III:1053
  complications of, III:1054
  current use of, III:85
  in dialysis fistula stenoses, III:739, III:740
  history of use of, III:1047
  in liver transplantation biliary tract strictures, III:518–520

in malignant biliary obstruction, III:478, III:479
  principles for use of, III:1047–1049
  in transjugular intrahepatic portosystemic shunt, III:532–533
Gianturco-Rösch Z stent
  in benign biliary obstruction, III:462–464
  in Budd-Chiari syndrome, III:1053
  history of use of, III:1047
  principles for use of, III:1048
Gianturco-Roubin FlexStent, III:89–90
  in coronary angioplasty, III:375
  current use of, III:85
Gidlund AS, 9, 68
Gidlund compressed-air injector, 171
Glands of Littre, III:616
Glass microspheres in embolization
  in hepatic malignancy, III:437
  in small-vessels or tissues, III:54
Glass tube for cooling of radiographic tube, 95
Glenn shunt, 844
Glial neoplasm, anaplastic, 333
Glidewire. *See also* Guidewires
  in biliary calculi removal, III:493
  in bronchial artery embolization, III:825
  in pulmonary arteriovenous malformation embolotherapy, III:846
  in ureteral stenting, III:574
  in varicocele embolization, III:694
Glioblastoma multiforme
  distal shift of cerebral vessels in, 333
  hemorrhage presenting in, 340–341
  of temporal lobe, 263
Glioma, vascular, 273
  in basal ganglia or brainstem, 340–341
Glomerular filtration rate (GFR), 54
Glomerulogram, 1122
Glomerulonephritis
  chronic, hypertension in, 1269
  renal vein thrombosis in, 1308, 1312
Glomus tumors, vascular malformations in, 337–339
Glomus-type of spinal dural arteriovenous fistulas, 378
Glucagon, 61–62
  in arterial portography, 1530
  dosage and preparation of, 53
  in percutaneous gastrostomy, III:548
  in superior mesenteric angiography, 1557
Glucagonomas, 1402, 1405, 1406
  glucagon and insulin concentrations in, 1430, 1431
Glucose
  hypertonic, in varicocele percutaneous embolization, III:696
  in interventional radiology emergency reactions, III:216
  in renal cyst sclerosis, III:663
Glues, liquid, III:65
Glutamic acid, III:120
Gluteal arteries
  anatomy of, 1022
  in arteriosclerosis, 1065
  in collateral circulation, 1067
  in pelvic fractures, III:873, III:875, III:877
  superior, 1022
Gluteal lymph nodes, 1878

Gluten-induced steatorrhea, 1568
Glycoprotein IIb/IIIa platelet antagonists, III:15
Goldvalve balloons, III:67, III:69
Gonadal arteries, 1220
  collateral circulation in renal ischemia and, 1281, 1283
  pelvic arteriography of, 1642
Gonadal shielding, 129–130
Gonadal veins, 1292, 1295, 1296
  drainage of, III:678, III:679–686
  for inferior vena cava collateral circulation, 951–954, 956, 957
  intravascular leiomyoma in, 1845
  varicocele and, 1857, III:693–699
  venography of, III:682
Gonococci
  in inflammatory urethritis, III:617
  in thoracic aortic aneurysms, 485
Goodwin percutaneous nephrostomy, III:561
Gore-Tex grafts, femoral arteriography after, 1717
Gorhman syndrome, 1901
GP IIb/IIIa complex, III:123, III:124
GP IIb/IIIa receptor, monoclonal antibody against, III:126
GR 32191B, III:15
Gradient-echo imaging, low-flip-angle, 1839
Gradual reversal, spin phase of magnetic resonance imaging and, 200
Grafts
  abdominal aorta aneurysm
    endoluminal, fluoroscopic-guided, 1093–1095
    postoperative infection of, 1095
  aortic, 549
  aortobifemoral
    femoral arteriography after, 1719, 1721
    thrombolysis of, in pelvic intraarterial fibrinolytic therapy, 1640, 1641
  in aortoiliac interventions
    failure after, 1693–1695, III:232–234, III:235
    infection after, 1686, 1691–1692
    thrombosis after, 1682, 1684, 1685, 1689, 1690
  atherectomy for, III:49. *See also* Atherectomy
  in atherosclerosis obliterans, 1709, 1710, 1717–1721, 1722
  autologous vein, 223–225, 226, color plates 10 and 11
  axillofemoral bypass. *See* Axillofemoral bypass
  in chronic mesenteric ischemia, 1633–1634
  coronary artery. *See* Coronary artery bypass grafts (CABG), arteriography after
  endovascular, in mechanical embolization, III:55, III:71
  in extremity, 1682, 1684, 1685, 1689, 1690
  femoropopliteal. *See* Femoropopliteal revascularization
  hemodialysis. *See* Dialysis graft
  interposition, in dialysis fistula thromboses, III:727

puncture approach for, in femoral arteri-
    ography, 1705
renal artery stenosis and, 1284–1287
skin, 1730
synthetic, sonography of changes and
    complications after, 222–223
for thoracic aortic aneurysms. *See* Tho-
    racic aortic aneurysms, stent-grafts
    for
thrombolysis in, III:144–146, III:147
Grainger RG, 14
Gram-negative bacteria in renal abscess,
    1182, 1183
Granulomas
    in colitis, 1607, 1608
    in enteritis, 1560, 1568
    epithelioid cell, in benign lymph node
        disease, 1925, 1926
    from lymphangiography contrast media,
        1867–1868, 1869
    in malignant metastatic lymph node dis-
        ease, 1927
    in polynephritis, 1276
    in pyelonephritis, 1193–1194, 1195
        renal cell carcinoma versus, 1154,
            1156
    Wegener, 1273, 1274
Granulomatous inflammatory changes in
    lymph nodes
    epithelioid cell, in benign disease, 1925,
        1926
    in malignant disease, 1927
Grasping forceps or catheters in foreign
    body removal, III:961, III:963
Gravity effects in pulmonary physiology
    and microstructure, 854, 855
Grawitz' tumor, 1137. *See also* Renal cell
    carcinoma
Gray scale imaging
    of breast disorders, 233
    for display of phase images, 191, 192
    of lymph nodes, 232–233
    physics of, 205–206, 207
    real-time patterns in, 217
    of varicocele, 232
Great arteries, transposition of. *See also*
    Great vessels
    aorticopulmonary window and, 464
    pulmonary valve stenosis in, 826
Great cardiac vein, 590, 591
Great vein of Galen, 275, 276
Great vessels. *See also* Great arteries, trans-
    position of
    buckling of, 397, 551
    truncus arteriosus of, 549, 551
Greater sphenoid wing, extraaxial lesions
    of, III:793
Greenbaum SS, 5
Greenfield filters
    complications with, 1044
    evaluation and comparison of
        stainless steel in, III:987, III:988
        titanium in, III:987, III:990–991
    for inferior vena cava, 970
    introduction of, III:984–985
    magnetic resonance venography and,
        1852
Greenfield transvenous vacuum cup, III:161
Grids
    in cardiac catheterization laboratory, 103
    in magnification angiography, 177–180

Gries H, 18
Griffiths E, 1426
Grishman A, 410
Groin complications after later angioplasty,
    1042
Grollman JH Jr, 768, 769
Grollman catheter, 773, 774
Groshong catheters for venous access cathe-
    ter placement, III:975, III:976, III:
    978
Gross I, 583
Gross' technique for postmortem coronary
    angiogram, 583–584
Grounding
    automatic injectors and, 172–173
    problems of, 130
Growth hormone, 56
Grüntzig A, III:25, III:294, III:300, III:
    366
Grüntzig percutaneous transluminal bal-
    loon angioplasty, III:294, III:298
    femoral balloon catheter system in, III:
        262, III:300–303
    history of, III:366
Guanethidine, 1306
Guglielmi detachable embolization coil,
    III:62–63
"Guidelines for Peripheral Percutaneous
    Transluminal Angioplasty of Abdom-
    inal Aorta and Lower Extremity Ves-
    sels," III:97, III:98
Guidewires. *See also* Glidewire
    in biliary calculi removal, III:493
    in bronchial artery embolization, III:825
    in cerebral angiography, 242–243
    in cholecystomy, III:484
    complications of, 1028–1029
    in coronary angioplasty, III:368–369,
        III:370
    in coronary arteriography, 556–558
    for dialysis fistula thrombolysis, III:729,
        III:730
    in femoral arteriography, 1704–1705
    in femoropopliteal revascularization, III:
        263, III:264
    in foreign body removal, III:960–963,
        III:964–966
    in hepatic arteriography with hepatic
        artery injuries, III:431
    hydrophilic coating to polyurethane
        jacket of, 242
    in hysterosalpingography, III:673, III:
        676
    in infrapopliteal revascularization, III:
        285
    in intraaxial central nervous system
        embolotherapy, III:766
    in mesenteric angioplasty, III:327
    metallic, with Teflon coating, 242
    in pediatric interventional angiography,
        III:904
    in pelvic angiography, 1028–1029,
        1638–1639
    in pulmonary arteriography, 772
    in pulmonary arteriovenous malforma-
        tion embolotherapy, III:846
    in renal angiography, 1102–1110, 1114,
        1115, 1117
        breakage of, 1109
        hazards of, 1103–1110

    in renal angioplasty, III:302–303, III:
        317, III:329
    in suction thromboembolectomy, III:
        161, III:162
    in superior mesenteric angiography,
        1555
    in superselective catheterization, 155–
        156
        balloon catheter, 155–156
        catheter controlled by, 161–164
        problems from, 166
        with superelastic nitinol core, 156
    in transfemoral catheterization, 1014
    in transhepatic cholangiography, III:474
    in ureteral stenting, III:574
    in varicocele embolization, III:694
Guns, automatic, with needles for biopsy,
    III:174
Gunshot wounds
    cerebral vascular effects in, 342–353
    in extremity
        arteriography in, III:858, III:862, III:
            863
        upper, 1757–1758
    femoral arteriography in, 1727–1728,
        1729
    in liver, III:422, III:424, III:429
    ureteral strictures after, III:578
Gunther vena cava filter, III:987
Guttadauro MA, 635
Gynecology
    lymphangiography in, 1929, 1932–1933
    pelvic angiography in, 1646–1648, 1649

H_1 and H_2 blockers, 1025, 1043, III:209
Haemophilus influenzae infections, 1472
Halpern N, 1587
Hamartomas
    hepatic, 1445
    renal, 1163–1165
        renal cell carcinoma versus, 1154
    of spinal cord, 386
    of spleen, 1482–1483
    superior mesenteric angiography in,
        1577
Hamate, osteoid osteomas of, 1789
Hand, hemangiomas of, 1805
Hand injectors in superselective catheteriza-
    tion, 171
Hanson HE, 391
Hardware in digital angiography, 144–146
Harp-string grid method of inferior vena
    cava plication, III:983
Harris HA, 891
Harwood-Nash catheters (DHN), 244,
    245
Haschek E, 3, 4, 13
HDLs (high-density lipoproteins), 1052
Head and neck
    carcinoma of, regional chemotherapy in,
        III:82, III:83
    complications of procedures for, 1032–
        1033
    hematoma of, carotid extravasation in,
        348
    imaging of
        cerebral vascular angiography and. *See*
            Cerebral angiography
        noninvasive methods for, 252
Head-tilt maneuver, 36
Healey JE, 1434

Heart
capillary network in, 589
contrast agent toxicity and, 27, 28
coronary artery anatomy of. *See* Coronary arteries
epicardial collaterals at apex of, 704, 707
historical notes on study of, 7–8
topography of, 586–590
Heart block, 43, 44, III:216
in coronary artery catheterization complications, 577
Heart disease
cardiac catheterization laboratory for broad spectrum of, 119–122
congenital. *See* Congenital heart disease
pulmonary, pulmonary arteriography in, 799–801
valvular, as indication for angiography, 637
Heart failure
congestive. *See* Congestive heart failure
intractable, with coronary disease, as indication for angiography, 637
pulmonary arteriography in, 786, 818–819
pulmonary hypervascularity in, 815–816
Heart rate, III:214–217
Heart-shaped collimators, 97
Heat
dissipation of, for radiographic tube
in cardiac catheterization, 94–95
in vascular intervention angiography, 134
feeling of, in systemic reactions to contrast agents, 29
Heel, hemangiomas of, 1803
Helander CG, 892, 933
Helicine arterioles, III:705
in penile arteriography, III:711, III:712, III:713
Helmsworth JA, 391, 394
HEMA. *See* 2-Hydroxyethyl methylacrylate (HEMA)
Hemachromatosis, biopsy and, III:183
Hemangioblastoma
cerebral vascular malformations in, 342
spinal angiography in, 384, 385–386
Hemangioendothelioma
of extremities, 1806
hepatic, III:905, III:908
arteriography in, 1441, 1443
Hemangioma, III:998–1000
adrenal gland, 1373
cavernous
femoral arteriography in, 1731–1733
hepatic arteriography in, 1439–1441, 1442, 1443
hepatic biopsy in, III:176, III:180, III:181
venous malformations and, III:1022–1026, III:1027
diagnosis of, III:998–999
distinguishing features of, III:999
of extremities, 1801–1804, 1805, 1806
in differential diagnosis, 1811
tumor embolization in, 1814–1815
incidence of, III:998
of jaw, 1816
natural history of, III:998
pancreatic, 1406
proliferative phase of, III:998

of spleen, 1482–1483
treatment of, III:999–1000
vertebral, 386
Hemangioma simplex, 1731
Hemangiopericytomas
of extremities, 1804, 1806
retroperitoneal, 1669
Hemangiosarcomas of spleen, 1483, 1484
Hematologic effects of contrast agents, 24–26
Hematoma. *See also* Hemorrhage
after arterial portography, 1530
after nephrostomy, III:569, III:570
after pulmonary angiography, 1031–1032
after renal angiography, 1109–1110
after transaxillary arteriography, 1031
axillary artery displacement by, 1008
epidural, in left carotid angiogram, 352
in extremity trauma, III:857
femoral, after angioplasty, 1042
of head and neck, carotid extravasation in, 348
intrahepatic, 1454–1455
as lithotripsy complication, III:607
perigraft, after dialysis fistula thrombolysis, III:736
perinephric, as stone removal complication, III:602
in puncture site complications, 1026–1027
in renal cell carcinoma, 1149, 1152, 1153–1154
in renal trauma, 1271–1272, III:895, III:898
retroperitoneal, 1232
angiographic findings in, 1671–1672, 1674, 1675
in coronary arteriography complication, 578
subcapsular, hepatic, 1454–1455
subdural, in carotid angiogram, 352
trauma and
blunt, to aorta and brachiocephalic arteries, 522, 531–532
renal, 1271–1272, III:895, III:898
venous access catheters and, III:979
Hematuria
after angiography, 1103–1107
in arteriovenous fistula, 1267
lithotripsy and, III:500, III:607
magnification angiography in, 181
in pelvic tumors, 1138
prostatic urethroplasty and, III:632
in renal cell carcinoma, 1138
renal cysts and, III:659
in trauma, 1230, 1233, 1234
Hemiazygos veins, 898, 1295, 1296
anomalous drainage of, into left atrium, 900, 910
esophageal location of, 898
for inferior vena cava collateral circulation, 951–953, 952, 955, 956, 957
variations in systemic venous return and, 900–910
Hemi-Kock pouch, III:646, III:648, III:653
Hemiplegia
dissecting aortic aneurysms with, 496, 497

in thoracic aortography complications, 398–399
Hemobilia
lithotripsy and, III:500
percutaneous cholecystostomy and, III:489
Hemochron machine, III:286
Hemodialysis. *See* Dialysis
Hemodialysis graft. *See* Dialysis graft
Hemodynamics
in angioplasty, III:367
in coronary arteriography, 568
Poiseuille's law and, 852, 854
in pulmonary arteriography, 769
in splenoportography
normal, 1498, 1500–1501, 1502–1505
in vascular obstruction, 1506–1512, 1517–1521
vasopressin and, 55
Hemolytic anemias, splenomegaly in, 1467
Hemoperitoneum, 1233
Hemoptysis
bronchial artery embolization for, III:819–828. *See also* Bronchial arteries, embolization of
from cystic fibrosis, III:905–906
defined, III:819
embolization for, transcatheter bronchial artery. *See* Bronchial arteries, embolization of
as lung biopsy complication, 1034–1035, III:185
pulmonary arteriography in, 770
superselective catheterization in, 167–168
Hemorrhage. *See also* Bleeding; Hematoma; Rupture
adrenal, angiography in, 1379–1380
after aortoiliac interventions, extremity angiography in, 1689–1690
after biliary drainage procedures, 1038
after cerebral angiography, 246
after percutaneous gastrostomy, 1038
after percutaneous transhepatic cholangiography, 1037
after pulmonary angiography, 1031–1032
after thrombolytic therapy, 1042–1043
after transaxillary arteriography, 1031
after transcatheter hepatic tumor ablation, 1037
after transpleural puncture, 1029–1030
in aortoenteric and paraprosthetic fistulas, 1692
central nervous system embolization and, III:767, III:778, III:782–784
in arteriovenous malformations, III:780, III:781
cerebral plexiform nidus aneurysms and, III:775–776, III:777
post-subarachnoid or subarachnoid intracranial angioplasty and pharmacologic vasodilation in, III:753–757, III:758
in cerebral vascular malformations and fistulas, 327–328
cholecystostomy and, III:489
duodenal, superselective catheterization in, 160

femoral arteriography in, 1726–1727
gastrointestinal. *See* Gastrointestinal system, bleeding in
intracranial, intraoperative angiography in, 252–253
intraparenchymal, mass effects on cerebral vessels and, 342
intraplaque, 1056
massive extraperitoneal, 1648
mechanical embolic agents for, III:64, III:74–75
nephrostomy and, III:568–569
pancreatic
   in pancreatitis, 1412, 1413
   superselective catheterization in, 168
parenchymal, cerebral angiography technique in, 251
pelvic
   in abscess drainage, III:954
   angiography in, 1648–1650, 1651, 1652
   in fractures, III:869–883. *See also* Pelvic fractures, interventional radiology in
   in renal tumors, 1158–1159
   transcatheter embolization for uncontrollable, 1650–1654, 1658–1661
in puncture site complications, 1026–1027
renal
   in cysts, III:659–660
   during or after nephrostomy, 1036
   in renal cell carcinoma, 1149, 1152, 1153–1154
   in renal pelvic tumors, 1158–1159
retroperitoneal. *See* Retroperitoneum, hemorrhage in
in splenoportography, 1500
subarachnoid, cerebral angiography technique in, 250–251
in transhepatic portal venography, 1425
Hemorrhagic transformation in stroke, III:746
Hemorrhoidal arteries, 1019, 1021, 1022
in arteriosclerosis, 1066
superior, 1589
   in inferior mesenteric arteriography, 1597, 1599
Hemorrhoidal plexuses for inferior vena cava collateral circulation, 954, 956, 957
Hemostasis
angiography and
   cerebral, 251–252
   of extremities for aortoiliac intervention problems, 1686
in bleeding after biopsy, III:180–183
contrast agent toxicity and, 25–26
in transaxillary catheterization, 1016
Hemothorax
after transpleural puncture, 1030
dissecting aortic aneurysms and, 500, 502, 503
Henle J, 700
Heparin
aortoiliac revascularization and, III:230
carotid angioplasty and, III:342
coronary angioplasty and, III:372, III:377

in coronary arteriography, 568–569, 575
detachable balloons in embolization and, III:68
in femoropopliteal revascularization, III:263
in heparin-bonded catheters, III:1034
in implantation for subcutaneous port, III:977
in infrapopliteal revascularization, III:286, III:290
lymphocele formation and, III:944
in mesenteric angioplasty, III:327
for pediatric interventional angiography, III:903
in pelvic digital angiography, 1638
penile vascularization and, III:710
   for erectile dysfunction, III:722
in preventing catheter or guidewire complications, 1029
in puncture site complications, 1027
in renal angiography, 1109
in renal angioplasty, 1041, III:306
in restenosis after balloon angioplasty, III:15
reversal of, in interventional radiology, III:215
in thoracic aortic aneurysm stent-graft procedure, III:360
in thrombolysis, III:126, III:127, III:128, III:137
   in aortoiliac disease, III:234
   in central nervous system, III:748
   in dialysis fistula, III:731, III:737–738
   in hemodialysis grafts, III:138, III:147
   in lower extremities, III:150–151
   in upper extremities, III:152
Hepatic abscess, 1438, 1440–1441
after arteriography, III:434
percutaneous drainage of, III:929–931
Hepatic adenomas, 1443–1445
Hepatic angiosarcoma, 1450
Hepatic arteries, 1018, 1020, 1434–1436. *See also* Hepatic arteriography
anomalous, computerized tomography during arterial portography of, 1543–1544
bleeding false aneurysm of, 1453–1454
common, 1018
   inadvertent dissection of, in superselective catheterization, 165
   occlusion of, in superior mesenteric angiography, 1554–1555
   in pancreatic vasculature, 1384
embolization in, III:428–434
   anatomy and, III:431
   complications of, 1037, III:429, III:434
   indications for, III:428–431, III:432
   interhepatic arterial injuries and, III:422–428, III:429
   success and failure of, III:434
   techniques for, III:431–434
   timing of angiography and, III:428, III:430–431
injuries to, III:422–435
   embolization in. *See* Hepatic arteries, embolization in
   interhepatic, III:422–428, III:429

timing of angiography and embolization in, III:428, III:430–431
in liver transplantation
   complications of, III:510–513
   in donor allograft preparation, III:509
   in pediatric embolization, III:910
   splenic renal artery anastomoses and, 1285
superselective catheterization in, 160–161, 165
   in liver trauma and tumor, 168
vasopressin infusion in, III:396
Hepatic arteriography, 1433–1456. *See also* Hepatic arteries
in benign tumors, 1439–1445
in cirrhosis, 1436–1438, 1439
in inflammatory disease, 1438, 1439, 1440–1441
in metastatic malignant disease, 1450–1451, 1452, 1453
normal anatomy in, 1434–1436
in primary malignant tumors, 1446–1450, 1451
technique of, 1433–1434
in trauma, 1451–1455
Hepatic biopsy, III:186–187
bleeding in, III:180, III:182
in metastatic adenocarcinoma of colon, III:167
Hepatic cirrhosis. *See* Cirrhosis
Hepatic failure
nephrotoxicity of contrast agents and, 23, 24
in renal cell carcinoma, 1139
Hepatic hamartomas, 1445
Hepatic inflammatory disease, 1438, 1439, 1440–1441
Hepatic lobe pseudolesion, computerized tomography during portography of, 1544–1545
Hepatic malignancy, III:436–454
arterial portography in, 1544
bland thrombus versus tumor thrombus in, 1855
carcinoid in, III:451–452
hepatobiliary obstruction and. *See* Hepatobiliary obstruction, malignant
hepatocellular carcinoma in, III:450, III:451
interventional therapy in, III:436, III:450, III:451
   chemotherapeutic and embolic agents for, III:437–438
   complications of, III:452–453
   patient selection for, III:438–439
   physiologic basis of, III:436–437
   repeated embolization in, III:440, III:445–446
   results of, III:450, III:451
   technique for, III:439–440, III:441–449
islet cell tumors in, III:451–452
metastatic. *See* Liver, metastases and survival in, III:439, III:450, III:451
Hepatic oil embolism from lymphangiography, 1869–1870
Hepatic trauma
ablation in, 1030, 1037
arteriography in, 1451–1455
superselective catheterization in, 168–169

Hepatic tumors. *See also* Hepatic malignancy
  ablation of, 1037
  benign, 1439–1445
Hepatic veins
  adrenal veins compared to, 1355
  sonography of, 231
  stenosis of, after transjugular intrahepatic portosystemic shunt, III:541–542
  thrombosis of, as contraindication to transjugular intrahepatic portosystemic shunt, III:538–541
  for transjugular liver biopsy, III:198
  for venous access catheters, III:975
  washout effects simulating filling defects of, 971
Hepatic-lienal-mesenteric trunk, 1434, 1435
Hepatitis
  infectious, 1438, 1439
  serum, 1438
Hepatobiliary obstruction, malignant, III:472–482
  anatomy and, III:473–476
  biliary drainage in, III:473–476
  diagnosis of, III:476, III:477
  management of patient in, III:477
  palliation in, III:477–481
Hepatocellular carcinoma, 1446–1450, 1451. *See also* Hepatic malignancy
Hepatofugal collateral circulation, 1506
Hepatomas, 1446–1450, 1451. *See also* Hepatic malignancy
Hepatopetal collateral circulation, 1506
Hereditary hemorrhagic telangiectasia (HHT), 1033, III:837
Hereditary nephritis, 1226, 1227
Hereditary polycystic disease, adult, 1226, 1227
Herniation, mesenteric, 1579
Herrick JB, 635
Hexabrix. *See* Sodium meglumine ioxaglate
Heyer-Schulte biliary stent, III:477
H1H (Hilal Modified Headhunter) catheter
  in bronchial artery embolization, III:822
  in pulmonary arteriovenous malformation embolotherapy, III:846
H3H (Hilal Modified Headhunter) catheter, 244, 246
HHT (hereditary hemorrhagic telangiectasia), 1033, III:837
Hibernomas, 1373
Hickman catheters, III:970, III:975, III:978
High-density lipoproteins (HDLs), 1052
High-flow priapism, 1661
High-osmolality contrast agents (HOCAs)
  cardiac toxicity and, 27, 28
  coronary artery catheterization complications from, 576, 577
  physiology of, 30–31
  renal toxicity and, 24
High-pass filtration, 144
High-pressure pulse in blunt trauma, 528
High-resolution television viewing systems, 102
High-voltage cables, 88
Hilal Modified Headhunter (H1H) catheter
  in bronchial artery embolization, III:822

in pulmonary arteriovenous malformation embolotherapy, III:846
Hilal Modified Headhunter (H3H) catheter, 244, 246
Hilar arteries, 1217, 1219, 1224
Hilar lymph nodes, middle, filling of, 1897, 1898
Hildebrand, 583
Hilton J, 891
Hinck Headhunters (H1P and H3P) catheters, pediatric, 244, 246
Hip arthroplasty, 1851
Hippuran, 1335
Hirsch S, 5, 6, 13
Hirudin, III:126
His bundle, 615, 621
Histamine
  blockers of, 1025, 1043. *See also* Antihistamines
  in pancreatic angiography, 1392
  in systemic reactions to contrast agents, 30
Histiocytomas, fibrous, malignant
  of extremities, 1799–1801, 1802
    in differential diagnosis, 1811
  retroperitoneal, 1669
Histiocytosis, sinus, malignant lymphoma versus, 1943
Histologic examination in biopsy, III:166–171
Histoplasmosis
  Addison disease secondary to, 1378
  in adrenal gland infection, 1379
  lymph node changes in, 1925
Historical notes, 3–12
History
  of balloon angioplasty, III:3–4
  of balloon catheters, III:24–25, III:26
  of cerebral vascular angiography, 241
  of coronary angioplasty, III:366
  of extremity trauma arteriography and transcatheter treatment, III:857
  of femoral arteriography, 1697
  of femoropopliteal angioplasty, III:262
  patient
    in percutaneous aortoiliac intervention, III:225–228
    in preinterventional assessment, III:206
  of peripheral vascular magnetic resonance angiography, 1822–1823
  of pulmonary arteriography, 768–769
  of renal transplantation angiography, 1330–1333
  of thoracic aortic aneurysm stent-grafts, III:356–357
  of thoracic aortography, 391
  of vascular stents, III:85
  of vena cava filter use, III:982–985
  of venography of extremities, 1743
  of vertebral and azygos vein study, 891–892
Hjortsjö C-H, 1506
HMPAO. *See* ^{99m}Tc-hexamethylpropyleneamine oxine (Tc^{99m}Tc HMPAO)
HOCAs. *See* High-osmolality contrast agents (HOCAs)
Hockey stick curved catheter, 159
  in penile transluminal therapy, III:722
  in urethral procedures, III:619

Hodgkin disease. *See also* Lymphoma, malignant
  biopsy and, III:172–173, III:184
  diagnostic accuracy in, 1950–1952
  histopathologic classification of, 1940
  lymph node patterns in, 1941–1942, 1943
  lymphedema in, 1915
  nodular sclerosing, 1950
    biopsy and, III:172–173
  radiotherapy effects in, 1915
  renal cell carcinoma versus, 1154
  spleen in, 1483, 1484
    enlarged, 1467
    rupture of, 1491
  surveillance abdominal films in, 1944–1946, 1947
Hoevels J, 1422
Hoey GB, 18
Hohn catheter, III:970, III:978
Holman E, III:1000
Holmium-YAG laser systems, III:380, III:381
Homans J, III:982
Honeywell MEDDARS display system, 118
Hook-tip guidewires or catheters in foreign body removal, III:961, III:962
Hoop strength of balloon catheter, III:26–27
Hoop stress, III:26
Hopff M, III:25
Hopff percutaneous transluminal balloon angioplasty for femoropopliteal revascularization, III:262
Hoppe JO, 15
Hormones
  in benign prostatic hyperplasia, III:627–628
  blood levels of, 169
Horseshoe kidney, 1221, III:590
Hot tip laser probes in infrapopliteal revascularization, III:293
Houston Fearless film processor, 112
H1P and H3P (Hinck Headhunters pediatric catheters), 244, 246
HS-1 and HS-2 catheters in spinal angiography, 368
Huber needle, III:977
Huebner, recurrent artery of, 261
Humeral artery, compression of, 1008
Humerus, chondrosarcomas of, 1786, 1788
Humoral factors, vascular smooth muscle cells and, 51
Hump sign, 499, 500, 501, 503
Hunter-Sessions balloon, III:984
Hutch diverticulum, III:618
Hydatidiform mole, 1646, 1647
Hydralazine, 1306, III:215
Hydration
  adjustment of, in preintervention assessment, III:207
  nephrotoxicity of contrast agents and, 23, 24
Hydrocele, III:641
Hydrocortisone, 48, III:216
Hydrogel-coated angioplasty balloons, III:39–42
Hydromer-coated Anthron catheter, 159

Hydronephrosis, 1202–1216
  angiographic findings in, 1203, 1204–
    1209
    in determining cause, 1209, 1210,
      1213–1214
    in infection and pyonephrosis, 1203–
      1213
    in treatment planning, 1204, 1207,
      1208, 1215
  hypertension and, 1276
  imaging of, 1203
  infected, 1199–1200
  from obstruction, 1202, 1203, 1213–
    1215
  renal angiography in, 1113, 1120
  renal cysts versus, 1173, 1175
  renal venography in, 1317, 1318–1319
  from ureteroileal anastomotic strictures,
    III:649, III:650
  Wilms tumor versus, 1135, 1136
  xanthogranulomatous pyelonephritis ver-
    sus, 1193
Hydrosalpinx, III:673, III:676
Hydroxyapatite renal calculi, III:606
2-Hydroxyethyl methylacrylate (HEMA),
  III:65–66
  in intraaxial central nervous system
    embolotherapy, III:696–698, III:
    766
Hydroxyzine, III:217
Hygroma, cystic, 1921
Hypaque. *See* Sodium diatrizoate
Hypaque 50%, 170
Hypaque 60%, 170
Hypaque-76, 576, 577
Hypaque–M 75%, 170
Hypaque–M 90%, 170
Hypercalcemia, 1138
Hyperemia
  occlusive, after central nervous system
    embolotherapy, III:767
  reactive, 83
Hypernephroma, 1137. *See also* Renal cell
    carcinoma
  in inferior vena cava obstruction, 960
Hyperparathyroidism, 1056
Hyperperfusion syndrome after brachio-
    cephalic angioplasty, 1041
Hyperplasia
  of adrenal glands
    in adrenogenital syndromes, 1368–
      1369
    in Cushing syndrome, 1364, 1366
  diffuse, in pancreatic islet-cell tumors,
    1403
  fibromuscular, of renal arteries, 1250–
    1257
  hepatic focal nodular, 1441–1443,
    1444
  intimal
    in coronary artery bypass graft, 763
    in dialysis fistula, III:726–727
    sonography of, 217
  islet cell. *See* Islet cell tumors
  lymph node
    in inflammations, 1923–1924, 1925
    in lymphedema, 1907, 1908, 1910,
      1918
    malignant lymphoma versus, 1943
    reactive, benign lymph node disease
      in, 1923, 1924, 1925

parathyroid glands and, 983
reactive follicular
    malignant lymphoma versus, 1944–
      1947
    repeat lymphography in, 1948, 1949,
      1950
  renal
    focal cortical, 1166, 1167, 1168
    medial arterial, 1253
Hyperreflexia, autonomic, 1036
Hypersensitivity to contrast agents, 29, 30,
    49. *See also* Contrast media
  symptoms and treatment of, 35
Hypersplenism, partial splenic ablation in,
    1492
Hypertensin. *See* Angiotensin amide
Hypertension
  agenesis of kidney and, 1313–1315,
    1316
  in aneurysm
    etiology of, 1073
    of renal artery, 1264–1266
  in arteriosclerosis, 1052
  in blunt trauma to aorta and brachio-
    cephalic arteries, 522
  cerebral vessels in, 310, 312
  in coarctation of aorta, 439, 440, 441
  in coronary arteriography complications,
    575
  dissecting aneurysm and
    aortic, 493, 494, 496, 503, 1276
    renal artery, 1251–1253, 1270–
      1271
  essential, 1259–1260
  induced, in cerebral vessel vasospasm,
    III:754–755
  interventional radiology in, 1287, III:
    214
  in lithotripsy complications, III:607
  malignant, semiselective renal angiogra-
    phy in, 1116, 1117
  in nonfunctioning kidney, 1313–1315
  normal renal arteriography in, 1245–
    1248, 1249
  in pheochromocytoma, 1372, 1373
  portal, III:525–546. *See also* Portal
    hypertension
  pulmonary. *See* Pulmonary hypertension
  renovascular. *See* Renovascular hyperten-
    sion (RVHTN)
  reserpine in, 59
  surgery in, angiography after, 1284–
    1287
Hyperthermia of prostate, III:614, III:
    634–636
Hyperthyroidism, 815–816
Hypertonic duodenography, 61
Hypertonic glucose in varicocele percutane-
    ous embolization, III:696
Hypertrophic subaortic stenosis, idiopathic,
    540
Hypervascularity, pulmonary, 786, 815–
    816
Hypnotics in premedication, 1713
Hypogastric arteries
  anatomy of, 1022
  claudication and, III:232, III:236.III:
    238
  in pelvic arteriovenous malformation,
    III:1017, III:1018
  in pelvic fractures, III:872, III:875

right, 1022, 1649
    transcatheter embolization of, 1651,
      1654, 1657, 1659, 1661, 1663
Hypogastric lymph nodes, 1878
Hypogastric veins, 1843, 1846, 1847
Hypoglossal artery, persistent, 281
Hypoglycemic reactions, III:216–217
Hypokinesis, ventricular, 561, 640
Hypophyseal aneurysm, superior, 320
Hypoplasia
  of innominate vein, 899, 900, 901–902,
    908
  of kidney, 1222–1224, 1225
    nonfunctioning, 1313–1315
  lung, in partial anomalous pulmonary
    venous connection, 883, 885, 886
  in lymphedema, 1907, 1908, 1909
  pulmonary arterial
    central, 831, 832
    left, 799
    peripheral, 842–843
  of transverse aortic arch, coarctation of
    aorta and, 437, 443, 445, 446
Hypotension, III:215
  in blunt trauma to aorta and brachio-
    cephalic arteries, 522
  in coronary arteriography complications,
    578
  in selective coronary artery catheteriza-
    tion, 568
Hypothalamic-pituitary-gonadal axis, III:
    688
Hypothenar hammer syndrome, 1758
Hypothermia of prostate, III:614
Hypovascularity, pulmonary, 786, 816
Hypoxia
  in cardiopulmonary resuscitation, 39, 45
  magnification angiography and, 181
Hyrtl J, 585, 700
Hysterectomy, ureteral strictures after, III:
    578
Hysterosalpingography, III:673, III:674,
    III:676

Iaccarino V, III:678
IADSA. *See* Intraarterial digital subtraction
    angiography (IADSA)
Iatrogenic injuries
  arterial, at chemotherapy infusion point,
    III:84
  in dissection
    of carotid artery, 348, 351
    in catheter or guidewire complica-
      tions, 1029, 1030
    to liver, III:422, III:425–427
  in renal trauma, III:895
Iatrogenic-induced shunting, sonography
    of, 216, 218
IBCA. *See* Isobutyl 2-cyanoacrylate (IBCA)
Ibuprofen, III:852
IC (intracavernosal) injections, III:706–
    707
ICA. *See* Carotid arteries, internal (ICA)
ICRP (International Commission on Radio-
    logical Protection), 124
ICRU (Internal Commission on Radiation
    Units and Measurements), 96
Idiopathic hypertrophic subaortic stenosis,
    540
Idiopathic pulmonary artery dilatation,
    796, 829, 830

Idiosyncrasy, 49, 1024–1025
thrombolytic therapy and, 1042–1043
Ifosfamide, III:81
in hepatic malignancy, III:437
in osteosarcomas, III:1033
[131]I-hippuran, 1335
Ileal arteries, 1020
in superior mesenteric angiography, 1550, 1551–1552
Ileal conduit
background of, III:645, III:646–647
complications related to, III:654, III: 655, III:656
with stones or stenoses, III:654, III:655
transconduit retrograde placement of nephrostomy catheter through, III: 574
Ileal loop, background of, III:645, III: 646–647
Ileitis, bleeding, III:400, III:401
Ileocecal carcinoma, 1568
Ileocolic arteries
anatomy of, 1020
in superior mesenteric angiography, 1550–1551, 1552
Ileofemoral bypass, 1690
Ileum, carcinoid of
metastatic to liver, 1451
superior mesenteric angiography in, 1576, 1577
Ileus in lithotripsy complications, III:500, III:607
Iliac arteries
anastomoses of renal arteries to, 1325, 1326, 1327
angiography after interventions of, 1681–1863. *See also* Aortoiliac disease, angiography of extremities after interventions for
angioplasty of, III:230–232, III:233
in obstruction, III:38, III:40, III:245, III:246
results in, III:98–100, III:245–247, III:248
arteriosclerotic disease of, 1058, 1059, 1060, 1638–1639
circumflex, in collateral circulation, 1067
common, 1017, 1019, 1021
collateral vessels circumventing, 1064
eccentric plaque in, digital angiography of, 1637
obstruction of, 1065, 1067, 1068
in pelvic magnetic resonance angiography, 1637
in renal transplant angiography, 1328, 1342
thrombosis in, arteriosclerotic disease and, 1058
extension of inflammatory abdominal aorta aneurysm into, 1076–1077
external, 1021
arteriosclerotic disease of, 1638–1639
collateral circulation of, 1067–1068, 1700–1702
obstruction of, 1069
in pelvic magnetic resonance angiography, 1637
in renal transplant angiography, 1343
2D-TOF magnetic resonance imaging of, 1826

fistulas between ureter and, after ureteral stenting, III:577
iatrogenic dissection of, 1029
internal, 1021, 1022
angiography technique for, 369
collateral circulation of, 1277, 1283, 1700, 1701, 1702
metal-based mechanical embolic agents for fistula and pseudoaneurysm of, III:58, III:59
obstruction of, 1067, 1069
in pelvic fractures, III:869–883. *See also* Pelvic fractures
in pelvic magnetic resonance angiography, 1637
in renal transplantation angiography, 1330
2D-TOF magnetic resonance imaging of, 1826
left, obstruction of, III:40, III:235
left common
collateral vessels circumventing, 1064
obstruction of, 1065
thrombosis in, arteriosclerotic disease and, 1058
magnetic resonance venography of, 1841
right, obstruction of, III:38, III:40, III: 232, III:245, III:246
right common, obstruction of, 1067
stent in, 1724
thrombolysis results in, III:250–253
2D-TOF magnetic resonance imaging of, 1824, 1826
Iliac lymph nodes, 1874–1876, 1878
external, 1931
Iliac stents, complications of, 1042
Iliac veins
angiography after interventions of, 1681–1863. *See also* Aortoiliac disease, angiography of extremities after interventions for
circumflex, for inferior vena cava collateral circulation, 954, 956
common
for inferior vena cava collateral circulation, 954, 956
left, streaming from, simulating thrombus, 971
magnetic resonance venography of, 1843, 1846
postoperative thrombus in, 967
venogram of, 1312
external
inferior vena cava and, 932, 954, 956
magnetic resonance venography of, 1843, 1846, 1847, 1850, 1851
filter for, complications with, 1044
internal
anomalous, 1849
magnetic resonance venography of, 1846, 1847, 1850
reflux into, 932, 933
magnetic resonance venography of, 1841, 1843, 1846, 1847, 1850, 1851
perforation of, in inferior vena cavography, 971
spurs from, inferior vena cava and, 972–973
stents for stenosis of, III:1052

thrombosis of, after renal transplant, 1345
2D-TOF magnetic resonance imaging of, 1824
varicosities of, 1579
Iliacus muscle, fluid collection in, III:945
Iliofemoral veins
phlebothrombosis of, 965, 966
pediatric thrombolysis in, III:917
stents in obstructions of, III:1051, III: 1052
Iliolumbar artery
in collateral circulation, 1067
in pelvic fractures, III:874, III:877
Ilium, lung cancer metastasis to, tumor embolization in, 1817
Image
sharpness or unsharpness of, in cardiac catheterization, 89
storage and display of, in digital angiography, 146
Image acquisition
pulsed-progressive, 142
using frame integration, 142, 143
for vascular intervention angiography, 135
Image display
in digital angiography, 146
in nonsubtraction imaging, 152
Image intensifiers
alignment of x-ray beam with, 127
in cardiac catheterization laboratory, 98–99
cesium iodide, 121
optics for, 99
ceiling suspension of, 105
cesium iodide, 98–99
contrast ratio of, 99
for coronary arteriography, 98
deterioration or obsolescence of, 127–128
dual-mode, in left ventriculography, 561
intrinsic contrast ratio and quantum detection efficiency of, 89
optical distributor in digital angiography video system and, 139, 140
in vascular intervention angiography, 134
Image optics in cine viewers, 111–113
Image processing hardware in digital angiography, 144–146
Image-guided biopsy, percutaneous, III: 166–194. *See also* Percutaneous image-guided biopsy
Imaging algorithm for peripheral vascular disease, 1834
Imaging equipment, in femoral arteriography
intraarterial, 1707
transvenous, 1707
Imaging modalities for vascular intervention, 135
Imaging physics in vascular sonography, 205–211
Imaging procedures
for benign biliary obstruction, III:457, III:458–459
in cerebral vessel occlusion studies, III: 768
Imidazoline derivatives, 57–58

Immobilization in pediatric interventional angiography, III:903
Immune-mediated systemic reactions to contrast agents, 29, 30
Immunohistochemical studies of lymphomas, III:170
Immunologic function of spleen, III:884–885
Impedance plethysmography, 1839–1840
Implantable subcutaneous ports, III:969, III:976–977
Impotence
    after pelvic fracture hemorrhage embolization, III:881
    aortoiliac intervention in, III:243–244
    aortoiliac occlusion and, III:226
    causes of, III:707
    implications of suboptimal results of transcatheter therapy for, III:723–724
    male
        pelvic angiography in, 1641–1645
        superselective catheterization in, 169
    venogenic, III:707–708
IMV. *See* Mesenteric veins, inferior (IMV)
¹¹¹In (Indium-111) scanning, 1693
    in infected renal cyst diagnosis, III:658
    of pelvic abscesses and fluid collections, III:946
Incompetent vein, sonography of, 216
Inderal. *See* Propranolol
Index finger malformation, 1756
Indiana pouch, III:646, III:648, III:649
Indium-111 (¹¹¹In) scanning, 1693
    in infected renal cyst diagnosis, III:658
    of pelvic abscesses and fluid collections, III:946
Indomethacin, 426
Induced hypertension in cerebral vessel vasospasm, III:754–755
Infant
    cardiac catheterization laboratory for, 122
    cardiopulmonary resuscitation in, 36, 39–40
    coarctation of aorta in, 434, 435
        clinical presentation of, 438–439
    congenital heart disease in. *See* Congenital heart disease
    patent ductus arteriosus in. *See* Patent ductus arteriosus (PDA)
    percutaneous transluminal angioplasty in, 458
    thoracic aortography in, 401–406
        aortic silhouette and, 401–404, 405
        ductus diverticulum and, 402, 403, 404, 405
        effect of increasing age and, 404–405
        opacified vessels and, 405–406
        recirculation in, 406
Infantile polycystic disease, 1135, 1136
Infarction
    bronchial, after embolization, III:827
    of gallbladder
        after hepatic arteriography, III:434
        after transcatheter tumor ablation, 1037
    of kidney, hypertension in, 1262–1264
    myocardial. *See* Myocardial infarction
    pulmonary, term, 806

splenic, 1477–1478, 1479
    in coronary arteriography complications, 578
Infection. *See also* Sepsis
    adrenal gland, 1379
    after percutaneous gastrostomy, III:556
    in aneurysms of thoracic aorta, 483–487
    angiography complications and, 1026
        coronary, 578
    in aortoenteric and paraprosthetic fistulas, 1692
    in asplenia, 1472
    balloon angioplasty restenosis and, III:17
    of caliceal diverticulum, 1199
    in endocarditis. *See* Infective endocarditis
    in fallopian tube obstruction, III:672
    of fluid drainage, preintervention assessment and, III:209–210
    of grafts after aortoiliac interventions, 1686, 1691–1692
    in hydronephrosis, 1199–1200
        angiographic findings in, 1203–1213
    in inflammatory urethritis, III:617
    lymph node, 1943
    neck, in pseudoaneurysms of extracranial cerebral arteries, 303, 305
    postsplenectomy, III:884
    of prosthetic grafts after aneurysm repair, 1095, 1097
    in pyonephrosis, 1199–1200
    renal. *See* Renal infection
    of tumor tissue, percutaneous drainage of, III:944, III:945
    venous access catheters and, III:979–980
    wound, in lymphangiography, 1867
Infectious hepatitis, 1438, 1439
Infectious mononucleosis, 1491
Infective aneurysms, term of, 483, 484
Infective endocarditis
    cerebral mycotic aneurysms and, 319
    patent ductus arteriosus and, 421
    thoracic aortic mycotic aneurysms and, 484
Inferior mesenteric angiography, 1587–1614
    in acute mesenteric ischemia, III:331–336
    anatomy in, 1588–1590
        artery origin in, 1589–1590
        artery size and branches in, 1590
        colon segments in, 1590
    in bleeding of left colon, 1608–1611, 1612–1613
        in angiodysplasia, 1608–1611
        detection rates and, 1611
        in diverticula, 1608, 1609
        in ischemic colitis, 1611, 1612–1613
    in carcinoma of colon, 1603–1605
    indications for, 1590
    in inflammatory disease of colon, 1605–1607, 1608
    in primary vascular abnormalities, 1591–1603
        acute vascular occlusion and, 1602–1603
        arteriosclerosis, stenosis, and occlusion in, 1593–1601, 1602
        collateral circulation to left colon and, 1591–1593, 1594–1597
        of intestinal ischemia, 1591

technique for, 1587–1588, 1589
    bradykinin and, 62
Inferior mesenteric arteries (IMA). *See* Mesenteric arteries, inferior (IMA)
Inferior mesenteric veins. *See* Mesenteric veins, inferior (IMV)
Inferior vena capnocavography, 936–937
Inferior vena cava (IVC), 932–975
    abnormal anatomy of, 941–947
        anomalies in, 943–947, 948
        embryogenesis in, 941–943, 945
    absence of, 898, 900, 904–908
        prerenal segment, 947, 949
    anomalies of, 943–947, 948
    bland thrombus in, tumor thrombus versus, 1852, 1853
    capnocavography of, 936–937
    cavography of, 932–934
        complications of, 971–972
        physiology and, 969–971
        pitfalls in diagnosis in, 969–971
        radionuclide, 941
        in renal cell carcinoma, 1143, 1154, 1302–1304, 1305
    collateral circulation and, 949–958
        intrarenal obstruction and, 951–957
        middle level obstruction and, 952–955, 957
        upper level obstruction and, 952–953, 955–956, 957–958
    color sonography of, 938, 939
    computerized tomography of, 940, 941, 942
    double, 945, 947
    drainage of, into left atrium, 898
    duplex sonography of, 938, 939
    embryology of, 1291–1292
    extrinsic obstruction of, 958–963
        anterior, 958
        aorta in, 959, 961, 962
        collateral circulation and, 949–958
        gastrointestinal tract in, 959
        left, 958
        lymph nodes in, 960, 962
        pancreas in, 959
        posterior, 958
        pregnancy in, 960–963
        right, 958
        soft tissue masses in, 960, 962
    filters in. *See* Inferior vena cava filters
    iliac vein spurs and, 972–973
    infrarenal, testicular drainage and, III:678, III:679
    intravascular biopsy in, III:196
    intravascular ultrasonography of, 938–939, 940
    intrinsic obstruction of, 963–965, 966
        collateral circulation and, 949–958
        infrarenal, 965, 966
        middle, 964–965
        upper, 963–964
    left, 908–910
        persistent, 900, 904
    in liver transplantation, III:515, III:516, III:517
        donor preparation and, III:510
    magnetic resonance imaging of, 940, 942, 943
    magnetic resonance venography of, 1843, 1845, 1846
    mirror image of, 947, 948

Inferior vena cava (IVC)—*Continued*
  normal vascular sonography flow patterns in, 214
  obstruction of, III:1046
    aorta and, 959, 961, 962
    effects of, 910
    extrinsic. *See* Inferior vena cava (IVC), extrinsic obstruction of
    gastrointestinal tract and, 959
    intrarenal, 951–957, 965, 966
    intrinsic. *See* Inferior vena cava (IVC), intrinsic obstruction of
    lymph nodes and, 960, 962
    middle, 952–955, 957, 964–965
    pancreas and, 959
    pregnancy and, 960–963
    soft tissue masses and, 960, 962
    stents in, III:1051–1055
    upper, 952–953, 955–956, 957–958, 963–964
  partial anomalous pulmonary venous connection to, 885
  partial interruption of, III:982–983
  percutaneous angioscopy of, 940–941
  persistent left, 900, 904
  plication of, 968, 969, III:982–983
  postoperative, 965–968, 969
  primary tumors of, 971, 972
  renal vein anatomy and, 1295, 1296, 1298
  in renal venography of carcinoma, 1290
  sarcomas of, III:1031
  sonography of, 230–231, 937–938, 939
  standard technique for visualizing, 934–936
  stenosis of, pediatric angioplasty in, III:914
  systemic venous return variations and, 900, 901–902, 904
  thrombus of, III:124, III:125
  for venous access catheters, III:973–975
Inferior vena cava filters, 968–969, 970
  complications of, 1043–1044
  pulmonary arteriography approach and, 771
  sonography of thrombosis and occlusion of, 219, 230
Inferior vena cavography, 932–934
  complications of, 971–972
  diagnostic pitfalls in, 969–971
  normal, 934, 935, 936
  physiology and, 969–971
  radionuclide, 941
  in renal cell carcinoma, 1143, 1154, 1302–1304, 1305
  before vena cava filter insertion, III:985
Inferior vermian veins, 279, 280
Infertility
  after pelvic fracture hemorrhage embolization, III:881
  varicocele in, III:699–701. *See also* Varicocele
    etiology of, III:688
Inflammations
  in abdominal aorta aneurysms, 1074–1077, 1080
  bone lesions in, 1782–1783
  of bronchial artery, transcatheter embolization for, III:819–828. *See also* Bronchial arteries, embolization of
  of cerebral vessels, 303–312, 313

  of colon, 1605–1607, 1608
  hepatic, 1438, 1439, 1440–1441
  hyperplastic changes in, 1923–1924, 1925
  in inflammatory bowel disease, III:414–415
  lymph node disease in
    benign, 1923–1925, 1926
    malignant lymphoma versus, 1943
    metastatic, 1927
  from lymphangiography contrast media, 1867–1868
  lymphedema in, 1908–1909, 1914
  mesenteric, 1560, 1573, 1575–1577
  retroperitoneal, 1676
  of seminal vesicle and prostate, III:640
  of thoracic duct, 1901
  in urethral strictures, III:617
  in urethritis, III:617
Inflation pressures of balloon catheter in renal angioplasty, III:298–300
Inflation times of balloon catheter, III:39
Inflow angiography, 188. *See also* Time-of-flight (TOF) enhancement in magnetic resonance angiography
Informed consent
  for pediatric interventional angiography, III:903
  in preinterventional assessment, III:206
Infrainguinal polytetrafluoroethylene grafts, III:145
Infrapopliteal revascularization, III:284–293
  atherectomy and, III:292–293
  balloon catheters for, III:284–285
  complications of, III:290–291
    embolization in, III:290–291
    thrombosis in, III:290
  equipment for, III:284–285
  guidewires in, III:285
  hot tip laser probes and, III:293
  patient selection for, III:284
  pharmacologic agents in, III:290
    anticoagulants as, III:290
    antispasmodics and vasodilators as, III:290
  physical examination before, III:285
  results of, III:291–292
  technique for, III:285–290
    balloon selection in, III:286
    follow-up arteriography and, III:286–289
    lesions traversal in, III:285–286
    postprocedural care in, III:286
    puncture in, III:285
Infrarenal aortic percutaneous transluminal angioplasty, III:247–250
Infundibulum
  junctional, 323
  of posterior communicating artery, 260–261, 323
  right ventricular, in single coronary artery anomalies, 748
Infusion thrombolysis
  complications of, III:155
  methods of, III:134–135
Inguinal crease, 1013, 1014
Inguinal ligament, 247, 248, 1013, 1014
Inguinal lymph nodes, 1876, 1877
  deep, 1874–1875
  fibrolipomatosis of, 1873

  fibromatosis of, 1923, 1924
Inguinal lymphadenectomy, 1914–1915
Inguinal lymphogranuloma, 1925
Injection
  of contrast agents. *See* Contrast media dye. *See* Dyes
Injectors in superselective catheterization, 170–173
Injury. *See* Trauma
Innominate artery
  aneurysms of, 489
  angioplasty of, III:761–763
  in extracranial brachiocephalic arterioplasty, III:352, III:354
  isolated, 548
  technique for catheterization of, 249
  vertebral flow reversal syndrome and, 552, 553
Innominate veins
  absence or hypoplasia of, 899, 900, 901–902, 908
  obstruction of, 900, 901–902
  persistent left, superior vena cava syndrome in, 926
  sonography of, 219
  stenosis of, 1777
  systemic venous return variations and, 900, 901–902
Inpatient
  postprocedure routine for, III:219
  preintervention assessment of, III:205–206
In-plane flow artifacts, 1829, 1830
Input to intensifying screen, 89
Instructions after interventional radiology, III:220–221
Insulin, III:207, III:216–217
Insulinomas, 1401, 1402, 1403–1405
  glucagon and insulin concentrations in, 1430, 1431
  pancreatic venography in, 1429
Intensifiers, image. *See* Image intensifiers
Intensifying screens
  in cardiac catheterization, 89
  closure of, 69
    intermittent, 81–82
  in large-field angiography, 81
Intensity transformation in image-processing hardware, 144
Intensity transformation table (ITT), 144
Interarterial coronary anastomoses, 711–712, 714–718
Interatrial septum, Kugel's anastomosis in, 714–715
Interaxial embolotherapy in central nervous system, III:765–788. *See also* Central nervous system, interaxial embolotherapy in
Intercommunication system during cardiac catheterization, 118
Intercoronary coronary collateral circulation, 703–711
Intercostal approach in renal stone removal, III:599
Intercostal arteries, 366, 1021, III:820–822
  aneurysms of, 489
  angiography technique for, 368
  anterior, in parathyroid arteriography, 979
  in arteriosclerosis, 1063, 1067

collateral circulation in renal ischemia and, 1277, 1283
thyroid carcinoma metastasis and, 387
Intercostal veins, 894, 896, 898
in infant aortography, 404
variations in systemic venous return and, 900, 901–902
Interdigital injection of vital dye in lymphangiography, 1864, 1865
Interferons in hepatic malignancy, III:437
Interleukins in hepatic malignancy, III:437
Interlobar artery, 1117, 1118
occlusion of, 1109
Interlobar veins
displacement of, 1317
in polycystic disease, 1317, 1320
Interlobular arteries, 1115, 1117, 1118, 1246, 1247
Intermediate follow-up after interventional radiology, III:219–221
Internal carotid artery. *See* Carotid arteries, internal (ICA)
Internal Commission on Radiation Units and Measurements (ICRU), 96
Internal elastic lamina after balloon angioplasty, III:5, III:13, III:18, III:19
Internal gland of prostate, III:622
Internal herniation, mesenteric, 1579
Internal iliac arteries. *See* Iliac arteries, internal
Internal iliac veins. *See* Iliac veins, internal
Internal jugular vein technique for venous access catheters, III:971–972, III:973
Internal mammary artery graft, 758–759
arteriography catheter selection and use for, 760
disease of, 764
International Commission on Radiological Protection (ICRP), 124
International Standards Organization photographic ratings of natural light, 105
Interobserver disagreement, 657
Interposition graft in dialysis fistula thromboses, III:727
Interrogation time, 72–73
Interstitial edema, septal, 863
Interstitial pressure, pulmonary, 855–856
Interventional radiology (IR)
in abnormal arteriovenous communications, III:998–1030. *See also* Arteriovenous communications, abnormal
in breast biopsy, III:1037–1046
of central nervous system, III:743–816. *See also* Central nervous system; Central nervous system, interventional radiology for
cholecystomy in, III:483–490
clinical trials of, III:202–203
complications of, 1032–1044, III:202
in abdominal biopsy, 1035
in abscess drainage, 1035–1036
in biliary drainage, 1038
in bronchial artery embolization, 1033
in extracranial embolization, 1033
in intracranial embolization, 1032–1033
in percutaneous gastrostomy, 1038–1039

in percutaneous hepatic tumor ablation, 1037
in percutaneous lung biopsy, 1033–1035
in percutaneous nephrostomy and nephrolithotomy, 1036–1037
in percutaneous transhepatic cholangiography, 1037–1038
in pulmonary artery fistula embolization, 1033
in removal of common duct stones, 1038, 1039
in thyroid biopsy, 1033
in transcatheter hepatic tumor ablation, 1037
in foreign body removal, III:959–968
pediatric, III:919
of gastrointestinal system, III:387–558. *See also* Gastrointestinal system
of genitourinary system, III:560–742. *See also* Genitourinary system
intermediate and long-term follow-up of, III:219–221
in intraarterial chemotherapy for sarcomas, III:1031–1036
intraprocedural management in
blood pressure in, III:214–217
blood sugar and, III:214–217
fluid balance and, III:214
heart rate and, III:214–217
immediate preprocedural, III:211–212
pain control in, III:212–214
renal function and, III:214–217
sedation in, III:212–214
in malignant hepatobiliary obstruction, III:472–482
patient care and, III:201–203
pediatric, III:901–921. *See also* Pediatrics, interventional angiography in
postprocedural care for, III:219–221
preintervention assessment for, III:204–210
allergy preparation and, III:209
antibiotics and, III:208–209
auxiliary personnel and, III:205
cardiac rhythm abnormalities and, III:209
coagulation deficits and, III:207–208
hydration adjustment and, III:207
immediate preprocedural, III:207–210
infected fluid drainages and, III:209–210
inpatient consultation in, III:205–206
medication adjustment and, III:207
outpatient consultation in, III:207
scope of clinical responsibilities in, III:204–205
of thorax. *See* Thorax, interventional radiology of
in trauma, III:855–900. *See also* Trauma
in urethral strictures, III:618–619
in vena cava filters, III:982–997. *See also* Vena cava filters
for venous access catheters, III:969–981. *See also* Venous access catheters
in venous thrombolysis and stenting, III:1046–1057. *See also* Venous thrombolysis and stenting
written instructions after, III:220–221

Interventional Therapeutics Corporation Detachable Silicone Balloon, III:65
Interventricular artery, posterior, 703, 704
Interventricular septum
collaterals of, 703, 704, 705
defect of, 787, 800
Interventricular vein, anterior, 590
Intestinal angina, 1631–1634
inferior mesenteric arteriography in, 1600
Intestinal decompression, percutaneous gastrostomy in, III:547
Intestinal intramural pressure measurements, 1632
Intestinal ischemia, 1591
Intestinal lymphangiectasis, 1919
Intestinal varices, 1535
Intimal fibroplasia
after balloon angioplasty, III:8–11, III:12–13
technical strategies and, III:14
coronary arteriography in, 692
of renal arteries, 1251–1252
Intimal flap
atherectomy in, III:44, III:49
in dissecting aortic aneurysms, 508–512
in extremity trauma, arteriography and, III:860, III:861
from iatrogenic dissection from catheter, 1029
Intimal hyperplasia
in coronary artery bypass graft, 763
sonography of, 217
Intimal injuries
femoral arteriography in, 1700, 1727–1729
in knife wounds of upper extremities, 1757
Intimal-medial plaque fracture after balloon angioplasty, III:4–5
Intraabdominal branches
of aorta. *See* Abdominal aorta, branches of
of vena cava, sonography of, 214, 230–231
Intraaortic injection in dissecting aortic aneurysms, 503
Intraaortic pressure pulse, 528
Intraarterial chemotherapy for sarcomas, III:1031–1036
complications of, III:1034–1035
technique for, III:1034–1035
Intraarterial contrast
in cerebral angiography, 242
in digital angiography, 139
Intraarterial digital subtraction angiography (IADSA)
2D-TOF MR angiogram compared to, 1832
in femoral arteriography, 1707
in pelvic fractures, III:877, III:878
in pulmonary arteriovenous malformations, III:838, III:846
Intraarterial femoral arteriography, 1707
Intraarterial fibrinolytic therapy, 1640–1641, 1642
Intraarterial infusion chemotherapy, III:82
Intraarterial pressure before revascularization, III:230
Intraarterial thrombolytic therapy in central nervous system, III:745–751, III:752, III:753

Intrabronchial pressure, 620, 622
Intracavernosal (IC) injections, III:706–707
Intracoronary collateral circulation, 703, 705, 711–712
Intracranial aneurysm. *See* Cerebral aneurysm
Intracranial angioplasty in post-subarachnoid hemorrhage vasospasm, III:753–757, III:758
Intracranial embolization, 1032–1033
Intracranial, extraaxial lesions, III:789–816
  anatomy and, III:791–795, III:799–800, III:809–812
  of anterior cranial base, III:793
  of cavernous sinus and parasellar region, III:794, III:799–800, III:809–812
  of convexity, III:791–793
  embolization of neoplastic, III:808–814
    complications in, III:814
  of falx cerebri, III:793
  functional embolization for, III:789
    agents in, III:791
  of greater sphenoid wing, III:793
  pathologic, III:795–808
    carotid-cavernous fistulas in, III:802–808
    dual arteriovenous malformations in, III:795–802
  of posterior fossa, III:794–795
  of tentorium cerebelli, III:794
Intracranial hemorrhage, intraoperative angiography in, 252–253
Intracranial neoplasms, embolization in, III:808–814
Intracranial pharmacologic vasodilation in post-subarachnoid hemorrhage vasospasm, III:753–757, III:758
Intracranial subarachnoid shunts, 280
Intradural arteriovenous fistulas. *See* Spinal dural arteriovenous fistulas
Intragraft stenoses in dialysis fistula, III:735, III:737
Intrahepatic gas after transcatheter tumor ablation, 1037
Intrahepatic hematoma, 1454–1455
Intrahepatic inferior vena caval obstruction, stents in, III:1053–1054, III:1055
Intrahepatic portal obstruction and collaterals, 1532–1535
Intrahepatic portosystemic shunt, perirectal varices after, 1850
Intrahepatic vascular circulation, 1504, 1506, 1507, 1514
  changes in, 1512–1526. *See also* Splenoportography, intrahepatic anatomic changes in
  obstruction of, 1506–1508, 1517–1521
Intralobar sequestration, 798
Intramural circulation, 589–590
Intramyocardial injection of contrast agents, 578
Intraobserver inconsistency, 657
Intraoperative cerebral angiography, 252–253
  in aneurysms, 322–323
Intraparenchymal cerebral hemorrhage or edema, 342
Intrapericardial injection of contrast agents, 578
Intraplaque hemorrhage, 1056

Intraprocedural management in interventional radiology, III:211–218. *See also* Interventional radiology (IR), intraprocedural management in
Intrarenal veins, 1292, 1293–1295
  arteriovenous fistulas and, III:1004
  obstruction of, collateral circulation and, 951–957
  in renal angiography, 1115, 1118, 1125
Intrathoracic tumors. *See* Lung cancer
Intrathrombotic antithrombin-III, III:126
Intraurethral prosthesis, III:632–634, III:635
Intrauterine balloon in tubal catheterization, III:676
Intravascular biopsy, III:195–200
  transvenous liver and kidney, III:197–199
  of vessel material, III:195–197
Intravascular stents. *See* Stents
Intravascular ultrasonography of inferior vena cava, 938–939, 940
Intravenous aortography in dissecting aortic aneurysms, 500, 503
Intravenous digital subtraction angiography (IVDSA), 1686–1688, 1690
Intravenous infusion in emergency treatment, 39
Intravenous pyelogram (IVP)
  in agenesis of kidney, 1316
  in circumaortic venous ring, 1317
  in renal cysts, III:659
  in renal fibrolipomatosis, 1320, 1321
  in renal trauma, III:892–893
  in renovascular hypertension diagnosis, III:112
Intravenous ultrasound in renal artery restenosis after angioplasty, III:11
Intravenous urography. *See* Urography, intravenous
Intravoxel phase dispersion, 189–191, 192
Introduction sheaths for superselective catheterization catheter, 157, 158
Intropin. *See* Dopamine
Intubation, tracheal, 38, 39
Intussusception, 1579
Involutive changes, benign lymph node disease in, 1923, 1924
Iobitridol, 19, 20
Iodine-containing compounds
  in arterial portography with computerized tomography, 1542
  content of, necessary for satisfactory opacification, 22
  coronary artery catheterization complications from, 576
  historical notes on early uses of, 7, 13–14
  incidence of reactions to, 34–35
  lymphangiography and, 1868
  in penile vascularization, III:710
  in varicocele embolization, III:698
  as vasodilator, 53, 60
[131]Iodine-labeled iodomethyl norcholesterol
  in adrenal scintigraphy, 1357, 1364
  in localization of adrenal remnants, 1376
Iodipamide, 16
Iodixanol, 19, 20
Iodomethyl norcholesterol, radiolabeled, 1357, 1364, 1376

Iodopyracet, 14, 15
  adverse reactions to, 397, 400
  early uses of, 7, 14
Iohexol, 17, 20
  coronary artery catheterization complications from, 576
  in pancreatic angiography, 1396
  reactions to, 1026
  in superior mesenteric angiography, 1556
Ionic contrast media. *See* High-osmolality contrast agents (HOCA)
Iopamidol, 17, 20
  coronary artery catheterization complications from, 576
  in pancreatic angiography, 1396
  in superior mesenteric angiography, 1556
  toxicity of, 25
Iopamiro. *See* Iopamidol
Iopax, early uses of. *See* Neoselectan, early uses of
Iopromide, 20
Iothalamate, 17, 20
  in superior mesenteric angiography, 1556
  in thoracic aortography, 395
Iotrol, 20
Iotrolan, 18, 19
  cardiac effects of, 27
Ioversol, 18, 20, III:710
  coronary artery catheterization complications from, 576
Ioxaglate, 16–17, 20
  coronary artery catheterization complications from, 576
  in pancreatic angiography, 1396
  reactions to, 1026
  in superior mesenteric angiography, 1556
Ioxilan, 18, 20
Ioxithalamate, 18, 20
IR. *See* Interventional radiology (IR)
Iris-type collimators, 97, 98
Irradiation damage. *See* Radiation damage
Irrigation in superselective catheterization procedures, 163, 164
Ischemia
  after thoracic aortography, 399–400, 401
  in aortoiliac disease, III:226–228
    as indication for treatment, III:241
  bile duct, in liver transplantation complications, III:518
  cerebrovascular
    after intraaxial embolotherapy for central nervous system, III:767, III:782–784
    pathophysiology of, III:746–747
    revascularization procedures in, III:745–764. *See also* Central nervous system, revascularization in
  in colitis
    inferior mesenteric angiography in, 1607, 1611, 1612–1613, III:327
    superior mesenteric angiography in, 1565–1566
  digital, from embolic occlusion, 1762
    lytic therapy in, 1762, 1763
  intestinal, 1591, 1602–1603
  limb
    clinical categories of, III:266

thrombolysis in, III:136, III:139–144, III:250

mesenteric, 1615–1635. *See also* Mesenteric ischemia

myocardial, 562. *See also* Angina pectoris; Myocardial infarction

cardiac catheterization and, 119–121

nephrogram in, 1248, 1258, 1259, 1263

renal, collateral circulation and hypertension in, 1276–1284

time of, arterial repair and, 1728

ureteral, renal transplant obstruction from, III:581

from wounds of extremity arteries, 1700, 1727–1729

Ischemic colitis

inferior mesenteric angiography in, 1607, 1611, 1612–1613, III:327

superior mesenteric angiography in, 1565–1566

Ischemic heart disease, cardiac catheterization laboratory for, 119–121. *See also* Angina pectoris; Myocardial infarction

Ischemic penumbra, III:746

Ischium, chondrosarcomas of, 1787

Islet cell tumors, 1401–1403, 1405

hormone assay and, 1430

in liver, III:451–452

pancreatic venography in, 1429, 1430

Isobutyl 2-cyanoacrylate (IBCA)

calibrated leak balloon with, III:65

in intraaxial embolotherapy for central nervous system, III:766–767

in selective embolization in gastrointestinal bleeding, III:403

in varicocele embolization, III:698

Isobutyl 6-cyanoacrylate monomer, 1651

Isopaque 280, 170

Isopaque 440, 170

Isoproterenol, 47, 59

in arterial portography, 1530

in cardiac standstill, 45

in heart block, 43, 44

recommended intravenous dosages for, 46

in sinus bradycardia, 43

strengths and volumes of, 48

in superior mesenteric angiography, 1557

Isordil, 627

Isotope imaging. *See* Radionuclide scanning

Isovist. *See* Iotrol

Isovolumetric contraction, left coronary blood flow during, 686

Isovue. *See* Iopamidol

Isthmus of aorta. *See* Aorta, isthmus

ITT (intensity transformation table), 144

Ivalon. *See* Polyvinyl alcohol (PVA) embolization

Ivalon plug of Porstmann, 427

IVDSA (intravenous digital subtraction angiography), 1686–1688, 1690

IVP. *See* Intravenous pyelogram (IVP)

J guidewire

in renal angioplasty, III:297, III:300

reproductive organ dose and, 129

James TN, 583, 589, 700, 701

James casts and studies of coronary arteries, 585

Jamieson Film Magazine Loader, 110

Jamieson film processor, 112, 113

Jamin F, 583

Jarre H, 66, 67

Jaundice, obstructive, III:486

Jaw, hemangiomas of, 1816

JB (Bentson-Hanafee-Wilson) catheters, 244, 245

JCAHO (Joint Commission on the Accreditation of Healthcare Organizations), 137

Jeffrey one-stick system in cholangiography, III:474–475

Jejunal arteries

aneurysm of, in pancreatitis, 1414

in superior mesenteric angiography, 1550, 1551–1552

Jejunum, adenocarcinomas of, 1578

Jenner E, 583

Johnson WD, 756

Johnstone AS, 891

Joint Commission on the Accreditation of Healthcare Organizations (JCAHO), 137

Joints, 1779–1780

angiography of

lesions of synovial origin in, 1808–1810

technique in, 1780–1781

inflammatory lesions of bone and, 1782–1783

tumors of

benign, 1808–1809

malignant, 1781–1782, 1809–1810

Jönsson G, 8, 9, 391, 394, 411, 635

J-tip

in coronary arteriography, 556

in pulmonary arteriography, 772, 773, 774

Judkins MP, 10, 556, III:3, III:24

Judkins catheters, 556–558

in coronary artery bypass grafts, 760, 761

in coronary artery catheterization, 557, 563, 565, 570

Judkins femoropopliteal angioplasty, III:262

Judkins technique for coronary arteriography, 557, 570

Judkins vascular stent, III:85

Jugular vein

for liver biopsy, III:198

for portal venography, 1425–1426

for pulmonary arteriography, 771, 774

for vena cava filter insertion, III:985

for venous access catheters, III:971–972, III:973

Jump graft insertion in coronary artery bypass graft, 758, 759

Junctional infundibulum, 323

Juvenile angiofibromas, 339–340

Juvenile-type of spinal dural arteriovenous fistulas, 378

Kahn DR, 702

Kahn P, 1587

Karnell J, 391

Kasabach-Merritt syndrome, III:998

Kassabian MK, 4

Keith JD, 392

Kensey atherectomy catheter, 1042

in femoropopliteal atherectomy, III:280

in infrapopliteal revascularization, III:293

Kerber (CK1) catheter, 244, 245

Keynes, thymic vein of, 987

Kidney

absence or agenesis of, 1222

renal venography in, 1313–1315, 1316

aplasia of, 1222

arteriovenous fistulas in, III:1004

biopsy of, III:188–189

carcinoma of

nephrostomy for, III:561, III:563, III:564, III:567, III:568

renal cell. *See* Renal cell carcinoma

renal venography in, 1291, 1299–1304, 1305

transitional cell, 1154–1158, 1160, 1303

tuberculosis versus, 1160

collecting system in, historical notes on study of, 7

congenital lobulation of, 1166

cystic, 1224–1226

dysplasia of, 1222, 1224

ectopic, III:590

fractured, 1272

fused, 1221, 1222–1223, 1224

horseshoe, 1221, III:590

hypernephroma of, 960

hypoplastic, 1222–1224, 1225

nonfunctioning, 1313–1315, 1316

infarction of, 1262–1264

magnification angiography of. *See* Renal angiography

malrotated, 1217, III:590

medullary sponge, 1226

metastases to, 168

nonfunctioning, 1313–1315, 1316

page

hypertension and, 1276

in renal artery stenosis after renal transplantation, 1340

phlegmon of, terminology, 1178

polycystic disease of, 1226, 1227

renal angiography of. *See* Renal angiography

transplantation of. *See* Renal transplantation

transvenous biopsy of, III:195, III:197–199

trauma to. *See* Renal trauma

tumor of. *See* Renal tumors

Kilovoltage, contrast and, 105, 106

Kimray Greenfield filter, III:987

Kink resistance of balloon catheter, III:31–37

Kinking

of aorta, 553

of catheter in coil embolization, III:59

Kissing balloon technique

in aortoiliac angioplasty, III:232, III:233

in renal angioplasty, III:303, III:305

Klippel-Trenaunay syndrome, III:1026–1029

spinal involvement in, 369

superior mesenteric angiography in, 1573

KLX (Kodak Liquid X-ray Developer), 109
Knee
cross section of, 1827
magnetic resonance venography and, 1842
synovial sarcoma of, 1810
Knife wounds
in cerebral vascular trauma, 342–353
of upper extremities, 1757–1758
Knowles DM, 1443
Kock pouches, III:652–653
complications from, III:654–655
Kodak cine films, 107
Kodak Liquid X-ray Developer (KLX), 109
Kommerell, diverticulum of, 416
Koordinat 3D ceiling-mounted patient support, 105
Kugel MA, 711
Kugel anastomosis in interatrial septum, 714–715
Kyphoscoliosis, 818–819

Labbé, vein of, 275, 276
Labetalol, III:215
in emergency reactions, III:216
in renal angioplasty, III:306
Labey, III:160
Lacerations of liver, 1455
Lacunae of corpus cavernosa, III:705
LACV (levo-atrial-cardinal vein), 881–883, 887
LAD. *See* Coronary arteries, left anterior descending (LAD)
Laking of contrast material in tumor, 1781
Laminated anode in tube, 95
Laminography, 1161
Landmarking technique in digital subtraction imaging, 151
Lang maneuver or position, 1002–1007
LAO projections. *See* Left anterior oblique (LAO) projection
Laparoscopic cholecystectomy, percutaneous cholecystolithotomy versus, III:505–506
Laplace's law, 861, III:297
Large-field angiography, 80–82
diabetic patient and, 84
film changers in, 81–82
Amplatz, 82
diabetic patient and, 84
long-leg, 81–82
principles of, 81
serial, in pulmonary arteriography, 776
alternatives to, 776–777
technical considerations for, 80–81
Larsen HA, 15
Laryngeal edema, 29
Laryngospasm, III:217
Laser angioplasty, III:14
complications of, 1028, 1041–1042, III:44, III:47–49
at puncture site, 1028
in coronary disease, III:380–381
femoropopliteal, III:280–281
balloon, III:281
infrapopliteal, III:293
lumen diameter after, III:7, III:13–14
Laser-induced occlusion in mechanical embolization, III:55, III:71
Lasix. *See* Furosemide
LASTAC laser system, III:380

Late mask, 150
Latex detachable balloons in embolotherapy, III:65–66, III:69
for central nervous system, III:766
Latitude, contrast and, 105, 106, 108
Laurell H, 849
Lawrence EA, 892
Laws
Laplace's, 861, III:297
Poiseuille's, 170, 852, 853, 854
LCX. *See* Coronary arteries, left circumflex (LCX)
LDLs (low-density lipoproteins), 1052
LE (lupus erythematosus)
cerebral arteries in, 307
pulmonary arteriography in, 802, 805
Lead apron for radiation protection, 128, 137
Leading as term in balloon catheter angioplasty, III:42–43
Leaking
of abdominal aorta aneurysm, suspected, 1094, 1095, 1096
after percutaneous gastrostomy, III:556
of anastomoses after Crohn disease surgery, III:942–943
of balloon, calibrated, III:65
of bile in liver transplantation, III:520–522
of puncture sites in dialysis shunt complications, 1771, 1772
of thoracic aortic aneurysm, 473, 474
of urine from renal calix into renal sinus and retroperitoneum, 1202–1203
Left anterior descending (LAD) coronary arteries. *See* Coronary arteries, left anterior descending (LAD)
Left anterior oblique (LAO) projection
in coronary arteriography, 561, 566–568, 592–593
of coronary ostium, 594, 595
of left coronary artery, 608, 609, 611, 612, 614
of right coronary artery, 603–607
of sinus node artery, 618
in left ventriculography, 561
Left ventricular ejection fraction (LVEF), 562, 574–575
Left ventricular end-diastolic pressure (LVEDP), 562
Leg
arteries of, normal flow patterns in, 211, 212
cross section of, 1827
retarded growth of, after coronary artery catheterization, 579
runoff vessels in, 1831
veins of, normal flow patterns in, 211
Leger L, 1497, 1527
Lehman JS, 635
Leiomyomas
in gonadal vein, 1845
of inferior vena cava, 971
superior mesenteric angiography in, 1577
Leiomyosarcomas
of inferior vena cava, 971, 972
intravascular biopsy of, III:196
metastatic to liver, 1452
pancreatic, 1406–1409

retroperitoneal, 1669, 1670, 1671, 1673, III:1031
Lenticulostriate arteries, 267, 268
arteritis of, 307, 310
medial, 261
Leonard catheter with Dacron cuff, III:970
Leptofibrila, III:124
Leriche syndrome, 1060–1061, 1062–1063
Lesser sac abscesses, percutaneous drainage of, III:936
Leukemias
ischemic colitis and, 1611, 1612–1613
spleen in, 1467, 1468, 1483, 1484
Leukocyte scintigraphy
in aortoenteric and paraprosthetic fistula diagnosis, 1693
in thoracic aortic aneurysm diagnosis, 469
Levarterenol bitartrate, 48. *See also* Norepinephrine
Levin DC, 605
Levo-atrial-cardinal vein (LACV), 881–883, 887
Levophed. *See* Levarterenol bitartrate
LGM (Vena Tech) filter
for inferior vena cava, 970
magnetic resonance venography and, 1852
Lichtwitz, 14
Lidocaine, 46, III:201, III:212, III:213, III:214, III:216
in arrhythmias after pulmonary angiography, 1031
in bronchial artery embolization, III:825
in coronary arteriography anesthesia, 559
in emergency reactions, III:216
in femoral arteriography, 1713
in implantation for subcutaneous port, III:976
intraductal, in biliary duct dilation, III:212
in percutaneous gastrostomy, III:549
in premature ventricular contractions, 44–45
prostatic biopsy and, III:636–637
recommended intravenous dosages for, 46
in seminal vesicle interventions, III:640
strengths and volumes of, 48
in superior mesenteric angiography, 1557
in transaxillary catheterization, 1016
in transfemoral catheterization, 1013
in upper extremity arteriography, 1755
in urethral lesion intervention, III:618
in ventricular fibrillation, 45
in ventricular tachycardia, 45
Liebel-Florsheim injector, 173
Life support, basic, 35–36
Life-Tech pump in penile vascularization, III:709
Ligaments, pelvic, rupture of, 1644–1645
Ligamentum arteriosum
calcification of, patent ductus arteriosus and, 423
subclavian artery course origin altered by, 418, 419
Ligation of spermatic veins, III:691–692

Light intensity, voltage output and, 141
Lima S, III:678
Limb amputation after cerebral angiography, 246
Limb ischemia
  clinical categories of, III:266
  thrombolysis in, III:136, III:139–144, III:250
Limb-sparing resection of extremity sarcomas, III:1032–1034
Lind J, 9
Lindblom A, 892, 933
Lindenthal OT, 3, 4, 13
Line of Zahn, III:124, III:125
Lingular artery, 782
Lipiodol
  complications of, in hepatocellular carcinoma therapy, 1037
  early uses of, 4–6, 13
  in hepatic malignancy embolization, III:437, III:438
  in lymphangiography, 1867
Lipomas
  intramuscular, in upper leg, 1812
  retroperitoneal, 1669
Lipoprotein metabolism, 1052
Liposarcomas
  of extremities
    in differential diagnosis, 1811
    femoral arteriography in, 1735, 1736–1737
  retroperitoneal, 1669, 1670, 1673
  of shoulder, 1818
Liposomal transfection of genes, III:16
Liposomes in hepatic malignancy embolization, III:437
Liquid embolization agents in small-vessels or tissues, III:54
Liquid glues. *See* Adhesives
Listeria, 485
Lithiasis, common duct, 1038, 1039
Litholytic agents in biliary calculi removal complications, III:497
Lithotripsy
  electrohydraulic, III:497, III:499
  extracorporeal shock wave. *See* Extracorporeal shock wave lithotripsy (ESWL)
Lithotriptors, III:607
Liver
  abscesses of, 1438, 1440–1441
    after arteriography, III:434
    percutaneous drainage of, III:929–931
  adenomas of, 1443–1445
  angiosarcoma of, 1450
  biopsy in, III:186–187
    bleeding and, III:180, III:182
    in metastatic adenocarcinoma of colon, III:167
  circulation of. *See* Intrahepatic vascular circulation
  cirrhosis of. *See* Cirrhosis
  complications of procedures for, 1030, 1037–1039
    in biopsy, 1035
  contusion or laceration of, 1455
  failure of
    after transjugular intrahepatic portosystemic shunt, III:538

nephrotoxicity of contrast agents and, 23, 24
  in renal cell carcinoma, 1139
fistula in, III:425–426, III:428, III:431
  techniques for, III:431–432
gas in, after transcatheter tumor ablation, 1037
hamartomas of, 1445
hemangioendothelioma of, embolization in, III:905, III:908
hematomas of, subcapsular, 1454–1455
hepatomas of, 1446–1450, 1451
iatrogenic injury to, III:422, III:425–427
inferior vena cava and, 932, 934
  obstruction of, 958
inflammatory disease of, 1438, 1439, 1440–1441
injury to, as stone removal complication, III:602
malignant tumors of
  arterial portography in, 1544
  bland thrombus versus tumor thrombus in, 1855
  metastatic. *See* Liver, metastases and
  primary, 1446–1450, 1451
  superselective catheterization in, 168–169
metastases and, 1450–1451, 1452, 1453
  adenocarcinoma of colon in, 183
  biopsy in, III:179
  colorectal, III:450–451
  ocular melanoma in, III:452
  omental, chemoembolization in, 167
  splenoportography in, 1522–1525
  superselective catheterization in, 168–169
oil embolism to, from lymphangiography, 1869–1870
portal obstruction and collaterals of, 1532–1535
portosystemic shunt of, perirectal varices after, 1850
pseudolesion of, computerized tomography during portography of, 1544–1545
rupture of, after transcatheter tumor ablation, 1037
sarcomas of, intraarterial chemotherapy for, III:1035
transplantation of, III:509–524
  arterial and venous reconstruction of allograft in, III:509–510
  biliary complications and interventions in, III:517–522
  biliary tract reconstruction in, III:516–517
  hepatic artery complications and interventions in, III:510–513
  in hepatic malignancy, III:438
  pediatric, III:510
  in portal hypertension with liver failure, III:526
  in variceal hemorrhage, III:526
  vascular sonography after, 232
  venous complications and interventions in, III:513–515, III:517
transvenous biopsy of, III:195, III:197–199
trauma to, III:422–435. *See also* Hepatic arteries, embolization in

amenable to transcatheter therapy, III:422–428
  hepatic arteriography in, 1451–1455
  superselective catheterization in, 168–169
  from tumor ablation, 1030, 1037
  types of, III:422
  tumors of
    ablation complications in, 1030, 1037
    benign, 1439–1445
    in inferior vena cava obstruction, 959
    malignant. *See* Liver, malignant tumors of; Liver, metastases and
Liver failure
  after transjugular intrahepatic portosystemic shunt, III:538
  nephrotoxicity of contrast agents and, 23, 24
  in renal cell carcinoma, 1139
Liver transplantation. *See* Liver, transplantation of
LMCA. *See* Coronary arteries, left main (LMCA)
LMG Vena Tech filters, III:987, III:988, III:992–994
Lobar emphysema, 799
Lobar nephronia, terminology, 1178, 1179
Lobo catheter, III:285
Local anesthesia
  in coronary arteriography, 559
  in prostatic biopsy, III:636–637
  in seminal vesicle interventions, III:640
  in transfemoral catheterization, 1013
  in translumbar catheterization, 1017
LOCAs. *See* Low-osmolality contrast agents (LOCAs)
Lock Clamshell Occluder, III:70
Logarithmic transformation, temporal subtraction and, 149
Long-leg film changers in large-field angiography, 81–82
  diabetic patient and, 84
Long-term follow-up after interventional radiology, III:219–221
  for pulmonary arteriovenous malformations, III:852, III:853
Look-up table (LUT), 144
Loop catheter for renal aortography, 1102
Loop graft hemodialysis shunt, 226, III:729, III:731
  thrombolysis in, III:731
Loopogram, ureteroileal anastomotic strictures and, III:649, III:650, III:655, III:656
Loop-snare catheters in foreign body removal, III:960–961, III:962–965
Lorazepam, III:213
Lord W Jr, 1527
Lordosis, 971
Loss index, III:8
Lossy compression algorithms, 148
Low profile balloon catheter, III:27, III:32
Low-density lipoproteins (LDLs), 1052
Lower R, 700
Lower extremities. *See also* Extremities
  arteriovenous malformations of, III:1006
  lymph nodes of, 1874–1875
  sonography of
    in arterial disease, 212, 222, 223
    in venous thrombosis, 217–220
  stents for vascular disease of, III:97–112

Lower extremities—*Continued*
superselective catheterization in, 169, 170
thigh in, cross section of, 1827
thrombolysis in, III:136, III:139–144, III:150–152
trauma to, 169, 170
Lower genitourinary tract, III:614–644
bladder in, III:614–615
prostate in, III:621–639. *See also* Prostate
scrotum in, III:641–642
seminal vesicles and ejaculatory ducts in, III:639–641
urethra in, III:615–621
Low-flip-angle gradient-echo imaging, 1839
Low-molecular–weight dextran in thrombolysis, III:127, III:128
for lower extremities, III:137
for upper extremities, III:152
Low-osmolality contrast agents (LOCAs)
in cerebral angiography, 242
indications for use of, 31
in pancreatic angiography, 1396
physiology of, 30–31
in pulmonary arteriography, 776
reactions to, 1026
cardiac toxicity in, 28
in coronary artery catheterization, 576–577
renal toxicity in, 24
Low-pass filtration, 144
LPA. *See* Pulmonary arteries, left (LPA)
LSCA (left subclavian artery), 415
Luer-Lok fitting, 558
Luetic aneurysms of thoracic aorta, 486–487
superior vena cava obstruction after, 923, 924
Lukes-Butler classification of Hodgkin disease, 1940
Lumbar aortography, 1013–1100
in abdominal aorta aneurysms, 1073–1100. *See also* Abdominal aorta aneurysms
abdominal aortography in, 1013–1023. *See also* Abdominal aortography
in abnormal abdominal aorta, 1052–1072. *See also* Arteriosclerosis, of abdominal aorta
complications of, 1024–1051. *See also* Complications
abdominal abscess in, 1035–1036
abdominal biopsy in, 1035
abdominal procedures in, 1035–1036
angioplasty in, 1039–1041
catheters and guidewires in, 1028–1029
diagnostic angiography in, 1024–1032, 1039–1044
head and neck procedures in, 1032–1033
interventional radiology in, 1032–1044
intracranial aneurysm embolization in, 1032
lasers, atherectomy, and stents in, 1041–1042
liver and biliary tree procedures in, 1030, 1037–1039

lung procedures in, 1033–1035
percutaneous nephrostomy and nephrolithotomy in, 1036–1037
pulmonary angiography in, 1031–1032
puncture site, 1026–1028
systemic, 1024–1026
thrombolytic therapy in, 1042–1043
transaxillary arteriography in, 1031
transbrachial arteriography in, 1030
translumbar aortography in, 1029–1030
transluminal angioplasty in, 1039–1041
vena cava filter placement in, 1043–1044
Lumbar arteries, 1021
in abdominal aorta arteriosclerosis and other diseases, 1064, 1067, 1068, 1069
collateral circulation and, 1067–1069
in renal ischemia, 1277, 1280, 1283
Lumbar ectopia of kidney, 1221, 1222, 1223
Lumbar enlargement, artery of, 361
Lumbar lymph nodes, 1879–1881
Lumbar spinal plexus, venography of, 933
Lumbar trunks, 1884, 1892, 1893
Lumbar veins. *See* Lumbar vessels
Lumbar vertebrae
angiography and, 368–369, 933
in inferior vena cava obstruction, 958
inferior vena cava relationship to, 933
Lumbar vertebral veins, 894, 895, 896, 897
Lumbar vessels, 1295
angiography technique for, 368–369, 933
azygos veins and, 894, 895, 896, 897
collateral circulation and, 1067–1069
for inferior vena cava, 900, 905, 951, 952, 955, 956, 958
in renal ischemia, 1277, 1280, 1283
washout effects simulating filling defects of, 971
Lumen geometry after balloon angioplasty, III:7, III:13–14
Lung
abscesses of, III:829–831
anatomy of, 851, 852
arteriovenous malformations in, 180, 181
biopsy complications and, 1033–1035
cancer of. *See* Lung cancer
complications of procedures for interventional radiology in, 1033–1035
lymphangiography in, 1868–1869
compression of
after empyema, 817
pulmonary hypovascularity in, 816
embryology of, 869, 870
hemoptysis from. *See* Hemoptysis
hypoplastic, in partial anomalous pulmonary venous connection, 883, 885, 886
injury to
in lithotripsy complication, III:607
in percutaneous stone removal complication, III:602

in pulmonary arteriography, 770, 780–783
of tumors, 810–813, 814, 815
regional variations in perfusion of, 849–850
sarcoma of, 815
sequestration in
arteriography in, 798–799
as developmental anomaly, 840–842
extralobar or intralobar, 798
thoracic aortography in, 396, 549, 550
small-cell cancer of
biopsy in, III:177, III:186
non-small–cell cancer versus, III:170
Lung cancer
metastases from
to adrenal gland, 1673, 1674
to ilium and femur, 1817
pulmonary arteriography in, 770, 810–815
in superior vena cava obstruction, 917–919, 920
thromboembolic disease in, 1749
Lung compliance, 865
Lung water, extravascular, 864, 865
Lupus erythematosus (LE)
cerebral arteries in, 307
pulmonary arteriography in, 802, 805
LUT (look-up table), 144
Luteinizing hormone–releasing hormone (LH-RH) analogue, III:627
Luxury perfusion, term of, 302
LVEDP (left ventricular end-diastolic pressure), 562
LVEF (left ventricular ejection fraction), 562, 574–575
Lymph, 1900
Lymph fistula, 1918, 1919–1920
Lymph nodes, 1871–1890
abscess in, 1925
along thoracic duct, 1897, 1898
aortic, 1879–1881
testicular tumor malignant metastatic spread to, 1930, 1935
axillary, 1882–1883, 1888, 1889
benign disease of, 1923–1926
external iliac chain of, 1931
fibromatosis of, 1927–1930, 1932–1934, 1936, 1937
in inferior vena cava obstruction, 958, 959, 960, 962
inguinal, 1875–1877
fibrolipomatosis of, 1873
fibromatosis of, 1923, 1924
lower extremity, 1874–1875
lumbar region, 1879–1881
in malignant lymphoma patterns, 1941–1942, 1943, 1944
metastases to, 1927–1939
clinical indications for lymphangiography in, 1929, 1932–1938
dislocation and absence in, 1930, 1933, 1934
filling defects in, 1927–1930, 1932–1934, 1936, 1937
formation of, 1927, 1928
principles of diagnosis in, 1927–1931, 1932–1934, 1936, 1937
size and shape of, 1929, 1930, 1936
necrotizing changes in, 1925

normal, 1871–1873
pelvic, 1876–1879
retrocrural, 1885, 1886
retrosternal, 1887, 1888
storage patterns of, 1872, 1873
structure of, 1872
supraclavicular, 1888, 1889
thoracic duct, 1883–1889. *See also* Thoracic duct
upper extremity, 1881–1882
vascular sonography of, 232–233
Lymph vessels. *See* Lymphatics
Lymphadenectomy
in cervical carcinoma, lymphocyst after, 1920
inguinal, lymphedema after, 1914–1915
Lymphadenitis, abscess-forming, 1925
Lymphangiectasis, intestinal, 1919
Lymphangiography, 1864–1952
of arm, 1866
in benign lymph node disease, 1923–1926
cardiovascular reactions to, 1870
cerebral oil embolism in, 1870
complications of, 1867–1870
in lung, 1868–1869
contrast media in, 1866–1867
false-positive, for malignancy, 1943
of foot, 1866
foreign-body reaction in, 1867–1868
hepatic oil embolism in, 1869–1870
instruments for, 1864
lumbar trunk visualization by, 1884
in lymphangiopathies, 1907–1922. *See also* Lymphangiopathies
lymphoscintigraphy and, 1902–1904
of malignant lymphomas, 1940–1952. *See also* Lymphoma, malignant
in malignant metastatic disease, 1927–1939
clinical indications for, 1929, 1932–1938
direct diagnostic signs in, 1927
formation of lymph node cancerous metastases in, 1927, 1928
metastatic triad in, 1927
principles of diagnosis in, 1927–1931, 1932–1934, 1936, 1937
secondary indirect symptoms in, 1927
neoplasm extension and, 1868
normal radiologic anatomy in, 1871–1890. *See also* Lymph nodes; Lymphatics
nuclear medicine and, 1902–1904
second-look, 1929
surgical dissection in, 1864–1865
technique of, 1864–1867
radiographic, 1865
thoracic duct in, 1891–1906. *See also* Thoracic duct
vital dyes in, 1866
vital staining for, 1864
wound infection in, 1867
Lymphangiomas
of bone, 1908, 1912–1913
cavernous, in axillary region, 1921
in retroperitoneum, 1921, III:168
of spleen, 1482
of thoracic duct, 1901
Lymphangiomyomas, 1921
Lymphangiopathia obliterans, 1907

Lymphangiopathies, 1907–1922
in lymph fistula, 1918, 1919–1920
lymphedema in, 1907–1909, 1910–1920
primary, 1907–1908, 1909–1913, 1918–1919
secondary, 1908–1909, 1914–1916, 1920
in lymphocele, 1920–1921
in lymphogenic neoplasm, 1921
in retroperitoneal fibrosis, 1915, 1916–1917
Lymphangiosarcomas, 1921
Lymphangitis, 1908–1909, 1914
Lymphatic aneurysms of thoracic duct, 1901
Lymphaticovenous anastomoses, 1909, 1931
Lymphatics, 1871–1890
lifting of, in lymphangiography, 1864, 1865
in malignant metastatic disease, 1930–1931, 1933–1936
normal, 1871–1873
posterior prefascial, 1875
subcutaneous
anterolateral, 1874
anteromedial, 1874, 1876
topographic anatomy of, 1874–1889
aortic region, 1879–1881
axillary region, 1882–1883
inguinal region, 1876, 1877
lower extremity, 1874–1875
lumbar region, 1879–1881
pelvic region, 1876–1879
thoracic duct, 1883–1889. *See also* Thoracic duct
upper extremity, 1881–1882
Lymphedema, 1907–1909, 1910–1920
congenital, 1907
noninflammatory lesions in, 1909
postoperative, 1909, 1914, 1920
primary, 1907–1908, 1909–1913, 1918–1919
secondary, 1908–1909, 1914–1916, 1920
Lymphedema praecox, 1907
Lymphoceles, 1920–1921
pelvic, percutaneous drainage of, III:944–946
Lymphocysts
lymphocele and, 1920–1921
postoperative, 1920
Lymphocytes
cutaneous T-cell lymphoma and, 1950
thoracic duct and, 1900
Lymphogenic neoplasm, 1921
Lymphogranuloma, inguinal, 1925
Lymphogranuloma venereum, 1925
Lymphography. *See also* Lymphangiography
false-positive, 1943
in malignant lymphomas, repeat, 1946–1950
second-look, 1929
Lymphoid hyperplasia, malignant lymphoma versus, 1944–1947
Lymphointestinal fistula, 1919
Lymphoma
adrenal gland, 1373

after immunosuppression in renal transplantation, 1346–1348
cutaneous T-cell, 1950
gastrointestinal, hemorrhage from, III:75
inferior vena cava capnocavography in, 937
intravascular biopsy of, III:196
malignant, 1940–1952
biopsy diagnosis in, III:169, III:190
diagnostic accuracy in, 1950–1952
differential diagnosis in, 1943–1944, 1945–1947
histopathologic classification of, 1940, 1941
lymph node patterns in, 1941–1942, 1943, 1944
mycosis fungoides and, 1950
repeat lymphography in, 1946–1950
surveillance abdominal films in, 1944–1946, 1947, 1948
mediastinal
subclavian vein occlusion in, 996
in superior vena cava obstruction, 917, 920
pancreatic, 1406, 1408
retroperitoneal, 1669
of spleen, 1484
Lymphosarcoma
in inferior vena cava obstruction, 962
retroperitoneal, 1672
irregular arterial stenosis in, in splenic arteriography, 1466, 1467
of spleen, 1483
Lymphoscintigraphy, 1902–1904
Lysine, plasminogen and, III:120
Lysis-resistant thrombi, III:126
Lytic stagnation, III:135, III:136–137

Maass double-helix barrel prosthesis, III:1047
Macklin C, 849
MacLeod J, III:678
Macleod's syndrome, 810
Macrofistula, term of, 1732
Macrophages in vascular wall after balloon angioplasty, III:5
MAG-3 (mercapto-acetyl-triglycine), III:112
Magic microcatheters, 165
Magnetic disks, on-line digital recording and, 147–148
Magnetic field gradient
bipolar, 200
encoding
first moment, 199
maximum, 201–202
position-dependent, 190, 199
spin-echos along, 189–190
Magnetic resonance angiography (MRA)
after renal transplantation, 1335, 1337
carotid angioplasty and, III:340
for cerebral studies, 252
for coronary artery studies, 692–693
in dural arteriovenous malformations, III:801
of extremities, 1822–1836. *See also* Peripheral vascular magnetic resonance angiography (PVMRA)
after aortoiliac interventions, 1695
in pancreatic disease, 1402

Magnetic resonance angiography (MRA)—
    Continued
  pelvic, 1636, 1637
  in preinterventional assessment, III:206
  in thoracic outlet syndrome, 1001–1002
Magnetic resonance imaging (MRI), 188–
    204
  in abdominal abscesses, III:926–927
  in abdominal aorta aneurysms, 1091,
      1092–1093
  in acute mesenteric venous thrombosis,
      1624
  of adrenal glands, 1358, 1359
  in aortoiliac intervention problems, 1695
  in arteriovenous malformations, III:
      1006, III:1009
  in biopsy, III:175
  in blunt trauma to aorta and brachio-
      cephalic arteries, 524
  for cerebral studies, 252
  in coarctation of aorta, 447–452
  compared to angiography in progressive
      stenosis, 285–286
  in coronary disease, 692–693
  in dissecting aortic aneurysms, 516–518
  in dural arteriovenous malformations,
      III:801
  effects of blood flow on signal in, 188–
      191, 192
  in gastrointestinal bleeding, III:389
  of heart at level of aortic root, 594
  in hepatobiliary malignant obstructions,
      III:476
  independent acquisitions for reconstruc-
      tion of images in, 201
  of inferior vena cava, 940, 942, 943
  of intracranial, extraaxial lesions, III:789,
      III:796–797, III:804–806, III:
      809–813
  in islet-cell tumors, 1403
  in pancreatic carcinoma, 1398
  in patent ductus arteriosus, 426
  of pelvic abscesses and fluid collections,
      III:946
  percutaneous nephrostomy and, III:565
  phase shifts and intravoxel phase disper-
      sion in, 189–191, 192
  projection techniques in, 198–202
    maximum encoding velocity parameter
        and, 201–202
    multidirectional phase contrast and,
        200–201
    phase contrast and, 199–201
  of prostate, III:623, III:624, III:625
  in pulmonary arteriovenous malforma-
      tions, III:838
  in renal cell carcinoma, 1140–1141,
      1144
  in renal vein thrombosis, 1309
  in sarcomas, III:1031
  in spinal dural arteriovenous fistulas
      (SDAVFs)
    of type I, 372–374
    of type II and III, 378–379, 380–381
    of type IV, 382–383, 385
  in stroke, III:748
  in thoracic aortic aneurysms, 471, 473
    with electrocardiogram, 471
  of thoracic duct, 1902–1904
  time-of-flight, 191–198

methods for improved background
    suppression in, 195–197
  physiologic motion and, 197–198
  saturation effects in, 193–195
  signal in, 188–189, 190
  two-dimensional (2D-TOF), 1823–
      1824, 1825
  in varicocele diagnosis, III:689, III:690
  in venous malformations, III:1023
Magnetic resonance lymphangiography,
    1902–1904
Magnetic resonance signal, bipolar gradient
    and, 200
Magnetic resonance venography, 1838–
    1852, 1853–1855
  ascending contrast venography compared
      to, 1838
  of brachiocephalic veins, 1856
  clinical diagnosis and, 1838
  contraindications to, 1852
  epidemiology and, 1837–1838
  of extremities, 1837–1863
  false-positive results in, 1852
  noninvasive studies compared to, 1838–
      1839
  optimization in, 1840, 1841
  in renal and portal venous systems,
      1852–1855
  techniques for, 1840–1843
    new contrast, 1855, 1856, 1857
  thrombus characterization in, 1852
  in venous mapping for vein grafts, 1856
Magnetic tape, digital archiving and, 148
Magnetization-prepared rapid acquisition
    gradient-echo (MP-RAGE) tech-
    nique, 198
Magnification, geometric, 143
Magnification angiography, 176–187
  direct geometric, 177–186
    clinical applicability of, 178, 179,
        180–186
    grids, screen, and film for, 177–180
    x-ray tubes and, 177
  electronic, 186
  photographic or optical, 176–177
Magnification cardioangiography, tubes
    for, 97
Malabsorption in superior mesenteric
    artery obstruction, 1568
Male erection. *See* Erection
Male impotence. *See also* Penile vascular
    catheterization in erectile dysfunc-
    tion
  assessment of, pelvic angiography in,
      1641–1645
  superselective catheterization in, 169
Male infertility
  etiology of, III:688
  varicocele in, III:699–701. *See also* Vari-
      cocele
Male urethra, III:615–616
Malecot catheter
  entrapped, as percutaneous stone
      removal complication, III:602–604
  in percutaneous nephrostomy, III:566,
      III:570
Malecot plastic urethral stent, III:633–634
Malecot retention mechanisms in percuta-
    neous gastrostomy, III:552
Malformations. *See* Anomalies and malfor-
    mations

Malignancy. *See also* Carcinoma; Neo-
    plasms
  after immunosuppression in renal trans-
      plantation, 1346
  in bone. *See* Bone tumors, malignant
  as contraindication to transjugular intra-
      hepatic portosystemic shunt, III:538
  hepatic, III:436–454. *See also* Hepatic
      malignancy
  intravascular biopsy of, III:195–200
  liver
    metastatic, 1450–1451, 1452, 1453
    primary, 1446–1450, 1451
  metastatic. *See* Metastases
  of ovaries, lymphatic malignant metasta-
      ses from, 1932–1933
  pain in, III:201–202
  in spleen, 1467, 1468, 1483–1484,
      1485, 1486
    intrahepatic, 1522–1524, 1525–1526
Malignant fibrous histiocytomas
  of extremities, 1799–1801, 1802
  in differential diagnosis, 1811
  retroperitoneal, 1669
Malignant hypertension, 1116, 1117
Malignant lymphomas, lymphangiography
    of, 1940–1952. *See also*
    Lymphoma, malignant
Malignant melanoma. *See* Melanoma,
    malignant
Malignant neurofibrosarcoma of thigh,
    1811
Malignant polyps of colon, 1604, 1605
Mallinckrodt Gastrostomy Set, III:549,
    III:551
Mallory-Weiss tears
  gastritis in, III:393
  vasopressin infusions and embolic ther-
      apy in, III:404, III:405
Malrotation
  of kidney, 1217
    renal stones in, III:590
  superior mesenteric angiography in,
      1579
Malunion theory of aortic arch develop-
    ment, 437
Mammary artery, internal
  graft of, 758–759
    arteriography catheter selection and
        use for, 760
    disease in, 764
  in infant, 404, 406
  in parathyroid arteriography, 978–979,
      991, 992
Mammary veins, internal, 954, 956
MAN (Mani) catheter, 244, 245
Mandril guidewire, III:484
Mani (MAN) catheter, 244, 245
Manifold in coronary arteriography, 558
Mannitol, 1528–1529, III:207, III:214
Manual dissection in postmortem studies,
    583, 584
MAO (monoamine oxidase), 54
Mapping
  for evaluating vein grafts, 1856
  technique for
    in digital subtraction imaging, 151
    in γ-mapping, 141
    in nonsubtraction imaging, 152
  velocity, in dissecting aortic aneurysms,
      516

Marcozzi G, 933
Marfan syndrome
  dissecting aortic aneurysms in, 493, 494,
    496
    chest x-ray and, 498, 499
  thoracic aortic aneurysms in, 487
    magnetic resonance imaging of, 471,
      473
Marginal artery, 1588, 1589, 1596
Marginal coronary arteries, obtuse, 674,
  675, 676–677, 682
Marginal irregularity in coronary arteriography, 641, 642–643
Marginal vein, right, 590
Marsupialization of renal cysts, III:665–
  666
Martin and Ellis needle biopsy, III:166
Mason F, 9
Mass
  abdominal, vascular sonography of, 230
  cerebral, 328–342
  mediastinal, 1900
    biopsy in, III:190
    in thoracic duct, 1895, 1901
  neck, 1900, 1901
  renal, diagnostic decision tree in, 1173.
    See also Renal tumors
  soft tissue, in inferior vena cava obstruc-
    tion, 960, 962
  supraclavicular, 1901
  vascular neoplastic, sonography of, 216
Massé, 6
Massive extraperitoneal hemorrhage, 1648
MAST (military antishock treatment), III:
  860
Matas test, III:768
Matrix, pixel, 143–144
Maxillary artery, 340
Maximum encoding velocity parameter,
  201–202
Maximum horizontal framing, 100
Maximum intensity pixel (MIP), 1824
Maximum intensity projection (MIP) ray
  tracing, 199
May-Thurber syndrome, 973
MCA (carotid arteries, main (MCA), bifur-
  cation of, 314, 316, 345
McAlpine WA, 583, 584
MCES (multiple cholesterol emboli syn-
  drome), 1029
McGahan catheter, III:952
McNamara modified method for
  intrathrombic infusion of thrombo-
  lytic agents, III:127
McPheeters HO, 6
MD. *See* Sodium diatrizoate
Mean velocity in leg arteries, 212, 213
Mean visual values in coronary arteriogra-
  phy, 658
Meandering mesenteric artery, 1067
  intestinal ischemia and, 1622, 1623,
    1632
Mean-diameter framing, 100
Meatotomy, ureteral, strictures after, III:
  578
Mechanical embolic agents, III:55–79
  adverse effects in, III:77
  balloons in, III:55, III:63–70
  bristle brushes in, III:55, III:71
  clinical indications for, III:71–76

comparison of detachable balloons and
    embolization coils in, III:71, III:72
  devices for occluding congenital heart
    defects and shunts and, III:55, III:
    70
  early descriptions of, III:55
  endovascular grafts in, III:55, III:71
  ideal agent in, III:55
  laser-induced occlusion in, III:55, III:71
  metal-based, III:55, III:56–63
  methods in, III:55
  plain threads in, III:55, III:71
Mechanical injectors
  electrically powered, 172–173
  powered by series of springs, 171–172
Mechanical resuscitation, 37
Mechanical thrombolysis, III:119
Meckel diverticulum, 1579
Medial plaque fracture after balloon angioplasty, III:4–5
Mediastinal abscesses, III:832–835
Mediastinal adenomas, 980
  anterior, 989–990
  left inferior thyroid arteriogram in, 977
  parathyroid angiography in, 988–990
  parathyroid hormone gradient in, 982–
    983
  posterior, 988–989
  thyroid arteries to, 985
  thyroid gland obscuring, 984
Mediastinal lymph nodes, 1886, 1897
  filling of middle, 1897, 1898
Mediastinal lymphoma, subclavian vein
  occlusion in, 996
Mediastinal myxoliposarcoma, 924
Mediastinal shifting in lung biopsy compli-
  cation, 1034
Mediastinal teratoma, 917
Mediastinal tumors, 1900
  biopsy and, III:185, III:186, III:187
  in superior vena cava obstruction, 917,
    920, 924
  in thoracic duct, 1895, 1901
Mediastinal veins, 956
Mediastinal widening or rupture
  in blunt trauma, 531
  in dissecting aortic aneurysms, 500, 502,
    503
Mediastinitis, fibrosing, 919, 921–922
Medications. *See* Drugs
Medrad injector, 173
Medullary cystic disease of kidney, 1226
Medullary sponge kidney, 1226
Medullary veins, 275
Megacalices, 1228
Megestrol acetate, III:627–628
Meige disease, 1907
Melanoma, malignant
  biopsy diagnosis in, III:168
  metastatic spread of, 1938
    filling defects in enlarged lymph nodes
      in, 1930, 1938
    to forearm, 1938
    to liver, III:452
    to lower leg, thigh, and inguinal
      nodes, 1735, 1736
    to spleen, 1485
Mellins HZ, 892
Melphalan, III:81
Membrane, congenital, in inferior vena
  cava obstruction, 964

Mengheni needles, III:174
MEN-ILA (multiple endocrine neoplasia),
  1370, 1402
Meningeal artery
  anatomic variations in, III:792–793
  anterior, 277
  middle, aneurysms of, 352
  posterior, 277
Meningiomas
  cerebral vascular malformations in, 334–
    335, 337
    complications of intracranial emboliza-
      tion of, 1032–1033
  petroclival, embolization in, III:809–
    814
Meperidine
  in idiosyncratic reactions to urokinase,
    III:155
  in interventional radiology procedures,
    III:213, III:215
  in premedication
    for coronary artery catheterization,
      568
    for femoral arteriography, 1713
  strengths and volumes of, 48
  in thoracic aortography, 398
  in thrombolytic therapy reactions, 1043
Mepivacaine, III:214
Mercapto-acetyl-triglycine (MAG-3), III:
  112
Merkel H, 583
Mesencephalic vein, posterior, 276, 280
Mesenchymal tumors
  of extremities, 1811
  retroperitoneal, 1669, III:169, III:190
Mesenteric angiography, 1549–1635
  bradykinin and, 62, 1557
  inferior, 1587–1614. *See also* Inferior
    mesenteric angiography
  in mesenteric ischemia, 1615–1635. *See
    also* Mesenteric ischemia
  superior, 1549–1586. *See also* Superior
    mesenteric angiography
Mesenteric angioplasty, III:326–338
Mesenteric arteries. *See also* Mesenteric vas-
    cular insufficiency
  hepatic branches from, superselective
    embolization of, 169
  inferior (IMA), 1019, 1021
    in arteriosclerotic disease, 1061, 1066
    balloon catheter in, III:32–33
    branches of, 1590
    colon segments and, 1590
    endovascular interventions for chronic
      mesenteric ischemia in, III:326–338
    level of origin of, 1589–1590
    occlusion of, 1557–1570, 1596–
      1597, III:334–335. *See also* Inferior
      mesenteric angiography
    in pelvic arteriovenous malformation,
      III:1019
    size of, 1590
    stenoses of, 1593–1601, 1602
  magnification angiography of, 181–182,
    183
  meandering, 1067
    ischemia and, 1622, 1623, 1632
  occlusion of, 1557–1570, III:334–335.
    See also Mesenteric angiography
  sonography in, 213–214, 229–230,
    231

Mesenteric arteries—*Continued*
  superior (SMA), 1015, 1018–1020, 1549–1552, 1553–1555. *See also* Superior mesenteric angiography
    aneurysms of, chronic intestinal ischemia and, 1631
    angiography technique and, 1391
    in arterial portography, 1527–1528. *See also* Arterial portography
    balloon catheter in, III:32–33
    embolus (SMAE) of, 1619–1620, 1621
    endovascular interventions for chronic mesenteric ischemia in, III:326–338
    intestinal collateral circulation and, 1594–1595, 1596–1597
    occlusion of, 1557–1570. *See also* Mesenteric angiography
    in pancreatic vasculature, 1389, 1411
    thrombosis (SMAT) of, 1620–1622, 1623
Mesenteric carcinoma, 1568, 1570
Mesenteric ischemia, 1615–1635. *See also* Mesenteric vascular insufficiency
  endovascular interventions for, III:326–338
    discussion of, III:336–337
    etiologies and, III:326, III:328
    results of, III:330–336
    techniques for, III:326–330
  sonography in, 214, 229–230, 231
Mesenteric root in inferior vena cava obstruction, 958
Mesenteric steal, 1568
Mesenteric thrombosis
  in coronary arteriography complications, 578
  ischemia in, 1622–1624
  vascular sonography in, 231
Mesenteric vascular insufficiency. *See also* Mesenteric ischemia
  abdominal angina in, 1631–1634
    inferior mesenteric arteriography in, 1600
  acute, 1616–1630
    mesenteric venous thrombosis in, 1622–1624
    nonocclusive, 1618–1619
    with occlusion, 1558–1566
    plan for diagnosis and therapy in, 1624–1628
    prognosis in, 1628–1630
    superior mesenteric artery embolus in, 1619–1620, 1621
    superior mesenteric artery thrombosis in, 1620–1622, 1623
  chronic, 1631–1634
    diagnosis and treatment in, 1632–1634
    obstruction in, 1553, 1560, 1565, 1566–1570
    results in, 1634
  endovascular interventions in, III:326–338
    discussion of, III:336–337
    etiologies and, III:326, III:328
    results of, III:330–336
    techniques for, III:326–330
  inferior mesenteric angiography in, 1591
  intestinal angina in, 1631–1634
    inferior mesenteric arteriography in, 1600

    obstruction in, 1553, 1560, 1565, 1566–1570
    papaverine infusion in, 1617, 1625–1629
    pathophysiologic changes in, 1615–1616
    persistent vasoconstriction in, 1616
    plan for diagnosis and therapy in, 1624–1628
    recurrent vascular, 1631–1634
    sonography in, 214, 229–230, 231
    superior mesenteric angiography in, 1557–1571. *See also* Superior mesenteric angiography
      with acute occlusion, 1559–1570
      with chronic obstruction, 1553, 1560, 1565, 1566–1570
Mesenteric veins. *See also* Mesenteric vascular insufficiency
  inferior (IMV)
    for inferior vena cava collateral circulation, 957
    stenoses in, 1593–1601
    transhepatic portal venography in, 1423
    magnification angiography of, 181–182, 183
  superior (SMV)
    compression of, 1394, 1397
    in pancreatic venography, 1426–1427
    thrombosis in, in acute mesenteric ischemia, 1622–1624
    varices of, III:397–400
    in vascular sonography, 231
Mesocaval shunt, 231–232
Mesonephric arteries, 1220–1221
Mesotheliomas, retroperitoneal, 1669
Messinetti S, 933
Metabolic acidosis, 39, 45
Metabolic diseases, coronary arteriography in, 692
Metabolic rate, myocardium and, III:367
Metaiodobenzylguanidine (MIBG), 1357, 1371
Metal microspheres in small-vessel or tissue embolization, III:54
Metal-based mechanical embolic agents, III:55, III:56–63
  bare wires in, III:62
  coil, III:56–62
  detachable balloons in, III:62
  imaging of, III:62
  materials for, III:56–57
  microspheres in, III:54
  modifications for, III:60–61
  pitfalls of, III:58, III:59–60
  spiderlon in, III:63
  technique in use of, III:57–59
  wire baffles in, III:62
  wire-induced electroocclusion in, III:62–63
  wires with threads in, III:56–62
Metallic artifact, 1828, 1829
Metallic stents. *See also* Stents; specific stent
  in arteriosclerotic disease of pelvic arteries, 1638, 1640
  in benign biliary obstruction, III:462–465, III:466
  biological response to implantation of, III:93–97

  ideal, III:86
  in liver transplantation complications, III:514–515, III:518–520
  in superior vena cava obstruction, 928–929
  ureteral, III:573
Metameric angiomatosis, 369
Metanephric arteries, 1220–1221
Metaraminol, 47
  recommended intravenous dosages for, 46
  strengths and volumes of, 48
Metastases
  adrenal gland, 1359, 1373, 1374, 1375
    biopsy in, III:190
    from lung cancer, 1673, 1674
  in biopsy needle track seeding, III:183–184
  to brain, cerebral vascular malformations in, 342
  from colon adenocarcinoma, 936, III:436, III:450–451
    to liver, biopsy in, III:167
  to kidney, 168, 1165
  to liver
    biopsy in, III:167, III:179
    from colon adenocarcinoma, 183, 1453, 1542, 1543, III:167, III:436, III:450–451
    hepatic arteriography in, 1450–1451, 1452, 1453
    obstructions in, III:472–482
    splenoportography of, 1522–1525
    superselective catheterization in, 168–169
  to lung, thromboembolic disease in, 1749
  from lung cancer
    to ilium and femur, 1817
    in superior vena cava obstruction, 917–919, 920
  lymphangiography in, 1927–1939
    clinical indications for, 1929, 1932–1938
    formation of lymph node cancerous metastases in, 1927, 1928
    principles of diagnosis in, 1927–1931, 1932–1934, 1936, 1937
  to omentum, superselective embolization in, 167
  to pancreas, 1406–1408
    islet-cell tumors versus, 1403, 1405
  perinephric, 941
  from renal cell carcinoma, 1139, 1154–1158
    femoral arteriography in, 1738
    to femur, 1808
    pancreatic islet-cell tumors versus, 1403, 1405
    to shoulder, 1807
  retroperitoneal, 1669
  skip, in Hodgkin disease, 1941
  to spinal column, 386–387
  to spleen, 1485, 1486
  from thyroid carcinoma, 917
  vertebral and azygos veins and, 892
  from Wilms tumor, 1133
Metastatic triad in lymphatic metastases, 1927
Metatarsal branches of plantar arteries, 1699

Methotrexate, III:80–81
  in hepatic malignancy, III:437
  in osteosarcomas, III:1032–1033
Methyl *tert*-butyl ether, III:504–505
  toxicity of, III:497
Methyldopa, 1306
N-Methylglucamine diatrizoate
  in coronary artery catheterization, 568,
    576
  in superior mesenteric angiography,
    1556
Methylparaben, allergy to, III:214
Methylprednisolone, 30, 48
Metoclopramide, III:214
Metrizamide, 20
  with absolute alcohol embolization, III:
    1013
    in pediatrics, III:906
  chemistry and characteristics of, 16, 17,
    20
Metrizoate, 20
  chemistry and characteristics of, 16, 17,
    20
MIBG (metaiodobenzylguanidine), 1357,
    1371
Michel NA, 1457
Michelsson catheter, 368
MIC-Key gastric button, III:555, III:556
Micro Ferret catheter, 1428
Microadenomatosis, pancreatic, 1403
Microballoons for intracranial angioplasty,
    III:755–756
Microcatheters
  in carotid-cavernous fistula embolization,
    III:807
  for coil introduction, III:57
  in extremity arteriovenous malformation,
    III:1020–1022
  Ferret, 1428
  with flexible segments and rigid body,
    163
  in superselective catheterization, 164–
    165, 166
Microcoils
  in arteriovenous malformations, III:
    1011, III:1012
  in intraaxial embolotherapy for central
    nervous system, III:766
Microcystic adenoma of pancreas, 1405
Microfibrillar collagen, III:52–53
Microfistula, term of, 1732
Microfocal spot tube, 95
Microgastrinoma, 1403
Microguidewires, 162
Microhistologic fragments in diagnosis, III:
    170–171
Microinjectors, 170–171
Micropuncture introducing sets, 157
Microspheres
  glass or metal, III:54
  starch, III:53
Microstructure, pulmonary, 849–867. *See
    also* Pulmonary physiology and
    microstructure
Microsurgical tubocornual anastomosis in
    fallopian tube obstruction, III:672
Midaortic syndrome, 1054, 1055, 1061
Midazolam, III:213
  in arterial portography preparation, 1528
  in cerebral angiography, 246
  in femoral arteriography, 1713, 1714

in gastrostomy, III:548
lidocaine and, III:201
in pelvic abscess drainage, III:947
in transjugular intrahepatic portosystemic
    shunt, III:532
in varicocele embolization, III:694
Midstream aortography, 158
Mikaelsson catheters, III:822
Mild arteriolar nephrosclerosis, 1260
Miles clip, III:983
Military antishock treatment (MAST), III:
    860
Miller Double Mushroom endoprosthesis,
    III:479
Mills intravascular biopsy, III:195–196
Milroy disease, 1907
Mini-balloon detachable balloon, III:68–
    69
MIP (maximum intensity pixel), 1824
MIP (maximum intensity projection) ray
    tracing, 199
Mirroring in Doppler imaging, 208
Mitomycin, III:81
  in gastrointestinal sarcomas, III:1035
  in hepatic malignancy, III:437, III:451
Mitoxantrone
  in breast carcinoma, III:82
  in hepatic malignancy, III:437
Mitral insufficiency, 637
Mixed partial anomalous pulmonary
    venous connection, 882
Mixed total anomalous pulmonary venous
    connection, 873, 879, 881
Mobin-Uddin umbrella, III:983–984
  evaluation and comparison of, III:987
Mobitz type heart blocks, 43, 44
Moderate arteriolar nephrosclerosis, 1260
Moderator band, collaterals in, 703
Modulation transfer function (MTF), 143–
    144
Mole, hydatidiform, 1646, 1647
Molecular genetics, balloon angioplasty
    restenosis and, III:16–17
Monitoring
  in femoral arteriography, 1714
  in interventional radiology procedures,
    III:212
  for patient safety in cardiac catheteriza-
    tion, 114–116
  radiation, 128, 129, 132
Moniz E, 6, 13, 19
  cassette changer of, 67
Monoamine oxidase (MAO), 54
Monoclonal antibody against GP IIb/IIIa
    receptor, III:126
Monoethanolamine, III:696
Mononucleosis, infectious, 1491
Monooctanoin, III:497
Monostic coronary circulation, 596
Monro, foramen of, 275
Moore DB, 892
Moretz clip, III:983
Morgan RH, 9
Morphine, 47, III:213
  in cholecystomy, III:485
  in gastrostomy, III:548
  lidocaine and, III:201
  recommended intravenous dosages for,
    46
  strengths and volumes of, 48

Morphine analogs for femoral arteriogra-
    phy, 1713, 1714
Morphine derivatives, III:212, III:213
Mortality. *See also* Death
  in abdominal abscesses, III:940
  in coronary arteriography, 572–575,
    690–691
  in pediatric and neonatal patients, 579
  in pulmonary arteriography, 783
  in splenic trauma, 1485
  in systemic reactions to contrast agents,
    29–30
Motion artifacts, 1828–1829, 1830
Motor vehicle accident in liver injury, III:
    422, III:423, III:428, III:430–431
Motorcycle riders, aortic trauma in, 522,
    528–529
MOTSA (multiple overlapping thin slap
    acquisitions), 196
Moving-slit radiography, 83–84
Moya Moya disease, 307, 310
MPA. *See* Pulmonary arteries, main (MPA)
MP-RAGE (magnetization-prepared rapid
    acquisition gradient-echo) tech-
    nique, 198
MRA. *See* Magnetic resonance angiography
    (MRA)
MRI. *See* Magnetic resonance imaging
    (MRI)
Mucin-containing tumors of pancreas,
    1405
Mucosal hemorrhage, gastric, III:392, III:
    404–405, III:406, III:407
Mueller catheter, abscess drainage and
    abdominal, III:930
    pelvic, III:951–952
Multichannel display and recording system,
    118
Multicystic kidney, 1135, III:658. *See also*
    Polycystic disease
Multidirectional phase contrast angiogra-
    phy, 200–201
Multilocular renal cysts, III:658
Multiple aneurysms
  of abdominal aorta, 1091
  of thoracic aorta, 475–477, 488
Multiple cholesterol emboli syndrome
    (MCES), 1029
Multiple congenital stenoses of pulmonary
    artery branches, 792
Multiple endocrine neoplasia (MEN-IIA),
    1370, 1402
Multiple overlapping thin slap acquisitions
    (MOTSA), 196
Multiple pulmonary artery stenoses, 792,
    793
Multiple renal arteries, 1217–1221, 1224
Multiple thin slice technique, 197
Multivessel coronary disease, 680–681,
    682–683
  angioplasty in, III:373–374
Mural thrombus, sonography of, 207, 228
Muscular pulmonary arteries, 769
Musculoskeletal system, biopsy and, III:
    190–192
Musculotendinous fibers of psoas minor
    muscle or diaphragmatic crura in
    renal artery compression, 1269–
    1270
Mustard syndrome, III:915
Mycosis fungoides, 1950

Mycotic aneurysms
of abdominal aorta, 1077, 1080
cerebral, 319–320
intracranial changes in, 303, 305
peripheral pulmonary artery, 843, 845
of thoracic aorta, 483–486
Mycotic pseudoaneurysms of extracranial
cerebral arteries, 303, 305
Myelitis, transverse, III:826–827
Myelography in spinal dural arteriovenous
fistulas, 373–374, 378–379, 380–
381
Myelolipomas, adrenal gland, 1373, 1374
Myelomas
biopsy diagnosis in, III:168
plasma cell, 1793–1794
Myelomeningocele, renal stones and, III:
598
Mylar membranes, 69, 77
Myocardial blush, 620
Myocardial bridging
in coronary arteriography, 686–689,
735, 736
in coronary artery anatomic variations,
751, 755
Myocardial infarction
acute, nonfatal, 573, 575–578
angioplasty in, III:373
restenosis after, III:8, III:14
coronary arteriography in
as complication, 573, 575–578
morphology and, 661
normal, 662
dissecting aortic aneurysms with, 496
multiple, as indication for angiography,
635–636, 637
Myocardial ischemia, coronary artery catheterization and, 562
Myocardial perfusion, 589–590
in coronary artery anomalies
altered, 740–745
unaltered, 746–748
Myocardial steal syndrome, 722
Myocardium
circulation in. *See* Myocardial perfusion
contraction of
contrast agents and, 27
left coronary blood flow during,
686
coronary arteriography complications
and, 577
metabolic rate and, III:367
operability of, 689
perforation of, in pulmonary arteriography, 783
Myocutaneous skin flaps, 1730–1731
Myointimal hyperplasia after balloon angioplasty, III:8–11, III:12–13
Myositis ossificans, 1812–1813
subclavius muscle, in thoracic outlet syndrome, 996
Myxofibrosarcomas of extremities, 1811
Myxoliposarcoma, mediastinal, 924

Naloxone, III:213, III:216
in fentanyl reversal, 246
strengths and volumes of, 48
Narcan. *See* Naloxone
Narcotics, III:212, III:213
in pleurisy, III:852

NASCET (North American Symptomatic
Carotid Endarterectomy Trial), 286,
287, III:339
Nasopharyngeal tumors, 339–340
angiofibroma as, III:905
National Council on Radiation Protection
and Measurements (NCRP) recom-
mendations
for cardiac catheterization laboratory, 124
on occupational dose limitations, 128
for vascular intervention angiography lab-
oratory, 136–137
National Electrical Code of National Fire
Protection Association, 130
National Electrical Manufacturers Associa-
tion (NEMA), 96
National Fire Protection Association
(NFPA), 130
National Heart, Lung, and Blood Institute
(NHLBI), III:366
National Heart Institute, 572
National Institute of Health Working Formulation for non-Hodgkin
lymphoma classification, 1940,
1941
National Standards for Cardiopulmonary
Resuscitation, 34
Natural light, photographic ratings of, 105
Nausea
during procedures, III:213, III:214
and vomiting from systemic reactions to
contrast agents, 29
NBCA (*N*-Butylcyanoacrylate embolization), III:791, III:802
in spinal dural fistulas, 376
NCRP (National Council on Radiation Protection and Measurements) recommendations
for cardiac catheterization laboratory,
124
on occupational dose limitation, 128
for vascular intervention angiography laboratory, 136–137
Nebesar RA, 1435
Neck
carcinoma of, regional chemotherapy in,
III:82, III:83
complications of procedures for, 1032–
1033
hemangiopericytomas of, 1806
hematoma of, carotid extravasation in,
348
imaging of
cerebral vascular angiography and. *See*
Cerebral angiography
in lumbar aortography, 1032–1033
noninvasive methods for, 252
masses in, 1900, 1901
mycotic pseudoaneurysms of extracranial
cerebral arteries in, 303, 305
Necrosis
coagulative, in prostatic hyperthermia,
III:635–636
of liver after hepatic arteriography, III:
434
lymph node, 1925
Needle
in biopsy, III:174
of kidney, III:189
in thoracic region, III:184–185
for cerebral angiography, 242

in dialysis fistula thrombolysis, III:729,
III:730
in lymphangiography, 1864–1865
in nephrostomy, III:566
in pelvic abscess drainage, III:947
in penile vascularization, III:709
for splenoportography, 1499
in stone removal, III:599–600
in subcutaneous port implantation, III:
977
in transfemoral catheterization, 1013–
1014
in venous access catheter placement, III:
973, III:975, III:977, III:978
Needle aspiration. *See* Aspiration
Needle track seeding in biopsy, III:183–184
Neff introducer system, III:952
NEMA (National Electrical Manufacturers
Association), 96
Nembutal, 568
Neodymium-yttrium aluminum garnet
laser systems, III:380, III:381
in femoropopliteal angioplasty, III:280,
III:281
Neointima
after stent placement, III:95–97
hyperplasia of, in dialysis fistula, III:
726–727
Neoiopax. *See* Uroselectan
Neonate
complications of coronary arteriography
in, 579–580
vertebral blood supply of, 365
Neoplasms. *See also* Carcinoma; Malignancy
arteriography in bleeding in, III:417
varices and, III:397–400
cystic, pancreatic, 1393, 1405–1406,
1407, 1408
intracranial
embolization in, III:808–814
monocompartmental or multicompart-
mental, III:809–811
lymphangiography of
extension of tumor in, 1868
metastatic skin malignancies in, 1937,
1938
lymphogenic, 1921
pelvic
angiography in, 1645–1646, 1647
transcatheter embolization for intractable hemorrhage from, 1658–1661
in spleen, 1467, 1468, 1482–1484
urethral strictures in, III:617
vascular, sonography of, 216
Neoselectan, early uses of, 7
Neo-Synephrine. *See* Phenylephrine
Neovascularity, tumor, 1781
pelvic angiography in assessment of,
1645–1646, 1647
Nephrectomy
in granulomatous pyelonephritis, 1194
in renal abscess, 1187, 1188, 1189
in renal cell carcinoma, 1154
in renal hypertension without main renal
arterial stenosis, 1262
Nephritis
bacterial
acute, 1178–1182, 1183
terminology, 1178
hereditary, 1226, 1227

Nephroblastoma, 1132. *See also* Wilms
   tumor
Nephrogram
   cortical, 1122–1124
   general, 1124
   in hydronephrosis, 1203, 1204, 1209
   in ischemia, 1248, 1258, 1259, 1263
   normal, 1246–1248
Nephrographic phase of renal angiography,
   1114, 1115, 1118, 1119, 1122–
   1124
Nephrolithotomy complications, 1036–
   1037
Nephropathy, contrast, 578–579
Nephrosclerosis
   arteriolar, 1260–1261
   magnification angiography in, 181
Nephrostomy
   catheter for. *See* Nephrostomy catheter
   complications of, 1036–1037
      renal vascular injuries in, 1230–1231
   percutaneous, III:561–572. *See also* Per-
      cutaneous nephrostomy (PCN)
   pyopneumothorax after, 1036
Nephrostomy catheter
   entrapped, in percutaneous stone
      removal complications, III:602–603
   in pelvic abscess drainage, III:952
   in renal transplant obstruction, III:581,
      III:582
   transconduit retrograde placement of,
      through ileal conduit, III:574
   in ureteral stenting, III:574, III:575–
      576
Nephrotomography
   antegrade, in urinomas, III:668, III:669
   percutaneous nephrostomy and, III:572
   in renal cysts, 1171
   in renal hamartoma, 1163, 1164–1165
Nephrotoxicity of contrast agents, 23–24
Nephroureteral obstruction, III:561–586
   antegrade catheter for, III:574
   extracorporeal shock wave lithotripsy
      and
      in complications, III:608
      in contraindications, III:606
   percutaneous nephrostomy in, III:561–
      572
      assessment and, III:561
      complications of, III:568–570
      contraindications to, III:566
      follow-up after, III:570–572
      results of, III:567–568
      technique for, III:562–566
   in renal transplants, III:581–584
   ureteral stenting in, III:572–578
      antegrade, III:574–576
      complications of, III:576–578
      materials for, III:572–573
      results of, III:576–578
      retrograde, III:576
      technique of, III:574
      ureteral stricture dilation in, III:576, III:
         578–581
      results of, III:580–581
      urinomas in, III:667, III:668
Nerve sheath tumors, 1811
Neural tumors, retroperitoneal, 1669
Neuralgia, femoral, in puncture site complications, 1028

Neurilemomas, retroperitoneal, 1669,
   1670
Neurinomas, 1577
Neuroblastomas
   adrenal gland, 1373
      angiography in, 1376, 1378
   extrarenal, retroperitoneal, 1669
   Wilms tumor versus, 1136
Neurofibromas, 1165
   pheochromocytoma and, 1370
   in renovascular hypertension, 1257–
      1258
   retroperitoneal, 1669, 1670
   vertebral artery changes in, 337
Neurofibromatosis
   pediatric, angiography in, III:911
   renal angioplasty results in, III:318, III:
      319
Neurofibrosarcoma of thigh, 1811
Neurogenic tumors, renal, 1165, 1166
Neurologic deficits
   central nervous system revascularization
      in, III:745–764. *See also* Central
      nervous system, revascularization in
   in cerebral vascular trauma, 348–353
   in extremity trauma, III:857–858
   spinal cord angiography and, 356–357
Neuropathy in coronary arteriography com-
   plications, 578
Neurotransmitters
   catecholamines and, 52–54
   in erection, III:705, III:707
   vascular smooth muscle cells and, 51
Nevus, blue rubber bleb, 1573
Newborn
   complications of coronary arteriography
      in, 579–580
   vertebral blood supply of, 365
Newton catheter, 244, 245
Newton guidewire, III:263, III:264
NFPA (National Fire Protection Association), 130
NHLBI (National Heart, Lung, and Blood
   Institute), III:366
Nicolas-Favre disease, 1925
Nicotine, transdermal, III:230
Nidus arteriovenous malformations in central nervous system, III:775–779
Nifedipine, 53, III:215
   calcium channel blockers and, 60
   in central nervous system embolother-
      apy, III:767
   in emergency reactions, III:216
   in extremity trauma, III:861
   in femoropopliteal revascularization, III:
      267
   in renal angioplasty, III:305
   in thrombolysis, III:138
   in varicocele embolization, III:694
   for vasospasm at puncture site in angiog-
      raphy, 1028, 1030
NIH Working Formulation for non-Hodgkin lymphoma classification, 1940,
   1941
Nimodipine, III:755
Nitinol basket, III:504
Nitinol filters, Simon, III:987, III:991–
   992
   complications with, 1044
   magnetic resonance venography and,
      1852

Nitinol guidewire, 156
   in infrapopliteal revascularization, III:
      285
Nitinol snare catheter in foreign body
   removal, III:961, III:962
Nitinol spring-coil stent, III:90, III:92
Nitrates, 58–59
   revascularization and, III:230
Nitric oxide (NO), 50, 58
   erection and, III:705, III:707
Nitrodilators, 50, 58
Nitrogen mustard, 1380, III:437
Nitroglycerin (NTG), 53, 58–59, III:215
   in cavernosometry, 1644
   in coronary angiography, 569, 627
   in emergency reactions, III:216
   intraarterial, before thrombolysis, III:
      138
   intraaxial embolotherapy for central ner-
      vous system and, III:767
   in pharmacologic erection, III:706
   in pulmonary arteriovenous malforma-
      tion embolotherapy complications,
      III:850
   for puncture site vasospasm, 1028, 1030
   in renal angioplasty, 1041, III:305–306
   revascularization and
      femoropopliteal, III:267
      infrapopliteal, III:290
      preparation for, III:230
   in varicocele embolization, III:695
   vasopressin and, 55
   vertebral artery angioplasty and, III:348
Nitroprusside, 58, III:215
   in pheochromocytoma, 1356, 1373
   renin determination and, 1306
Nitroso compounds, 58
NO (nitric oxide), 50, 58
   erection and, III:705, III:707
Node of Aschoff and Tawara, 617
Nodular hyperplasia, focal hepatic, 1441–
   1443, 1444
Noise amplitude in subtraction image, 150
NOMI. *See* Nonocclusive mesenteric ischemia (NOMI)
Nondetachable occlusion balloons, III:63–
   65
   potential complications of, III:64
Non-Hodgkin disease, III:184. *See also*
   Lymphoma, malignant
   diagnostic accuracy in, 1950–1952
   histopathologic classification of, 1940,
      1941
   lymph node patterns in, 1942, 1943
   surveillance abdominal films in, 1944–
      1946, 1948
Noninvasive vascular testing for percutaneous aortoiliac intervention, III:228–
   229
Nonionic contrast media. *See* Low-osmolality contrast agents (LOCA)
Nonocclusive mesenteric ischemia (NOMI)
   acute, 1618–1619
   superior mesenteric angiography in,
      1563–1565, 1566
Nonossifying fibromas, 1798
Nonpenetrating trauma of upper extremities, 1758
Nonselective renal angiography, 1113
   catheter for, 1102, 1103
Nonspecific arteritis, 1054

Nonsteroidal antiinflammatory agents
    oral hypoglycemics and, III:217
    in postembolization syndrome, III:440
Nonsubtraction imaging, 151–152
Nontropical sprue, 1568, 1569
Nontunnel catheters for venous access, III:969, III:978
Nonvascular foreign bodies, removal of, III:963–967
Noonan syndrome, 1901
    central pulmonary artery stenosis and, 831
    pulmonary valve stenosis in, 826
Norcholesterol, radiolabeled iodomethyl, 1357, 1364, 1376
Nordenstrom B, 893
Norepinephrine, 47, 48
    action of, 52, 53
    clinical indications for, 54
    dosage and preparation of, 52
    in erection reversal, III:706
    in pancreatic angiography, 1392
    pheochromocytoma producing, 1369
    recommended intravenous dosages for, 46
Normal sinus rhythm, 43, 44
North American CPTA Register, III:343, III:345
North American Symptomatic Carotid End-arterectomy Trial (NASCET), 286, 287, III:339
NP-59 adrenal scintigraphy, 1357, 1364
    in adrenogenital syndromes, 1369
    in localization of remnants, 1376
NTG. *See* Nitroglycerin (NTG)
Nucleoside release, contrast agent osmolality and, 24
Nurses and nursing staff
    cardiac catheterization laboratory, 131–132
    vascular intervention angiography laboratory, 136
Nussbaum A, 585
Nutcracker phenomenon, III:688
Nutritional support, percutaneous gastrostomy in, III:547
Nuvoli I, 8, 10
Nylon balloons, scratch-resistance of, III:39
Nylon-tufted stainless steel coils, III:403
Nyquist frequency limit, 209, 210

Obesity, renal stones and, III:597
Obliterative pulmonary diseases, 801–803, 804–806
Obstetric procedures, III:881
Obstetrics, pelvic angiography in, 1646, 1647. *See also* Pregnancy
Obstruction. *See also* Occlusion
    biliary. *See* Biliary obstruction
    of extrahepatic vascular circulation, 1499, 1508–1512, 1513–1517
    fallopian tube, III:672–677
    hepatobiliary, malignant, III:472–482. *See also* Hepatobiliary obstruction, malignant
    hydronephrosis from, 1202, 1203, 1213–1215
    of innominate veins, 900, 901–902
    of intrahepatic vascular circulation, 1506–1508, 1517–1521

intrarenal inferior vena cava, collateral circulation and, 951–957
    nephroureteral, III:561–586. *See also* Nephroureteral obstruction
    of portal veins. *See* Portal veins
    of pulmonary artery, pulmonary hypovascularity in, 816
    of pulmonary vascular bed, progressive, 853, 859–861
    of renal arteries, transcatheter thrombo-embolectomy, 1287
    of renal transplants, III:581–584
    of small coronary artery branches as coronary arteriography pitfall, 736–737
    thoracic duct, 1901–1902
        upper extremity angiography in, 1762, 1764
    in total anomalous pulmonary venous connection, 874–875
    upper airway, 36
Obstructive jaundice, percutaneous cholecystostomy in, III:486
Obstructive pulmonary diseases, percutaneous biopsy complications in, III:178, III:187
Obturator arteries, 1022
    embolization of, 1662
Occipital artery vasospasm in trauma, 344
Occipital veins, 276
Occlusion. *See also* Obstruction
    after gunshot wounds of upper extremity, 1757, 1758
    aortic
        abdominal, in arteriosclerosis and other diseases, 1058–1060
        sonography of, 229
    of basilar artery
        with telangiectasia, 307, 310
        of unknown etiology, 312, 313
    of celiac arteries. *See* Celiac arteries, occlusion of
    of cerebrovascular vessels
        pathophysiology of, III:746–747
        revascularization procedures in, III:745–764. *See also* Central nervous system, revascularization in
    in congenital heart disease, mechanical embolization in, III:55, III:70
    of coronary arteries, 643, 649–650
        causes of, other than arteriosclerosis, 691–692
        in coronary artery catheterization complications, 575, 579
        in hemodynamically significant disease, 688
        recanalization of thrombi in, as arteriography pitfall, 575
        in small vessels, 736–737
    in dialysis shunt complications, 1771, 1772, 1775, 1776–1778
    of esophageal varices, 1422
    femoral arteriography in, 1700, 1727–1729
    femoropopliteal, angioplasty in, III:263–264, III:274, III:277
    hepatic vein, 231
    and hyperemia after central nervous system intraaxial embolotherapy, III:767
    inferior vena cava, 230
    of interlobar artery, 1109

mesenteric, 214, 229–230, 231, 1557–1570. *See also* Mesenteric angiography
    inferior mesenteric angiography in, 1593–1601, 1602
    in peripheral angioplasty, 1040
    portal vein, 231
    in puncture site complications, 1027
    in renal angioplasty, 1041
    of renal artery after angioplasty, 1041
    renal vein, after transplant, 212
    sonography flow patterns in
        arterial, 214–215, color plate 3
        venous, 215–216, color plate 4
    of splenic vein, 1480
    thromboembolic, in renal angiography, 1109
    of tumor vessels, 1781
    of vertebral artery, angioplasty in, III:761–763
Occlusion angiography, 84
Occult parathyroid adenoma, 167
Occupational dose limitation recommendations, 128
Ochsner A, III:982
Octreotide acetate, 56
    in carcinoid crisis, 1037
Ocular melanoma, III:452
Ocular vessels, sonography of, 233
Ödman P, 394, 1383, 1433, 1527, 1555
Ödman radiopaque polyethylene catheter, 394
    in pancreatic angiography, 1389, 1391
    in superior mesenteric angiography, 1555
Olbert Catheter System, III:762
Oligemia, term of, 850
O'Loughlin BJ, 932–933
Omentum, hepatoma metastases to, chemoembolization in, 167
Omnipaque. *See* Iohexol
Ondansetron, III:214
One-rescuer cardiopulmonary resuscitation, 37
On-line disk storage in digital angiography, 146–148
Onuigbo WIB, 892
Open chest cardiac massage, 40
Operability in coronary disease, 688–689
Ophthalmic artery, 257–260
    aneurysm of, 316, 317
    sonography of, 233
OPSI (overwhelming postsplenectomy infection), III:884
Opta 5 catheter, III:330
Optical disks, digital archiving and, 148
Optical distributor in digital angiography video system, 139, 140
Optics, 176–177
    contrast ratio in, 99
    image, in cine viewers, 111–113
    for image intensifiers in cardiac catheterization, 99
Optiray. *See* Ioversol
Oral contraceptives
    hepatic adenomas and, 1444
    hypertension and, 1276
    pulmonary embolism and, 809
Oral hypoglycemics, III:216–217
Orbitofrontal arteries, 266–267, 268, 270

Organ ablation, mechanical embolic agents for, III:76
Organ Injury Scaling Committee of the American Association for the Surgery of Trauma, III:422, III:428
Organic nitrates, 58
Orthopedic surgery, III:881
Osborne ED, 7, 13
Oscilloscopic recording for cardiac monitoring, 118
Osler-Weber-Rendu syndrome, 369, 377, III:74
Osmolality
  contrast agent
    cardiac complications and, 26–27, 28, 29
    physiology and, 30–31
    renal toxicity and, 24
    vascular and hematologic effects of, 24–26
  of perfusate, 24–26
Osteoarthritis, 996
Osteoblastomas, 1788, 1791
Osteochondromas, 1783, 1785
Osteogenic sarcoma of femur, 1734
Osteoid osteomas, 1770, 1787–1788, 1789
Osteomas
  osteoid, 1787–1788, 1789, 1790
  of spleen, 1482
Osteomyelitis, 1782–1783
  in mycotic aneurysms, 1077
Osteophytes in diagnostic pitfalls, 971
Osteosarcomas, 1788–1792, 1793–1795
  chemotherapy for, III:1032–1033
Ostia, coronary. *See* Coronary ostia
Otic artery, persistent, 281
Outflow occlusion, arterial, in dialysis shunt, 1776–1778
Outflow vein, dialysis shunt, complications in, 1770, 1773–1776, 1777
Outpatient
  postprocedure routine for, III:219
  preintervention assessment of, III:207
Ovarian arteries, 1021
  collateral circulation in renal ischemia and, 1277, 1280, 1283
Ovarian veins
  for inferior vena cava collateral circulation, 956, 957
  recurrent embolization of pulmonary vessels from, 966, 967
  varicocele of, III:700, III:701
Ovarian-parametrial venous complex, 951–953, 956
Ovaries
  carcinoma of, 1485
  lymphatic malignant metastases from, 1932–1933
  vascular sonography of, 233
Overframing in cinefluorography, 100–101
Overhead supports in cardiac catheterization laboratory, 105
Overwhelming postsplenectomy infection (OPSI), III:884
Oxidized cellulose in selective embolization, III:403
Oxycel. *See* Oxidized cellulose
Oxygen, III:212, III:216
  in resuscitation, 39, 45

p53 tumor suppressor protein, III:17
PAC (premature atrial contractions), 43, 44
Pacemaker, 615
  in cardiac standstill, 45
  external, in cardiac catheterization laboratory, 107
  in heart block, 43, 44
  in sinus bradycardia, 43
Pachyfibrils, III:124
PACS (Picture Archiving and Communication Systems), 148
PAD. *See* Pelvic abscess percutaneous drainage (PAD)
Page kidney, 1276, 1340
Paget-Schroetter syndrome, III:1050
Pain
  in acute mesenteric ischemia, 1627
  after ureteral stenting, III:578
  cancer, III:201–202
  chest, after bronchial artery embolization, III:827
  in deep vein thrombosis, 1750, 1752
  in dissecting aortic aneurysms, 496, 497
  electrocorporeal shock wave lithotripsy and, III:500
  in femoral arteriography, 1713–1714
  in hepatic embolization, III:440
  interventional radiology and, III:201–202
  intraprocedural control of, III:212–214
  in pancreatic venography, 1429
  in peripheral angioplasty, 1040
  postembolization syndrome and, III:202
  in renal angioplasty, III:297–298
  in renal cell carcinoma, 1138
  in renal hamartoma, 1163
  in systemic reactions to contrast agents, 29
PAIs (plasminogen activator inhibitors), III:123
Pako film processor, 112
Palmaz stent, III:86–87
  in aortoiliac interventions, III:101–108, III:234, III:236–238, III:252–253, III:254
  balloon angioplasty catheter compatibility with, III:39
  balloon-expandable intraluminal, III:86–87
  in benign biliary obstruction, III:462–464
  complications of, 1042, III:1054–1055, III:1056
  current use of, III:85
  deformation of, in dialysis fistula stenoses, III:740
  in external iliac artery stenosis after transplant, 1343
  in extracranial brachiocephalic angioplasty, III:352–354
  history of use of, III:1047
  lumen diameter after, III:7
  in malignant biliary obstruction, III:478–479
  in mesenteric ischemia, III:329–330
  principles for use of, III:1048
  in renal angioplasty, III:321
  in restenosis after balloon angioplasty, III:14–15, III:321
  sizes of, III:87

in transjugular intrahepatic portosystemic shunt, III:532–533
Palmaz-Schatz stent
  in coronary angioplasty, III:375–376
  current use of, III:85
  lumen diameter after, III:7
  in renal artery disease, III:115–116
  in restenosis after balloon angioplasty, III:14–15
Pampiniform plexus, III:678
Pancoast tumors, 996
Pancreas. *See also* Pancreatic disease
  abscesses of, III:935–936
  biopsy of
    complications of, 1035
    percutaneous image-guided, III:187–188
  carcinoma of. *See* Pancreatic carcinoma
  cysts of, vascular displacement in, 1465
  hemorrhage of, superselective catheterization in, 168
  in inferior vena cava obstruction, 958, 959
  injury to, in extracorporeal shock wave lithotripsy complication, III:607
  pseudocysts of, 1465
  transplants of, 1415
Pancreatic angiography, 1383–1548
  anterior (AP) projection in, 1385, 1392
  arterial portography and, 1527–1548. *See also* Arterial portography
  bradykinin and, 62, 1392, 1394
  complications of, 1396
  hepatic arteriography and, 1433–1456. *See also* Hepatic arteriography
  in pancreatic disease, 1390, 1391, 1393–1395, 1396–1415
    of angiomatous lesions, 1404, 1406–1409
    of cystic neoplasms, 1393, 1405–1406, 1407, 1408
    of insulinoma and gastrinoma, 1403–1405
    of islet cell tumors, 1401–1403, 1405
    of leiomyosarcoma, reticulum cell sarcoma, and other retroperitoneal tumors, 1406–1409
    of pancreatic carcinoma, 1390, 1391, 1393–1395, 1396–1401
    of pancreatitis, 1400, 1401, 1410–1414
    of pseudocysts and abscesses, 1401, 1402, 1408, 1409, 1413, 1414–1415
    in Rendu-Osler-Weber disease, 1404, 1406–1409
    with transplantation, 1415
    of trauma, 1409, 1415
    of uncommon tumors, 1404, 1406–1409
    of VIPomas, glucagonomas, somatostatinomas, PPomas, and carcinoid tumors, 1405, 1406
  portal and pancreatic venography in, 1422–1432
  right posterior oblique (RPO) projection in, 1386, 1392
  splenic arteriography and, 1457–1496. *See also* Splenic arteriography
  splenoportography and, 1497–1526

Pancreatic angiography—*Continued*
  technique for, 1389–1396
    contrast material and filming, 1395–
      1396
    pharmacoangiography, 1385–1387,
      1390, 1392–1394
    routine, 1392
    simultaneous and sequential
      approaches in, 1391
    superselective angiography, 1388–
      1389, 1394–1395
    vascular anatomy in, 1383–1389, 1390,
      1391
      arterial, 1383–1389, 1390, 1391
      venous, 1385–1387, 1389
Pancreatic artery
  dorsal, 1387, 1388–1391
  magnification angiography of, 181
  transverse, 1387
Pancreatic branches of splenic artery,
    1458–1460
  to body and tail of pancreas, 1385–1387
  caudal, 1459, 1460
  dorsal, 1458, 1459, 1460
  superior, of Testus, 1458, 1459, 1460
Pancreatic carcinoma
  angiography in, 1390, 1391, 1393–
    1395, 1396–1401
  cystadenocarcinoma and, 1407, 1408
  diagnosis of, 1390, 1391, 1393–1401
    differential, 1398–1399
  irregular arterial stenosis in, 1465, 1466
  pancreatitis versus, 1413–1414
  resectability and operability of, 1400–
    1401, 1402
    inoperable carcinoma in, 1397
  superior mesenteric angiography in,
    1568, 1570
  vascular displacement in, in splenic arteri-
    ography, 1465
  venography in, 1429
Pancreatic cysts, vascular displacement in,
    1465
Pancreatic disease. *See also* Pancreas
  abdominal abscesses in, III:932–936
  pancreatitis in
    after in biliary calculi removal, III:
      492–493
    biopsy in, III:187–188
    electrocorporeal shock wave lithotripsy
      and, III:500
Pancreatic magna artery, 1385–1387
Pancreatic pseudocysts, 1465
Pancreatic transplants, 1415
Pancreatic veins
  anatomy of, 1426–1427, 1428
  in arterial portography, 1532
  catheterization of
    complications of, 1428–1429
    in endocrine tumors, 1429–1431
    indications for, 1428
    technique of, 1428
  magnification angiography of, 181
  transverse, 1427, 1428
Pancreatic venography, 1426–1432
  anatomy in, 1426–1427, 1428
  complications of, 1428–1429
  in endocrine tumors, 1429–1431
  indications for, 1428
  technique of, 1428
Pancreaticoduodenal arcade, 1018

Pancreaticoduodenal artery, 1384–1387,
    1390, 1391
  in arterial portography, 1543, 1544
  inferior, in superior mesenteric angiogra-
    phy, 1550–1551
Pancreaticoduodenal trunk, 1019
Pancreaticoduodenal veins
  posterior inferior (PIPD), 1426
  posterior superior (PSPD), 1426, 1427,
    1429
Pancreatitis, 1400, 1401, 1410–1414
  acute, 1409
    recurrent, 1400, 1401, 1409–1411
  after pancreatic angiography, 1396
  after partial splenic ablation, 1493
  chronic, 1401, 1402, 1411–1414
    compression of splenic vein in, 1400
    pancreatic venography in, 1429
    with pseudocyst in tail of pancreas,
      1401
    with recurrent acute pancreatitis,
      1400, 1401, 1409–1411
    superior mesenteric angiography in,
      1568, 1570
Pancuronium bromide, 48
Pantopaque
  in bronchial artery embolization, III:826
  with cyanoacrylates in arteriovenous mal-
    formation embolization, III:1015,
    III:1016
  in renal cyst sclerosis, III:663, III:665
Papaverine, 53, 57
  action of, 52, 53
  in acute mesenteric ischemia, 1617,
    1625–1629
  in arterial portography, 1530
  in cavernosometry, 1643–1645
  in extremity trauma, III:861
  in infrapopliteal revascularization, III:
    290
  intraaxial embolotherapy for central ner-
    vous system and, III:767
  metabolism of, 49
  in pancreatic angiography, 1392
  in penile duplex sonography, III:719
  in pharmacologic erection, III:706–707,
    III:708
  for vasospasm at puncture site, 1028
Papillary tumors of kidney, 1154–1158
PAPVC. *See* Partial anomalous pulmonary
    venous connection (PAPVC)
Paraaortic adenopathy
  in inferior vena cava obstruction, 962
  in malignant lymphoma, 1942
Paradoxical embolization of balloon or
    coils in pulmonary arteriovenous
    malformations, III:845, III:850
Paraganglioma in pelvis, 1370
Parallel cine technique for digital archiving,
    149
Parallelogram design of x-ray platform,
    134
Paralysis, phrenic, 816
Paralytic ileus, lithotripsy and, III:500
Parapelvic cyst, III:658, III:665
Paraplegia
  after surgery for thoracic aneurysm
    repair, 483
  after thoracic surgery, III:364
  dissecting aortic aneurysms with, 496,
    497

Paraprosthetic fluid aspiration after aorto-
    iliac interventions, 1694, 1695
Parasagittal surfaces of skull vault,
    extraaxial lesions of, III:791–793
Parasellar region, intracranial, extraaxial
    lesions of, III:794, III:799–800,
    III:809–812
Parathyroid adenomas
  below thyroid lobe, 981
  intrathymic, 979
  left inferior, 978
  occult, superselective catheterization in,
    167
  previous unsuccessful surgery and, 980
  thyroid arteries to, 985
Parathyroid angiography, 976–994
  complications of, 984
  in mediastinal adenomas, 988–990
  parathyroid venous sampling in, 984–
    988
  percutaneous aspiration for parathyroid
    hormone assay in, 977
  procedure and uses of, 977–980, 981–
    986
  for transcatheter therapy, 990–992
Parathyroid glands
  ectopic superior, 988
  hyperplastic, 983
  magnification angiography of, 186
  normal, 980
Parathyroid hormone (PTH)
  gradient of, in thyroid vein, 987
    mediastinal adenomas and, 982–983
  percutaneous aspiration for assay of, 977
Parathyroid venous sampling, 984–988
Paratracheal lymph nodes, 1887
Parenchyma
  cerebral
    hemorrhage or edema in, 251, 342
    vascular malformations of cerebral
      arteries and, 323, 324
  pulmonary, biopsy of, III:185
  renal
    benign disease of, 1315–1320
    biopsy and, III:189
    malformation of, 1222–1228
Paresthesias after transaxillary arteriogra-
    phy, 1031
Parietal artery, posterior, 271
Parietal collateral network, 957, 958,
    1063, 1065, 1067–1069
Parietal lobe, blood supply to, 270
Parietes-retroperitoneal portal collaterals,
    957, 958
Parietooccipital arteries, 274
Parkes Weber syndrome, III:1028, III:
    1029
Parodi endovascular stent-graft placement
    in thoracic aortic aneurysms, III:
    357
Partial anomalous pulmonary venous con-
    nection (PAPVC), 879–887
  anatomy of, 881–883
  angiography of, 882, 886–887
  atrial septal defect in, 880–887
  cardiac, 884, 886
  clinical aspects of, 884
  embryology of, 881, 882
  physiology of, 883–884
  plain films of, 883, 884–886

scimitar syndrome or sign in, 882–883, 885, 886, 887
Partial thromboplastin time (PTT), III: 207, III:208
  intraarterial chemotherapy and, III:1034
  transcatheter thrombolysis and, III:1047
Parvus waveform, 222, 224–225
Patch
  in coarctation of aorta repair, 453, 454, 455, 456
  in dialysis fistula thromboses, III:727
  in renal transplantation, 1325, 1326
Patency rates in iliac artery angioplasty, III: 245, III:246, III:247
Patent blue-violet dye in lymphangiography, 1866
  allergy to, 1868
Patent ductus arteriosus (PDA), 415–433, 833, 838, 839
  anatomy of, 416–417
  aorticopulmonary window and, 464, 465
  central pulmonary artery stenosis and, 831
  clinical features of, 418–420
  coarctation of aorta and, 435, 444, 445
  complications of, after therapy, 429–430
  definition of, 415
  differential diagnosis of, 420
  ductal closure and, 417–418, 419
  embryology of, 415–416
  incidence of, 415
  management of, 426–430
    complications of, 427
    nonsurgical, 427–430
    surgical, 426–427
  natural history of, 420–421
  pulmonary arteriography in, 796, 798
  radiology in, 416, 417, 421–426
    angiography, 416, 417, 422–426
    chest x-ray, 421–422, 423
    echocardiography, 422, 423
    magnetic resonance imaging, 426
  thoracic aortic aneurysms and, 488
  thoracic aortography in, 396
  in total anomalous pulmonary venous connection, 873
Patient
  cardiac catheterization
    exposure in, 129–130
    monitoring in, 114–119
    radiation exposure calculation for, 129
    safety for, 114–116
    supports for, 103–105
  femoral arteriography
    positioning for, 1707–1711
    preparation for, 1713
  pediatric, preparation of, III:903–904
  positioning of
    for arterial portography, 1529–1530
    for femoral arteriography, 1707–1711
    for transaxillary catheterization, 1016
Paulin S, 1743
PAVMs. *See* Pulmonary arteriovenous malformations (PAVMs)
Pavulon. *See* Pancuronium bromide
PBD (percutaneous biliary drainage) in malignant obstructions, III:473–476
PC angiography. *See* Phase contrast (PC) angiography

PCCL (percutaneous cholecystolithotomy), III:487–489
PCN. *See* Percutaneous nephrostomy (PCN)
PCOM. *See* Communicating arteries, posterior (PCOM)
PCV (precentral cerebellar vein), 278
PDA (posterior descending artery), left, 614. *See also* Patent ductus arteriosus (PDA)
Peak detected x-ray exposure, 139, 140
Peak velocity
  in arterial occlusion and stenosis, 215
    of mesenteric artery, 229–230
  in arterial thromboses, 217
  in carotid arteries, 220
    Doppler velocity ratio and, 223
  in leg arteries, 212, 213
Pedal veins
  dorsal, in venography, 1744
  runoff, 1831
Pediatrics
  cardiac catheterization laboratory for, 122
  complications of coronary arteriography in, 579–580
  interventional angiography in, III:901–921
    anesthesia for, III:903
    angioplasty in, III:910–916, III:917
    cardiac catheterization laboratory for, 122
    cardiopulmonary resuscitation in, 36, 39–40
    coagulation and, III:903
    complications of, III:908, III:917–920
    consent for, III:903
    diet and medications and, III:904
    embolization techniques for, III:904–908, III:909, III:910
    foreign-body removal in, III:919
    immobilization for, III:903
    new directions for, III:920
    patient preparation for, III:903–904
    postoperative care for, III:904
    radiation dose and fluids and, III:904
    temperature control and, III:904
    thrombolysis in, III:153–154, III:916–919
PEG (percutaneous endoscopic gastrostomy), III:547. *See also* Percutaneous gastrostomy
Peirce EC II, 391, 394, 1013
Pelvic abscess percutaneous drainage (PAD), III:939–955
  access route in, III:948–951
  analgesics in, III:947
  catheters in
    insertion of, III:952
    lavage and irrigation of, III:952
    management of, III:952–953
    problems with, III:953–954
    selection of, III:951–952
    withdrawal of, III:952–953
  common sites and etiologies of abscess in, III:939–940
  complications and failures in, III:954
  consultation for, III:947
  in Crohn disease, III:942–943
  diagnostic aspiration and, III:947–948

fluid collections and, III:944, III:945
  common sites and etiologies of, III: 939
  imaging method for, III:946–947
  in infected tumors, III:944, III:945
  interventional rounds in, III:953–954
  intravenous drugs in, III:947
  in lymphoceles, III:944–946
  in periappendicular abscess, III:941–942
  principles for, III:941–946
  in sigmoid peridiverticular abscess, III: 941
  tools and technique for, III:947–954
  transabdominal, III:948–949
  transgluteal, III:949–951
  transrectal, III:951
  transvaginal, III:951
  in tuboovarian abscesses, III:944
  in urinomas, III:946
Pelvic angiography, 1636–1668. *See also* Abdomen and pelvis
  in aortoiliac disease before revascularization, III:230
  in arteriosclerotic disease of pelvic arteries, 1637, 1638–1640
  digital angiography in, 1636–1638
  in gynecology, 1646–1648, 1649
  in intraarterial fibrinolytic therapy, 1640–1641, 1642
  magnetic resonance angiography in, 1636, 1637
  in male impotence assessment, 1641–1645
  in obstetrics, 1646, 1647
  in pelvic arteriovenous malformations, 1654–1658
  in pelvic hemorrhage diagnosis, 1648–1650, 1651, 1652
    technique for, 1650, 1651, 1652
  in pelvic neoplasms, 1645–1646, 1647
  in pelvic venography, 1664, 1665
  in superselective chemotherapy and chemoembolization, 1661–1665
  in transcatheter embolization
    for high-flow priapism, 1661
    for intractable hemorrhage from neoplastic disease, 1658–1661
    for uncontrollable hemorrhage from pelvic organs, 1650–1654
Pelvic arteries
  arteriosclerosis of, 1637, 1638–1640
  in renal angiography, 1114, 1118, 1119, 1120–1122, 1124
  thrombolysis in, III:136, III:139–144
Pelvic arteriovenous malformations, 1654–1658
Pelvic exenteration, ureteral strictures after, III:578
Pelvic fractures
  in blunt trauma, 523–524
  hemorrhage from, III:869–883. *See also* Pelvic fractures, interventional radiology in
  interventional radiology in, III:869–883
    angiography in, III:871–877, III:878
    embolization in, III:877–881
    hemorrhage in, III:869–871
    in obstetric procedures, III:881
    in orthopedic surgery, III:881
    in penetrating trauma, III:881
  mechanisms of injury in, III:870

Pelvic pressure, normal, 1202
Pelvic tumors
  embolization in, 1814–1815
  pelvic angiography in, 1645–1646, 1647
  renal, 1154–1161
    diagnostic evaluation of, 1159–1160,
      1161, 1162
    differential diagnosis of, 1160–1161
    pathology of, 1154–1158
    symptoms and signs of, 1158–1159
    treatment of, 1161
  superselective catheterization in, 169
  transcatheter embolization in, 1658–
    1661
Pelvic veins, venography of, 1664, 1665
  magnetic, in deep vein thrombosis, 1850
Pelvis. *See also* Abdomen and pelvis; Pelvic
    angiography
  abscess of, percutaneous drainage in, III:
    939–955. *See also* Pelvic abscess per-
    cutaneous drainage (PAD)
  adhesions and varicosities in, III:397,
    III:399
  arteriovenous malformations in, III:
    1016–1018, III:1019, III:1020
    absolute alcohol embolization for, III:
      1015
    clinical features of, III:1006, III:1007
  collateral vessels of, III:681, III:687
  fluid collections in, percutaneous drain-
    age of, III:944, III:945. *See also* Pel-
    vic abscess percutaneous drainage
    (PAD)
  fractures of. *See* Pelvic fractures
  hemorrhage in
    diagnosis of, 1648–1650, 1651, 1652
    from fractures, III:869–883. *See also*
      Pelvic fractures, interventional radiol-
      ogy in
  lymph nodes of, 1876–1879
  neoplasms in. *See* Pelvic tumors
  paraganglioma in, 1370
  trauma to
    erectile dysfunction after, 1644–1645
    fractures in. *See* Pelvic fractures
      hemorrhage from, III:869–883, 1727.
        See also Pelvic fractures, interven-
        tional radiology in
    superselective catheterization in, 169
  tumors of. *See* Pelvic tumors
Pelviureteric varices, 1311–1314, 1315
PE-MT5 catheter, III:330
Penetrating trauma
  of extremities
    arteriography indications in, III:858–
      859
    upper, 1756, 1757–1758
  pelvic interventional radiology in, III:
    881. *See also* Pelvic fractures
Penicillin, 1492
Penile artery
  anatomic variants of, III:711–712
  common, 1544, 1644, 1645
    branches of, III:711
  dorsal, 1645
    embolization of, 1661
Penile vascular catheterization in erectile
    dysfunction, III:705–725
  background of, III:707–708
  cavernosal pulse amplitude in, III:717,
    III:718

cavernosography in, III:715–721
diagnostic, III:707–710
duplex sonography in, III:719–721
indications for, III:708–709
interpretation of, III:708, III:710
methodology in study of, III:708, III:
  709–710
pharmacocavernosometry in, III:716–
  717
physiology of erection in, III:705–
  707
suboptimal results in, III:723–724
transluminal therapy in, III:714–715,
  III:720, III:721–723
yield in, III:708
Penile vein
  anatomy of, III:719
  deep dorsal, 1642
    on cavernosography, III:715–716, III:
      719, III:721
  leakage from, mechanical embolic agents
    for, III:76
Penile venoablation in erectile dysfunction,
  III:715, III:720–721, III:722–723
Penis. *See also* Male impotence
  carcinoma of, 1933, 1935
  collateral circulation to, III:712, III:
    714–715
  vascular sonography of, 232
Pentothal, 398
Peptic ulceration, III:392, III:404–405,
  III:406, III:408–410
Peptides, gastroenteropancreatic, 56
Per-Abrodil. *See* Iodopyracet
Percent diameter stenosis, 657
Perception of x-ray images in magnification
  angiography, 178–179
Percuflex endoprosthesis
  in malignant hepatobiliary obstructions,
    III:479–480
  as ureteral stent, III:573
Percutaneous abscess drainage
  abdominal, III:925–938. *See also*
    Abdominal abscesses, percutaneous
    drainage of
  mediastinal, III:832–835
  pelvic, III:939–955. *See also* Pelvic abscess
    percutaneous drainage (PAD)
  peridiverticular sigmoid, III:941
  perirenal, III:936
Percutaneous angioplasty. *See also* Angio-
    plasty
  femoral arteriography in, 1709
  sonography of, 226–227, 228, color
    plates 1 and 2
Percutaneous angioscopy of inferior vena
  cava, 940–941
Percutaneous aortoiliac intervention
  angioplasty in, III:98–100, III:230–232,
    III:233
    complications of, III:254–256
    results of, III:98–100, III:244–254
    stents with, III:100–108
  atherectomy in, III:234–240
  clinical evaluation for, III:225–229
  complications of, III:244, III:254–256,
    III:257
  conclusions for, III:256–258
  contraindications to, III:244
  factors influencing outcome of, III:240

in femoropopliteal disease, III:262–283.
  See also Femoropopliteal revascularization
history before, III:225–228
iliac, III:245–247, III:248
indications for, III:227, III:228, III:
  235, III:240–244, III:256–257
in infrapopliteal disease, III:284–293.
  See also Infrapopliteal revascularization
infrarenal, III:247–250
noninvasive vascular testing before, III:
  228–229
patient preparation for, III:229–230,
  III:231
physical examination before, III:225–
  228
progression of, after intervention, 1682,
  1685, 1687–1689, 1690–1695
results of, III:98–100, III:244–254
  angioplasty in, III:245–247, III:248
  atherectomy in, III:254
  infrarenal aortic percutaneous translu-
    minal angioplasty in, III:247–250
  intravascular stents in, III:236–237,
    III:251–254, III:255
  stents in, III:236–237, III:251–254,
    III:255
  thrombolysis in, III:228, III:250–
    255
SCVIR guidelines for, III:240–241
stents in, III:100–108, III:234, III:
  236–238
  results of, III:236–237, III:251–254,
    III:255
techniques for, III:230–232, III:233
thrombolysis in, III:232–234, III:235
  results of, III:250–255
in tibial occlusive disease, III:284. *See
  also* Infrapopliteal revascularization
Percutaneous approach. *See also* Percutaneous catheterization
in aortoiliac disease. *See* Percutaneous
  aortoiliac intervention
in atherosclerosis obliterans, 1719,
  1721, 1723, 1724
in nephrolithotomy and nephrostomy,
  1036–1037
to portal vein, 1424–1426
retrograde transfemoral
  in aortic arch anomalies, 547
  in dissecting aortic aneurysms, 503
in transhepatic cholangiography, 1037–
  1038
in transluminal angioplasty. *See* Percutaneous transluminal angioplasty
  (PTA)
Percutaneous aspiration for parathyroid
  hormone assay, 977
Percutaneous biliary calculi removal, III:
  491–508
  cholecystolithotomy in, III:501–507
  complications in, III:496–501
  morbidity and mortality in, III:501
  patient preparation for, III:491–492
  through T-tube tract, III:492–495
  transhepatic choledocholithotomy and,
    III:495–496
  transjejunal choledocholithotomy and,
    III:496

Percutaneous biliary drainage (PBD) in malignant hepatobiliary obstructions, III:473–476
Percutaneous biopsy, image-guided. *See* Percutaneous image-guided biopsy
Percutaneous catheterization. *See also* Percutaneous approach
  in atherectomy, 226–227, 228, color plates 1 and 2
  in cisterna chyli cannulation, 1901–1902
  in hepatic tumor ablation, 1037
  in renal artery thrombolysis after transplant, 1338
  technique for, 1014
  transaxillary, 1016
  transfemoral, 1013–1016. *See also* Percutaneous approach, retrograde transfemoral
    in inferior mesenteric arteriography, 1587
  translumbar, 1016–1017
Percutaneous cholecystolithotomy (PCCL), III:487–489, III:501–507
  complications of, III:500
  extracorporeal shock wave lithotripsy in, III:505
  gallstone dissolution therapy and, III:504–505
  laparoscopic cholecystectomy versus, III:505–506
  morbidity in, III:500
  preferred methods for, III:502–504
  in removal of biliary calculi, III:501–507
  results of, III:505–507
  techniques for, III:501–502
Percutaneous cholecystostomy, III:483–490
  complications of, III:489
  diagnostic indications for, III:485–486
  history of, III:483
  interventional indications for, III:485, III:486–487, III:488
  percutaneous cholecystolithotomy in, III:487–489
  technical considerations in, III:483–485
Percutaneous drainage of abscesses
  abdominal, III:925–938. *See also* Abdominal abscesses, percutaneous drainage of
  mediastinal, III:832–835
  pelvic, III:939–955. *See also* Pelvic abscess percutaneous drainage (PAD)
  peridiverticular sigmoid, III:941
  perirenal, III:936
Percutaneous endoscopic gastrostomy (PEG), III:547. *See also* Percutaneous gastrostomy
Percutaneous endoscopy in biliary calculi removal complications, III:500–501
Percutaneous fluid collection drainage, III:939–955
Percutaneous gastrojejunostomy
  advantages and disadvantages of, III:557
  complications of, III:556–557
  contraindications to, III:548
  gastrostomy versus, III:547–548
  indications for, III:547–548
  management of, III:554–555
  results of, III:556

technique of, III:549–552, III:553
  procedural modifications in, III:552–554
Percutaneous gastrostomy, 1038–1039, III:547–558
  advantages and disadvantages of, III:557
  button placement in, III:555–556
  complications of, III:556–557
  contraindications to, III:548
  gastrojejunostomy versus, III:547–548
  gastrostomy button placement in, III:555–556
  indications for, III:547–548
  management of, III:554–555
  results of, III:556
  technique of, III:548–549, III:550–552
    procedural modifications in, III:552–554
  tube removal after, III:555
Percutaneous image-guided biopsy, III:166–194
  of breast, III:1037–1046
  complications of, III:178–184
    bleeding in, III:180–183
    needle track seeding in, III:183–184
    pneumothorax in, III:178–179
    protective measures in, III:182–183
  contraindications to, III:178
  history of, III:166
  indications for, III:178
  of lung, complications of, 1033–1035
  in malignant hepatobiliary obstructions, III:476
  pathology and, III:166–171, III:172–173
  regional considerations for, III:184–192
    adrenal gland, III:189–190
    hepatic, III:186–187
    musculoskeletal system, III:190–192
    pancreatic, III:187–188
    peritoneal and retroperitoneal, III:190
    renal, III:188–189
    thoracic, III:184–186, III:187
  in renal transplant dysfunction, 1335
  technical considerations in, III:171–177
    complications and, III:182
    devices and, III:174
    guidance modalities and, III:175–177
    technique and, III:174–175
Percutaneous infundibuloplasty, III:595
Percutaneous large-core breast biopsy, III:1037–1046. *See also* Percutaneous image-guided biopsy
Percutaneous nephrostomy (PCN), III:561–572
  catheter in. *See* Nephrostomy catheter
  complications of, 1036–1037, III:568–570
    renal vascular injuries in, 1230–1231
  contraindications to, III:566
  follow-up after, III:570–572
  postprocedural care for, III:219–221
  puncture site for, III:565–566
  pyopneumothorax after, 1036
  results of, III:567–568
  technique for, III:562–566
Percutaneous pelvic abscess drainage, III:939–955. *See also* Pelvic abscess percutaneous drainage (PAD)
Percutaneous removal of calculi
  biliary, III:491–508. *See also* Percutaneous biliary calculi removal

renal (PCNL), III:587–603, III:604. *See also* Percutaneous renal calculi removal (PCNL)
Percutaneous renal calculi removal (PCNL), III:587–603, III:604
  complications of, III:602–603, III:604
  contraindications to, III:601–602
  electrohydraulic lithotripsy with, III:601
  extracorporeal shock wave lithotripsy with, III:588–589
  flexible ureteroscopy with, III:595
  indications for, III:587–599
    abnormal body habitat in, III:597, III:598
    anatomic abnormalities in, III:597, III:598
    certainty of final results in, III:597–598
    compromised urinary drainage in, III:590–596, III:597
    staghorn calculi in, III:588–590, III:591, III:592
    stone composition in, III:596–597
    stone size in, III:587–588, III:589
    symptomatic stones during pregnancy in, III:598–599
    urinary obstruction in, III:590–596, III:597
  multiple access tracts in, III:600–601
  retrograde approach in, III:599–600
  technique for, III:599–601
  ultrasonic lithotripsy with, III:601
Percutaneous revision of surgical portosystemic shunts, III:528–530
Percutaneous stent, III:71. *See also* Stents
Percutaneous suction thromboembolectomy, III:160–165
  background of, III:160–161
  drawbacks of, III:162–163
  indications for, III:161
  investigational devices in, III:164
  method of, III:161–163
  results of, III:163–164
Percutaneous transhepatic approach
  in cholangiography. *See* Percutaneous transhepatic cholangiography (PTC)
  in malignant hepatobiliary obstructions, III:473–476
  in portal hypertension and esophageal varices, III:526
  to portal vein, III:397, III:398
  in primary sclerosing cholangitis, III:466–467, III:468, III:469
Percutaneous transhepatic cholangiography (PTC)
  in benign biliary obstructions, III:458, III:460
  complications of, 1037–1038
    in hepatobiliary malignancy, III:473
  in liver transplantation complications, III:509
  in malignant hepatobiliary obstructions, III:473–476
Percutaneous transhepatic variceal embolization, III:526–528, III:529
Percutaneous transluminal angioplasty (PTA), 457–460
  angiotensin II and, 51
  aortic. *See* Percutaneous aortoiliac intervention
  with bypasses, III:241, III:244

Percutaneous transluminal angioplasty
(PTA)—*Continued*
catheter in. *See* Balloon catheter
in chronic mesenteric ischemia, 1633–
1634
complications of, 459–460, 1039–1041
at coarctation site, 459
at femoral puncture site, 459–460
intravascular stenting for, III:85–86.
See also Stents
coronary arteriography in choice of, 684
endothelins and, 51
in erectile dysfunction, III:714–715, III:
720–721, III:722
extracranial brachiocephalic. *See* Extracranial brachiocephalic arterioplasty
extremity angiography in, 1690
factors influencing outcome of, III:240
femoral arteriography after, 1712
femoropopliteal. *See* Femoropopliteal
revascularization
"Guidelines for Peripheral Percutaneous Transluminal Angioplasty of
Abdominal Aorta and Lower
Extremity Vessels" and, III:97,
III:98
history of catheter for, III:24–25, III:26
iliac, III:98–100
stents with, III:100–108
imaging follow-up after, 460
indications and patient selection for,
457–458, III:240–244
in infant, 458
infrapopliteal. *See* Infrapopliteal revascularization
in liver transplantation biliary tract reconstruction, III:515–517
long-term efficacy of, III:241–242
mortality in, 572
nitrates and, 58
overuse of, III:205
pathophysiologic mechanisms of, III:3–
5, III:6. *See also* Balloon angioplasty
postintervention care for, III:219–221
in renal angioplasty. *See* Renal angioplasty
in renal artery dysplasia, 1257, 1287
in renal artery stenosis after renal transplantation, 1339–1340
restenosis after, III:5–19. *See also* Balloon angioplasty, restenosis after
results of, 458–459
SCVIR guidelines for, III:240–241
in subclavian, innominate, and vertebral
vessels, 1765, III:761–763
technique of, 458
Percutaneous transluminal coronary angioplasty (PTCA). *See also* Coronary
angioplasty; Percutaneous transluminal angioplasty (PTA)
angiotensin II and, 51
coronary arteriography in choice of, 684
Percutaneous transluminal coronary angioplasty (PTCA) Registry, III:366
Percutaneous transluminal renal angioplasty (PTRA), III:112, III:113–
115, III:294. *See also* Renal angioplasty
Percutaneous varicocele embolization, III:
693–699
results of, III:699

Percutaneous vena cava filter placement,
III:985–986
Pereiras R, 7, 8, 391, 392
Perey O, 893
Perforating arteries
of adrenal gland, 1352–1353
in renal angiography, 1118
Perforating branches of profunda femoris
artery, 1698, 1699
Perforation
of iliac vein, 971
myocardial, 783
in percutaneous stone removal complications, III:602, III:603–604
septal, 637
of spleen in percutaneous nephrostomy,
III:569
of stomach by gastrostomy tube, III:556
in superselective catheterization, 166
of viscus, abscesses after, III:925
Perfusate, osmolality of, 24–26
Perfusion, pulmonary, regional variations
in, 849–850. *See also* Lung
Periappendicular abscess, percutaneous
drainage of, III:941–942
efficacy and rational of, III:940
Periarterial fibroplasia of renal arteries,
1255–1256
Periarteritis nodosa, 1273
Pericallosal segment of anterior cerebral
artery, 264–266
Pericardiophrenic veins, 955
Pericarditis, 497
Pericatheter thrombosis as complication of
transgraft thrombolysis, III:155
Peridiverticular abscess drainage, sigmoid,
III:941
Perineal abscess after prostatic
urethroplasty, III:632
Perineal trauma, 1644–1645
Perinephric abscess, 1185, 1190–1191,
1676
Perinephric hematoma after stone removal,
III:602
Perinephric metastases, 941
Peripelvic renal cysts, III:658
Peripelvic vessels in renal ischemia, 1276–
1284
Peripheral angiography
bradykinin and, 62
nitrates and, 58
optimal resources for, 133. *See also*
Equipment, angiographic
without film changer, 83–84
Peripheral angioplasty, complications of,
1039–1041
Peripheral arterial disease, sonography of,
222–227, 228, color plates 1, 2, 10
and 11
Peripheral artery aneurysms, 1709–1711
Peripheral artery arteriovenous fistulas,
1709–1711
Peripheral bypass grafts
causes of occlusion in, III:145
thrombolysis in, III:144–146, III:147
Peripheral pulmonary arteries, developmental anomalies of, 839–844
aneurysms in, 843, 845
arteriovenous malformations in, 844,
846
hypoplasia in, 842–843

pulmonary sequestration in, 840–842
stenosis in, 843, 844
supplied by systemic arteries, 840, 841,
842
Peripheral runoff
in femoral arteriography, 1706–1707,
1712, 1713
in magnetic resonance angiography,
1823, 1831, 1832
Peripheral vascular disease
cross-sectional anatomy of, 1826–1828
diagrams of, 1826, 1827
femoral arteriography in, 1707–1709
imaging algorithm for, 1834
magnetic resonance angiography in,
1822–1836. *See also* Peripheral vascular magnetic resonance angiography (PVMRA)
Peripheral vascular magnetic resonance
angiography (PVMRA), 1822–1863
after aortoiliac interventions, 1695
artifacts in, 1828–1829, 1830
axial angiography in, 1824–1825
contrast angiography compared to,
1831–1833
aortoiliac system and, 1831–1833
runoff vessels and, 1831, 1832
cross-sectional vascular anatomy in,
1826–1828
examination time for, 1833
gadolinium in, 1829–1831
noninvasive imaging and, 1822
overestimation of occlusive disease in,
1833
peripheral runoff in, 1823, 1831, 1832
pitfalls of, 1833
techniques for, 1823–1824, 1825
uses of, 1833–1835
introduction and, 1822–1823
venography in, 1837–1863. *See also* Venography, of extremities
Peripherally inserted central catheters
(PICC), III:969
Perirectal varices, 1850
Perirenal abscesses, percutaneous drainage
of, III:936
Peritoneal dialysis, 1850
Peritoneum
biopsy of, III:190
inferior vena cava obstruction and, 958
Peritonitis
abscesses after, III:925
after percutaneous gastrostomy, 1038
bile, III:489
Peritubular plexus, 1118
Periureteric stenosis, renal transplant
obstruction from, III:581
Periureteric vessels in renal ischemia,
1276–1284
Periurethral abscess, III:618
Peroneal arteries
anterior, 1698
arteriovenous fistula of, in puncture site
complications, 1027, 1028
collateral circulation of, 1703
posterior, 1698
Peroneal vein, 1744, 1747
Persantine. *See* Dipyridamole
Persistent cardinal or supracardinal veins,
945, 947

Persistent circumaortic venous ring, 947, 950
Persistent hypoglossal artery, 281
Persistent left inferior vena cava, 900, 904
Persistent left innominate vein, 926
Persistent left superior vena cava, 900, 909, 920–927
    superior vena cava syndrome in, 926
Persistent mesenteric vasoconstriction, 1616
Persistent otic artery, 281
Persistent trigeminal artery, 281, 548
Persistent truncus arteriosus. *See* Truncus arteriosus
Personnel
    in cardiac catheterization laboratory, 130–133
        exposure of, 128–129
    for cerebral angiography, 247
    for vascular intervention angiography, 135–136
PET (positron emission tomography), 660
Peter Bent Brigham Hospital classification of dissecting aortic aneurysms, 495, 504
Petrén T, 1426
Petroclival meningioma, embolization in, III:809–814
Petrosal sinus
    dural arteriovenous malformations of, III:800, III:801
    superior, 280
Petrosal veins, 279, 280
    sampling from, for adrenocorticotropic hormone, 253
Petrous carotid artery aneurysm, III:768–769
Pfeiffer H, 18
PGE₁. *See* Prostaglandin E₁ (PGE₁)
PGF₂α (prostaglandin F₂α), 60–61, 1394
PGI₂ (prostacyclin), 61, III:15
Pharmacoangiography, 49–65
    agents in, 52–60
        bradykinin as, 62
        dopamine as, 61
        general characteristics of, 49
        glucagon as, 61–62
        prostaglandins as, 60–61
        vasoconstrictor, 52–56
        vasodilator, 57–60
    cell biology and physiology of blood vessels in, 50–52
    in pancreatic angiography, 1385–1387, 1390, 1392–1394
    in portal system in arterial portography, 1530
    in superior mesenteric angiography, 1557, 1558
Pharmacoangiography in erectile dysfunction, III:708
Pharmacocavernosography, III:708, III:715–721
Pharmacocavernosometry, III:708, III:716–717
Pharmacologic control of bleeding in portal hypertension, III:525
Pharmacologic erection, III:706–707
    pharmacoangiography and, III:708
Pharmacologic maintenance erectile flow (PMEF), III:708, III:710, III:716–717, III:720–721

Pharmacologic vasodilation in post-subarachnoid hemorrhage vaso-spasm, III:753–757, III:758
Pharmacomechanical thrombolysis, pulse-spray. *See* Pulse-spray pharmaco-mechanical thrombolysis (PSPMT)
Pharyngeal artery, ascending, 340
Phase contrast (PC) angiography, 189–191, 192
    basic principle of, 199–200
    computed phase differences in, 200, 201
    multidirectional, 200–201
    projection techniques in, 199–200
Phase ghosting, 1829, 1830
Phase images, 191, 192
Phase shifts and intravoxel phase disper-sion, 189–191, 192
Phasing-in time, 72–73
Phenol
    in celiac ganglion block, III:201
    in renal cyst sclerosis, III:663
Phenomena
    nutcracker, III:688
    Raynaud's, 1759, 1760
Phenoxybenzamine, 57–58
    in adrenal angiography with pheochro-mocytoma, 1356, 1372
    in benign prostatic hypertrophy, III:627–628
    in pharmacologic erection, III:706
Phentolamine, 53, 57–58
    in arterial portography, 1530
    in catecholamine action reversal, 54
    in emergency reactions, III:216
    metabolism of, 49
    with papaverine in pharmacologic erection, III:706–707, III:708, III:710
    in pheochromocytoma, 1356, 1373
Phenylalanine mustard, III:437
Phenylephrine, 48
Phenytoin, 45
Pheochromocytoma, 1253, 1257
    adrenal angiography in, 1369–1373
        complications of, 1356
    ectopic ACTH production in, 1365
Philipson J, 394
Phillips Poly Diagnost C system, 104
Phillips Sones support unit, 104
Phlebothrombosis, 965, 966
Phlegmasia cerulea dolens, III:152
Phlegmon of kidney, terminology, 1178
Photoconductive tube, 140–141
Photographic magnification, 176–177
Photographic ratings of natural light of International Standards Organiza-tion, 105
Photoplethysmographic tracings in aorto-iliac disease, III:228
PHPT (primary hyperparathyroidism), 976. *See also* Parathyroid angiography
Phrenic arteries, 1021
    bleeding from, III:823
        arteriographic appearance of, versus adrenal glands, III:393, III:394
    inferior, 1352, 1353, 1354
Phrenic paralysis, 816
Phrenic veins, 1295
    for inferior vena cava collateral circula-tion, 954, 955, 956, 957

Physical examination
    before percutaneous aortoiliac interven-tions, III:225–228
    in preinterventional assessment, III:206
Physicians
    in cardiac catheterization laboratory, 131
    of vascular intervention angiography lab-oratory, 135–136
Physics, imaging, 205–211
Physiologic studies and equipment in car-diac catheterization, 114–119
Physiology
    anomalous pulmonary venous connec-tion
        partial, 883–884
        total, 873
    of blood vessels and cell biology, 50–52
    of contrast media, 22–33. *See also* Emer-gency treatment
        emergency treatment of, 34–48
        osmolality and, 30–31
    inferior vena cavography and, 969–971
    monitoring of, in cardiac catheterization, 114–119
    pulmonary, 849–867. *See also* Pulmo-nary physiology and microstructure
        blood flow redistribution in, 859
        gravity effects in, 854, 855
    renal angiography and, 1124–1126
    of spinal dural arteriovenous fistulas
        of type I, 370–372
        of type II and III, 377–378
    of thoracic outlet, 996–998
Pial parenchymal vascular malformations or fistulas, 323, 324
Pial plexus, 362
Pial veins, 367
PICAs (posterior inferior cerebellar arter-ies), 277–278
    aneurysms of, 318
    emboli in, 298
PICC (peripherally inserted central cathe-ters), III:969
Picker cassette changer with computer pro-grammer, 71, 72
Picker-Amplatz vacuum contact system, 71
Pickup tube for video systems, 140–141
Picture Archiving and Communication Sys-tems (PACS), 148
Piezoelectric crystals, 205
Pigmented villonodular synovitis, 1808–1809
Pigtail catheter
    in aortic arch injections, 243–244, 249
    in coronary arteriography, 560, 561, 562
    in gastrostomy, III:549
    in left ventriculography, 561
    in nephrostomy, III:566
    in patent ductus arteriosus, 424
    in penile vascularization, III:709
    in pulmonary arteriography, 772, 773, 775
    in renal angiography, 1102, 1103
    in thoracic aortic aneurysm stent-grafts procedure, III:360
    in transaxillary catheterization, 1016
    in transfemoral catheterization, 1015
    in ureteral stenting, III:575, III:576
    in ureteroenteral anastomotic strictures, III:653
    in ventriculography, 120

PIOPED (Prospective Investigation of Pulmonary Embolism Diagnosis) study, 769–770, 805, 1031
PIPD (posterior inferior pancreaticoduodenal vein), 1426
Pitressin. *See* Vasopressin
Pixel matrix, 143–144
Pixel value, 190–191
Placenta, embolization of, 1646
Placenta previa, 1646
Plain threads in mechanical embolization, III:55, III:71
Plantar arch, 1699
Plantar arteries, 1828
    tarsal branches of, 1699
Plaque
    in arteriosclerosis, 1052. *See also* Arteriosclerosis
        degenerative changes in, 1056
        in posterior wall of aorta, 1058
        in subclavian artery, 1007
    atherectomy catheter in removal of, III:44
    atypical formation of, 692
    eccentric, in common iliac artery, 1637
    in extracranial neck arteries, 221
    fracture of, after balloon angioplasty, III:4
    gray-scale imaging principles and, 206, 207, 217
Plasma cell myelomas, 1793–1794
Plasmin, III:120–121
    rate of thrombi lysis of, III:123
    tissue-type plasminogen activator and, III:121
Plasminogen, III:120
Plasminogen activator inhibitors (PAIs), III:123
Plasminogen activators, III:120–121
Plastic urethral stent, double Malecot, III:633–634
Platelet adherence after arterial injury, III:11, III:18
Platelet aggregation, 61
Platelet infusions before arterial portography, 1528
Platelet inhibitors in extremity trauma conservative management, III:860
Platelet trapping, hemangioma and, III:998
Platelet-derived growth factor, III:12–13
Platelets, III:123–124
    activation of, III:123
    antifibrinolytic properties of, III:123–124
    intrathrombotic, III:124
Platinum in metal-based mechanical embolization, III:62–63
    in extremity trauma, III:863–867
    in hepatic malignancy, III:437
    in intraaxial embolotherapy for central nervous system, III:766
    in pediatrics, III:906
    in renal trauma, III:897
Platinum analogues, III:81
Platinum guidewire
    in bronchial artery embolization, III:825
    in infrapopliteal revascularization, III:285
Platinum radiopaque marker, 163, 166
Pleonemia, term of, 850

Plethysmography, impedance, 1839–1840, III:228
Pleural disease, hemoptysis in, III:824
    bronchial artery embolization results for, III:827
Pleural effusion, 865
    in dissecting aortic aneurysms, 502
Pleural injury as percutaneous stone removal complication, III:602
Pleurisy after pulmonary arteriovenous malformation embolotherapy, III:852
Plexiform nidus arteriovenous malformations, III:775
Plexus
    aortic, of sympathetic nervous system, 958
    brachial, 996
    hemorrhoidal, 954, 956, 957
    internal pudendal, 957
    pampiniform, III:678
    pial, 362
    preprostatic, 1642
    sacral venous, 893, 894, 895, 896
    vertebral, 893, 894, 896–897, 951, 952, 958
Plication, inferior vena cava, 968, 969, III:982–983
Plumbicon photoconductive tube, 140
PMEF (pharmacologic maintenance erectile flow), III:708, III:710, III:716–717, III:720–721
Pneumatic power injectors, 171, 172
Pneumococcal infection
    in asplenia, 1472
    in thoracic aortic aneurysms, 485
Pneumococcal vaccine, polyvalent, 1492
Pneumonia
    after percutaneous gastrostomy, III:557
    chemical, after lymphangiography, 1868–1869
    pulmonary arteriography in, 802
Pneumoperitoneum after percutaneous gastrostomy, III:557
Pneumothorax
    after biliary drainage procedures, 1038
    in biopsy, 1034, III:178–179
    pulmonary arteriography in, 816–818
    pulmonary hypovascularity in, 816
    venous access catheters and, III:979
Point source in magnification angiography, 177
Poiseuille JLM, 849
Poiseuille's law, 170, 852, 853, 854
Polar arteries, 1217, 1219, 1224
    splenic artery branches and, 1461
Polidocanol, III:696
Polyarteritis nodosa, 305–307
Polycystic disease, 1224–1226
    adult hereditary, 1226, 1227
    hypertension and, 1276
    infantile, Wilms tumor versus, 1135, 1136
    of liver as contraindication to transjugular intrahepatic portosystemic shunt, III:538
    renal, type of cysts in, III:658
    renal cell carcinoma versus, 1154, 1157, 1158
    renal venography in, 1317, 1320
Polycythemia, 1138

Polyethylene
    compliance of, III:26, III:27
    in delivery-inflation catheters, III:66, III:67, III:69
    scratch-resistance of, III:39
Polymyalgia rheumatica, 998
Polynephritis, 1276
Polyps of colon
    bleeding from, III:411, III:412
    malignant, 1604, 1605
Polysplenia, 1472
    azygos continuation of inferior vena cava in, 949
Polytetrafluoroethylene (PTFE)
    in dialysis graft, III:726
    in femoropopliteal percutaneous transluminal angioplasty, III:262
    in grafts
        in dialysis shunts, 226, 1767, 1770
        femoral arteriography after, 1717, 1719
    in infrainguinal grafts, thrombolysis in, III:145
    in portosystemic shunt, III:526
Polyurethane in delivery-inflation catheters, III:66, III:68
Polyvalent pneumococcal vaccine, 1492
Polyvinyl alcohol (PVA) embolization
    in arteriovenous malformations, III:1011–1013, III:1014–1015
        of central nervous system, III:778–779
    in bronchial artery embolization, III:825, III:826
    in hemorrhage of pelvic organs, 1651
    in hepatic malignancy, III:437, III:438
    in intracranial, extraaxial lesion embolization, III:790, III:791
        in dural arteriovenous malformations, III:802
        in neoplasms, III:811–814
    in pediatric interventional angiography, III:904
    in small-vessels or tissues, III:53–54
    spiderlon and, III:63
    in spinal vascular metastatic lesions, 386
    spring embolus and, III:61
    in varicoceles, III:698–699
Polyvinyl chloride
    in balloon angioplasty catheter, III:3
    compliance of, III:26, III:27
Pontine veins, transverse, 280
Pontomesencephalic cerebellar (APMC) vein, anterior, 279, 280
Pooling of contrast material in tumor, 1781
Popliteal arteries
    aneurysm of, 1724–1725
    collateral circulation of, 1700–1703
    in diabetes mellitus, 1715, 1717
    dissection of, 1825
    in femoral arteriography, 1706
    occlusion of
        after balloon angioplasty, III:8–10
        thrombolysis in, III:139–144
        percutaneous suction removal of occluding thrombus in, III:162, III:163
    stenoses in, 222
        after femoropopliteal revascularization, III:275–276

2D-TOF magnetic resonance imaging of, 1826, 1834
wounds of, 1728, 1729
Popliteal veins
    duplication of, 218
    sonography of, 218, 220
    venography of, 1744
Porstmann W, III:837
Porstmann's balloon catheter, III:24
Porstmann's Ivalon plug, 427
Port, implantable subcutaneous, III:969, III:976–977
Portacath, fractured segment of, III:963
Portacaval shunt, 1538, 1539
Portal circulation. *See also* Portal veins
    arterial portography of
        in extrahepatic obstruction, 1535, 1536, 1537
        in intrahepatic obstruction and collaterals, 1532–1535
    splenoportography of. *See* Splenoportography
    superselective catheterization in, 160–161
    velocity of flow in, 1500, 1506
    venography of. *See* Portal venography
Portal hypertension, III:525–546
    azygos veins in, 911
    beta-adrenergic blockers in, III:397
    in cirrhosis, hepatic arterial–portal venous shunts and, 1436, 1437
    endoscopic therapy in, III:525–526
    hepatomas and, 1448
    percutaneous management of, III:526–530
    pharmacologic control of bleeding in, III:525
    portosystemic shunt surgery in, III:526
    splenic arteriography in, 1478, 1479
    splenoportography in. *See* Splenoportography
    superior mesenteric angiography in, 1573
    transhepatic portal venography in, 1423, 1424
    transjugular intrahepatic portosystemic shunt in. *See* Transjugular intrahepatic portosystemic shunt (TIPS)
    vascular sonography in, 231
    vasopressin and, 55
Portal veins, 1018, 1020, 1422–1424, 1425
    anomalies of, 1422, 1425
    arterial portography of
        computerized tomography during, 1543, 1544
        in extrahepatic obstruction, 1535, 1536, 1537
        in intrahepatic obstruction and collaterals, 1532–1535
    compression of, 1397, 1402
    inferior vena cava relationship to, 932, 934
    collateral circulation and, 953, 955–957, 958
    liver transplantation and
        angioplasty and, III:514
        complications and interventions for, III:513–515
        donor liver preparation and, III:509
        stents and, III:514–515

magnetic resonance venography of, 1852–1855
    obstruction of, 1543, 1544
        extrahepatic, 1535, 1536, 1537
        intrahepatic, collaterals in, 1532–1535
        stents in, III:1053
    patency of, III:439
    renal vein spontaneous communication with, 1314
    sonography of, 231–232
        in follow-up after procedures, 231–232
        normal flow patterns in, 214, 215
        in occlusion and thrombosis, 231
    splenoportography of. *See* Splenoportography
    superselective catheterization in, 160–161
    thrombosis of
        arterial portography in, 1535
        as contraindication to TIPS, III:538–541
        splenomegaly in, 1467
        splenoportography disadvantages and, 1497, 1499
    total anomalous pulmonary venous connection to, 878, 881
    venography of. *See* Portal venography
Portal venography, 1422–1426
    anatomy in, 1422–1424, 1425
    approaches in, 1424–1426
Portography, arterial, 1527–1548. *See also* Arterial portography
Portosystemic collateral circulation, 1422, 1424
Portosystemic encephalopathy (PSE) after transjugular intrahepatic portosystemic shunt, III:537
Portosystemic shunt, III:526
    percutaneous revision of, III:528–530
    perirectal varices after, 1850
    transjugular intrahepatic (TIPS), III:204, III:530–542. *See also* Transjugular intrahepatic portosystemic shunt (TIPS)
    vascular sonography after, 232
Port-wine mark cirsoid aneurysm, 1731
Position
    of patient. *See* Patient, positioning of
    of personnel for radiation protection, 128–129
Position-dependent magnetic field gradients, 190, 199
Positive exercise test, 690
Positron emission tomography (PET), 660
Postembolization care in central nervous system arteriovenous malformations, III:782–784
Postembolization syndrome, III:202
    hepatic artery, 1037
    in hepatic embolization, III:440, III:452–453
Posterior fossa, intracranial, extraaxial lesions of, III:794–795
Postmortem studies
    after false negatives in coronary arteriography, 656
    of coronary artery anatomy, 583–585
        dye and corrosion techniques in, 585
        dye techniques in, 583–584, 585
        manual dissection in, 583, 584

Postoperative care after interventional radiology, III:219–221
    in coronary angioplasty, III:372
    in pediatrics, III:904
Postoperative changes
    after aortic arteriography in arteriosclerosis and other diseases, 1069, 1070
    after peripheral arterial surgery, 222–227, 228
    in inferior vena cava, 965–968, 969
    renal venography of, 1315, 1317
Postoperative complications. *See also* Complications
    after abdominal aorta aneurysm repair, 1095–1096, 1097, 1098
    after aortoiliac interventions
        immediate, 1689–1690
        late, 1690
    after peripheral arterial surgery, sonography of, 222–227, 228
    gastric bleeding in, III:411, III:412
    infection of prosthetic grafts after aneurysm repair in, 1095, 1097
    lymphedema in, 1909, 1914, 1920
    pelvic abscesses in. *See* Pelvic abscess percutaneous drainage (PAD)
Postpartum pseudothrombi, 1849
Postpartum pulmonary embolism, 808–809
Postprocedural care for interventional radiology, III:219–221
    in coronary angioplasty, III:372
    in pediatrics, III:904
Postrenal vena cava, double, 945, 947
Postrevascularization syndrome as complication of transgraft thrombolysis, III:155
Postsplenectomy infection, III:884
Poststenotic dilatation
    pulmonary arteriography in, 788–793
    of subclavian artery, 1002, 1005
Post-subarachnoid hemorrhage vasospasm, III:753–757, III:758
Posttreatment effects in malignant lymphomas, 1948, 1949
Posture, renin determination and, 1306, 1308
Potassium chloride, 48
Potter type 3 adult polycystic disease, 1226
Pourcelot index, 212, 213
Povidone-iodine as sclerosant, III:946
Powdered tantalum with cyanoacrylates, III:1015, III:1016
Power, electrical, in cardiac catheterization, 94, 95
PPACK (D-Phe-Pro-Arg chloromethyl ketone), III:15
PPomas, pancreatic, 1405, 1406
Precentral cerebellar vein (PCV), 278, 279
Prednisolone, 30, 48
Prednisone, 1607, III:999
Pregnancy
    dissecting aortic aneurysms in, 493, 494
    extremity swelling in, 1750
    in inferior vena cava obstruction, 960–963
    pelvic angiography in, 1646, 1647
    in percutaneous stone removal indications, III:598–599
    tubal, 1646, 1648
    varicosities and, 1753, III:700–701

Preinfundibular artery, 604
Preintervention assessment, III:204–210
  allergy preparation and, III:209
  antibiotics and, III:208–209
  auxiliary personnel and, III:205
  cardiac rhythm abnormalities and, III:209
  coagulation deficits and, III:207–208
  hydration adjustment and, III:207
  immediate preprocedural, III:207–210
  infected fluid drainages and, III:209–210
  inpatient consultation in, III:205–206
  medication adjustment and, III:207
  outpatient consultation in, III:207
  scope of clinical responsibilities in, III:204–205
Premature atrial contractions (PAC), 43, 44
Premature ventricular contractions (PVCs), 44–45
  in coronary artery catheterization complications, 575
Premedication, III:206
  in coronary angioplasty, III:369
  in coronary arteriography, 568
  in femoral arteriography, 1713
  in thoracic aortography, 391–392
  hazards and, 398
Preoperative evaluation
  of abdominal aorta aneurysms, 1074–1075, 1076, 1082–1095
    angiography in, 1074–1075, 1086–1091
    choice of method in, 1091–1093
    magnetic resonance imaging in, 1091, 1092–1093
    spiral volumetric computed tomography in, 1091, 1093
    ultrasonography in, 1076
  renal vein, venography in, 1315, 1317
Preoperative radiation therapy in extremity sarcomas, III:1032
Prep room in vascular intervention angiography laboratory, 136
Prepackaged angiography trays for cerebral studies, 242
Preprostatic plexus, 1642
Preshaped catheters
  in mesenteric angioplasty, III:327
  pigtail, in pulmonary arteriography, 772
  for superselective catheterization, 159, 160
Pressure
  alveolar, 854–855
  in cardiac catheterization, 114–117
  interstitial, pulmonary, 855–856
  in pulmonary arteriography, 769, 774–776
  static burst, of microcatheter, 166
  in superselective catheterization, 166
Pressure injectors, 171–173
Pressure pulses in blunt trauma, 528
Preventricular artery, 604
Prevesical spaces, III:939
Priapism, high-flow, 1661
Primaquine idiosyncrasy, 49
Primary beam limitation in radiation protection, 125

Primary hyperparathyroidism (PHPT), 976. *See also* Parathyroid angiography
Primary lymphedema, 1907–1908, 1909–1913, 1918–1919
Primary pulmonary hypertension, 813–815
Primary Raynaud's phenomenon, 1759
Primary sclerosing cholangitis (PSC), III:465–470
  diagnosis of, III:466–467
  endoscopy in, III:467–468
  percutaneous radiologic management of, III:468, III:469
  surgery in, III:468–470
  treatment of, III:467–470
Primary tumors
  of bile duct, 1450, 1451
  of inferior vena cava, 971, 972
  of liver, 1446–1450, 1451
  of spinal column, 386–387
Primicon photoconductive tube, 140
Prinzmetal variant angina, 569, 638, 685–687, 732–733
Priscoline. *See* Tolazoline
Probe, laser, in infrapopliteal revascularization, III:293
Probe catheter in penile transluminal therapy, III:722
Procainamide, 47
  in premature atrial contractions, 43
  in premature ventricular contractions, 45
  recommended intravenous dosages for, 46
  strengths and volumes of, 48
Procaine, III:214
Procedure room
  for cardiac catheterization, 87
  for vascular intervention angiography, 136
Processing, cine
  in cardiac catheterization laboratory, 106–111, 112, 113
  features to consider when purchasing equipment for, 109–111, 112, 113
  quality control for, 123–124
Prochlorperazine, III:214
Procoagulants, III:123
Professional nursing personnel
  in cardiac catheterization laboratory, 131–132
  in vascular intervention angiography laboratory, 136
Profunda femoris arteries
  angiography and
    femoral, 1698
      pelvic magnetic resonance, 1637
      postaortoiliac intervention, 1690
  collateral circulation of, 1700–1703
  in diabetes mellitus, 1715
Profunda femoris veins, 1843, 1846
Progressive scanning, 141, 146
Projections
  in abdominal aorta aneurysm detection, 1081–1082, 1083, 1084–1085
  for coronary arteriography, 566–568, 629–631
  in magnetic resonance angiography, 198–202
  in thoracic aortography, 394–395
Promethazine, III:214
Pronestyl. *See* Procainamide

Propranolol, 47
  in atrial fibrillation, 43
  in atrial flutter, 43
  in esophageal varices, III:397
  in portal hypertension, III:525
  in premature atrial contractions, 43
  in premature ventricular contractions, 45
  recommended intravenous dosages for, 46
  renin determination and, 1306
  strengths and volumes of, 48
Prospective Investigation of Pulmonary Embolism Diagnosis (PIOPED) study, 769–770, 805, 1031
Prostacyclin (PGI$_2$), 61, III:15
Prostaglandin E, 60–61
Prostaglandin E$_1$ (PGE$_1$), 60–61
  as adjunctive agent in pulse-spray thrombolysis, III:137
  male erection and, 56
  in pancreatic angiography, 1394
  in penile duplex sonography, III:719
  in pharmacologic erection, III:706, III:707
  in superior mesenteric angiography, 1557
  in thrombolysis action, III:126
  for vasospasm at puncture site, 1028
Prostaglandin F$_1$, 1530
Prostaglandin F$_{2\alpha}$ (PGF$_{2\alpha}$), 60–61
  in pancreatic angiography, 1394
  in superior mesenteric angiography, 1557
Prostaglandins, 60–61
  contrast agent osmolality and, 24–26
  in infant with coarctation of aorta, 438
  metabolism of, 49
  in restenosis after balloon angioplasty, III:15
  in superior mesenteric angiography, 1557
Prostate, III:621–639
  anatomy of
    pathologic, III:623–624, III:625
    surgical, III:621–622
    zonal, III:622–623, III:624
  benign hyperplasia of, III:625–634, III:635
    diagnosis of, III:626
    indications for intervention in, III:626
    interventional therapy in, III:628–634, III:635
    medical therapy in, III:626–628
    pathogenesis in, III:626
    surgery for, III:626
  biopsy of, III:636–639
    results of, III:638–639
  carcinoma of, 1664
    metastatic spread in, 1933, 1936
    percutaneous nephrostomy in, III:568
  examination of, III:625
  functions of, III:625
  hyperthermia of, III:614, III:634–636
  hypothermia of, III:614
  inflammations of, III:640
  resection of
    strictures after, III:578, III:579
    transurethral, III:626
  screening algorithm for, III:639
  stents for, III:632–634, III:635
  suspicious nodules of, III:625, III:638

urethroplasty of, III:628–632
  complications of, III:632
Prostatectomy
  strictures after, III:578, III:579
  transurethral, III:626
Prostheses
  esophageal, bowel segment for transplantation for, 1590
  intraurethral, III:632–634, III:635
  renal artery stenosis and, 1284–1287
  atherectomy catheter for, III:49
Prosthetic grafts. *See* Grafts
Protamine sulfate, 568–569, III:215
Protein C, 1623
Protein S, 1623
Proteus
  in renal abscess, 1183
  in xanthogranulomatous pyelonephritis, 1193
Prothrombin time (PT), III:208
Prothrombotic factors, III:123–124
Protooncogenes, III:16
pro-UKA (single-chain urokinase plasminogen activator), III:122
pro-uPA (single-chain urokinase plasminogen activator), III:122
Provocative tests in cerebral plexiform nidus aneurysms, III:776–777
Proximal as term in balloon catheter angioplasty, III:42
Proximal fallopian tube obstruction (PTO), III:672
Proximal interventricular septum, variations in blood supply to, 612
PSC (primary sclerosing cholangitis), III:465–470
PSE (portosystemic encephalopathy) after transjugular intrahepatic portosystemic shunt, III:537
Pseudoaneurysms. *See also* False aneurysms
  after aneurysm repair, 1095, 1098
  after angioplasty, 1693, 1694
  after aortoiliac interventions, 1686, 1691–1694
  after endarterectomy, 1693
  after femoral catheterization, 1693, 1694, 1695
  after gunshot wounds of upper extremity arteries, 1757, 1758
  after renal transplantation, 1344–1346, 1347, 1348
  at anastomotic site in coronary artery bypass graft, 759
  angioplasty and, III:256, III:257
  of carotid artery in trauma, 350, 354
  from cerebral angiography, 246
  in coronary arteriography complication, 578
  in dialysis shunt complications, 1771, 1772
  of femoral circumflex arteries, 1652
  of hepatic artery anastomosis in liver allograft, III:512–513
  mechanical embolic agents for, III:58, III:59, III:72–74
  mycotic, of extracranial cerebral arteries, 303, 305
  percutaneous renal stone removal and, III:568, III:602
  pulmonary artery bleeding in, III:820, III:823

in puncture site complications, 1027–1028
  sonography of, 216, 227, color plates 6 and 7
  of thoracic aorta in trauma, 477–483
  traumatic
    arteriography and, III:860, III:862
    arteriovenous fistula and, III:1002
    in extremity, III:860, III:862, III:864–867
    renal, III:896
    transcatheter management and, III:864–867
  of vertebral artery, 343
Pseudocalculus of common bile duct, III:500
Pseudocoarctation of aorta, 437, 553
  thoracic aortography in, 396, 553
Pseudocysts
  abdominal abscesses and, III:933, III:934–935
  pancreatic, 1401, 1402, 1408, 1409, 1413, 1414–1415, III:933, III:934–935
    chronic pancreatitis with, 1401
    in splenic arteriography, 1465
Pseudolesion, hepatic lobe, computerized tomography during arterial portography of, 1544–1545
Pseudomonas, 1183
Pseudothrombus
  in inferior vena cava computerized tomography, 940, 942
  postpartum, 1849
Pseudotruncus arteriosus, 788–789
Pseudotumors, renal, 1165–1166, 1167–1170, 1226–1228
  chronic atrophic pyelonephritis and, 1198
  pyelonephritic, venography in, 1317
Pseudovein versus vascular malformation, III:391, III:393
Pseudoxanthoma elasticum, carotid-cavernous fistulas in, III:802
Psoas abscesses, percutaneous drainage of, III:936–937
Psoas muscles, 958, 1269–1270
PSPD (posterior superior pancreaticoduodenal vein), 1426, 1427, 1429
PSPMT. *See* Pulse-spray pharmacomechanical thrombolysis (PSPMT)
PT (prothrombin time), III:208
PTA. *See* Percutaneous transluminal angioplasty (PTA)
PTC. *See* Percutaneous transhepatic cholangiography (PTC)
PTCA. *See* Percutaneous transluminal coronary angioplasty (PTCA)
PTFE. *See* Polytetrafluoroethylene (PTFE)
PTH. *See* Parathyroid hormone (PTH)
PTO (proximal fallopian tube obstruction), III:672
PTRA (percutaneous transluminal renal angioplasty), III:112, III:113–115, III:294. *See also* Renal angioplasty
PTT. *See* Partial thromboplastin time (PTT)
Pubic bone tumors, 1785
Puboprostatic ligament, rupture of, 1644–1645
Puck rapid film changers, 74–75, 76

Pudendal arteries, 1022
  anatomy of, III:711–712
  internal, 1642–1643, 1644, 1645, 1650
    in penile vascularization, III:709
    transcatheter embolization of, 169, 1660, 1662
  obstruction of, III:712, III:714–715
  in pelvic fractures, III:872–876
Pudendal plexus, internal, 957
Pudendal veins
  internal, 1642
  superficial external, III:678
Pullback atherectomy catheter, III:47, III:379, III:380
  in femoropopliteal atherectomy, III:280
  in infrapopliteal revascularization, III:293
Pull-through method for recanalization, III:38
Pulmonary angiography in pulmonary arteriovenous malformations, III:838, III:839–845
Pulmonary arteries. *See also* Pulmonary arteriography
  anomalous coronary artery origin from, 741–744, 799, 800
  anomalous origin of, 832–833, 836
  aorticopulmonary window and, 464–466
  arteriovenous malformations in, 858, 859
    detachable balloons for, III:1011, III:1012
  atresia of, 789, 790, 791, 796–798, 799
  bleeding from, III:820, III:823
  central
    coarctation of, 796–798
    developmental anomalies in. *See* Pulmonary developmental anomalies
    stenosis of, 831–832, 833–835
    varying degrees of distention of, 860
  coarctation of, 796–798, 799
  coronary artery bypass graft from, 756, 757, 758
  dilatation of, idiopathic, 796, 829, 830
  elastic, 769
  fistulas of
    embolization complications in, 1033
    to left anterior descending artery, 741
  historical notes on study of, 6
  left (LPA)
    aplasia of, 799
    ascending branch of, 782
    congenital absence of, 833, 836
    descending branch of, 782–783
    hypoplasia of, 799
    patent ductus arteriosus and, 415, 833, 836
    in pulmonary arteriography, 778, 779–781, 782
  left-to-right shunts from aorta into, 796
  main (MPA)
    ductus arteriosus and, 415
    in pulmonary arteriography, 777, 781
  multiple stenoses of, 792, 793
  muscular, 769
  obstruction of
    in patent ductus arteriosus, 418, 419
    pulmonary hypovascularity in, 816
  peripheral, 780
    developmental anomalies of, 839–844

Pulmonary arteries—*Continued*
  physiology of. *See* Pulmonary physiology
    and microstructure
  prostaglandins and, 61
  right
    ascending branch of, 781
    descending branch of, 781–782
    pulmonary arteriography in, 778, 779,
      780
    rupture of, patent ductus arteriosus and,
      420
    size of, 852
    subclavian artery anastomoses with,
      549–551
    surgical anastomosis of superior vena
      cava with, 844
    thrombolysis in, III:152–153
      pediatric, III:917, III:918
    truncus arteriosus of, 549, 551
    velocity of blood flow in, 856–858,
      859
Pulmonary arteriography, 768–867. *See*
    also Pulmonary arteries
  in acquired abnormalities, 799–819
    aortic arch aneurysm in, 818
    atelectasis in, 816–818
    Behçet disease in, 819
    embolism in, 805–810, 811, 812
    emphysema in, 801, 802, 803
    heart disease in, 799–801
    heart failure in, 818–819
    hypertension in, 800, 801, 813–815
    hypervascularity in, 786, 815–816
    hypovascularity in, 786, 816
    intrathoracic tumors in, 810–813,
      814, 815
    kyphoscoliosis in, 818–819
    lung cancer in, 810–813, 814, 815
    obliterative pulmonary diseases in,
      801–803, 804–806
    pneumothorax in, 816–818
    Rasmussen aneurysms in, 819
    Takayasu arteritis in, 819
  anatomic and functional considerations
    in, 769
  complications of, 783, 1031–1032
  in congenital abnormalities, 786–799,
      800
    anomalous coronary artery origin from
      pulmonary artery in, 799, 800
    aorticopulmonary window in, 464,
      796, 798
    arteriovenous fistula in, 794–795,
      796, 797
    atresia and coarctation in, 796–798,
      799
    coronary artery–pulmonary artery fis-
      tula in, 799
    idiopathic pulmonary artery dilatation
      in, 796
    lobar emphysema in, 799
    multiple pulmonary artery stenoses in,
      792, 793
    patent ductus arteriosus in, 796, 798
    pathophysiology in, 786–788, 789–
      791
    sequestration in, 798–799
    sling in, 794
    stenosis and poststenotic dilatation in,
      788–793
  contrast agent toxicity and, 29

  in developmental anomalies, 822–848.
      See also Pulmonary developmental
      anomalies
  film changers for, 68
  history of, 768–769
  indications for, 769–770
  magnification in
    geometric, 179, 180, 181
    normal, 178
  normal findings in, 777–783
    in left lung, 782–783
    in left pulmonary artery, 778, 779–
      780
    in main pulmonary artery, 777, 781
    in pulmonary artery branches, 780
    in right lung, 780–782
    in right pulmonary artery, 778, 779
  physiology and microstructure in, 769,
      849–867. *See also* Pulmonary physi-
      ology and microstructure
  selective, 770–777
    alternatives to large-film serial arteriog-
      raphy in, 776–777
    approach routes for, 771–772
    catheterization in, 773–774, 775
    catheters for, 772
    contrast medium injections in, 776
    guidewires for, 772
    imaging in, 776–777
    large-film serial arteriography in, 776
    monitoring in, 771
    preparation for, 770–771
    pressures in, 774–776
    transbrachial route for, 771–772
    transfemoral route for, 771, 773–774,
      775
    transjugular route for, 771, 774
Pulmonary arterioles, 769
Pulmonary arteriovenous fistulas, 770,
    794–795, 796, 797
Pulmonary arteriovenous malformations
    (PAVMs), III:72, III:837–854
  anatomic types of, III:838–840, III:
    841–845
  blood flow and, 858, 859
  detachable balloons for, III:71, III:74
  developmental, 844, 846
  diagnosis of, III:838, III:846
  embolization complications in, 1033
  embolotherapy in, III:845–847, III:848,
    III:849
    air embolus in, III:850–851
    complications of, III:850–852
    delayed pleurisy after, III:852
    devices for, III:846–847, III:848–851
    goals for, III:845
    long-term follow-up after, III:852,
      III:853
    paradoxical embolization of balloon or
      coils in, III:850
    reperfusion after, III:852
    selective catheterization and, III:846,
      III:847
    serial growth after, III:852, III:853
    venous complications of, III:852
  neurologic manifestations of, III:837
  symptoms and signs of, III:837–838
Pulmonary arteritis, 181
Pulmonary artery sling, 832, 836
  pulmonary arteriography in, 794

Pulmonary artery–coronary artery fistula,
    799
Pulmonary banding, pediatric angiography
    in expansion of, III:917
Pulmonary circulation
  drug effects on, magnification angiogra-
    phy in, 181
  normal values for, 852
  West's model of, 850, 851
Pulmonary conus branch of coronary arter-
    ies, 586–587
Pulmonary conus collaterals, 703–704,
    706–708
Pulmonary developmental anomalies. *See
    also* Congenital abnormalities, pul-
    monary arteriography in
  in central pulmonary arteries, 822–838,
    839
    absence of pulmonary valve in, 828–
      829
    anomalous coronary artery origin in,
      833, 837, 838
    anomalous pulmonary artery origin in,
      832–833, 836
    aorticopulmonary window in, 829
    central pulmonary artery stenosis in,
      831–832, 833–835
    embryology and, 822, 823–824
    hypoplastic central pulmonary arteries
      in, 831, 832
    idiopathic pulmonary artery dilatation
      in, 829, 830
    normal anatomy and, 824
    patent ductus arteriosus in, 833, 838,
      839
    pulmonary valve atresia in, 828
    pulmonary valve stenosis in, 826–828
    truncus arteriosus and, 822, 824–827
  in peripheral pulmonary arteries, 839–
    844
    aneurysms in, 843, 845
    arteriovenous malformations in, 844,
      846
    hypoplasia in, 842–843
    pulmonary sequestration in, 840–842
    stenosis in, 843, 844
    supplied by systemic arteries, 840,
      841, 842
  venous. *See* Anomalous pulmonary
    venous connection
Pulmonary diseases
  chronic obstructive, percutaneous biopsy
    complications in, III:178, III:187
  obliterative, 801–803, 804–806
Pulmonary ductal diverticulum, 418, 419
Pulmonary edema, 864, 865
  in coronary arteriography complications,
    578
  septal interstitial, in hypertension, 863
Pulmonary embolism
  after renal venography, 1311
  after thrombolytic therapy, 1042
  in coronary arteriography complications,
    578
  deep vein thrombosis and, 1751
  incidence of, III:982
  as indication for pulmonary arteriogra-
    phy, 770
  inferior vena cava recanalization for pre-
    vention of, 966, 967

magnetic resonance angiography of, 197–198
magnification angiography of, 179, 181
mortality in, III:982
from oil in lymphangiography, 1868, 1869
peripheral pulmonary artery stenoses versus, 843, 844
postpartum, 808–809
prophylaxis for, III:986
pulmonary arteriography in, 805–810, 811, 812
recurrent, III:982
from ovarian veins, 966, 967
streptokinase-accelerated lysis of, 809
term of, 806
Pulmonary emphysema, 801, 802, 803
Pulmonary heart disease, 799–801
Pulmonary hypertension
after pulmonary angiography, 1031
arterial, 853, 859–861
contrast agent toxicity and, 29
magnification angiography in, 181
patent ductus arteriosus and, 422
pulmonary arteriography in, 800, 801
after procedure, 1031
as indication, 770
in primary hypertension, 813–815
in secondary hypertension, 815
venous, 861–865
alveolar edema in, 863–864
extravascular lung water in, 864, 865
lung compliance in, 865
radiologic stages of, 862
septal interstitial edema in, 863
upper zone flow redistribution in, 861–863
Pulmonary hypervascularity, 786, 815–816
Pulmonary hypovascularity, 786, 816
Pulmonary infarction, term, 806
Pulmonary microcirculation, 863
Pulmonary motion, 197–198
Pulmonary perfusion, regional variations in, 849–850
Pulmonary physiology and microstructure, 849–867
alveolar pressure in, 854–855
anatomy and, 850, 851, 852
arterial hypertension in, 853, 859–861. *See also* Pulmonary hypertension
background in, 849–851
blood flow redistribution in, 859
early studies of, 849–851
flow-caliber relationship in, 856–858, 859
functional considerations of arteriography in, 769
gravity effects in, 854, 855
interstitial pressure in, 855–856
motion and, 197–198
Poiseuille's law in, 852, 854
vascular resistance in, 852, 853
venous hypertension in, 861–865. *See also* Pulmonary hypertension
Pulmonary sarcoid, hemoptysis in, III:819
Pulmonary sequestration
arteriography in, 798–799
as developmental anomaly, 840–842
extralobar or intralobar, 798
thoracic aortography in, 396, 549, 550

Pulmonary shunts, coil bronchial artery embolization for, III:826
Pulmonary stenosis, 788–793
Pulmonary torsion in pneumothorax, 1034
Pulmonary trunk, common (CPT), 871, 872
Pulmonary valve
absence of, 828–829
atresia of, 828
anomalous coronary artery origin and, 833, 838
patent ductus arteriosus and, 838
peripheral pulmonary arterial hypoplasia and, 842
pulmonary artery aneurysm and, 843
stenosis of, 826–828
central pulmonary artery stenosis and, 831
congenital, 792, 793
Pulmonary vascular bed, progressive obstruction of, 853, 859–861
Pulmonary vascular resistance, 769, 852, 853
early studies of, 849
Pulmonary veins
anomalous connection of, 868–890. *See also* Anomalous pulmonary venous connection
common, 869, 870, 871
embryology of, 869, 870
historical notes on study of, 6
prostaglandins and, 61
size of, 852
velocity of blood flow in, 856–858, 859
Pulmonary venous connection, anomalous, 868–890. *See also* Anomalous pulmonary venous connection
Pulsatility index, 213
Pulse
absent, in blunt trauma, 522
cardiac arrest and, 36–37
cardiopulmonary resuscitation and, 41
discrepancy between carotid and brachial or femoral, 437
high-pressure, in blunt trauma, 528
Pulse deficit in extremity trauma, III:857, III:858
Pulse flip angle, 195
Pulse volume recordings (PVRs), infrapopliteal revascularization and, III:284
Pulsed Doppler applications, 207
Pulsed excimer laser systems, III:380, III:381
Pulsed-progressive image acquisition
in nonsubtraction imaging fluoroscopy, 151
in vascular intervention angiography, 142
Pulse-spray pharmacomechanical thrombolysis (PSPMT)
age of thrombus and, III:125
clinical application of, III:127
complications of, III:154–155
in dialysis fistula revascularization, III:138, III:146–147, III:148, III:149, III:728–735
for pelvic and lower extremity arteries, III:136, III:139–144
for peripheral bypass grafts, III:145, III:146, III:147
principles of, III:119, III:126

resistant arterial clots in, III:732–733, III:734, III:735
for upper extremity arteries, III:148–149, III:150, III:151
Pulsewidth variation for exposure control, 94
Punch-card control system, 75
Puncture
in abdominal aortography, 1026–1028
in cerebral angiography, 246–249
in coronary arteriography, 558–560
in dialysis shunt, 1771, 1772
in femoral arteriography, 1703–1706
in renal angiography, 1102
in transaxillary catheterization, 1016
in transfemoral catheterization, 1013, 1014
transhepatic, for removal of common duct stones, 1038, 1039
Pupillary response to cardiopulmonary resuscitation, 40–41
Purkinje fibers, 615
Push technique for acrylic adhesive embolization, III:1016
Pushability of balloon catheter, III:37, III:38
PVA embolization. *See* Polyvinyl alcohol (PVA) embolization
PVCs (premature ventricular contractions), 44–45
in coronary artery catheterization complications, 575
PVMRA. *See* Peripheral vascular magnetic resonance angiography (PVMRA)
PVRs (pulse volume recordings), III:284
Pyelitis cystica, III:572
Pyelography
antegrade, of hydronephrosis, 1202, 1203
retrograde
of hydronephrosis, 1202, 1203, 1204
of renal pelvic tumors, 1160
Pyelonephritis
acute, 1178–1182, 1183
focal, terminology, 1179
suppurative, 1178–1182, 1183
chronic
atrophic, 1197–1198
hypertension in, 1268–1269
as renal pseudotumor, 1166, 1168
renal venography in, 1317
severe, terminology, 1179
xanthogranulomatous, 1193–1194, 1195
renal cell carcinoma versus, 1154, 1156
Pyelophlebitis, III:929
Pyonephrosis
in hydronephrosis, 1203–1213
infected, 1199–1200
xanthogranulomatous pyelonephritis versus, 1193, 1199
Pyopneumothorax after nephrostomy, 1036
Pyrexia
after coronary arteriography, 578
in renal cell carcinoma, 1138

Quain J, 891
Quality improvement
in cardiac catheterization, 122–124
complications and, 580

Quality improvement—*Continued*
in radiation protection, 126–128
in established laboratory, 126–128
in new facility, 126, 127
for vascular intervention angiography, 137
Quantitative ventriculography during cardiac catheterization, 117
Quantitization error, digitization and, 142
Quantum mottle, 89
excessive, improper cine processing and, 106
Quantum noise of video system, 140
Quick-Core guide cannula for transjugular liver biopsy, III:198
Quinidine
in atrial fibrillation, 43
in premature atrial contractions, 43
in premature ventricular contractions, 45

Rabinov K, 1743
Rabinov technique for extremity venography, 1743–1744
Racemose aneurysms, 1731–1733
Racine M, 635
Radial artery
in Brescia-Ciminno shunts, 1767, 1768, 1769
congenital anomaly of, 1755, 1756
thrombolysis for, III:149, III:151
Radial lymph nodes, 1881–1882
Radiation damage
cerebral vascular, 310, 342
enteritis and, 1579
fibrosis in, 1926
lymphedema and, 1909, 1915, 1916
renovascular hypertension in, 1273–1276
Radiation dose, 137
Radiation monitoring for personnel, 128, 129
Radiation safety
beam limitation in, 124–125
calculation of patient exposure in, 129
in cardiac catheterization laboratory, 124–128
control room and, 87–88
in established laboratory, 126–128
fluoroscopic timer in, 126
in new facility, 126, 127
physiologic monitors and recorders and, 107
quality control in, 126–128
scatter limitation in, 125–126
for vascular intervention angiography, 136–137
Radiation technologists, cross-training of, 133
Radiation therapy
embolization with, III:779–781
in extremity sarcomas, preoperative, III:1032
fibrosis after, 1926
lymphedema in, 1909, 1915, 1916
in pediatric interventional angiography, III:904, III:920
with surgery for arteriovenous malformations in central nervous system, III:779–781
Radicular arteries, 357–358
embryology of, 357

spinal dural arteriovenous fistulas and, 370–372
Radiculomedullary arteries, 357
angiography technique for, 367
anterior spinal artery and, 358
hairpin configurations of, 358, 359
regional supply of spinal artery and, 360–361
spinal dural arteriovenous fistulas and, 371–372
Radiculopial arteries, 357
angiography technique for, 367
hairpin configurations of, 359
spinal dural arteriovenous fistulas and, 371–372
Radiofrequency balloon angioplasty, III:14, III:42
Radiofrequency pulses, 205
Radiographic contrast agents. *See* Contrast media
Radiographic film
for cardiac catheterization laboratory, 105, 106, 107, 108
color response of, 105
Radiographic tubes. *See* Tube
Radioiodinated hippuran, 1335
Radiolabeled leukocytes, 1693
Radiologic technologist. *See* Technologist, radiologic
Radiology
in arteriovenous malformations, III:1006–1009
in coronary angioplasty, III:368, III:369–370
interventional (IR). *See* Interventional radiology (IR)
in lymphangiography, 1865, 1866
Radionuclide scanning. *See also* specific isotope
in accessory splenic tissue, 1471
of adrenal gland, 1356–1357, 1364
in adrenogenital syndromes, 1369
in coronary disease, role of, 660
in gastrointestinal bleeding, III:389–390
in inferior vena cavography, 941
in pelvic abscesses, III:946
in pulmonary arteriovenous malformations, III:838
in renal cell carcinoma, 1140, 1141
in thoracic aortic aneurysms, 469
in varicocele, III:689
Radiotherapy. *See* Radiation therapy
Radner S, 8, 391, 392, 393, 635
Radon gold seeds, 1662
Raeth, 13, 14
RAM (random access memory), 144
Rami perforantes, 362–363
Ramus intermedius, 614
Ramus limbi dexter, 617
Ramus medianus, 589
in anatomic variations of coronary arteries, 752–753, 754
Ramus ostii venae cavae superioris, 587
Ramus septi fibrosi, 617
Ramus superior septi ventriculorum, 617
Random access memory (RAM), 144
Ranganathan R, 19
Ranniger K, 893
RAO projection. *See* Right anterior oblique (RAO) projection

Rapid film changers, 66–85
Amplatz see-through, 77–78, 79, 80
CGR roll-film, 78–80
Elema roll-film, 75–76, 77
Franklin roll-film, 76–77, 78
history of, 9, 66–68
in large-field angiography, 80–82
peripheral angiography without film changer and, 83–84
phasing-in time and, 72–73
principles of, 69
Puck, 74–75, 76
resolution capacity of, 68
roll-film versus cut-film changers in, 68–69
Schönander cut-film, 73–74, 75
technical considerations in use of, 69–71
zero time and, 72
Rapid serial radiography
generators for, 91–92
historical notes on, 8
tubes for, 97
Rappaport classification for non-Hodgkin lymphoma, 1940, 1941
Rare-earth screen, 177–178
Rashkind double-disk umbrella occluder, 427–428, 429, 430, III:70
in pediatric embolization, III:908
Rasmussen aneurysms, 819
Raster scanning, 141
Rath C, 7
Rayleigh scattering, 205
Raynaud's disease, 1759, 1760
Raynaud's phenomenon, 1759, 1760
Ray-tracing algorithm, 199
RC catheter in bronchial artery embolization, III:822
Reactive follicular hyperplasia
malignant lymphoma versus, 1944–1947
repeat lymphography in, 1948, 1949, 1950
Reactive hyperemia in peripheral angiography, 83
Reactive hyperplasia, lymph node
benign, 1923, 1924, 1925
malignant, 1927
Real-time digital archival recording, 148–149
Real-time gray scale patterns in vascular sonography, 217
Reboul H, 635
Recanalization
in fallopian tube, III:672–677
of occluding thrombi
after balloon angioplasty, III:8–10
in arterial portography, 1535
in arteriosclerotic disease of pelvic arteries, 1638–1640
in coronary arteriography as pitfall, 735–736
in inferior vena cava for pulmonary emboli prevention, 968
long-term efficacy of, III:240–241
in percutaneous revision of surgical portosystemic shunts, III:528–530
Recirculation, cine film processing and, 109, 110
Recoarctation of aorta, 449, 454, 455
after percutaneous transluminal angioplasty, 459

Recombinant single-chain urokinase plasminogen activator (r-sctPA), III:122

Recombinant tissue type of plasminogen activator (RT-PA), 1640, III:233

Reconstruction
  of images, independent acquisitions for, 201
  of splanchnic arteries, in chronic mesenteric ischemia, 1633–1634

Recording system for cardiac catheterization monitoring, 118

Records of radiation exposure
  of patient, 129
  of technician, 132

Recovery room in vascular intervention angiography laboratory, 136

Rectum
  bleeding from, arteriography in, III:414–415
  carcinoma of, malignant metastatic spread of, 1936–1938, III:436, III:450–451
  varices around, after transjugular intrahepatic portosystemic shunt, 1850

Recumbent dedicated stereotactic breast biopsy equipment, III:1037, III:1038

Recurrent artery of Huebner, 261

Recurrent pulmonary embolism from ovarian veins, 966, 967

Recurrent vascular mesenteric ischemia, 1631–1634

Redistribution
  of blood flow, pathologic, 859
  upper zone flow, in pulmonary venous hypertension, 861–863

Redman HC, 1436

Reflux
  catheter, superselective catheterization, 166
  chylous, 1907
  of contrast material into sinus of Valsalva, 726–727, 729
  of embolic material into extremity, III:881
  gastroesophageal, gastrojejunostomy tube in, III:548
  in ovarian vessels in varicocele, III:700–701
  ureteral, after urinary diversions, III:650, III:651
  in varicocele, patterns of, III:691
  venous, sonography of, 220

Regional chemotherapy, III:80–84
  clinical applications of, III:82, III:83
  complications of, III:82–84
  drug classes and mechanisms of action of, III:80–82
  pharmacokinetics of, III:80

Regional enteritis, mesenteric angiography in
  inferior, 1605–1607, 1608
  superior, 1575

Regional variations in pulmonary perfusion, 849–850

Regional wall motion, 561

Registered nurses
  in cardiac catheterization laboratory, 131–132
  in vascular intervention angiography laboratory, 136

Regitine. *See* Phentolamine

Regurgitation, silent aortic valve, 546

Reichardt W, 1426

Reimplantation procedures in chronic mesenteric ischemia, 1633–1634

Rejection of transplantation
  of kidney, III:581
    acute, 1331, 1333, 1339
    chronic, 1332, 1336
    superimposed on chronic rejection, 1332, 1333
    ultrasonography in, 1334
  of liver, III:518
  lymphocele formation and, III:944

Remnants, adrenal, 1376

Renal abscess, 1182–1193
  clinical findings in, 1183–1184
  extension of
    into collecting system, 1184–1185, 1189, 1199
    perinephric, 1185, 1190–1191
  radiologic findings in, 1184, 1185–1188
  renal carcinoma versus, 1154, 1155, 1185–1193
  of renal sinus, 1123
  Wilms tumor versus, 1135
  xanthogranulomatous pyelonephritis and, 1187, 1188, 1191

Renal adenocarcinoma, 1137. *See also* Renal cell carcinoma

Renal adenoma, biopsy in, III:190

Renal agenesis, 1313–1315, 1316

Renal allografts. *See* Renal transplantation

Renal angiography, 1101–1351
  in adrenal disease, 1352–1382. *See also* Adrenal glands
  anatomy in, 1113–1125
    in arterial phase, 1114, 1116–1122
    in nephrographic phase, 1114, 1115, 1118, 1119, 1122–1124
    in venous phase, 1115, 1118, 1125
  in anomalies and malformations, 1217–1229. *See also* Renal anomalies and malformations
  arterial phase of, 1114, 1116–1122
  bradykinin and, 61
  contrast media for, 1110–1113
    complications of, 23–24, 1110–1113
    techniques of, 1110
  dopamine and, 61
  film changers for, 68
  glucagon and, 61
  guidewires, catheters, and catheterization technique for, 1102–1110, 1114, 1115, 1117
  hazards of, 1101–1113
    guidewire, catheter, and catheterization, 1103–1110
    subintimal dissection in, 1103–1107, 1108
    thromboembolic, 1107–1109
  in hydronephrosis, 1202–1216. *See also* Hydronephrosis
  in hypertension, 1244–1289. *See also* Renal arteriography
  in infection, 1178–1201. *See also* Renal infection
  nephrographic phase of, 1114, 1115, 1118, 1119, 1122–1124

nonselective or semiselective, 1113
    catheter for, 1102, 1103
  physiology and, 1124–1126
  preparation for, 1101
  puncture site for, 1102
  of renal pelvic tumors, 1159, 1160–1161
  in renal transplantation, 1325–1351. *See also* Renal transplantation
  renal tumor versus renal cyst in, 1132–1177. *See also* Renal tumors
  semiselective, 1113
    catheter for, 1102, 1103
    magnification in, 1113, 1115
    in malignant hypertension, 1116, 1117
  technique for, 1101–1113
    guidewire, catheter, and catheterization, 1102–1110, 1114, 1115, 1117
    nonselective or semiselective, 1113
    radiographic, 1113, 1114, 1115
    selective, 1113
  in trauma, 1230–1243. *See also* Renal trauma
  venography in, 1290–1324. *See also* Renal venography
  venous phase of, 1115, 1118, 1125

Renal angioplasty, 230, III:294–325
  attempted, III:36
  complications of, 1041, III:307
  indications for, III:294–295
  mechanism of, III:296
  in obstruction or occlusion, III:247–250
  patient management in, III:305–307
  principles of, III:296–300
    balloon diameter in, III:297–298
    balloon material and inflation pressures in, III:298–300
    crossing stenosis in, III:296–297
    renal vascular stents and, III:321–322
    renovascular evaluation in, III:295–296
  restenosis after, III:11, III:311
  results of, III:307–320
    in arteriosclerotic disease, III:308–311, III:312
    in fibromuscular dysplasia, III:311–316
    in neurofibromatosis, III:318, III:319
    in renal allografts, III:316–318
    in renal insufficiency, III:318–320
    in Takayasu arteritis, III:318
  rupture after, III:307
  spasm and, III:305–306
  stenosis in
    after procedure, III:11, III:311
    crossing of, III:296–297
    etiology of, III:294
  techniques for, III:300–303, III:304, III:305
  vascular spasm in, III:304–305, III:306

Renal anomalies and malformations, 1217–1229
  ectopy in, 1221, 1222–1224
  multiple renal arteries in, 1217–1221, 1224
  parenchyma in, 1222–1228
  renal pelvis in, 1228, 1252–1253

Renal aortography, catheters for, 1102

Renal arteries. *See also* Renal arteriography
  accessory, 1217–1221, 1224
    hydronephrosis and, 1210, 1213–
      1215
    normal arteriography of, 1245–1246,
      1258, 1263
    right lower pole, 1089
  anastomosis of, in transplantation, 1325,
    1326
  anatomy of, 1015, 1020–1021
  aneurysms of
    after transplantation, 1344–1346,
      1347, 1348
    dissecting, 1251–1253, 1270–1271
    hypertension and, 1251–1253, 1264–
      1266, 1270–1271
  arteriosclerosis of, 1250, 1251, 1278
  arteriovenous fistulas of, III:1004
    after transplantation, 1344–1346,
      1347, 1348
  branches of, 1114, 1116–1119, 1120
  caliber of, 1116
  course of, 1116
  direct catheterization of, 9
  dorsal, 1114, 1118
    ligated at pyelolithotomy, 1119
  dysplasia of
    in renovascular hypertension, 1250–
      1257
    total, 1222
    without hypertension, 1257
  extrinsic compression of, 1269–1270
    hypertension in, 1269–1270
  fibroplasia of, 1250–1257
    intimal, 1251–1252
    medial, with aneurysm, 1254, 1255
    periarterial, 1255–1256
    perimedial, 1255, 1256
  hyperplasia of
    fibromuscular, 1250–1257
    medial, 1253
  inferior vena cava relationship to, 932,
    934
  injection of contrast medium into, 1111
  injuries of, 1231–1236, 1237
  intimal tear of, 1231, 1233
  lumbar lymph nodes and, 1881
  magnetic resonance angiography of,
    physiologic motion and, 197–
    198
  medial dissection of, 1252–1253
  multiple, 1217–1221, 1224. *See also*
    Renal arteries, accessory
  normal arteriography of, 1245, 1246,
    1247
  obstruction or occlusion of
    after angioplasty, 1041
    transcatheter thromboembolectomy
      in, 1287
  origin of, 1116
  pseudoaneurysms of, after transplanta-
    tion, 1344–1346, 1347, 1348
  segmental supply of primary branches of,
    1114, 1116–1119, 1120
  spasm of, 1248, 1249
  stenosis of
    after transplantation, 1339–1340,
      1341–1343
    atherectomy catheter in, III:49
    attempted angioplasty of, III:36
    balloon catheter in, III:32–36

    branch, 1258–1259
    congenital, 1258
    crossing, in angioplasty, III:296–297
    etiology of, III:294
    sonography of, 229
  supplementary, 1217, 1219, 1220
    ectopic kidney and, 1221
  surgical approach to disease of, III:115
  thrombolysis in, III:153, III:154
  thrombosis of, after transplantation,
    1338, 1339
  trauma to, 1231–1236, 1237
Renal arteriography. *See also* Renal arteries
  in abscess, 1185–1189
  in acute pyelonephritis, 1179–1182,
    1183
  after interventional radiology in hyperten-
    sion, 1287
  after surgery in renovascular hyperten-
    sion, 1284–1287
  angioplasty and, III:310–311
    renovascular hypertension and, III:
      295, III:298
  in arteriolar nephrosclerosis, 1260–1261
  in arteriovenous fistula, 1266–1268
  in carcinoma, 1142, 1151
  catheter for, 1102, 1103
  in chronic glomerulonephritis, 1269
  in collateral circulation in renal ischemia,
    1276–1284
  in dissecting aneurysm of renal artery,
    1252–1253, 1270–1271
  in essential hypertension, 1259–1260
  in extrinsic compression of renal artery,
    1269–1270
  in hamartoma, 1164–1165
  in hydronephrosis, 1205–1208, 1211
  in infarction of kidney, 1262–1264
  magnification in, 1113, 1114, 1115
  normal, 1245–1248, 1249
  in pelvic tumors, 1161
  in pseudotumor, 1167, 1168
  in renal artery aneurysm, 1264–1266
  in renal vein thrombosis, 1311
  in renovascular hypertension, 1248–
    1259, 1278
    arteriosclerosis in, 1250, 1251, 1278
    branch stenosis in, 1258–1259
    congenital stenosis in, 1258
    diagnosis of, 1248–1249
    neurofibromatosis in, 1257–1258
    renal artery dysplasia in, 1250–1257
    without main renal arterial stenosis,
      1262
  in trauma, 1271–1272, 1274, III:895–
    896, III:897
  in unilateral irradiation damage, 1273–
    1276
Renal arteriosclerosis, 1250, 1251, 1278
  semiselective renal angiography in, 1116,
    1117
Renal arteriovenous fistulas, 1266–1268
Renal artery bypass, 1284–1287
Renal biopsy, III:188–189
Renal blood flow, magnification angiogra-
  phy of, 181
Renal calculi, III:587–613
  extracorporeal shock wave lithotripsy in,
    III:603–608, III:609. *See also* Extra-
    corporeal shock wave lithotripsy
    (ESWL)

  percutaneous stone removal in, III:587–
    603, III:604. *See also* Percutaneous
    renal calculi removal (PCNL)
  renal transplant obstruction from, III:
    581
  staghorn
    in percutaneous stone removal indica-
      tions, III:588–590, III:591, III:592
    in urinary diversion complications, III:
      656
  in ureter, III:608–611
    after stenting, III:577
    chronic, strictures with, III:578, III:
      580
Renal cell carcinoma, 1137–1154
  abscess versus, 1185–1193
  after immunosuppression in transplanta-
    tion, 1346
  angiography in, 1114, 1141–1154
  bland thrombus versus tumor thrombus
    in, 1854
  circumaortic venous ring and, 950
  cyst versus, III:660
  diagnostic evaluation of, 1139–1154
    angiography in, 1114, 1141–1154
    bone scan and, 1154
    chest examination and, 1154
    computed tomography in, 1140,
      1142, 1143
    inferior vena cavography in, 1143,
      1154
    intravenous urography in, 1139–1140
    isotope imaging in, 1140, 1141
    magnetic resonance imaging in,
      1140–1141, 1144
    renal venography in, 1142, 1154
    ultrasonography in, 1140
  hypertension and, 1276
  inferior vena cava and
    obstruction of, 963, 965
    ultrasonography of, 938
  metastases from
    femoral arteriography in, 1738
    to femur, 1808
    pancreatic islet-cell tumors versus,
      1403, 1405
    to shoulder, 1807
  pathology of, 1137–1138
  sonography of renal vein and, 230–231
  symptoms and signs of, 1138–1139
  vascularity in, 1141, 1144, 1145, 1146
Renal cysts
  capsular posterolateral, as pseudotumor,
    1169–1170
  carcinoma versus, III:660
  cortical
    simple, III:658
    urinomas after rupture of, III:667
  diagnostic evaluation of, 1170–1173,
    1174, 1175, III:658, III:659
    angiography in, 1171–1173, 1174
    computed tomography in, 1171, 1173
    decision tree in, 1173
    differential, 1173, 1175
    intravenous urography in, 1171, 1172
    nephrotomography in, 1171
    ultrasonography in, 1171
  incidence of, 1170
  in infantile polycystic disease, Wilms
    tumor versus, 1135, 1136
  infected, 1199

interventional radiology in, III:658–666, III:670–671
cyst puncture and aspiration in, III:660–662
marsupialization and, III:665–666
sclerosis and, III:662–666
symptoms and diagnosis in, III:658
types of cysts and, III:658
multilocular, III:658
parapelvic, III:658, III:665
pathology of, 1170, 1171
peripelvic, III:658
puncture and aspiration of, III:660–662
renal stones in, III:590
renal tumors versus, 1132–1177, 1154, 1155–1158, 1173. *See also* Renal tumors, renal cysts and
surgery in, III:665–666
symptoms and signs of, 1170
treatment of, 1173
Renal dysplasia
in renovascular hypertension, 1250–1257
total, 1222
Renal ectopy, 1221, 1222–1224
Renal failure
after pulmonary angiography, 1031–1032
after renal angioplasty, III:307
calcification of abdominal vessels in, 1056
in contrast media reactions, 1025–1026
Renal fibrolipomatosis, 1166, 1317–1320, 1321
renal cysts versus, 1173
Renal function, 1125–1126
in hydronephrosis, 1202, 1203
in interventional radiology, III:214–217
preservation of, percutaneous transluminal angioplasty for, III:113–115
renal angioplasty results in, III:318–320
Renal hamartomas, 1163–1165
renal cell carcinoma versus, 1154
Renal hypertension. *See* Renovascular hypertension (RVHTN)
Renal infection, 1178–1201
abscess as, 1182–1193
clinical findings in, 1183–1184
differentiation of, from renal carcinoma, 1185–1193
extension of, into collecting system, 1184–1185, 1189, 1199
perinephric extension of, 1185, 1190–1191
radiologic findings in, 1184, 1185–1188
acute bacterial nephritis in, 1178–1182, 1183
after renal transplant, 1344
angiography role in, 1200
in cysts, 1199, III:658, III:659
fungal, 1200
infected caliceal diverticulum as, 1199
infected hydronephrosis or pyonephrosis as, 1199–1200
pyelonephritis in
acute, 1178–1182, 1183
chronic atrophic, 1197–1198
suppurative, 1178–1182, 1183
tuberculosis as, 1195–1197

xanthogranulomatous pyelonephritis as, 1193–1194, 1195
Renal insufficiency, renal angioplasty results in, III:318–320
Renal ischemia
collateral circulation in, hypertension and, 1276–1284
nephrogram in, 1248, 1258, 1259, 1263
Renal magnification angiography, 180, 181
Renal mass lesions. *See* Renal tumors
Renal parenchyma
benign disease of, 1315–1320
injury to
in lithotripsy complications, III:607
in percutaneous stone removal complications, III:602
malformation of, 1222–1228
masses in, within renal allografts, 1346–1348
Renal pelvis
duplications of, 1228
malformation of, 1228, 1252–1253
tumors of, 1154–1161
carcinoma in, 1159
diagnostic evaluation of, 1159–1160, 1161, 1162
differential diagnosis of, 1160–1161
pathology of, 1154–1158
symptoms and signs of, 1158–1159
treatment of, 1161
Renal pseudotumors, 1165–1166, 1167–1170, 1226–1228
chronic atrophic pyelonephritis and, 1198
Renal reaction in thoracic aortography, 399
Renal scintigraphy
in acute pyelonephritis, 1179
captopril, 1245
in rejection after renal transplantation, 1334–1335, 1336
Renal sinus
abscess of, 1123
course of, in angiography, 1119–1120, 1121–1123
Renal transplantation, 169, 1325–1351
angiography in, 1327–1329, 1330
donor, 1325–1327
in dysfunction and complications, 1338–1348
historical review of, 1330–1333
in parenchymal masses within allografts, 1346–1348
in renal artery aneurysms, pseudoaneurysms, and arteriovenous fistulas, 1344–1346, 1347, 1348
in renal artery stenosis, 1339–1340, 1341–1343
in renal artery thrombosis, 1338, 1339
in renal vein abnormalities, 1342–1343, 1344
venous, 1330
angioplasty results in, III:316–318
atherectomy for stenosis after, III:49
current evaluation of dysfunction in, 1333–1338
obstructed, III:581–584
rejection of
acute, 1331, 1332, 1333, 1339

chronic, 1332, 1336
lymphocele formation in, III:946
with renal vein thrombosis, 1311, 1312
strictures after, III:578
superselective embolization after, 169
surgical techniques for, 1325, 1326
urinomas after, III:667, III:668
vascular sonography after, 230
Renal trauma, 169, 1230–1243, III:892–899
anatomy in, III:892
angiography in, 1231–1243, III:895–898
arterial injuries and, 1231–1236, 1237
embolization and, 1231, 1236–1238
timing of, 1231, 1236–1238
blunt, III:892, III:894
classification of, 1230, 1231, III:892, III:893
embolization in, 1232, 1239–1243, III:896–898
classification of trauma and, 1231
complications of, 1243
indications for, 1232, 1239, 1240, 1241
successes and failures of, 1237, 1243
techniques for, 1232, 1239, 1240, 1242
timing of, 1231, 1236–1238
hypertension in, 1271–1272, 1274
mechanism of injury in, 1230–1231, 1232, III:892–893
in narrow tract injuries, 1230–1231
in wide impact or tract injuries, 1230, 1231, 1232
penetrating, III:892, III:894–895, III:897
radiologic evaluation in, III:894–895, III:896
silent, 1237, 1238
superselective catheterization in, 169
transcatheter embolization and, III:896–898
Renal tuberculosis, 1276
Renal tumors, 1132–1177
adenoma in, 1161–1163
classification of, 1132, 1133
death from, 1132
diagnostic decision tree in, 1173
in extrinsic compression of renal artery, 1270
fibroma in, 1165
hamartoma in, 1163–1165
in inferior vena cava
magnetic resonance imaging of, 940, 943
obstruction and, 959, 960
metastases of, 1165, 1933–1936
neurofibroma in, 1165
neurogenic, 1165, 1166
pelvic, 1154–1161
angiography of, 1159, 1160–1161
carcinoma in, 1159
computed tomography of, 1159–1160
cystoscopy of, 1160
cytologic examination of urine in, 1160
diagnostic evaluation of, 1159–1160, 1161, 1162
differential diagnosis of, 1160–1161

Renal tumors—*Continued*
  pelvic—*Continued*
    intravenous urography of, 1159, 1160
    pathology of, 1154–1158
    renal venography of, 1160, 1162
    retrograde pyelography of, 1160
    symptoms and signs of, 1158–1159
    treatment of, 1161
    ultrasonography of, 1159–1160
  pseudotumors and, 1165–1166, 1167–
      1170, 1226–1228
    chronic atrophic pyelonephritis and,
      1198
  renal cell carcinoma in, 1137–1154
    angiography in, 1141–1154
    bone scan and, 1154
    chest examination and, 1154
    computed tomography in, 1140,
      1142, 1143
    diagnostic evaluation of, 1139–1154
    differential diagnosis in, 1154, 1155–
      1158
    inferior vena cavography in, 1143,
      1154
    intravenous urography in, 1139–1140
    isotope imaging in, 1140, 1141
    magnetic resonance imaging in,
      1140–1141, 1144
    pathology of, 1137–1138
    renal venography in, 1142, 1154
    symptoms and signs of, 1138–1139
    treatment of, 1154
    ultrasonography in, 1140
  renal cysts and, 1170–1173, 1174, 1175
    in differential diagnosis, 1132, 1154,
      1155–1158, 1173
  schwannoma in, 1165
  superselective catheterization in, 169
  Wilms, 1132–1137
Renal urinomas, III:667–670
Renal valves, 1299, 1300, 1301
Renal vascular stents, III:321–322
Renal vein renin analysis, III:112, III:295
Renal veins, 1291–1299
  abnormalities of, after transplantation,
    1342–1343, 1344
  absence of, 1313–1315, 1316
  adrenal, 1354
  anastomoses of, in transplantation, 1325
  arteriovenous fistulas and, III:1004
  collateral vessels and, III:681, III:686–
    687
  crossing ureteropelvic junction, 1219
  embryology of, 1291–1292
  in inferior vena cava ultrasonography,
    938, 939
  intrarenal, 1292, 1293–1295
  invasion of, in renal cell carcinoma,
    1146, 1151
  left, 1293–1299, 1301
    anatomy of, 1293–1299, 1301
    for inferior vena cava collateral circula-
      tion, 951–957
    in inferior vena cava ultrasonography,
      938, 939
    retroaortic, 947, 948
  lumbar lymph nodes and, 1881
  magnetic resonance venography in,
    1852–1855
  occlusion of, after transplant, 212

    preoperative and postoperative evalua-
      tion of, 1315, 1317
    in renal angiography, 1115, 1118, 1125
    in renal cell carcinoma, 1299–1302
    renin determination and, 1305–1308
    renin ratios in, 1308
    right, 1292–1293, 1294–1296
      in inferior vena cava ultrasonography,
        938
    spontaneous communication of, with
      portal vein, 1314
    thrombolysis in, III:153, III:154
    thrombosis of
      hypertension and, 1276
      magnetic resonance venography in,
        1840
      renal venography in, 1308–1311,
        1312, 1320
      sonography of, 230–231
    valves in, 1299, 1300, 1301
    varices of, 1315
      venography in, 1311–1314, 1315
    in varicocele embolization, III:695
    washout effects simulating filling defects
      of, 971
Renal venography, 1290–1324
  in acute pyelonephritis, 1180–1181
  applications of, 1299–1320
    in benign renal parenchymal disease,
      1315–1320
    in carcinoma of kidney, 1291, 1299–
      1304, 1305
    in nonfunctioning kidney, 1313–
      1315, 1316
    in preoperative and postoperative eval-
      uation, 1315, 1317
    in renal cell carcinoma, 1142, 1154
    in renal pelvic tumors, 1160, 1162
    in renin determination, 1305–1308
    in renovascular hypertension, 1304–
      1305
    in retroperitoneal tumors, 1304
    in thrombosis, 1308–1311, 1312,
      1320
    in varices, 1311–1314, 1315
  complications of, 1291
  renal vein anatomy in, 1291–1299
    intrarenal, 1292, 1293–1295
    left, 1293–1299, 1301
    right, 1292–1293, 1294–1296
    valves in, 1299, 1300, 1301
  technique for, 1290–1291
  in varicocele embolization, III:695
Rendu-Osler-Weber syndrome, 1406–
    1409, III:1003
  islet-cell tumors versus, 1404
  pulmonary arteriovenous malformations
    in, 1033
  spinal involvement in, 369, 377
Renin, 1244
  in aldosteronism, 1361
  measurement of, 1305–1308
    accuracy of, 1308
    technique of venous sampling in,
      1306–1308
  renal vein, III:295
    in renovascular hypertension diagnosis,
      III:112
Renin-angiotensin system, 1244
Renografin. *See* Sodium diatrizoate
Renografin 60%, 170

Renografin 76%
  in coronary artery catheterization, 568
    complications from, 576, 577
  viscosity of, 170
Renovascular evaluation, angioplasty and,
    III:295–296
Renovascular hypertension (RVHTN),
    1248–1259, 1278, III:294
  angiography after surgery in, 1284–
    1287
  arteriolar nephrosclerosis in, 1260–1261
  arteriosclerosis in, 1052, 1250, 1251,
    1278
  in arteritis, 1272–1273, 1274, 1275
  branch stenosis in, 1258–1259
  in chronic glomerulonephritis, 1269
  in chronic pyelonephritis, 1268–1269
  collateral circulation in renal ischemia
    and, 1276–1284
  congenital stenosis in, 1258
  diagnosis of, 1248–1249, III:112
  dissecting aortic aneurysm repair and,
    1276
  in dissecting renal artery aneurysm,
    1251–1253, 1270–1271
  in extrinsic compression of renal artery,
    1269–1270
  hydronephrosis and, 1276
  incidence of, 1244
  in infarction of kidney, 1262–1264
  interventional radiology in, 1287
  neurofibromatosis in, 1257–1258
  oral contraceptives and, 1276
  page kidney and, 1276
  percutaneous renal transluminal angio-
    plasty for, III:113, III:114
  polycystic disease and, 1276
  in renal arteriovenous fistula, 1266–
    1268
  in renal artery aneurysm, 1264–1266
  renal artery dysplasia in, 1250–1257
  in renal artery stenosis after renal trans-
    plantation, 1339
  renal cell carcinoma and, 1276
  renal dysplasia in, 1250–1257
  in renal trauma, 1271–1272, 1274
  renal vein thrombosis and, 1276
  renal venography in, 1304–1305
  solitary cyst and, 1276
  stents in, III:112–116
  treatment of, III:112–116
  tuberculosis and, 1276
  umbilical artery catheterization and,
    1276
  in unilateral irradiation damage, 1273–
    1276
  without main renal arterial stenosis,
    1262
  xanthogranulomatous polynephritis and,
    1276
Renovist, 170
Renovist II, 170
Repeat lymphography in malignant lympho-
    mas, 1946–1950
Reperfusion after pulmonary arteriovenous
    malformations embolotherapy, III:
    852
Replenishment in cine film processing,
    109, 110
Reproducibility of results, 657

Reproductive organ dose in radiation exposure, 129–130
Reserpine, 53, 59
    renin determination and, 1306
    for vasospasm at puncture site in angiography, 1028
Residual urine, III:618
Resistance, pulmonary vascular, 852, 853
    early studies of, 849
Resistive index, 212, 213
Resolution
    of rapid film changers, 68
    of test phantom
        of cine cameras, 100
        in spot-film fluorography, 101
    of video system, 102
    for vascular intervention angiography, 135
Resolving power, 179
Respirations
    in inferior vena cava computerized tomography, 940, 941
    pulmonary microcirculation and, 849, 850
Respiratory distress, III:212
    in pulmonary angiography, 1031–1032
Respiratory equipment for emergency treatment, 47–48
Respiratory motion in pulmonary magnetic resonance angiography, 197–198
Respiratory reactions
    to contrast agents, 30
    to thoracic aortography, 399
Restenosis
    after balloon angioplasty, III:5–19
        angiographic diagnosis of, III:6–8, III:9–11
        catheter in, III:39–42
        clinical diagnosis of, III:6, III:8
        combined maneuvers and, III:16, III:17
        in coronary vessels, III:373, III:377
        histopathologic diagnosis of, III:6, III:8–11
        infection and, III:17
        molecular genetics and, III:16–17
        newer concepts and potential therapeutic implications in, III:17–19
        pathogenesis of, III:11–14
        pharmacologic maneuvers and, III:15–16
        strategies for prevention of, III:14–17
        technical approach and, III:14–15
        thrombus replacement theory of, III:17, III:18
        vascular remodeling theory of, III:17–19
    vascular endoprosthesis, atherectomy catheter for, III:49
Resuscitation
    during cardiac catheterization, 118–119
    cardiopulmonary. *See* Cardiopulmonary resuscitation
    mechanical, 37
Rete arteriosum urogenitale, 1220
Retention of urine after prostatic urethroplasty, III:632
Rethrombosis
    concurrent, III:125–127
    delayed, III:126–127

Reticulum cell sarcoma
    of bone, 1797
    pancreatic, 1406–1409
    spleen in, 1483, 1484, 1485
    in superior mesenteric artery, 1568
Retroaortic left renal vein, 947, 948
Retrocaval ureter, 945, 946
Retrocrural lymph nodes, 1885, 1886
Retroesophageal aortic diverticulum, 548
Retrograde approach
    in aortography
        in aortic arch anomalies, 547
        brachial, 8, 11, 392, 547
        carotid, 392–393
        historical notes on, 8, 11
        transfemoral, 394
        in vascular ring diagnosis, 547
    in pyelography
        of hydronephrosis, 1202, 1203, 1204
        of renal pelvic tumors, 1160
        of retrocaval or circumcaval ureter, 945, 946
    transfemoral
        in aortography, 394
        in arteriography, 1703–1705
        percutaneous, in dissecting aortic aneurysms, 503
    in ureteral stenting, III:574, III:576
    in ureteroileal anastomosis catheterization, III:650
    in urethrography (RUG), III:616, III:618, III:619
        before prostatic urethroplasty, III:628–631
    in urography, 1142
Retroperitoneal angiography, 1669–1677
    differential diagnosis in, 1676
    findings in
        in hematomas, 1671–1672, 1674, 1675
        in inflammatory disease, 1676
        in tumor, 1670–1671, 1672, 1673
    role of, in retroperitoneal masses, 1676–1677
    types of tumors in, 1669–1670
Retroperitoneal tumors
    angiography in. *See* Retroperitoneal angiography
    biopsy in, III:168, III:190
    inferior vena cavogram in, 936
    leiomyosarcomas in, III:1031
    lymphosarcoma in, 1466, 1467
    metastatic colon adenocarcinoma and, 936
    pancreatic, 1406–1409
    renal venography in, 1304
    splenic arteriography in, 1466, 1467
    types of, 1669–1670
Retroperitoneal vein, 1292
Retroperitoneum
    abscess in, 1676
    angiography and. *See* Retroperitoneal angiography
    biopsy in, III:168, III:190
    collateral vessels of, III:681, III:684–685
    dissection in, lymphocele formation and, III:944
    fibrosis in, 1054, 1055
        in inferior vena cava obstruction, 962

lymphangiopathies in, 1915, 1916–1917
    renal stones after, III:591
    hemorrhage in, 1232
        after dialysis fistula thrombolysis, III:736
        after transpleural puncture, 1030
        angiographic findings in, 1671–1672, 1674, 1675
        in coronary arteriography complication, 578
        from fractures, III:869–871
        in renal angiography, 1109
    inflammatory disease and, 1676
    lymphangiomatosis in, 1921
    surgery of, renal venography before, 1315
    tumors of. *See* Retroperitoneal tumors
Retrosternal lymph nodes, 1887, 1888
Retroviral vectors for genes, III:16
Retzius space, III:939
Reuter SR, 1436, 1587
Revascularization, III:223–385
    of aorta and aortic branches, III:283–385. *See also* Aorta, and aortic branches, revascularization of
    in atherosclerosis obliterans, 1709, 1717–1722
    in central nervous system, III:745–764. *See also* Central nervous system, revascularization in
    for chronic mesenteric ischemia, III:326–338
        discussion of, III:336–337
        etiologies and, III:326, III:328
        results of, III:330–336
        techniques for, III:326–330
    of dialysis fistula, III:726–742. *See also* Dialysis fistula
    in donor liver preparation, III:509–510
    femoropopliteal, III:262–283. *See also* Femoropopliteal revascularization
    infrapopliteal, III:284–293. *See also* Infrapopliteal revascularization
    percutaneous aortoiliac intervention and, III:225–261. *See also* Percutaneous aortoiliac intervention
    renal angioplasty in, III:294–325. *See also* Renal angioplasty
Revascularization in Treatment of Angina (RITA) trial, III:382–383
Reverse-curve catheter
    in bronchial artery embolization, III:822, III:825
    in mesenteric angioplasty, III:327
Rhabdomyosarcomas
    of extremities
        in differential diagnosis, 1811
        femoral arteriography in, 1735, 1737
    retroperitoneal, 1669
Rhenium tungsten molybdenum in tube, 95
Rheumatic valvulitis, 543
Rheumatoid arthritis, III:173
Rheumatoid nodule in biopsy, III:173
Ribs
    cervical, in thoracic outlet syndrome, 996
    in translumbar catheterization, 1017
Rice CO, 6

Richter transjugular intrahepatic portosystemic shunt, III:530. *See also* Transjugular intrahepatic portosystemic
shunt (TIPS)
Ricketts HJ, 10, 556, 635
Right anterior oblique (RAO) projection
in coronary arteriography, 561, 566–
568, 592–593
of atrial arteries, 615
of left coronary artery, 607, 608, 611,
612, 613
of right coronary artery, 603, 604
in left ventriculography, 561
Right coronary arteries. *See* Coronary arteries, right
Rigler LG, 68, 76, 1527
Ring
aortic, 503
circumaortic venous, 1315, 1317
persistent, 947, 950
supravalvular, normal anatomy of, 593
of Vieussens, collaterals of, 703–704,
706–708
Ring's template for cortical branches of
middle cerebral artery, 270, 271
Ring endoprosthesis in malignant hepatobiliary obstructions, III:479
Ring-Kerlan endoprosthesis, III:479
Riolan artery, 1458, 1460
RITA (Revascularization in Treatment of
Angina) trial, III:382–383
Road-mapping technique
in digital subtraction imaging, 151
in arteriovenous malformations, III:
1010
in extremity arteriovenous malforma-
tion, III:1021
in infrapopliteal revascularization, III:
285
in nonsubtraction imaging, 152
Robb GP, 8, 768
Robb needle, 392
Robin ED, 769
Robins and Bookstein intravascular biopsy,
III:195
Robinson LS, 892
Rodbard S, 850
Rodes CB, III:837
Roentgen WC, 3
Roentgen rays, electrical energy conversion
to, 94
Roentgen-area-product meter, 129
Roll-film changers
CGR, 78–80
cut-film changers versus, 68–69
Elema, 75–76, 77
Franklin, 76–77, 78
history of, 66–68
Romazicon, 246
Rösch and Hanafee transjugular intrahe-
patic portosystemic shunt, III:530.
See also Transjugular intrahepatic
portosystemic shunt (TIPS)
Rösch transjugular liver biopsy, III:197
Rosen wire, III:31, III:34–35
in chronic mesenteric ischemia interven-
tions, III:329
in femoropopliteal revascularization, III:
263, III:264
Roseno A, 7
Rosenthal, veins of, 274, 275, 276

Rotablator atherectomy catheter, 1042
Rotational scanography, 83
Rotoblator atherectomy catheter, III:45,
III:47, III:378, III:379–380
in femoropopliteal atherectomy, III:280
in infrapopliteal revascularization, III:
293
Rousthöi P, 7, 391, 393, 635
Roux-en-Y choledochojejunostomy, III:
516–517
Roux-en-Y hepaticojejunostomy, III:477
Roux-en-Y loop, bile duct dilations and,
III:461–462, III:465
in primary sclerosing cholangitis, III:469
r-sctPA (recombinant single-chain urokinase plasminogen activator), III:122
RT-PA (recombinant tissue type of plasminogen activator), 1640, III:233
Rubella, 831
RUG (retrograde urethrography), III:616,
III:618, III:619
before prostatic urethroplasty, III:628–
631
Ruggles H, 66
Runoff vessels
in femoral arteriography
filming equipment for, 1706–1707
positioning and, 1707
visualizing distal, 1712, 1713
in peripheral vascular magnetic resonance angiography, 1823, 1831,
1832
Rupture. *See also* Hemorrhage
of abdominal aorta aneurysms. *See*
Abdominal aorta aneurysms, rupture
of
of aortic sinus aneurysm, thoracic aortography in, 396
of arteriosclerotic thoracic aortic aneurysm, 473, 474
of azygos veins, 911
of balloon in peripheral angioplasty,
1040
bulbomembranous urethral, III:617
of capsular artery, 1106, 1108
of liver, 1037
in percutaneous transluminal angioplasty
for coarctation of aorta, 459
of puboprostatic ligament or urogenital
diaphragm, 1644–1645
of pulmonary artery, 420
of renal cyst, III:659–660
splenic, 1490, 1491
in superselective catheterization, 166
of Valsalva aneurysms, 488
of veins after dialysis fistula thrombolysis, III:736
Rutherford scale for femoropopliteal revascularization results, III:265
Rutherford-Becker criteria for femoropopliteal revascularization results, III:
265, III:270
Rye classification of Hodgkin disease, 1940

Saccular aneurysms
of abdominal aorta, 1058, 1059, 1074–
1075, 1078
infrarenal, 1074–1075, 1078
mycotic, 1080
inferior mesenteric angiography in, 1601
of splenic artery, 1475

Sacral arteries, 362
anatomy of, 1021
angiography technique for, 369
in pelvic fractures, III:876
Sacral ectopia of kidney, 1222–1223
Sacral lymph nodes, 1878
Sacral venous plexuses, 893, 894, 895,
896
percutaneous abscess drainage and, III:
949
Sacral vertebral angiography, 933
Saddle embolus in pulmonary artery, 810
Safety
electrical, 130
patient
in cardiac catheterization laboratory,
114–116
emergency equipment and, 118–119
equipment for, 117–118
measurements in, 116–117
radiation. *See* Radiation safety
Sagittal sinus
dural arteriovenous malformations of,
III:800
superior, 274, 276
occlusion of, in gunshot wound, 274,
276, 351
thrombosis of, 303
Salicylic acid before pediatric angioplasty,
III:911
Saline in superior mesenteric angiography,
1557
Salmonella
in abdominal aortic aneurysms, 1077,
1080
in thoracic aortic aneurysms, 485
Salpingography, selective, III:672–677
Salt depletion, 1306, 1308
Salt solutions as sclerosant, III:946
Saltzman GF, 411
Sampling, venous
parathyroid, 984–988
in renin determination, 1306–1308
Sanchez-Perez JM, 67–68
Sanchez-Perez cassette changer, 70, 71
Sandostatin. *See* Octreotide acetate
Sandwich technique for staghorn calculi,
III:588
Saphenous artery, 1698
variants of, 1700
Saphenous veins
femoropopliteal revascularization and,
III:274
grafts of, 756, 757, 758
for inferior vena cava collateral circulation studies, 954, 956
magnetic resonance venography of,
1842, 1846
mapping of, before vein grafts, 1856
thrombolysis in grafts of, III:144–146
in venography, 1751
vertebral veins and, 898
Sarcoid, pulmonary, III:819
Sarcoidosis
lymph node changes in, 1925, 1926
pulmonary, pulmonary arteriography in,
802, 805
Sarcomas
in bone, 1797
classification of, III:1031
etiology of, III:1031

Ewing, 1794–1797
in extremities, 1811, 1812
limb-sparing resection in, III:1032–1034
preoperative radiation therapy in, III:1032
in femur, 1734
in inferior vena cava, 971, 972
intraarterial chemotherapy for, III:1031–1036
complications of, III:1034–1035
technique for, III:1034–1035
in lung, 815
mesenchymal, 1811
biopsy diagnosis in, III:169, III:190
natural history of, III:1031
osteogenic, 1734
in pancreas, 1406–1409
pleomorphic, 1812
reticulum cell
of bone, 1797
of pancreas, 1406–1409
of spleen, 1483, 1484, 1485
of superior mesenteric artery, 1568
retroperitoneal, 1669, 1670
soft tissue, III:1033–1034
spindle cell, 1669, 1670
in spleen, 1483, 1484, 1485
staging of, III:1031
in superior mesenteric artery, 1568
synovial, 1809–1810
femoral arteriography in, 1735
undifferentiated, 1669
Sarfeh and Rypins portosystemic shunt, III:526
Sasahara AA, 768
Satellite anastomotic circulation, 701
Saticon photoconductive tube, 140
Saturation losses in distal portions of vessels, 196
SCA&I. *See* Society for Cardiac Angiography & Intervention (SCA&I)
Scanning
delayed, 1545
progressive or sequential, 141, 146
radionuclide. *See* Radionuclide scanning
raster, 141
target, 141–142
Scanography, rotational, 83
Scatter
in gray scale imaging, 205, 206
limitation of, in radiation protection, 125–126
Rayleigh, 205
and veiling glare (SVG), 149
Schaper technique for postmortem coronary angiogram, 584–585
Schaper W, 584, 585, 700
Schlesinger MJ, 584, 701
Schlumpf M, III:25
Schneider Wallstent. *See* Wallstent
Schönander cut-film changers, 73–74, 75
closure time in, 72
Schoonmaker-King technique for coronary arteriography, 571
Schroy PC, 1434
Schwannoma
carotid artery supply to, 335–337
renal, 1165
Schwarten catheter, III:285
Sciatic artery, persistent, 1699

Sciatic nerve, percutaneous abscess drainage and, III:949–951
Scimitar syndrome or sign, 882–883, 885, 886, 887
Scintigraphy
of adrenal glands, 1356–1357, 1364
in adrenogenital syndromes, 1369
leukocyte
in aortoenteric and paraprosthetic fistula diagnosis, 1693
in thoracic aortic aneurysm diagnosis, 469
renal
in acute pyelonephritis, 1179
captopril, 1245, 1335
in rejection after renal transplantation, 1334–1335, 1336
in renovascular hypertension diagnosis, III:112
in varicocele diagnosis, III:689
Scleroderma, 802, 803, 805
Sclerosants. *See also* Embolization
after lymphocele percutaneous drainage, III:945–946
in renal cyst sclerosis, III:663
Sclerosing agents. *See* Embolization
Sclerosing cholangitis, primary, III:465–470
Sclerosing mediastinitis, 919, 921–922
Sclerosis
of renal cyst after aspiration, III:662–666
tuberous, 1370
Sclerotherapy
endoscopic, in esophageal varices, 1422
in portal hypertension, history of, III:525–526
in renal cyst, III:662–666
somatostatin and, 56
vascular sonography after, 232
Scoliosis, renal stones and, III:597, III:598
Scomazzoni G, 589, 701, 711
Scopix RP IC cine films, 107
Scopolamine, 398
Scratch-resistance of balloon catheter, III:39
Screen in magnification angiography, 177–180
Screening for abdominal aorta aneurysms, 1096–1098
Scrotum, III:641–642
collateral vessels and, III:681, III:687
Scrub nurse in cardiac catheterization, 131
scuPA (single-chain urokinase plasminogen activator), III:122
scu-UKA (single-chain urokinase plasminogen activator), III:122
SCVIR (Society of Cardiovascular and Interventional Radiology) guidelines for percutaneous interventions, III:240–241
SDAVFs. *See* Spinal dural arteriovenous fistulas (SDAVFs)
Seat belt trauma, 528, 529, 532–533
Second degree heart block, 43, 44
Second septal perforator branch, 611
Secondary lymphedema, 1908–1909, 1914–1916, 1920
Secondary pulmonary hypertension, 815
Secondary Raynaud's phenomenon, 1759

Second-look lymphography, 1929
Secretin
in pancreatic angiography, 1392, 1394
in superior mesenteric angiography, 1557
Sedation
for cerebral angiography, 246
in gastrostomy, III:548
intraprocedural, III:212–214
in nephrostomy, III:563–564
in renal angiography, 1101
in transjugular intrahepatic portosystemic shunt, III:532
Seeding of needle tract
in biopsy, III:183–184
in abdomen, 1035
of lung, 1035
in percutaneous ablation of liver tumors, 1037
See-through film changers, 77–78, 79, 80
Segmental branches of abdominal aorta, 1021
Segmented k-space acquisition, 198
Seizures, 327
Seldinger SI, 9, 1013
Seldinger technique, 155, 156
in abdominal aortography, 1013, 1014
in abscess drainage
hepatic, III:929
mediastinal, III:835
pelvic, III:951, III:952
thoracic, III:830
transvaginal percutaneous, III:951
in arterial portography, 1529
in femoral arteriography, 1704, 1705
in hepatic arteriography, 1433
in pancreatic pseudocyst drainage, III:933
in renal cyst sclerosis, III:662–663
in thoracic aortography, 472
for thoracic empyema drainage, III:832
Selectan, early uses of, 7
Selectan Neutral, 14
Selective angiocardiography, historical notes on, 8. *See also* specific procedure
Selective arteriography in bronchial artery embolization, III:823
Selective catheterization in pulmonary arteriovenous malformations, III:846, III:847
Selective embolization in gastrointestinal bleeding, III:400–403
from diverticula, III:411–414
Selective salpingography, III:672–677
Selective thrombolysis, III:119–131. *See also* Thrombolysis
transcatheter parathrombic, III:127
in stroke, III:748, III:750–751
Self-expanding stents, III:90–93, III:94–95
Semen analysis, varicocele and, III:699–700
Semilunar ganglion, 958
Semilunar valves
aorticopulmonary window and, 464, 465
leaflets of, normal anatomy of, 593
Seminal vesicles, III:639–641

Seminal vesiculitis, III:640
Seminoma, testicular, 1933, 1934
Semiselective renal angiography, 1113
   catheter for, 1102, 1103
   magnification in, 1113, 1115
   in malignant hypertension, 1116, 1117
Sensitivity testing, 392
Sensitometers, 124
Sepsis. *See also* Infection
   asplenia and, 1472
   biliary drainage procedures and, 1038
   nephrostomy tube and, III:569, III:572
   percutaneous cholecystostomy and, III:489
   percutaneous transhepatic cholangiography and, 1037
   stone removal complications and
      complicated biliary, III:496
      lithotripsy in, III:500, III:608
      percutaneous, III:602
Septal branch compression during ventricular systole, 686
Septal defects
   aortic, 464–466
      thoracic aortography in, 396
   atrial. *See* Atrial septal defect (ASD)
   ventricular
      aorticopulmonary window and, 464
      pulmonary arteriography in, 787, 789, 800
      truncus arteriosus of, 551
Septal interstitial edema, 863
Septal perforation, 637
Septal perforator, first, 611, 612
   superimposed in arteriography over obstructions, 734, 735
Septal veins, anterior, 275
Septic arthritis of knee, 1043
Septicemia, 1038
Septum
   defects of. *See* Septal defects
   interatrial, Kugel's anastomosis in, 714–715
   interventricular
      collaterals of, 703, 704, 705
      defect of, pulmonary arteriography in, 787, 800
Sequential scanning, 141
Sequestration, pulmonary
   arteriography in, 798–799
   as developmental anomaly, 840–842
   extralobar or intralobar, 798
   thoracic aortography in, 396, 549, 550
Serial radiography
   in abdominal aorta aneurysms, 1081–1082, 1083, 1084–1085
   biplane. *See* Biplane radiography
   in cardiac catheterization laboratory, 87, 101–102. *See also* Cardiac catheterization laboratory
   in femoral arteriography, 1706–1707
   for ischemic heart disease study, 121
   in pulmonary arteriography, 776–777
   rapid
      generators for, 91–92
      tubes for, 97
Serotonin
   reserpine and, 59
   somatostatin and, 56
Serous cystadenoma of pancreas, 1405, 1407

Serum creatinine, 23–24
Serum hepatitis, 1438
Seurat spleen, III:887
Sex veins, 951–953, 956, 957
SFA (superficial femoral artery), dissection of, 1040
Sharpness of image, 89
Shearing forces in liver injury, III:422, III:423
Sheaths
   arterial access, for balloon catheter, III:27
   for cerebral angiography, 249
      removal of, 251–252
   Cook introducer, in percutaneous cholecystolithotomy, III:504
   in coronary arteriography, 558, 559
   French catheter-introducing. *See* French catheter-introducing sheath
   French hemostatic, in transjugular intrahepatic portosystemic shunt, III:532
   Teflon-needle
      in percutaneous gastrostomy, III:549, III:551
      in ureteral stenting, III:574
Shepherd's crook catheter
   in adrenal angiography, 1354
   in bronchial artery embolization, III:822
   in mesenteric angioplasty, III:327
   in spinal angiography, 369
Shielding
   dose and, 137
   gonadal, 129–130
Shirey EK, 556, 635
Shock syndrome, III:209
Shock waves in lithotripsy complications, III:607
Short left main coronary artery, 564–565
Shotguns. *See* Gunshot wounds
Shoulder
   arteriovenous malformations of, 1761
   liposarcoma of, 1818
   renal cell carcinoma metastases to, 1807
Shrapnel wounds, 1729, 1730
Shunt
   arterial portography in, 1537–1538, 1539
   arteriovenous. *See* Arteriovenous fistula
   in congenital heart disease, mechanical embolization in, III:55, III:70
   dialysis. *See* Dialysis; Dialysis fistula; Dialysis shunt angiography
   Glenn, 844
   hepatic arterial–portal venous, 1436, 1437
   iatrogenic-induced, 216, 218
   left-to-right
      from aorta into pulmonary arteries, 796
      in partial anomalous pulmonary venous connection, 883–884
      pulmonary artery hypertension and, 860
      in total anomalous pulmonary venous connection, 873
   mesocaval, 231–232
   portacaval, 1538, 1539
   portosystemic
      transjugular intrahepatic, perirectal varices after, 1850
      vascular sonography after, 232

pulmonary
   in arteriovenous malformations. *See* Pulmonary arteriovenous malformations (PAVMs)
   coil bronchial artery embolization for, III:826
   right-to-left, 873
   spinal arteriovenous. *See* Spinal dural arteriovenous fistulas (SDAVFs)
   splenorenal
      arterial portography after, 1538
      surgical, 1478, 1481
      transhepatic portal venography in, 1424
      vascular sonography after, 231–232
   ventriculoatrial, broken fragment of, III:966
   ventriculopleural, 923
      abscess formation and, III:948
Shunt-type varicocele, III:689
Sicard JA, 4, 13
Side-to-side anastomosis, 758, 759
Sidewinder catheter, 1016
   in iliac artery obstruction, III:38
   in renal angioplasty, III:302
Siemens Angioskop C system, 104
Siemens cardiac contour collimator, 98
Siemens cine viewer, 115
Sigmoid artery, 1588, 1589
Sigmoid peridiverticular abscess, III:941
Sigmoid sinus, dural arteriovenous malformations of, III:800
Signal loss
   flip angle and, 195
   saturation, minimizing, 196–197
Signal-to-noise ratio (SNR), 140, 142
Silastic spheres in embolization, III:781
Silicon-controlled rectifier (SCR) contacting generators, 91
Silicone
   in detachable embolization balloon, III:65–66, III:69–70
   for central nervous system, III:766
   for varicocele, III:696–698
   on runners of cine camera, 123
   in ureteral stents, III:573
SIM1. *See* French Simmons catheters
Simmons catheters
   in bronchial artery embolization, III:822
   in internal iliac artery angiography, III:877
   in renal arteriography in trauma, III:895
Simon Nitinol filter, III:987, III:991–992
   complications with, 1044
   magnetic resonance venography and, 1852
Simple cortical renal cyst, III:658
Simpson AtheroCath catheter, 1042, III:44–45, III:46
   in aortoiliac disease, III:234–240
   in coronary disease, III:377, III:378
   in dialysis fistula stenoses, III:735, III:737
   in femoropopliteal atherectomy, III:278–280
   in infrapopliteal revascularization, III:292–293
   in intravascular biopsy, III:196
   in malignant hepatobiliary obstruction biopsy, III:476

Simpson AtheroTrack, III:240
  in infrapopliteal revascularization, III:
    292–293
Single coronary artery, 596–598, 599,
  747–748
Single photon emission computed tomography (SPECT), 660, III:777
Single wall arterial puncture, 248
Single-chain urokinase plasminogen activator (pro-UKA; scu-UKA), III:122
Single-stage cassette changers, 70
Sinoatrial node artery, 750
Sinus
  aortic
    in infant, 401
    ruptured aneurysm of, 396
  cavernous, 276
    approaches to, 253
  coronary venous, 623
  dural, 274, 276
  renal, abscess of, 1123
  sagittal, superior
    occlusion of, in gunshot wound, 274,
      276
    thrombosis of, 303
  sphenoparietal, 275
  straight, 274, 275, 276
  transverse, 274
  of Valsalva. *See* Valsalva, sinus of
  venous, thrombosis of, 303
Sinus arrest, 568
Sinus bradycardia, 43, 44, III:216
  in selective coronary artery catheterization, 568
Sinus histiocytosis, malignant lymphoma
  versus, 1943
Sinus node, 615
Sinus node artery (S-N), 587, 589, 616,
  619
  collateral circulation and, 714–715,
    720
Sinus rhythm, normal, 43, 44
Sinus tachycardia, 43, 44
Sinus venosus atrial septal defect, 880,
  881, 882
Sinusoids of corpus cavernosa, III:705
Sipple syndrome, 1370
SIST (summation of intensities following
  soft thresholding), 1844
Skeletal system
  biopsy and, III:190–192
  pain from malignancy and, III:201–202
  sarcomas of, III:1035
Skin
  magnification angiography of, 186
  metastatic neoplasms of, 1937, 1938
Skin grafts, 1730
Skiodan. *See* Abrodil
Skip metastases in Hodgkin disease, 1941
Skull base tumors, III:814
Skull vault, extraaxial lesions of parasagittal
  surfaces of, III:791–793
SLE (systemic lupus erythematosus), 307
Sling, pulmonary artery, 794
Slit radiography, 83–84
Slow-scan mode, 142
SMAE (superior mesenteric artery embolus), 1619–1620, 1621
Small bowel
  adenocarcinomas of, 1577–1578
  localization of bleeding in, III:394

Small-cell lung cancer
  biopsy in, III:177, III:186
  versus non-small-cell, III:170
Small-vessel embolization, III:52–54
SMANCS, III:437
SMAT (superior mesenteric artery thrombosis), 1620–1622, 1623
Smoking. *See* Cigarette smoking
Smooth muscle cells of vessels, 50–51
  in intimal hyperplasia, III:4–5, III:12–13
  restenosis after balloon angioplasty and,
    III:16–17, III:39
Smooth muscle relaxants, 56
  in pharmacologic erection, III:706
S-N (sinus node) artery, 587, 589, 616,
  619
  collateral circulation and, 714–715, 720
Snow plow technique in femoropopliteal
  revascularization, III:264
SNR (signal-to-noise ratio), 140, 142
Society for Cardiac Angiography & Intervention (SCA&I), 658–659
  registry of complications of, 572, 574,
    575, 580
  standards of, 1024, 1025
Society of Cardiovascular and Interventional Radiology (SCVIR) guidelines, III:240–241
  in femoropopliteal revascularization, III:
    271–272
Sodium acetrizoate
  adverse reactions to, 397
  chemistry and characteristics of, 15
Sodium bicarbonate, III:216
  in cardiac standstill, 45
  in emergency treatment, 39, 41, 45
  recommended dosages for, 46
  strengths and volumes of, 48
  in ventricular fibrillation, 45
Sodium chloride, 25, 27
Sodium citrate, 27
Sodium diatrizoate, 20
  chemistry and characteristics of, 15, 20
  in coronary artery catheterization, 568
    complications from, 576, 577
  in hepatic arteriography, 1433
  in superior mesenteric angiography,
    1556
  in thoracic aortography, 395
  toxicity of, 25, 400
    cardiac, 29
  as vasodilator, 60
Sodium EDTA, 27
Sodium iodide, early uses of, 5, 6, 7, 13
Sodium meglumine ioxaglate
  in adrenal angiography, 1354
  chemistry and characteristics of, 16–17, 20
  coronary artery catheterization complications from, 576
  in thoracic aortography, 395
Sodium monoiodohippurate, 14, 15
Sodium morrhuate, III:696
Sodium nitroprusside, 58
Sodium salts as sclerosants, 576, 577, III:
  946
Soft tissue
  anatomy of, 1779–1780
  angiography of
    femoral, 1711
    inflammatory lesions of bone and,
      1782–1783

technique of, 1780–1781
  tumor appearance in, 1781–1782
  myositis ossificans of, 1812–1813
  tumors of, 1810–1813
    benign, 1782, 1798, 1799, 1801–
      1806
    embolization of, 1813–1819
    femoral arteriography in, 1711
    fibrous origin of, 1798–1801, 1802
    in inferior vena cava obstruction, 960,
      962
    malignant, 1798–1801, 1802, 1806–
      1809
    metastatic, 1807–1808, 1809
    sarcomas in, III:1033–1034
    vascular origin of, 1801–1806
Sohendral kit
  in biliary calculi removal, III:493, III:
    495
  in percutaneous cholecystolithotomy,
    III:504
Solitary renal cysts, 1276
Solu-Cortef. *See* Hydrocortisone
Solu-Medrol. *See* Methylprednisolone
Somatostatin, 56
Somatostatin analogues, III:15
Somatostatinomas, 1402, 1405, 1406
Sones FM Jr, 10, 556, 635
Sones technique for coronary arteriography, 557, 570
Sonnenberg catheter, III:930, III:951
Sonography. *See* Ultrasonography
Sos spring guidewires, 162–163
Sotgiu G, 1497
Sovak M, 18, 19, 20
Space of Retzius, III:939
Space requirements
  for cardiac catheterization laboratory,
    87–89
  for vascular intervention angiography,
    136
Spalteholz W, 584
Spasm. *See* Vasospasm
Spatial convolution, 144–146
Spatial filtration, 152
Spatial resolution, 68
Speck U, 18
SPECT (single photon emission computed
  tomography), 660, III:777
Spermatic arteries, 1021, 1292
  in inferior vena cava obstruction, 958
Spermatic cord, III:639–640
Spermatic veins
  anatomy of, III:679–681
  collateral vessels for, III:681–686, III:
    687
    in varicocele recurrence after surgery,
      III:692, III:693
  external, III:679
  internal, III:678
  lack of venous valves in, III:688
  ligation of, III:691–692
  varicocele embolization in, III:693–699
Spermatic venogram, III:680, III:682–
  687
  after surgical ligation of varicocele, III:
    692
  in varicocele diagnosis, III:689, III:690
Sphenoid, wing of greater, III:793
Sphenoparietal sinus, 275
Spiderlon, III:63

Spiders, III:61
  in pediatric embolization, III:908
Spin echo imaging, 1839
Spin phase of magnetic resonance imaging,
    200
Spinal angiography, 356–388
  in cavernous angiomas, 385
  classification of vascular malformations
      in, 369
  embryology and, 357
  in hemangioblastomas, 384, 385–386
  indications for, 356
  intradural arteriovenous fistulas in
      complications of, 1032
      of type I, 369–376
      of type II and III, 376–382, 383
      of type IV, 382–385
  normal blood supply in, 357–366, 367
    anterior spinal artery and, 358–359.
        See also Spinal arteries, anterior
    intrinsic spinal cord supply and, 362–
        364, 365
    pial plexus and, 362
    posterior spinal arteries and, 362. *See
        also* Spinal arteries, posterior
    radicular arteries and, 357–358
    regional supply to anterior spinal
        artery and, 359–362, 363
    superficial spinal cord arterial system
        and, 358–362, 363
    veins and, 364–366, 367
    vertebral supply and, 363–364, 365,
        366
  in primary and metastatic tumors of spi-
      nal column, 386–387
  in spinal column lesions, 386–387
  technique for, 366–369
  in vertebral hemangiomas, 386
Spinal arteries
  anterior, 358–359
    bidirectional flow of, 360
    regional supply to, 359–362, 363
    to spinal cord, 362–363, 364, 365
    in bronchial artery embolization, III:
        822, III:823, III:825, III:826–
        827
    embryology of, 357
    hairpin configurations of, 358, 359
  posterior, 362
    to spinal cord, 362–363, 364, 365
    in spinal dural arteriovenous fistulas of
        type II and III, 379, 382–383
    in spinal dural arteriovenous fistulas of
        type II and III, 379, 382–383
    superficial, to spinal cord, 358–362, 363
Spinal column
  primary tumors of, 386–387
  spinal angiography of, 386–387
Spinal cord
  blood supply to
    in bronchial artery embolization, III:
        822, III:823, III:825, III:826–827
    intrinsic, 362–364, 365
    normal, 357–366, 367
    superficial arterial, 358–362, 363
    in superselective catheterization, 168
    venous system and, 364–366, 367
  magnification angiography of, 186
Spinal dural arteriovenous fistulas
    (SDAVFs)
  complications of embolization in, 1032

of type I, 369–376
  anatomy and pathophysiology of,
      370–372
  angiography of, 373–374, 375
  clinical features of, 369–370
  diagram of, 370
  radiology of, 372–373
  treatment of, 374–376
of type II and III, 376–382, 383
  anatomy and pathophysiology of,
      377–378
  angiography of, 379, 382–383
  clinical features of, 376–377
  diagram of, 376
  radiology of, 378–379, 380–381
  treatment of, 379–382
of type IV, 382–385
  diagnosis and treatment of, 382–385
  diagram of, 383
Spinal dysraphism, III:598
Spinal veins, 364–366, 367
  posterior, 364–366
Spindle cell sarcomas, 1669, 1670
Spine
  cervical, osteoblastomas of, 1791
  magnification angiography of, 186
Spin-echo imaging, 189–191, 192
Spiral arteries, 1118
Spiral computed tomography
  in abdominal aorta aneurysms, 1091,
      1093, 1094
  in coronary disease, 692
  in dissecting aortic aneurysms, 516
  of subclavian artery, 996
  in thoracic aortic aneurysms, 471
Spironolactone, 1361, III:536–537
Splanchnic arteries
  arteriosclerosis of, 1399
    chronic intestinal ischemia and, 1631–
        1632
  arteritis of, 1399
  blood pressure and, 1616
  cardiac output and, 1615
  method for assessing, 1631
  reconstruction or dilation of, in chronic
      mesenteric ischemia, 1633–1634
  vasopressin infusion in, III:396
Splanchnic circulation. *See also* Splanchnic
    arteries
  blood pressure and, 1616
  cardiac output and, 1615
  method for assessing, 1631
Spleen
  abnormalities of, 1467–1492. *See also*
      Splenic vascular bed abnormalities
  abscesses of, 1491–1492, III:931–932
  accessory, 1405, 1471
  arteriography of, III:886–887
  benign tumors in, 1482–1483
  blood supply to. *See* Splenic arteries;
      Splenic veins
  cysts in, 1480–1482, 1483
  immunologic function of, III:884–885
  infarction of, 1477–1478, 1479
    in coronary arteriography complica-
        tions, 578
  injury to
    interventional radiology in, III:884–
        891
    as percutaneous stone removal compli-
        cation, III:602

malignant tumors in, 1467, 1468,
    1483–1484, 1485, 1486
  intrahepatic, 1522–1524, 1525–1526
metastases to, 1485, 1486
neoplasms in, 1467, 1468, 1482–1484
removal of, III:884
rupture of, 1490, 1491
trauma to, 1485–1491
wandering or ectopic, 1468–1471
Splenectomy
  arterial portography after, 1535–1537
  infection after, III:884
  trauma and, 1485
Splenic arteries, 1464–1492. *See also*
    Splenic arteriography
  abscess and, 1491–1492
  accessory spleen and, 1471
  after surgery, 1478, 1481
  anatomy of, 1017, 1020, 1457–1458
  aneurysm of, 1474–1475, 1476, 1477
    in pancreatitis, 1412, 1413, 1414
    splenoportography and, 1500
  anomalies of
    number, 1471–1472
    position, 1459, 1461, 1468–1471
  arteriosclerotic, 1473–1474
  arteriovenous fistula in, 1475–1477,
      1478
  arteritis in, 1474
  asplenia and, 1471–1472
  branches of, 1458–1461, 1462
    arteria pancreatica magna in, 1459,
        1460, 1463
    caudal pancreatic, 1459, 1460
    celiac artery and, 1462
    dorsal pancreatic, 1458, 1459, 1460
    gastric, 1460, 1463
    gastroepiploic, 1461–1463
    incidence of visualized, in splenic arte-
        riography, 1459, 1460, 1462–
        1463
    interventional techniques in, 1492
    left gastroepiploic, 1461, 1462
    origin of, 1459, 1460, 1462–1463
    pancreatic, 1458–1460
    partial ablation of, 1492–1493
    polar arteries and, 1461, 1463
    short gastric, 1460, 1463
    superior pancreatic, of Testus, 1458,
        1459, 1460
    terminal, 1460, 1461
  circulation time in, 1464
  congenital, 1459, 1461, 1468–1472
  cysts in, 1480–1482, 1483
  diameters in, 1463, 1464
  distribution of, 1457–1458
  dysplastic, 1474
  irregular stenosis in, 1465–1467
  length and configuration of, 1464
  neoplasms in, 1467, 1468, 1482–1484
    benign, 1482–1483
    malignant, 1467, 1468, 1483–1484,
        1485, 1486
  occlusion of
    interventional techniques in, 1492
    partial ablation in, 1492–1493
  origin of, 1457
  in pancreas, 1384
    abnormalities of, 1464–1467
  polysplenia and, 1472
  portal hypertension and, 1478, 1479

in portography, 1500, 1527–1528, 1531–1532. *See also* Arterial portography
retrograde filling of, from inferior mesenteric artery, 1593
segmentation of, 1458
length and configuration in, 1464
of splenic vascular bed, 1473–1492. *See also* Splenic vascular bed abnormalities
infarction and, 1477–1478, 1479
splenic vein occlusion and, 1480
in splenomegaly, 1467–1468
surgical amputation of, in renal trauma, 1236
thrombosis in, 1478, 1479, 1480
tortuosity of, 1458
trauma of, 1485–1491
variants of normal spleen and, 1459, 1461, 1468
vascular displacement of, 1465
vasopressin infusion in, III:396
wandering spleen and, 1468–1471
Splenic arteriography, 1457–1496. *See also* Splenic arteries
of abnormal splenic artery, 1464–1492
abscess in, 1491–1492
in congenital anomalies, 1459, 1461, 1468–1472
diagnostic decision pathway in, 1493
interventional techniques and, 1492–1493
neoplasms in, 1467, 1468, 1482–1484
in pancreas, 1464–1467
primary abnormalities of splenic vascular bed and, 1473–1482. *See also* Splenic vascular bed abnormalities
in splenomegaly, 1467–1468
trauma in, 1485–1491
diagnostic decision pathway in, 1493
interventional techniques in, 1492–1493
of normal vessels, 1462–1464
Splenic arteriovenous fistula, 1475–1477, 1478
Splenic cysts, 1480–1482, 1483
false, 1481
Splenic vascular bed abnormalities, 1473–1482
after surgery, 1478, 1481
arterial aneurysm in, 1474–1475, 1476, 1477
arterial dysplasia in, 1474
arterial thrombosis in, 1478, 1479, 1480
arteriosclerosis in, 1473–1474
arteriovenous fistula in, 1475–1477, 1478
arteritis in, 1474
cysts in, 1480–1482, 1483
infarction in, 1477–1478, 1479
portal hypertension in, 1478, 1479
venous occlusion in, 1480
Splenic veins
anatomy of, 1018
in arterial portography, 1531–1532. *See also* Arterial portography
compression of, 1397, 1399–1400, 1410
Doppler waveform sampling in, 211
occlusion of, 1480
splenic arteriography in, 1480

in splenoportography, normal variants of, 1505
thrombosis of
splenomegaly in, 1467
splenoportography of, 1512–1515
Splenomegaly
partial splenic ablation in, 1492
splenic arteriography of, 1467–1468
Splenoportal axis, patent but nonvisualized, 1539–1541
Splenoportography, 1497–1526
complications of, 1500
disadvantages of, 1497
extrahepatic anatomic changes in, 1512–1526
hemodynamics in
normal, 1498, 1500–1501, 1502–1505
in vascular obstruction, 1506–1512, 1517–1521
indications for, 1497–1498, 1499
intrahepatic anatomic changes in, 1512–1526
cirrhosis of liver and, 1512–1521
in malignant tumors, 1522–1524, 1525–1526
normal, 1502–1505
portal vein variants in, 1505–1506
and portal hypertension, 1497–1526
technique for, 1498–1500
vascular anatomy in, 1498, 1501–1506, 1507, 1514
extrahepatic, 1498, 1501–1504, 1505–1506, 1526
intrahepatic, 1504, 1506, 1507, 1512–1526
vascular obstruction in, 1506–1512, 1517–1521
extrahepatic, 1499, 1508–1512, 1513–1517
intrahepatic, 1506–1508, 1517–1521
Splenorenal shunt
arterial portography after, 1538
spontaneous, transhepatic portal venography in, 1424
surgical, 1478, 1481
vascular sonography after, 231–232
Splenorrhaphy, 1491
Splenosis, accessory splenic tissue versus, 1471
Spontaneous chylothorax, 1920
Spontaneously occurring vasospasm, 685–686, 731–733
Spot-film fluorography
automatic stabilization system for brightness in, 93–94
beam limitation in, 124–125
cameras for, 101
collimators for, 97
generators for, 91
image intensifiers for, 99
for ischemic heart disease study, 121
transformer for, 94
tubes for, 97
Spring embolus, III:56–57, III:61
Spring guidewires, 162–163
Spring-coil stents, III:90, III:92
Spring-loaded biopsy gun, III:637
Sprue, 1568, 1569
Stab wounds
arteriography in, III:858

femoral arteriography in, 1726, 1727–1729
of superficial femoral artery, false aneurysm from, 1726
Staffing
for cardiac catheterization, 130–133
for vascular intervention angiography, 135–136
Staghorn calculi
in percutaneous stone removal indications, III:588–590, III:591, III:592
intraoperative film in, III:601
ureteral access catheter in, III:600
in urinary diversion complications, III:656
Staging of sarcomas, III:1031
Stagnation, lytic, III:135, III:136–137
Staining
for lymphangiography, 1864
of arm, 1866
of foot, 1866
tumor, 1781
in renal cell carcinoma, 1141, 1145, 1146
Stainless steel coil embolization
in arteriovenous malformations, III:1011
in gastrointestinal bleeding, III:403
in pediatrics, III:906
in splenic trauma, III:888
in transhepatic varices, III:526
in transjugular intrahepatic portosystemic shunt, III:533
Stainless steel Greenfield filters, III:987, III:988
Stainless steel spiders, III:61
Stainless steel Z-stent in thoracic aortic aneurysms, III:359
Standing vein compression, 220
Standing wave pattern in arteriography, 1733
Stanford classification of dissecting aortic aneurysms, 495
Staphylococcus aureus
in mycotic aneurysms, 1077
in renal abscess, 1182
in thoracic aortic mycotic aneurysms, 485
in xanthogranulomatous pyelonephritis, 1193
Staphylococcus epidermidis, 1095
Staple modification of Dotter and Judkins femoropopliteal angioplasty, III:262
Starch microspheres in embolization, III:53
in hepatic malignancy, III:437, III:451
Stationary artery wave pattern in arteriography, 1733
Steal phenomenon
in dialysis shunts, 1776–1778
femoral arteriography in, 1718
Stealth catheter, III:285
Steatorrhea, 1568
Steel coils. *See also* Stainless steel coil embolization
barbed, III:61
for biopsy tracks, III:76, III:183
in extremity trauma, III:863–867
spring, III:56–57
Steerable microguidewires, 162
in infrapopliteal revascularization, III:285

Steering wheel trauma, 528
Steinberg I, 8, 768
Steinberg MF, 410
Steinstrasse, III:608
Stenoses
  aortic. *See* Aortic stenosis
  arterial, sonography in, 207–208, 209,
    214–215, color plate 3
  cervical vertebral, angioplasty of nonori-
    fice, III:350
  coronary artery, 641, 646–647, 657
    in bypass graft, 763
    congenital, 744, 745–746
    coronary flow reserve and, 657
    eccentric, as arteriography pitfall, 731
    hemodynamically significant, 688, 723
    of main left coronary artery as arteriog-
      raphy pitfall, 727–729
    percent diameter, 657
  in dialysis fistula, 1769–1775, 1777, III:
    733–737. *See also* Dialysis fistula,
    revascularization of
  femoropopliteal, angioplasty in, III:262–
    263, III:272, III:274
  hepatic vein, after transjugular intrahe-
    patic portosystemic shunt, III:541–
    542
  of ileal conduits, III:654, III:655
  of mesenteric vessels, 1557–1570. *See
    also* Mesenteric angiography
  of portosystemic shunts, percutaneous
    revision of, III:528–530
  pulmonary artery
    in branches, congenital, 792, 843,
      844
    dilatation after, 788–793
    multiple, 792, 793
    pulmonary arteriography in, 788–793
  pulmonary valve, 826–828
    central pulmonary artery stenosis and,
      831
    congenital, 792, 793
  renal artery
    after renal transplantation, 1339–
      1340, 1341–1343
    branch, 1258–1259
    congenital, 1258
    in renovascular hypertension, 1258–
      1259
    sonography of, 229
  subaortic
    idiopathic hypertrophic, 540
    thoracic aortography in, 540–543
  of subclavian artery
    arteriography in, 1002–1007
    brachiocephalic angioplasty for, 1041
    as coarctation of aorta variant, 437,
      439–440
    in thoracic outlet syndrome, 997, 998
    ureteral, renal transplant obstruction
      from, III:581
  venous
    postoperative, after bypass graft, 223
    vascular sonography flow patterns in,
      215–216, color plate 4
Stents, III:71, III:85–118
  in aortoiliac disease, III:234, III:236–
    238
    with percutaneous transluminal angio-
      plasty, III:98–108
    results of, III:251–254, III:255

balloon catheter compatibility with, III:
  39, III:40–42
balloon-expandable, III:86–89
  in benign obstructions, III:1048, III:
    1049–1053
    biliary, III:456, III:462–466
    in Budd-Chiari syndrome, III:1052–
      1053
    of iliofemoral veins, III:1051, III:
      1052
    of inferior vena cava, III:1051, III:
      1052
    of portal vein, III:1053
    related to hemodialysis, III:1049, III:
      1050, III:1051–1052
    of subclavian vein, III:1048, III:
      1050–1051, III:1052
    unrelated to hemodialysis, III:1048,
      III:1049–1051
  biological response to implantation of,
    III:93–97
Bookbinder, III:89–90
clinical experience and applications of,
  III:1048, III:1049–1054, III:1055
complications of, 1041–1042, III:44,
  III:47–49, III:1054–1055, III:
  1056
Cordis, III:89
in coronary angioplasty, III:374–377
current experience with, III:85
in dialysis fistula stenoses, III:739–740
in dissecting aortic aneurysm repair, 519
in extracranial brachiocephalic arterioplasty, III:352–354
femoral arteriography after, 1721, 1724
  projections for, 1709
in femoropopliteal percutaneous transluminal angioplasty, III:110–112, III:
  262
Fontaine-Dake, III:89, III:90
Gianturco Z. *See* Gianturco Z stents
Gianturco-Rösch Z. *See* Gianturco-Rösch
  Z stent
Gianturco-Roubin FlexStent, III:89–90
  in coronary angioplasty, III:375
  current use of, III:85
history of use of, III:85, III:1047
in iliac disease, III:100–108
iliac percutaneous transluminal angioplasty and, III:98–100
long-term efficacy of, III:240–241
for lower extremity vascular disease, III:
  97–112
in malignant obstructions
  of hepatobiliary system, III:477, III:
    478
  of inferior vena cava, III:1053–1054,
    III:1055
  of superior vena cava, III:1053, III:
    1054
metallic
  in arteriosclerotic disease of pelvic
    arteries, 1638, 1640
  in benign biliary obstruction, III:462–
    465, III:466
  biological response to implantation of,
    III:93–97
  ideal, III:86
  in liver transplantation biliary tract
    strictures, III:518–520

for portal veins in liver transplantation
  complications, III:514–515
in superior vena cava obstruction treatment, 928–929
ureteral, III:573
Nitinol spring-coil, III:90, III:92
Palmaz. *See* Palmaz stent
in portosystemic encephalopathy after
  transjugular intrahepatic portosystemic shunt, III:540
postprocedural care in, III:1055
principles of, III:85–86, III:1047–1049
for prostate, III:632–634, III:635
renal artery
  angioplasty and, III:321–322
  in atherosclerotic disease, III:112–116
  in renovascular hypertension, III:112–
    116
in renal artery dysplasia, 1287
in restenosis after balloon angioplasty,
  III:14–15
results of, III:236–237, III:251–254,
  III:255
in right common iliac artery obstruction
  with balloon angioplasty, III:38
Schneider, III:90–92, III:93
self-expanding, III:90–93, III:94–95
Strecker, III:86, III:88
subclavian artery angioplasty and, III:
  352, III:353
techniques for, III:234, III:236–238
terminology for, III:42
for thoracic aortic aneurysms. *See* Thoracic aortic aneurysms, stent-grafts
  for
in transjugular intrahepatic portosystemic
  shunt, III:532–533
in treating iatrogenic dissection, 1029
types of, III:86–93, III:94–95
ureteral, III:572–578
  antegrade, III:574–576
  complications of, III:576–578
  materials for, III:572–573
  results of, III:576–578
  retrograde, III:576
  technique of, III:574
  in urinomas, III:669
in ureteroenteral anastomotic strictures,
  III:653
in ureteroileal anastomotic strictures, III:
  651, III:652
urethral, III:619–621
  retrieval of, III:962
venous, thrombolysis and, III:1046–
  1057. *See also* Venous thrombolysis
  and stenting
Wiktor, III:89, III:90
Stephens HB, 392
Stereotactic breast biopsy
  recumbent dedicated equipment for, III:
    1037, III:1038
  techniques in, III:1041–1044
Sternum, fractured, 522, 532, 533
Steroids, III:209
  in allergic reaction to contrast media, 30
  in lymphangiography, 1868
  in coronary artery catheterization compli-
    cations, 579
  in emergency treatment, 47
  in hemangioma, III:999
  lymphocele formation and, III:944

in neurologic deficits, 357
in restenosis after balloon angioplasty, III:15
Stewart-Treves syndrome, 1908
Stimulants, 43
Stomach, ulcers in, III:405, III:408, III:409, III:410
Stone baskets in biliary calculi removal, III:492, III:493
Stop-type varicocele, III:689
Storage of data in digital angiography, 146–149
Straight catheter in superselective catheterization, 159
Straight interposition graft hemodialysis shunt, 226
Straight sinus, 274, 275, 276
Straight-line sign, 1543, 1544
Strain gauge transducers, 118
Strecker stent, III:86, III:88
    current use of, III:85
    in dialysis fistula stenoses, III:739
    in percutaneous transluminal angioplasty
        aortoiliac, III:101–108
        coronary, III:375, III:376
        femoropopliteal, III:111
    in renal artery disease, III:115–116
    in transjugular intrahepatic portosystemic shunt, III:532
Streptococci, 485
Streptokinase, III:121–122
    comparison of, to other plasminogen activators, III:122, III:123, III:127
    history of use of, III:133, III:1046
    in pelvic artery fibrinolysis, 1640
    in pulmonary embolism, 809
    in renal artery thrombolysis, 1338
    in thrombolysis
        for pulmonary arteries, III:153
        for renal artery, III:153, III:154
    tissue-type plasminogen activator versus, III:121, III:122
Streptozotocin, III:437
Striate arteries, 267, 268
Strictures
    in biliary calculi removal, III:496
    in liver transplantation biliary tract complications, III:518–520
    ureteral
        dilation of, III:576, III:578–581
        impassable, neotract creation in, III:576
        nephrostomy for, III:570
        stenting for, III:580–581
    of urethra, III:617–621
        after resections, III:578
String sign, 285, 288
String-of-beads pattern in splenic artery dysplasia, 1474
String-of-pearl pattern in arteriography, 1733
String-of-sausage pattern in nonocclusive mesenteric ischemia, 1618
Stroke, 297–303
    after intracranial, extraaxial lesion embolization in carotid-cavernous fistulas, III:808
    carotid artery angioplasty and, III:339–347
    cerebral angiography and
        complications of, 245–246
        technique of, 250

in coronary arteriography complications, 576
    degree of atherosclerosis and, 285
    endarterectomy in, III:752–753
    hemorrhagic transformation in, III:746
    pathophysiology of, III:746–747
    pretreatment evaluation of, III:747, III:751–753
    revascularization procedures in, III:745–751, III:752, III:753. *See also* Central nervous system, revascularization in
    results of, III:751
    vertebral artery angioplasty and, III:347–350
Ström BG, 1587
Strongyloides stercoralis enteritis, 1568
Strontium bromide, early uses of, 5, 6, 13
Struvite renal calculi, III:606
Sturm RE, 9
Suabanejew, III:160
Sub-4 catheter, III:285
Subacute cerebral infarction, 302. *See also* Stroke
Subaortic stenosis
    idiopathic hypertrophic, 540
    thoracic aortography in, 540–543
Subarachnoid hemorrhage, 250–251, III:753–757, III:758
Subarachnoid shunts, 280
Subarachnoid space, tuberculosis and, 304, 306
Subcapsular hematoma
    after nephrostomy, III:569, III:570
    hepatic, 1454–1455
    from renal trauma in hypertension, 1272, 1274
Subcapsular vein, 1292, 1299
Subclavian artery, 995
    aberrant
        as coarctation of aorta variant, 439–440
        patent ductus arteriosus, 838, 839
    aneurysms of, 489
        in thoracic outlet syndrome, 996, 997
    angioplasty of, III:761–763
    blunt trauma to, 527, 528
    catheterization of
        superselective, 168
        technique for, 249, 570
    collateral circulation of, 996–998
    course origin of, altered by ligamentum arteriosus, 418, 419
    ductus arising from, 416
    embryology of, 435–436
    in extracranial brachiocephalic arterioplasty, III:350–352, III:353
    gun wound of, 1757
    inadvertent catheterization of, III:64
    left (LSCA), patent ductus arteriosus and, 415
    obstruction of, arteriography in, 1002, 1003
    poststenotic dilatation of, 1002, 1005
    pulmonary artery anastomoses with, 549–551
    regional chemotherapy in, III:82
    spiral computed tomography of, 996
    stenosis of, 287, 292
        arteriography in, 1002–1007

brachiocephalic angioplasty for, 1041
    as coarctation of aorta variant, 437, 439–440
    in thoracic outlet syndrome, 997, 998, 1762, 1764
    thrombus in, 298
    vertebral flow reversal syndrome and, 552, 553
Subclavian flap technique, 453, 454, 455, 456
Subclavian pulmonary artery anastomoses, 549–551
Subclavian steal, 287, 291
    upper extremity angiography in, 1762–1765
Subclavian vein
    arteriovenous fistulas of, III:1004
    in dialysis shunts, 1767
        stenosis of, 1775, 1777, III:735, III:737
    mediastinal lymphoma and, 996
    neoplasm compression of, 1008
    obstructions of, stents in, III:1048, III:1050–1051, III:1052
    port catheter in, 927, 928–929
    sonography of, 212, 219
    in superior vena cava obstruction treatment, 927, 928–929
    thrombolysis in, III:149, III:150, III:152
    thrombus in, 1857
    in venous access catheters, III:969–971
Subclavius muscle lesions, 996
Subcostal arteries, 1021
Subcutaneous ports, implantable, III:969, III:976–977
Subdural hematoma, 352
Subependymal veins, 274, 275
Subintimal dissection
    of coronary artery, 575
    of hepatic artery, 1396
    of renal artery, 1103–1107, 1108
Subintimal injection, 1110
Subphrenic abscess, III:926–927
Subtotal overframing, 100–101
Subtraction, temporal, 149–151
Subtraction techniques for adrenal glands, 1371
Subvalvular stenosis, 540–543
Succinylcholine chloride, 48
Suction thromboembolectomy, percutaneous, III:160–165
Sulcocommissural arteries, 362, 364, 365
Sulfamethoxazole and trimethoprim, III:628
Sulfonamides, oral hypoglycemics and, III:217
Sulfonylureas, III:216
Sulfur colloids, radiolabeled, III:389–390
Sulotroban, III:15
Summation of intensities following soft thresholding (SIST), 1844
Super ROTALIX Ceramic tube, 95
Superficial external pudendal vein, III:678
Superficial femoral arteries. *See* Femoral arteries, superficial (SFA)
Superior mesenteric angiography, 1549–1586, III:330–336
    in acute mesenteric ischemia, 1616–1618
    in adhesions, 1579

Superior mesenteric angiography—
Continued
  anatomy in, 1549–1555
    arterial, 1549–1552, 1553–1555
    venous, 1552–1555
  in aneurysms, 1570–1571, 1572
  in arteriovenous communications, 1550–
    1551, 1564–1565, 1568, 1570–
    1573
    with angiomatous lesions, 1550–
      1551, 1564–1565, 1570–1573
    with fistulas, 1568, 1573
  bradykinin in, 61, 1557
  complications of, 1555–1556
  in ilial varicosities, 1579
  in inflammations, 1560, 1573, 1575–
    1577
  in internal herniation, 1579
  in intussusception, 1579
  in malrotation, 1579
  in Meckel diverticulum, 1579
  in mesenteric vascular insufficiency,
    1557–1570
    with acute occlusion, 1558–1566
    with chronic obstruction, 1553, 1560,
      1565, 1566–1570
  in nonocclusive mesenteric ischemia,
    1618–1619
  in occlusion of superior mesenteric ar-
    teries, 1553, 1554–1555
  pharmacoangiography in, 1557, 1558
  physiologic considerations in, 1555
  in portal hypertension, 1573
  in radiation enteritis, 1579
  superior mesenteric vein in, 1552–1555
    in acute occlusion, 1561–1563
    in ischemic colitis, 1565–1566
    in nonocclusive disease, 1563–1565,
      1566
  technique of, 1554, 1555–1556
  in tumors, 1574, 1576, 1577–1579
  in volvulus, 1579
Superior mesenteric arteries (SMA). *See
    also* Superior mesenteric angiog-
    raphy
  balloon catheter in, III:32–33
  endovascular interventions for chronic
    mesenteric ischemia in, III:326–
    338
Superior mesenteric arteriography. *See*
    Superior mesenteric angiography
Superior mesenteric veins (SMV), varices
    of, III:397–400
Superior vena cava (SVC), 915–931
  anastomosis of
    to inferior vena cava for collateral cir-
      culation, 957, 958
    right pulmonary artery surgical, arterio-
      venous malformations after, 844
  anatomy of, 915–916
  angiography of
    in persistent left superior vena cava,
      920–927
    in superior vena cava syndrome, 915,
      916–920, 921–925. *See also* Supe-
      rior vena cava (SVC), occlusion of
    technique for, 916
  anomalous entrance of, into left atrium,
    898, 900, 909
  collateral circulation to, 1511
  intravascular biopsy in, III:197

obstruction of, III:1046
  benign, III:1048
  malignant, III:1053, III:1054
occlusion of, 916–920, 921–925
  effects of, 910
  treatment of, 927–929
partial anomalous pulmonary venous connection to, 884, 885
persistent left, 898, 900, 909, 920–927
  superior vena cava syndrome after,
    926
sonography of, 230–231
thrombus in, magnetic resonance venography in, 1857
total anomalous pulmonary venous connection to, 875–876, 877
variations in systemic venous return and,
  900, 903
Superior vena cava (SVC) syndrome, 915,
  916–920, 921–925
  atherectomy catheter for, III:49, III:50
  effects of, 910
  treatment of, 915, 916–920, 921–925
Supernumerary coronary arteries, 599–602
Superselective catheterization, 155–175.
  See also Catheterization, superselective
Superselective cerebral angiography, III:
  776, III:777
  in intracranial tumor embolization, III:
    811
Superselective chemotherapy and chemoembolization
  in gastrointestinal bleeding, III:400–
    403
  pelvic angiography in, 1661–1665
Superselective pancreatic angiography,
  1388–1389, 1394–1395
Supplementary renal artery, 1217, 1219,
  1220
  ectopic kidney and, 1221
Supply room for cardiac catheterization laboratory, 89
Support personnel in cardiac catheterization laboratory, 131–132
Supports, patient and equipment, 103–105
Suppression
  background, 195–197
  of superimposed anatomy, 151
Suppurative pyelonephritis, 1178–1182,
  1183
  acute, 1178–1182, 1183
  terminology, 1178
Supracardiac total anomalous pulmonary
  venous connection, 871, 876, 879
Supracardinal veins, 945–947
Supraclavicular lymph nodes, 1888, 1889,
  1897
Supraclavicular masses, 1901
Supraclinoid internal carotid artery aneu-
  rysm, III:773
Supraclinoid segment of internal carotid
  artery, 257–261, 262, 263
Supracondylar fracture, brachial artery
  occlusion after, III:917, III:919
Suprarenal arteries, 1021
Suprarenal caval venous access, III:975
Suprarenal veins, 955
Supratentorial veins, 274–277, 279
  deep, 274, 275–276, 279
  superficial, 274–275

Supravalvular aortic stenosis
  with congenital coronary atresia, 744–
    745
  thoracic aortography in, 542, 544–545
Supravalvular ring, 593
Supraventricular tachycardia (SVT), 580,
  III:216
Sural artery, 1698, 1699
Surgery
  in abdominal abscesses, III:925
  for arteriovenous malformations in cen-
    tral nervous system, III:779–781
  in bile duct injuries, III:455
  in intracranial tumors, III:811
  portosystemic shunt, III:526
    percutaneous revision of, III:528–
      530
  in primary sclerosing cholangitis, III:
    468–470
  splenic abnormalities after, 1478, 1481
  in varicocele, III:691–693, III:694
  vascular damage during, intraoperative
    angiography in, 252–253
Surgical dissection in lymphangiography,
  1864–1865, 1866. *See also* Dissec-
  tion
Sussman ML, 410
Sustained ventricular ectopy, III:216
Suture plication for partial interruption of
  inferior vena cava, III:982–983
SVG (scatter and veiling glare), 149
SVT (supraventricular tachycardia), 580
Sweep generator of camera control unit,
  141
Swick M, 14, 19
Swick N, 7
Swyer-James syndrome, 810
Sylvian point, 268
Sylvian triangle, 268–269, 270
Sympathetic nervous system, aortic plexus
  of, 958
Sympathicoblastoma of adrenal gland,
  1936
Sympathomimetic amines, 49, 55
Synchronization method, 141–142
Synovial origin of lesions, 1808–1810
Synovial sarcomas, 1809–1810
  femoral arteriography in, 1735
Synovitis, pigmented villonodular, 1808–
  1809
Synthetic vascular bypass grafts, 222–223
Syphilis
  aortic aneurysms in
    abdominal, 1077, 1078, 1080–1081
    superior vena cava obstruction after,
      923, 924
    thoracic, 486–487
  aortitis in, 486–487
  in complete aortic occlusion, 1061
  coronary arteriography in, 691–692
  in inflammatory urethritis, III:617
  lymphatic vessels and, 1901
Systemic blood pressure. *See* Blood pressure
Systemic complications of angiography,
  22–33, 1024–1026
Systemic effects in contrast agent complications, 29–30
Systemic lupus erythematosus (SLE)
  cerebral arteries in, 307
  pulmonary arteriography in, 802, 805

Systemic-pulmonary collateral network
developmental anomalies and, 840, 841, 842
in pulmonary valve atresia, 828
Systemic-systemic collateral network, 1063, 1065, 1067–1069

T anchor
in cholecystolithotomy, III:504
in gastrostomy, III:549, III:553, III:554
T lymphocytes, 1900
Table
for cardiac catheterization, 105
for vascular intervention angiography, 134
Tachycardia
sinus, 43, 44
supraventricular (SVT), 580, III:216
ventricular, 44, 45
Tagarno cine viewer, 115
Takayasu arteritis
angioplasty in, III:247–250
pediatric, III:911
renal, III:318
cerebral vascular angiography and, 305, 306
lumbar aortography and, 1054
pulmonary arteriography and, 819
Talc as sclerosant, III:946
Tantalum with cyanoacrylates, III:1015, III:1016
Taper guidewire in hysterosalpingography, III:673
TAPVC. *See* Total anomalous pulmonary venous connection (TAPVC)
Tardus waveform, 222, 224–225
Target angle of radiographic tube, 95–96
Target guidewire, 162, 164
Target microcatheter with flexible segments and rigid body, 163
Target scanning, 141–142
Target steerable microguidewires, 162
Target Tracker catheter, 163, 164, III:57, III:59. *See also* Embolization
Target vessel revascularization, III:8
Taybi's classification of supravalvular aortic stenosis, 542
⁹⁹ᵐTc HMPAO (technetium 99m-labeled hexamethylpropyleneamine oxine), 1693
in cerebral vessel occlusion studies, III:768, III:777
in pelvic abscesses and fluid collections, III:946
⁹⁹ᵐTc-DMSA renal scintigraphy, 1179
⁹⁹ᵐTc-DTPA, 1335, 1336
in renal flow scanning, III:112
⁹⁹ᵐTc-hexamethylpropyleneamine oxine (Tc⁹⁹ᵐTc HMPAO), 1693
in cerebral vessel occlusion studies, III:768, III:777
in radionuclide scanning of pelvic abscesses and fluid collections, III:946
⁹⁹ᵐTc-MAG3, 1335
⁹⁹ᵐTc-sulfur colloid, radioactive, 1471, III:389–390
TCD (transcerebral Doppler imaging), III:754
T-cell lymphoma, 1950

tcuPA (UK) (two-chain urokinase plasminogen activator), III:121, III:122
TEC atherectomy catheter, III:280
Technetium-labeled radioisotopes. *See* ⁹⁹ᵐTc *entries*
Technician, cardiopulmonary or darkroom, 132
Technologist, radiologic, 132
cross-training of, 133
of vascular intervention angiography laboratory, 136
TEE. *See* Transesophageal echocardiography (TEE)
Teflon catheters, III:24, III:25, III:66
Teflon clip, 968, 969
Teflon dilator, 560
Teflon-sheathed needle, III:549, III:551
TEGwire
in chronic mesenteric ischemia revascularization, III:329
in infrapopliteal revascularization, III:285
in renal angioplasty, III:303, III:304, III:317
Teichman's mixture, 3, 4
Telangiectasia
basal occlusive disease with, 307, 310
hereditary hemorrhagic, pulmonary arteriovenous malformations in, 1033
inferior mesenteric arteriography in, 1609
in pelvic neoplastic hemorrhage, 1659
Telebrix. *See* Ioxithalamate
Temperature
cine film processing and, 107, 110
in pediatric interventional angiography, III:904
of testicle, III:688
Temporal arteries
anterior, 267, 268
posterior, 266, 269, 271, 274
Temporal arteritis, 304–305
in splanchnic arteries, 1399
Temporal filtration, 152
Temporal lobe glioblastoma multiforme, 263
Temporal subtraction, 149–151
Temporary occlusion balloons, III:63–65
Temp-Tip nephrostomy catheter, III:570
Tennant R, 639
Tentorial incisura, dural arteriovenous malformations of, III:800, III:801
Tentorium cerebelli, intracranial, extraaxial lesions of, III:794
Teratoma, mediastinal, 917
Terumo Guidewire, 156
in bronchial artery embolization, III:825
in infrapopliteal revascularization, III:286
in pulmonary arteriovenous malformation embolotherapy, III:846
in varicocele embolization, III:694
Terumo microcatheter, 163
Test phantom
of cine identification frames, 123
resolution of
of cine cameras, 100
in spot-film fluorography, 101
of video system, 102
Test shot procedure in digital angiography video system, 140

Testicle
magnification angiography of, 186
temperature of, III:688
toxic metabolites of, III:688
tumors of. *See* Testicular tumors
ultrasonography of, III:641
vascular sonography of, 232
venous drainage of, III:678, III:679
Testicular arteries
anatomy of, 1021
collateral circulation in renal ischemia and, 1277, 1283
Testicular feminization syndrome, 1907
Testicular torsion, 232
Testicular tumors
malignant metastatic spread of, 1933, 1934
in aortic lymph nodes, 1930, 1935
seminoma in, malignant metastatic spread of, 1933, 1934
Testosterone, III:627
Tetracaine, III:214
Tetracyclines
in renal cyst sclerosis, III:663, III:665
as sclerosant after lymphocele percutaneous drainage, III:946
Tetradecyl sulfate, III:526
Tetralogy of Fallot, III:916
absence of pulmonary valve in, 828–829
anomalous coronary artery origin in, 833, 838
anomalous left coronary artery–pulmonary artery fistula in, 800
aorticopulmonary window and, 464
arteriography in, 787–788
balloon dilatation after repair of, III:916
Blalock-Taussig procedure for, 549–551
central pulmonary artery stenosis and, 831, 833, 836
coarctation of central pulmonary artery in, 796
patent ductus arteriosus and, 838, 839
pulmonary artery aneurysm and, 843
pulmonary artery hypoplasia in
central, 831
peripheral, 842
pulmonary valve stenosis in, 826
systemic-to-pulmonary collateral arteries and, 840, 842
Texture in sonographic terminology, 217
Thalamic vein, 276
Thalamoperforate arteries, 271, 273
anterior, 260
Thalamostriate veins, 274, 275
Thalamus, 185, 186
Thal-Quick Chest Tube, III:832
Thebesian valve, 590
Theoretical point source, 177
Thermal balloon angioplasty, III:14
Thermodilution method for cardiac output measurement, 117
Thermography in varicocele diagnosis, III:689
Thermoluminescent dosimeter (TLD), 128
Thigh
cross section of
lower, 1827
upper, 1826
fibrosarcoma of, 1800
neurofibrosarcoma of, 1811
Thiosulfate, III:82

Third coronary artery, 587
  in vivo angiography and, 601
Third degree heart block, 43–44
Thoracic aorta
  aneurysms of. *See* Thoracic aortic aneurysms
  coarctation of, 437
    dilatation in, 441, 442
Thoracic aortic aneurysms, 467–492
  acquired, 396, 488
  aortography in, 396, 397, 471–473
    trauma and, 479, 481
  arteriosclerotic, 473–477
  chest radiography in, 468
  computerized tomography of, 469–471
  congenital, 487–488
  death from, 467–468
  diagnosis of, 468–473
  etiology of, 468
  fluoroscopy in, 468
  incidence of, 467
  in intrathoracic branches, 489
  luetic, 486–487
  magnetic resonance imaging of, 471, 473
  multiple, 475–477, 488
  mycotic, 483–486
  natural history of, III:356–357
  pathogenesis of, 473, 474
  radionuclide evaluation of, 469
  signs and symptoms of, 467, 475
  stent-grafts for, III:356–365
    clinical experience in, III:360–364
    covered Z, III:94
    endovascular treatment of, III:357–358
    history and, III:356–357
    patient considerations and, III:358
    postprocedural monitoring in, III:360
    procedure in, III:359–360
    surgical treatment of, III:357
    technical considerations and, III:358–359
  surgical intervention in, 477, III:357
  survival in, 473–474
  traumatic, 477–483
    chronic, 483
    diagnostic algorithm for, 483
    diagnostic imaging and findings in, 478–481, 482–483
    location of, 477–478
    mechanism of injury in, 477
    signs and symptoms of, 478
    surgical treatment of, 483, 484
  types of, 467, 468
  ultrasound in, 468–469
Thoracic aortography, 391–414
  age and hazards of, 398
  anesthesia for, 391–392
    hazards and, 398
  in aneurysms, 396, 471–473
    from trauma, 479, 481
  in aortic arch anomalies, 547–548
  aortic diameter and aortic wall in, 412
  in aortic graft evaluation, 549
  in aortic insufficiency, 543–546, 547
  aortic spindle in, ductus diverticulum versus, 410–411
  in aortic stenosis, 397, 540–543, 544–545
  in brachiocephalic vessel study, 552, 553

  in bronchial artery embolization, III:822
  for buckling of great vessels, 551
  cardiovascular reactions to, 399
  cerebral reactions to, 399
  in child and adult, 406–409
    diameter and aortic wall in, 412
  in coarctation of aorta versus narrowing of isthmus, 402, 404, 410, 411, 445. *See also* Aorta, coarctation of
  complications of, 397–401
  condition of patient and hazards of, 398
  death in, 397–398
    mode of, 398
  ductus diverticulum in, 402, 403, 404, 405
    aortic spindle versus, 410–411
  dynamic aspects of, 410
  electrocardiography and, 395
  gangrene after, 399–400
  history of, 8, 10, 391
  indications for, 396, 397
  in infant, 401–406
  injection in, 395
  ischemia after, 399–400
  medium employed in, 395
  number of films in, 395
  postaortography measures after, 395
  preliminary films in, 394
  premedication for, 391–392
    hazards and, 398
  in pseudocoarctation, 553
  radiographic projections in, 394–395
  respiratory reactions to, 399
  sensitivity testing before, 392
  in sequestration of lung, 549, 550
  severe nonfatal reactions to, 398–399
  for subclavian pulmonary artery anastomoses evaluation, 549–551
  in supravalvular aortic stenosis, 542
  technique of, 391–395, 396
    angiocardiography, 393
    catheter aortography, 393–394
    direct puncture, 392
    left ventricular puncture, 393
    retrograde brachial aortography, 392
    retrograde carotid aortography, 392–393
    route of injection in, 392–394
  in truncus arteriosus, 549, 551
  urogram and, 395
  volume of medium in, 395, 396
  vomiting after, 399
Thoracic duct, 1891–1906. *See also* Thoracic outlet
  abdominal section of, 1883–1884
    radiologic anatomy of, 1892–1893, 1894
  ampullaceous trunks of, 1888, 1889
  anatomy of, 1883–1889, 1891–1892
    radiologic, 1892–1897
  beaded appearance in, 1884, 1896, 1897
  cervical section of, 1887–1889
    radiologic anatomy of, 1894–1895, 1896
  doubling of, 1898, 1899
  embryology of, 1891
  functional and experimental aspects of, 1899–1900
  lumbar section of, 1884–1885
  lymph nodes along, 1897, 1898

  magnetic resonance imaging of, 1902–1904
  new imaging techniques of, 1902–1904
    direct cannulation and interventions in, 1904
  obstruction of, 1901–1902
    malignant metastases in, 1931
    upper extremity angiography in, 1762, 1764
  radiologic studies of, 1892, 1893
  thoracic section of, 1885–1887
    radiologic anatomy of, 1893–1896
  valves of, 1896, 1897
  variations in, 1895, 1897–1899
    congenital disorders in, 1901
    inflammation in, 1901
    mediastinal masses in, 1895, 1901
    obstruction in, 1901–1902
    radiologic aspects of abnormal, 1895, 1900–1902
    tumors in, 1901
Thoracic outlet, 976–1010. *See also* Thoracic duct
  anatomy of, 995–996
  parathyroid angiography in, 976–994. *See also* Parathyroid angiography
  thoracic outlet syndrome in. *See* Thoracic outlet syndrome
Thoracic outlet syndrome, 995–1010, III:1050
  anatomy in, 995–996
  arteriography in, 1002–1007
    findings and interpretation of, 1003–1007
    technique for, 1002–1003, 1004–1005
  clinical examination in, 998–999
  color Doppler sonography in, 999–1001
  magnetic resonance angiography in, 1001–1002
  pathophysiology in, 996–998
  venography in, 1007–1008
Thoracic spine, fracture of, 522–523
Thoracoabdominal veins for inferior vena cava collateral circulation, 954, 956
Thoracolumbar region
  angiography technique for, 368
  spinal artery in, 359–360, 361
Thoracoplasty, 816
Thoracostomy, tube, III:179
Thorax, 389–1010
  abscesses of, III:829–836
  aneurysms of thoracic aorta and, 467–492. *See also* Thoracic aortic aneurysms
  anomalies of aortic arch and, 547–548
  aortic grafts and, 549
  aortic insufficiency and, 543–546, 547
  aortic septal defect and, 464–466
  aortic stenosis and, 540–543, 544–545
  aorticopulmonary window and, 464–466, 796, 798
  aortography and, 391–414. *See also* Thoracic aortography
  biopsy and, III:184–186, III:187
  blunt trauma to aorta and brachiocephalic arteries in, 521–539. *See also* Blunt trauma, to aorta and brachiocephalic arteries
  brachiocephalic vessels and, 552, 553
  buckling of great vessels and, 551

coarctation of aorta and, 434–463. *See also* Aorta, coarctation of
coronary arteriography and. *See* Coronary arteriography
deformity of, pulmonary hypovascularity in, 816
dissecting aortic aneurysms and, 493–520. *See also* Dissecting aneurysms, of aorta
empyema in, III:831–832, III:833, III:834
interventional radiology of, III:817–854
in abscesses, III:829–836
bronchial artery embolization for inflammation or hemoptysis in, III:819–828. *See also* Bronchial arteries, embolization of
in pulmonary arteriovenous malformations, III:837–854. *See also* Pulmonary arteriovenous malformations (PAVMs)
large systemic venous systems of anomalous pulmonary venous connection in, 868–890. *See also* Anomalous pulmonary venous connection
inferior vena cava in, 932–975. *See also* Inferior vena cava (IVC)
superior vena cava in, 915–931. *See also* Superior vena cava (SVC)
vertebral and azygos veins in, 891–914. *See also* Vertebral and azygos veins
patent ductus arteriosus and, 415–433. *See also* Patent ductus arteriosus
pseudocoarctation and, 553
pulmonary arteriography in, 768–867. *See also* Pulmonary arteriography
sequestration of lung and, 549, 550
subclavian pulmonary artery anastomoses and, 549–551
truncus arteriosus and, 549, 551
veins on, normal vascular sonography flow patterns in, 212
Thorium dioxide
chemistry and characteristics of, 16
historical notes on early uses of, 13
Thorotrast. *See* Thorium dioxide
Threads in mechanical embolization, III:55, III:71
Three-dimensional time-of-flight (3D-TOF) magnetic resonance imaging, 193
gadolinium-enhanced, 1831
Three-stopcock manifold, 558
Thrombin
coils soaked in, III:61
inhibitors of, in thrombolysis, III:127, III:128
in selective embolization in gastrointestinal bleeding, III:403
Thrombin-antithrombin III complex, III:126
Thromboangiitis obliterans
femoral arteriography in, 1726, 1727
upper extremity arteriography in, 1759, 1760
Thrombocytopenia, hemangioma and, III:998
Thromboembolectomy, transcatheter, 1287
first use of, III:160
percutaneous suction, III:160–165

Thromboembolism. *See also* Embolism; Thrombosis
after carotid angioplasty, III:344
detachable balloons in embolization and, III:68
femoral arteriography in, 1722–1723, 1725
hazards for, in renal angiography, 1107–1109
transcatheter removal of, 1287
venography in, 1743, 1746–1749, 1750–1752
Thromboendarterectomy, 1070
Thrombogenic balloon, III:70
Thrombolysis, III:119–131
of aortobifemoral arterial bypass graft, 1640, 1641
clinical applications of, III:127–128, III:132–159
in aortoiliac disease, results of, III:250–251
in axillary and subclavian veins, III:150, III:152
in central nervous system, III:745–751, III:752, III:753
choice of agent in, III:133–134
complications in, III:154–155
contraindications in, III:132–133
in hemodialysis grafts, III:146–147, III:148, III:149
indications in, III:132–133
in lower extremity arteries, III:150–152
methods in, III:134–138, III:139
in pediatric applications, III:153–154
in pelvic and lower extremity arteries, III:136, III:139–144
in peripheral bypass grafts, III:144–146, III:147
in pulmonary arteries, III:152–153
in renal artery and vein, III:153, III:154
in upper extremity arteries, III:148–149, III:150, III:151
complications of, 1042–1043, III:154–155, III:1054–1055, III:1056
concurrent rethrombosis in, III:125–127
dynamic nature of, III:125–127
fibrinolytic system in, III:119–123
history of, III:133, III:1046
long-term efficacy of, III:240–241
mechanical, III:119
pediatric, III:916–919
complications of, III:917–919
indications for, III:917, III:918, III:919
postprocedural care in, III:1055
principles of, III:1046–1047
prothrombotic sequelae of, III:125–126
pulse-spray pharmacomechanical. *See* Pulse-spray pharmacomechanical thrombolysis (PSPMT)
of renal artery thrombosis after transplant, 1338
results of, III:228, III:250–251
in superior vena cava syndrome, 927
systemic versus selective, III:119, III:127
techniques for, III:232–234, III:235
thrombus composition in, III:123–125

transcatheter, III:127. *See also* Pulse-spray pharmacomechanical thrombolysis (PSPMT)
complications of, III:155
history of use of, III:1046
poor outcome in, III:139–140, III:141–144
principles for, III:1046–1047
venous, III:1046–1057. *See also* Venous thrombolysis and stenting
Thrombolytic agents. *See also* Fibrinolytic therapy
choice of, III:133–134. *See also* specific agent
for dialysis fistula, III:727, III:731
history of use of, III:1046
in stroke, III:747
early uses of, III:745–746
Thrombophlebitis
with oral contraceptives, 809. *See also* Thrombosis
pediatric thrombolysis in, III:917
in pulmonary arteriovenous malformation embolotherapy complications, III:852
Thrombosis. *See also* Thrombus
after inferior vena cava surgery, 966, 967
after percutaneous transluminal angioplasty for coarctation of aorta, 459
after thrombolytic therapy, 1042–1043
after transaxillary arteriography, 1031
aortoiliac, chronic, 1060–1061
arterial
real-time gray scale sonography patterns in, 217, color plates 8 and 9
in thoracic aortography complications, 399
in arteriosclerotic disease, 1054, 1055
of aortoiliac junction, 1058–1060
with calcifications, 1062
in complete aortic occlusion, 1061, 1062–1063
in iliac arteries, 1058, 1060
in Bird's Nest filter, 940
of brachial artery after transbrachial arteriography, 1030
central nervous system intraaxial embolotherapy and, III:767
in cerebral vessels, 297, 298. *See also* Stroke
computed tomography in thoracic aortic aneurysm and, 469–471
contrast agent toxicity and, 25–26
in coronary arteriography complications, 575, 578, 579
as pitfall, 735–736
deep vein, 1743. *See also* Magnetic resonance venography
extracorporeal shock wave lithotripsy and, III:607
extremity, 1752
sonography of, 217–220
of femoral vein after renal angiography, 1110
graft
after aortoiliac interventions, 1682, 1684, 1685, 1689, 1690
extremity angiography in, 1689–1690
thoracic aortography in, 549
gray-scale imaging principles and, 206

Thrombosis—*Continued*
　of hepatic arteries in liver allograft, III:
　　510–513
　hepatic vein, 231
　　as contraindication to TIPS, III:538–
　　　541
　in iliofemoral venous system, 965, 966
　inferior vena cava
　　computerized tomography in, 940,
　　　942
　　intravascular ultrasonography of, 939,
　　　940
　　sonography of, 230
　infrapopliteal revascularization and, III:
　　290
　intraarterial chemotherapy and, III:1035
　magnetic resonance venography of, 1852
　mesenteric
　　in coronary arteriography complica-
　　　tions, 578
　　ischemia in, 1620–1624
　　sonography in, 231
　mural, 207, 228
　pediatric angioplasty and, III:916
　pericatheter, as complication of
　　transgraft thrombolysis, III:155
　in peripheral angioplasty, 1040
　portal vein
　　arterial portography in, 1535
　　as contraindication to TIPS, III:538–
　　　541
　　in liver allograft, III:513–515
　　sonography of, 231
　　splenoportography disadvantages and,
　　　1497, 1499
　in puncture site complications, 1027
　　after arterial portography, 1530
　renal artery
　　after transplantation, 1338, 1339
　　as angiography hazard, 1107–1109
　　in angioplasty, 1041
　　in infarction, 1262–1264
　renal vein
　　hypertension and, 1276
　　sonography of, 230–231
　　venography in, 1308–1311, 1312,
　　　1320
　sonography of
　　in extremities, 217–220
　　real-time gray scale patterns in, 217
　　renal vein in, 230–231
　in splenic abnormalities, 1478, 1479,
　　1480
　of splenic veins, 1512–1515
　in superior mesenteric artery, 1620–
　　1622, 1623
　tumor, in inferior vena cava obstruction,
　　963, 965
　　intravascular ultrasonography of, 939,
　　　940
　at vena caval filter site, III:985
　vena caval filters for. *See* Vena cava filters
　venous access catheters and, III:980
　in venous malformations, III:1023
　in venous sinuses, 303
Thromboxane A$_2$, 61
Thromboxane A$_2$-receptor inhibitors, III:
　15
Thrombus. *See also* Thrombosis
　age of, III:125
　composition of, III:123–125

　of inferior vena cava, III:124, III:125
　lysis-resistant, III:126
　percutaneous suction thromboembolec-
　　tomy removal of, III:160–165
　white, III:124
Thrombus replacement theory of balloon
　　angioplasty restenosis, III:17, III:18
Thumb, arteriovenous malformation of,
　　1757
Thurmond-Rösch Hysterocath, III:673
Thymic arteries, 979
Thymic veins, 987–988
　of Keynes, 987
　in parathyroid arteriography, 979
Thyrocervical trunk, 978
Thyroid
　arteriography of, 983
　biopsy complications of, 1033
　magnification angiography of, 186
　metastases from carcinoma of, 387, 917,
　　III:191
　sonography of, 233, color plate 12
Thyroid arteries, 977, 978, 981
　inferior
　　left, 977, 978
　　right, 978
　to mediastinal parathyroid adenoma, 985
　selective injection of, 980
　small, 979
　superior, 983
Thyroid veins
　inferior
　　common, 987
　　left, 978, 988
　parathyroid hormone gradient in, 987
　valves of, 987
Thyroidea ima artery, 979–980, 981
TIA (transient ischemic attack)
　cerebral angiography technique in, 250
　degree of atherosclerosis in, 285
　vascular sonography and, 221
Tibia, osteosarcoma of, 1795
Tibial angioplasty, III:284–293
Tibial artery
　anterior, 1698
　　stenoses of, III:30–31
　　2D-TOF magnetic resonance imaging
　　　of, 1826, 1835
　　variants of, 1700, 1701
　　wounds of, 1728
　posterior, 1698, 1699
　　mechanical embolic agents for, III:
　　　72–73
　　stenoses in, after femoropopliteal revas-
　　　cularization, III:277
　　2D-TOF magnetic resonance imaging
　　　of, 1826–1827, 1835
　　variants of, 1700
Tibial vein, anterior, 1744
Tibioperoneal arteries, stenoses of, III:30–
　31
　after femoropopliteal revascularization,
　　III:275–276
Ticlopidine, 927, III:15
Time-of-flight (TOF) enhancement in mag-
　　netic resonance angiography, 188–
　　189, 190
　blood flow and signal in, 188–189, 190
　methods for improved background sup-
　　pression in, 195–197
　physiologic motion and, 197–198

　saturation effects in, 193–195
　three-dimensional, 193
　　gadolinium-enhanced, 1831
　two-dimensional, 1823–1824, 1825
　　in deep venous thrombosis, 1839
Timer, fluoroscopic, 126
Timing cycle of film changers, 72–80
　diagram of, 73
Tip of balloon catheter, III:37
TIPS. *See* Transjugular intrahepatic porto-
　　systemic shunt (TIPS)
Tissue embolization, III:52–54
Tissue factors in bleeding with biopsy, III:
　180–181
Tissue-type plasminogen activator (tPA),
　　1640, III:121, III:122
　comparison of, to other plasminogen
　　activators, III:122, III:123, III:127
　in dialysis fistula thrombolysis, III:731
　history and use of, III:133–134
　in thrombolysis
　　in aortoiliac disease, III:233
　　for renal artery, III:154
Titanium filters, 970, III:987, III:990–991
Titanium stent, intraurethral, III:633, III:
　634
TLD (thermoluminescent dosimeter), 128
Tobacco. *See also* Cigarette smoking
　in aortoiliac disease, III:227
　restenosis after balloon angioplasty and,
　　III:8, III:14
TOF. *See* Time-of-flight (TOF) enhance-
　　ment in magnetic resonance angiog-
　　raphy
Tolazoline, 52, 53, 57–58
　in arterial portography, 1530, 1542
　in extremity trauma, III:861
　in pancreatic angiography, 1385, 1392,
　　1394, 1397
　in pelvic angiography, 1644
　revascularization preparation and, III:
　　230
　in superior mesenteric angiography,
　　1557, 1558, 1617
　in upper extremity arteriography, 1759
　for vasospasm at puncture site, 1028
Tolbutamine, III:216
Tongue, carcinoma of, III:82, III:83
Tonometers, balloon, 1632
Topography, cardiac, 586–590
Toposcopic catheter, 159, 160
Torcular Herophili, 276
Torsion
　pulmonary, 1034
　testicular, 232
Torsional attenuating diameter, III:31
Tortuous vessels
　in abdominal aorta arteriosclerosis,
　　1058, 1059
　coronary arteriography in, 643, 652
　splenic artery in, 1458
　　arteriosclerosis and, 1473–1474
Total anomalous pulmonary venous con-
　　nection (TAPVC), 868–879, 880,
　　881
　anatomy in, 871–873
　angiography in, 877–881
　cardiac, 871–873, 876, 879, 880
　cardiac catheterization in, 878
　clinical aspects of, 873–874
　embryology of, 868–871

epidemiology of, 868
infracardiac, 873, 876, 879, 880
to left vertical vein, 875, 876, 877, 879
left-sided, 871, 875, 879
mixed, 873, 879, 881
nonobstructed, 875
obstructed, 874–875
physiology of, 873
plain films of, 874–878
to portal vein, 878, 881
prominent venous structures in, 872, 875–878
right-sided, 871, 875, 879
to superior vena cava, 875–876, 877
supracardiac, 871, 876, 879
Total overframing, 101
Total quality management (TQM), 580
Total renal dysplasia, 1222
Touhy-Borst adaptor, III:69, III:729
Toxicity
contrast dose-related, 49. *See also* Contrast media
of testicular metabolites, III:688
TP (transverse pancreatic) vein, 1427, 1428
tPA. *See* Tissue-type plasminogen activator (tPA)
TQM (Total quality management), 580
Tracheal compression
dissecting aortic aneurysms and, 503
patent ductus arteriosus and, 421
Tracheal edema, 29, 30
Tracheal intubation, 38, 39
Trackability of balloon catheter, III:29–31, III:32–36
Tracker catheter
assembly and irrigation systems for, 164
in bronchial artery embolization, III:825
in embolization. *See also* Embolization
of arteriovenous fistula after renal transplant, 1345
coils for, 164
in pelvic arteriography, 1652, 1657, 1664
of penile artery, 1661
of splenic artery, 1492
floppy tip of, 163
in hepatic arteriography, III:431
in hysterosalpingography, III:673
in pancreatic venography, 1428
in parathyroid ablation, 991
in pelvic digital angiography, 1638
static burst pressure of, 166
in stroke thrombolysis, III:748
for wire emboli, III:57, III:59
Trac-Wright atherectomy catheter, III:46–47
Trailing as term in balloon catheter angioplasty, III:42–43
Transabdominal percutaneous drainage of pelvic abscess, III:948–949
Transarterial digital subtraction angiography (DSAA), 525, 526
Transaxillary arteriography
complications of, 1031
technique of, 1016
Transbrachial arteriography
complications of, 1030
for pulmonary arteriography, 771–772
for renal angiography, 1102

Transcatheter embolization. *See* Embolization; Tracker catheter
Transcatheter management in extremity trauma, III:861–867. *See also* Extremities, trauma to
Transcatheter thromboembolectomy in renal artery obstruction, 1287
Transcatheter thrombolysis, III:127. *See also* Pulse-spray pharmacomechanical thrombolysis (PSPMT); Thrombolysis
complications of, III:155
history of use of, III:1046
poor outcome in, III:139–140, III:141–144
principles for, III:1046–1047
Transcaval ureter, 945
Transcerebral Doppler imaging (TCD), III:754
Transconduit retrograde placement of nephrostomy catheter, III:574
Transducer
in gray scale imaging, physics of, 205–206, 207
strain gauge, during cardiac catheterization, 118
Transducer leads, 117
Transesophageal echocardiography (TEE)
in blunt trauma to aorta and brachiocephalic arteries, 524
in thoracic aortic aneurysm diagnosis, 469
in trauma, 479
Transfemoral catheterization
in pelvic venography, 1665
percutaneous retrograde, in dissecting aortic aneurysms, 503
for pulmonary arteriography, 771, 773–774, 775
technique of, 1013–1016
in upper extremity arteriography, 1755
for venous access catheter, III:974
Transformer for serial radiography, 94
Transgluteal percutaneous drainage of pelvic abscess, III:949–951
Transhepatic approach for venous access catheter, III:975
Transhepatic cholangiography, percutaneous, 1037–1038
Transhepatic choledocholithotomy, III:495–496
Transhepatic portal venography, 1424–1425
complications of, 1425
in liver cirrhosis and portal hypertension, 1423
Transhepatic puncture for removal of common duct stones, 1038, 1039
Transhepatic variceal embolization, III:526–528, III:529
Transient ischemic attack (TIA), III:761–763
cerebral angiography technique in, 250
degree of atherosclerosis in, 285
vascular sonography and, 221
Transitional cell carcinoma
fluid collections in, III:944, III:945
of kidney, 1154–1158
nephrostomy and, III:563, III:564
renal veins in, 1303
tuberculosis versus, 1160
of urethra, III:617

Transjejunal choledocholithotomy, III:496
Transjugular approach
in hepatic biopsy, III:182
to portal vein in venography, 1425–1426
complications of, 1426
for portosystemic shunt. *See* Transjugular intrahepatic portosystemic shunt (TIPS)
for pulmonary arteriography, 771, 774
Transjugular intrahepatic portosystemic shunt (TIPS), III:204, III:530–542
complications of, III:535
hepatic encephalopathy after, III:537–541
magnetic resonance venography before, 1855
parallel shunts in, III:534
perirectal varices after, 1850
portosystemic encephalopathy after, III:537
postintervention care for, III:219–221
preintervention assessment for, III:204
procedural complications of, III:537–541
results of, III:534–537, III:538–539
shunt biology and patency in, III:541–542
stents for, III:85, III:86, III:92
technique for, III:530–534
Translumbar approach for venous access catheter placement, III:974
Translumbar arteriography
in abdominal aorta aneurysm, 1068
in angiography of extremities after aorto-iliac interventions, 1681, 1684
complications of, 1029–1030
femoral arteriography and, 1705–1706
with French over-the-needle catheters, 158
historical notes on, 6, 9
long-leg film changers in, 81
in renal angiography, 1102
Transluminal angioplasty. *See* Percutaneous transluminal angioplasty (PTA)
Transluminal balloon dilatation of pelvic arteries, 1638–1640
Transluminal extraction atherectomy catheter, III:47, III:378, III:379
Transluminal placement of thoracic aortic stent-grafts. *See* Thoracic aortic aneurysms, stent-grafts for
Transluminal therapy in erectile dysfunction, III:715, III:720–723. *See also* Penile vascular catheterization in erectile dysfunction
Transplantation
bowel segment, for esophageal prosthesis, 1590
of liver. *See* Liver, transplantation of
pancreatic, 1415
rejection of
of kidney, III:581
of liver, III:518
lymphocele formation and, III:944
renal, 1325–1351. *See also* Renal transplantation
Transpleural puncture complications, 1030
Transport of film in cine viewers, 113–114, 115

Transposition of great arteries
aorticopulmonary window and, 464
pulmonary valve stenosis in, 826
Transrectal percutaneous drainage of pelvic
abscess, III:951
Transrectal ultrasound (TRUS)
of prostate, III:638–639
of seminal vesicles, III:640
Transshunt embolization in portosystemic
shunt, III:528–530
Transsomatic vertebral angiography, 933
Transthoracic echocardiography (TTE),
516, 518
Transurethral resection of prostate
(TURP), III:626
Transurethral ureteroscopy, III:609–611
Transvaginal percutaneous drainage of pel-
vic abscess, III:951
Transvenous approach in femoral arteriog-
raphy, 1706, 1707
Transvenous digital subtraction angiography (DSAV), 525
Transvenous imaging equipment in femoral arteriography, 1707
Transvenous liver and kidney biopsy, III:
195, III:197–199
Transverse gradient-echo images, 190
Transverse magnetization, 191
Transverse myelitis, III:826–827
Transverse sinus dural arteriovenous malformation, III:796–797, III:800
Trauma, III:855–900
to aorta
and brachiocephalic arteries, 477–483,
521–539
in thoracic aorta aneurysms, 477–483
thoracic aortography in, 396, 397
in carotid-cavernous fistulas, III:802
cerebral angiography technique in, 251
cerebral vessel abnormalities in, 342–
353
symptoms of, 347
chylothorax from, 1920
coronary arteriography in, 692
dissecting aortic aneurysms and, 493
in extracorporeal shock wave lithotripsy
complications, III:607
to extremities, III:857–868. *See also*
Extremities, trauma to
femoral arteriography in, 1726–1730
hepatic
hepatic arteriography in, 1451–1455
superselective catheterization in, 168–
169
to hepatic arteries, III:422–435. *See also*
Hepatic arteries, embolization in
iatrogenic, in upper extremity arteriography, 1755, 1756
intimal, femoral arteriography in, 1700,
1727–1729
for kidney, III:892–899. *See also* Renal
trauma
to lower extremity, superselective catheterization in, 169, 170
pancreatic, 1409, 1415
pelvic
arteriovenous malformations from,
1654–1658
erectile dysfunction after, 1644–1645
fractures in, III:869–883. *See also* Pelvic fractures

hemorrhage from, 1727, III:869–883.
See also Pelvic fractures
superselective catheterization in, 169
in percutaneous stone removal complications, III:602
renal, III:892–899. *See also* Renal
trauma
to spleen, III:884–891, 1485–1491
to upper extremities
nonpenetrating, angiography of, 1758
penetrating, angiography of, 1756,
1757–1758
superselective catheterization in, 169,
170
urethral strictures from, III:617
Traveras injector, 171
Trendelenburg position after air embolism,
1035
Triage in blunt trauma, 521–522
Tricuspid valve atresia, 826
Trigeminal artery, persistent, 281, 548,
III:802
Trigonum fibrosum dextrum, 616
Triiodinated benzoic acids, 576
Trimethoprim, sulfamethoxazole and, III:
628
Trocar technique in drainage
of hepatic abscess, III:929
of mediastinal abscess, III:835
of pancreatic pseudocyst, III:933
of renal cyst, III:662–663
of thoracic abscess, III:830
of thoracic empyema, III:832
Trolard vein, 274, 276
True-Cut needles, III:174
for transjugular liver biopsy, III:198
Truncus arteriosus, 549, 551, 822, 824–
827
aorticopulmonary window versus, 464–
466, 796, 798
classification of, 822, 825
pulmonary arteriography in, 788
thoracic aortography in, 396, 549, 551
TRUS (transrectal prostatic ultrasound),
III:638–639
Trypsin, 1392
T3.0S infusion wire, III:57
in bronchial artery embolization, III:825
T-tube
for common duct stones, 1038, 1039
in liver transplantation biliary tract reconstruction, III:516–517
complications from, III:520–522
percutaneous removal of biliary calculi
through, III:492–495
Tubal ligation, ureteral strictures after, III:
578
Tubal pregnancy, 1646, 1648
Tube
in cardiac catheterization laboratory,
94–97
ceiling suspension of, 105
for cinefluorography, 96–97
in magnification angiography, 177
photoconductive, in vascular intervention angiography, 140–141
pickup, for video systems in digital angiography, 140–141
for spot-film fluorography, 97
variable current of, 94
variable potential of, 93–94

for vascular intervention angiography,
134
Vidicon-style, in vascular intervention
angiography, 140
Tube thoracostomy, III:179
Tuberculosis
in adrenal gland infection, adrenal angiography in, 1379
aneurysms in, 319, 484
hemoptysis in, III:819
hypertension and, 1276
in inflammatory urethritis, III:617
intracranial changes in, 304, 306
lymph node changes in, 1925
lymphatic vessels and, 1901
pulmonary arteriography in, 801–802,
803, 804
renal, 1195–1197
superior vena cava syndrome after, 925
transitional cell carcinoma of kidney versus, 1160
ureteral strictures and, III:580
Tuberous sclerosis
hamartoma in, 1164–1165
pheochromocytoma and, 1370
Tubocornual anastomosis, III:672
Tuboovarian abscess, III:944
Tubular ectasia, benign, 1226
Tubular necrosis, acute (ATN), 1331, III:
250
Tubular wire mesh, intraurethral, III:633
Tulloch W, III:678
Tumor. *See also* specific organ or system
ablation of. *See* Embolization
angiographic appearance of, 1781–1782
benign, 1782
femoral, 1733–1737, 1738
hepatic, 1446–1451, 1452, 1453
malignant, 1781–1782
pulmonary, 810–813, 814, 815
superior mesenteric, 1574, 1576,
1577–1579
arteriovenous shunts in, 1781–1782
carcinoid. *See* Carcinoid
cerebral angiography technique in, 251
displacement of vessels in, 1781
encasement of, 1781
extension of, 1781
infected tissue of, percutaneous drainage
of, III:944, III:945
intracranial, extraaxial lesion embolization in, III:808–814
intravascular biopsy of, III:195–200
large draining abdominal veins in, 1782
lymphangiography in, 1929, 1932–1938
malignant
angiographic appearance of, 1781–
1782
metastatic, hepatic arteriography in,
1450–1451, 1452, 1453
primary, hepatic arteriography in,
1446–1450, 1451
neovascularity of, 1781
pelvic angiography in, 1645–1646,
1647
nerve sheath, 1811
occlusion of vessels in, 1781
inferior vena cava and, 939, 940, 959,
960
superior vena cava and, 917, 920, 924
Pancoast, 996

pelvic superselective catheterization in, 169

pooling or laking of contrast material in, 1781

urothelial

percutaneous nephrostomy for, III: 561, III:563

renal stones in, III:591

venous course abnormalities in, 1782

venous invasion of, 1782

Tumor blush, 1781

in renal cell carcinoma, 1141, 1145, 1146

Tumor markers, 169

Tumor necrosis factor, III:437

Tumor staining, 1781

in renal cell carcinoma, 1141, 1145, 1146

Tumor suppressor proteins, III:17

Tumor thrombus in inferior vena cava obstruction, 963, 965

intravascular ultrasonography of, 939, 940

Tunnel catheters

with Dacron cuff, III:970

for venous access, III:969, III:975–976, III:977

Turner syndrome

coarctation of aorta in, 435

lymphedema in, 1907

TURP (transurethral resection of prostate), III:626

Twin catheters for dialysis, III:978

Twining's line, 274

Two-chain molecule tissue-type plasminogen activator, III:121, III:122

Two chain urokinase plasminogen activator [tcuPA (UK)], III:121, III:122

Two-dimensional time of flight (2D-TOF) magnetic resonance imaging, 1823–1824, 1825

in deep venous thrombosis, 1839

Two-rescuer cardiopulmonary resuscitation, 37

Two-stage cassette changers, 70

Two-valved detachable balloon, III:70

U-arm equipment

in craniocaudal and caudocranial imaging, 103–105

radiation safety and, 88, 124, 125, 126, 127

for vascular intervention angiography, 134

UFCT (ultrafast computed tomography), 471

Ulceration

in coronary disease, 645, 654

peptic, III:392, III:404–405, III:406, III:408–410

Ulcerative colitis, 1606–1607, 1608, III: 414–415

Ulnar lymph nodes, 1881–1882

Ultrafast computed tomography (UFCT), 471

Ultrasonography, 205–238

in abdominal abscesses, III:925–927

of liver, III:929

of spleen, III:931–932

of abdominal aorta and its branches, 228–230

in aneurysms, 1076, 1084–1085, 1090–1091

of adrenal glands, 1359

of aneurysms and pseudoaneurysms, 207, 216, color plates 6 and 7

abdominal aortic, 1076, 1084–1085, 1090–1091

thoracic aortic, 468–469

in aorticopulmonary window, 466

in biopsy, III:175–177

of breast, III:1037–1038, III:1040–1041, III:1043–1045

of kidney, 1335, III:189

of prostate, III:636–637

carotid

compared to angiography in progressive stenosis, 285, 286

duplex, 252

color flow studies in. *See* Color flow imaging

in dialysis fistula blood flow analysis, III: 738

Doppler. *See* Doppler imaging

of extracranial neck arteries, 220–222

of extremities

after aortoiliac interventions, 1693

in arteriovenous malformations or fistulas, 216, 1693, color plate 5

in deep venous thrombosis, 1839

in peripheral arterial disease, 222–227, 228, color plates 1, 2, 10, 11

in trauma, III:860

in venous thrombosis, 217–220

in fallopian tubal catheterization, III:676

flow patterns in

abnormal, 214–216

normal, 211–214, 215

in hepatobiliary malignant obstructions, III:476

of iatrogenic-induced shunting, 216, 218

imaging physics in, 205–211

Doppler, 206–211

gray scale, 205–206

of incompetent vein, 216

in liver transplantation complications, III:509

mesenteric

in acute venous thrombosis, 1624

superior mesenteric arteries in, 1549

pancreatic

in carcinoma, 1398

in islet-cell tumors, 1403

patterns of interest in, 211–217

abnormal flow patterns and, 214–216

intimal hyperplasia and, 217

normal flow patterns and, 211–214, 215

real-time gray scale and, 217

in pelvic abscesses, III:942, III:946–947

in penile visualization, III:719–721

in percutaneous thrombectomy, III:164

in periappendiceal abscesses, III:942

of portal vein, 231–232

of postoperative changes and complications, 222–227, 228

in preinterventional assessment, III:206

renal

in abscess, 1184

in acute transplant rejection, 1334, 1335

in calculi removal, III:599

in cysts, 1171, III:659, III:660

in hydronephrosis, 1202, 1203, 1213

in pyelonephritis, 1179, 1193, 1197

in renal cell carcinoma, 1140

in renal pelvic tumors, 1159–1160

in renal vein thrombosis, 1309

in tuberculosis, 1196

of retroperitoneal space, 1670, 1676

in scrotal interventions, III:640–641

of seminal vesicles, III:640

of small parts, 232–233, color plate 12

in thoracic empyema drainage, III:831–832

transrectal, III:623

in urinomas, III:668

of Valsalva maneuver, 216

in varicocele, III:689, III:690

of vascular neoplastic masses, 216

of vena cava and branches, 230–231

inferior, 937–939, 940

in venous access catheter placement, III: 971, III:972

of venous insufficiency, 216, 220

Ultravist. *See* Iopromide

Umbilical artery

catheterization of, hypertension and, 1276

in thoracic aortography, 394

Umbilical vein

for inferior vena cava collateral circulation, 954, 956

for portal vein approach, 1426

Umbrella occluder of Rashkind, 427–430, III:70, III:908

Unconscious patient, resuscitation in, 36

Underprediction in coronary arteriography, 650

Undifferentiated sarcomas, retroperitoneal, 1669

Unexplained cyanosis in vertebral and azygos vein variations, 911

Unistep Wallstent, III:92

Unsharpness of image, 89

Unstable angina pectoris. *See* Angina pectoris

Upper airway obstruction, 36

Upper extremities. *See also* Extremities

angiography of, 1755–1766

in arteriosclerosis, 1758–1759, 1765

in arteriovenous malformations, 1756, 1757, 1759–1760, 1761

in bone and soft tissue tumors, 1765–1766

in Buerger's disease, 1759, 1760

in embolization, 1762, 1763

in nonpenetrating trauma, 1758

in penetrating trauma, 1756, 1757–1758

in Raynaud's phenomenon, 1759, 1760

in subclavian steal, 1762–1765

in thoracic outlet obstruction, 1762, 1764

lymph nodes of, 1881–1882

malignant fibrous histiocytomas of, 1802

sonography of

in arterial disease, 222

in venous thrombosis, 219–220

superselective catheterization in, 169

Upper extremities—*Continued*
thrombolysis in, III:148–149, III:150, III:151
trauma of
nonpenetrating, 1758
penetrating, 1756, 1757–1758
superselective catheterization in, 169
venography in, 1743–1754. *See also* Magnetic resonance venography
venous access catheters and, III:972–973
Upper zone flow redistribution in pulmonary venous hypertension, 861–863
Upscanning, 146
Ureter
calculi in
distal, III:609–611
extracorporeal shock wave lithotripsy for, III:608–611
midureteral, III:609
percutaneous nephrostomy for, III:561, III:562
proximal, III:609
transurethral ureteroscopy for, III:609–611
catheterization of, strictures after, III:578
ureteroenteral anastomotic, III:653
fistula from, nephrostomy in, III:563
mechanical embolic agents for, III:76
obstruction of. *See* Nephroureteral obstruction
reflux into, after urinary diversions, III:650, III:651
reimplantation of, renal stones after, III:591
renal transplant obstruction from ischemia of, III:581
retrocaval or circumcaval, 945, 946
stenosis of, renal transplant obstruction from, III:581
stenting in, III:572–578
after ureteral stricture dilation, III:579
antegrade, III:574–576
complications of, III:576–578
materials for, III:572–573
occlusion of, III:576–577
results of, III:576–578
retrograde, III:574, III:576
technique of, III:574
in urinomas, III:669
stricture of
dilation of, III:576, III:578–581
nephrostomy for, III:570
in ureteroenteral anastomoses of continent diversions, III:649, III:652–653
in ureteroileal anastomoses, III:649, III:650–652
transcaval, 945
in ureteroileal-ureteroenteric anastomosis extravasation, III:648
Ureteral meatotomy, strictures after, III:578
Ureteral reflux after urinary diversions, III:650, III:651
Ureteric vein, 1292
for inferior vena cava collateral circulation, 951–954, 956

Ureteroenteral anastomoses, strictures in continent diversions from, III:649, III:652–653
Ureteroileal anastomoses, strictures from, III:649, III:650–652
Ureteroileal-ureteroenteric anastomosis, extravasation at, III:648
Ureteroileostomy
background of, III:645, III:646–647
enteroenteral fistulas after, III:648
Ureterolithotomy, III:562
renal stones after, III:591
ureteral strictures and, III:578, III:580
Ureteroneocystostomy, III:576
renal transplant obstruction from, III:581, III:582–584
strictures after, III:578
Ureteropelvic junction (UPJ), urinary obstruction in, III:590–593
Ureteroscopy
flexible, percutaneous stone removal with, III:595
in ureteral stone removal, III:609–611
Ureterosigmoidostomy, III:645, III:646
Ureteroureterostomy in renal transplant obstruction, III:583
Urethra
bulbomembranous rupture of, III:617
female, III:616–617
male, III:615–616
strictures of, III:617–621
after resections, III:578
Urethral stents, III:619–621
as foreign body, retrieval of, III:962
Urethritis, inflammatory, III:617
Urethroplasty, prostatic, III:628–632
Uric acid renal calculi, III:606
Urinary bladder. *See* Bladder, urinary
Urinary diversions, III:645–657
background of, III:645, III:646–647
complications of, III:645–655, III:656
related to conduit, III:654–655, III:656
ureteroenteral anastomotic strictures in continent diversions in, III:649, III:652–653
ureteroileal anastomotic strictures in, III:649, III:650–652
continent
background of, III:645, III:646–647
complications related to conduit in, III:654–655
ureteroenteral anastomotic strictures from, III:649, III:652–653
contrast studies of, III:648, III:649
by percutaneous nephrostomy, III:563
Urinary drainage, compromised, stone removal and, III:590–596, III:597
Urinary tract
dehiscent anastomosis of, percutaneous nephrostomy in, III:563
fistulas of, mechanical embolic agents for, III:76
obstruction of, in percutaneous stone removal indications, III:590–596, III:597
Urine
cytologic examination of, 1160
perinephric collections of. *See* Urinomas
residual, III:618

retention of, after prostatic urethroplasty, III:632
Urinomas, 1036
iatrogenic, III:667
interventional radiology in, III:667–671
diagnosis and, III:668–669
therapy and, III:669–670
percutaneous drainage of, III:946
Urogenital diaphragm rupture, 1644–1645
Urogenital ridge tumors, 1669
Urografin. *See* Sodium diatrizoate
Urography
antegrade, 1210–1211
excretory, 1210–1211
in hydronephrosis, 1202, 1203, 1209, 1210–1211
intravenous
in chronic atrophic pyelonephritis, 1197, 1198
in hydronephrosis, 1202, 1203, 1209, 1210–1211
in renal cell carcinoma, 1139–1140
in renal cysts, 1171, 1172
of renal pelvic tumors, 1159, 1160, 1163
in renal vein thrombosis, 1310, 1311
in renal cell carcinoma, 1142
in renovascular hypertension, 1249
retrograde, 1142
thoracic aortography and, 395
Urokinase
after embolization of posterior tibial artery, III:277
carotid angioplasty and, III:343–344
comparison of, to other plasminogen activators, III:121, III:122, III:123, III:127
before femoropopliteal revascularization, III:273
in fibrinolytic therapy, 810, III:122–123
for peripheral bypass grafts, III:145, III:146
history of use of, III:133, III:1046
idiosyncratic reactions to, III:155
in pediatric interventional radiology, III:917
in pelvic intraarterial fibrinolytic therapy, 1640, 1641
in pulse-spray pharmacomechanical thrombolysis, III:127, III:128, III:135–137
for hemodialysis grafts, III:138, III:147, III:148
for pelvic and lower extremity arteries, III:139–144
for upper extremities, III:149, III:150, III:151–152
rigors during infusion of, 1043
in superior vena cava obstruction treatment, 928
in thrombolysis, III:34, III:1047. *See also* Urokinase, in pulse-spray pharmacomechanical thrombolysis
in aortoiliac disease, III:233–234, III:235
in central nervous system embolization, III:748
for dialysis fistula, III:727, III:731
for pulmonary arteries, III:153
tissue-type plasminogen activator versus, III:121

Urokinase Reaction Registry, 1043
Urokon. *See* Sodium acetrizoate
Uroselectan
  chemistry and characteristics of, 14
  early uses of, 6, 7
Uroselectan B, 14
Urothelial tear, III:602, III:603–604
Urothelial tumors
  nephrostomy for, III:561, III:563, III:
    564, III:567, III:568
  renal stones in, III:591
Urovist, 25
Urticaria, 29, 30, III:217
Useful drugs in emergency treatment, 45–
  47
Uterine arteries, 1022–1023
Uterus
  arteriovenous malformation in, III:1018
  carcinoma of
    lymphatic spread of, 1931, 1932
    radiation fibrosis after therapy for,
     1916
Utricle of prostate, III:622

V-18 Control Wire, III:285
V SYNC (vertical synchronization) pulse,
  141
VACA (Valvuloplasty and Angioplasty of
  Congenital Anomalies) Registry,
  458, 459
Vaccines, polyvalent pneumococcal,
  1492
Vacuum cup hysterosalpingography device,
  III:673, III:674, III:676
Vagina, carcinoma of, 1932–1933
Valium, 568
Valsalva, sinus of
  anatomy of, 591, 593
  arterial origins from
    all coronary artery, 748, 749
    circumflex artery, 746, 747
    left coronary artery, 744, 746–747
  congenital aneurysms of, 487–488
  normal anatomy of, 591, 593
  reflux of contrast material into, 726–
    727, 729
Valsalva maneuver, 216
Valves
  aortic. *See* Aortic valves
  in renal veins
    anatomy of, 1299, 1300, 1301
    renal venography and, 1291
Valvular heart disease, 637
Valvuloplasty and Angioplasty of Congeni-
  tal Anomalies (VACA) Registry,
  458, 459
Van Andel catheter in femoropopliteal
  revascularization, III:263, III:264
Van Andel modification of Dotter and Jud-
  kins femoropopliteal angioplasty,
  III:262
Van de Maele M, 67
Van Praagh and Van Praagh classification
  of truncus arteriosus, 825
Vancomycin, III:209
Vanguard cine viewer, 115
van Sonnenberg catheter, III:930, III:951
Variable pulsewidth, 94
Variable tube current, 94
Variable tube potential, 93–94

Variant angina, 569, 638, 685–687, 732–
  733
Vari-Cath cine films, 107
Varices
  arterial portography in, 1533–1537
  arteriography in
    esophageal, 1533–1535, 1537, III:
     397, III:403–404, III:405
    mesenteric, 1579, III:397–400
  arteriovenous fistulas and, III:1002
  bleeding from, 232
  endoscopic variceal band ligation of, III:
    526
  esophageal
    in arterial portography, 1533–1535,
     1537, III:403–404, III:405
    partial splenic ablation in, 1492
    portal venography in occlusion of,
     1422
  gastric
    in arterial portography, 1533–1535,
     1536, 1537
    partial splenic ablation in, 1492
  as gastrostomy tube contraindication,
    III:548
  history of endoscopic therapy for, III:
    525–526
  ilial, 1579
  intestinal, 1535
  in Klippel-Trenaunay syndrome, III:
    1027
  partial splenic ablation in, 1492
  percutaneous transhepatic embolization
    in, III:526–528, III:529
  perirectal, 1850
  portal venography in, 1422
  renal venography in, 1311–1314, 1315
  of saphenous vein, 1751
  somatostatin and, 56
  vascular sonography after therapy for,
    232
Varicocele, III:678–704
  anatomy in, III:678–686, III:687
  definition of, III:678
  diagnosis of, III:689–691
  etiology of infertility in, III:688
  history of treatment of, III:678
  incidence of, III:678
  magnetic resonance venography in, 1857
  mechanical embolic agents for, III:76
  ovarian, III:700, III:701
  pathophysiology in, III:686–688
  percutaneous embolization in, III:693–
    699
    complications of, III:695–696, III:
     699
    results of, III:699
    technical success or failure of, III:
     695–696, III:699
  pregnancy rates and, III:700–701
  recurrence of, after surgery, III:692–
    695, III:696
  in renal cell carcinoma, 1139
  semen analysis and, III:699–700
  shunt-type, III:689
  sonography of, 232
  stop-type, III:689
  surgical correction of, III:691–693, III:
    694
Varicosities. *See* Varices
Varikocid, III:696

Vasa brevia, 1588
Vasa vasorum after balloon angioplasty,
  III:5
Vascular access site complications, 577–
  578
Vascular bypass grafts. *See* Grafts
Vascular catheterization, penile, III:705–
  725. *See also* Penile vascular catheter-
  ization in erectile dysfunction
Vascular contractility, contrast agents and,
  27
Vascular damage
  in extremity trauma. *See* Extremities
  during surgery, 252–253
Vascular dissections. *See* Dissection
Vascular dysplasia. *See* Dysplasia
Vascular ectasia. *See also* Angiodysplasia
  in arteriosclerosis, 1716
  benign tubular, 1226
  inferior mesenteric arteriography in,
    1609
Vascular endothelium, contrast and, 24–26
Vascular hamartomas of spinal cord, 386
Vascular impotence, 169
Vascular insufficiency, mesenteric. *See* Mesenteric vascular insufficiency
Vascular intervention angiography. *See also*
  specific procedure
  complications of. *See* Interventional radi-
    ology, complications of
  equipment for
    digital angiography in, 138–152. *See*
     also Digital angiography
    optimal, 133–138
    radiographic environment for, 134–135
Vascular malformations
  arteriovenous. *See* Arteriovenous malfor-
    mations (AVMs)
  cerebral, 323–328
    aneurysms associated with, 323, 325–
     326
    complications of embolization of,
     1032
    dural, 323, 327
  inferior mesenteric arteriography in,
    1609
  magnification angiography in, 180, 181
  pediatric, embolization in, III:905–906
  pseudovein versus, III:391, III:393
  spinal, classification of, 369. *See also* Spi-
    nal angiography; Spinal dural arterio-
    venous fistulas (SDAVFs)
Vascular mesenteric ischemia, recurrent,
  1631–1634
Vascular neoplastic masses, sonography of,
  216
Vascular obstruction or occlusion
  inferior mesenteric angiography in,
    1602–1603
  splenoportography in, 1506–1512,
    1517–1521
    extrahepatic, 1499, 1508–1512,
     1513–1517
    hemodynamics and, 1506–1512,
     1517–1521
    intrahepatic, 1506–1508, 1517–1521
Vascular remodeling theory of balloon
  angioplasty restenosis, III:17–19
Vascular resistance, pulmonary, 769, 852,
  853
  early studies of, 849

Vascular ring
  patent ductus arteriosus, 838, 839
  retrograde brachial aortography in, 547
Vascular signal, pulse flip angle and, 195
Vascular smooth muscles
  calcium channel blockers and, 60
  cells of, 50–51
    contractility of, contrast agents and,
    27
  digitalis and, 56
  papaverine as, 56
Vascular sonography. *See* Ultrasonography
Vascular spasm. *See* Vasospasm
Vascular stents. *See* Stents
Vascular supply. *See* Blood flow
Vascular testing, noninvasive, III:228–229
Vascular wall histopathology after balloon
  angioplasty, III:4–5
Vasculitis
  in acute transplant rejection, 1331
  cerebral, 303–312, 313
  chronic mesenteric ischemia and, III:326
  isolated central nervous system, 307,
    308–309
  pediatric, angioplasty in, III:911
  pulmonary, 805
  renovascular hypertension and, 1272–
    1273
  in systemic lupus erythematosus, 805
Vasoconstriction
  drugs in, 52–56
    in pancreatic angiography, 1390,
      1392, 1393
    proposed sites of action of, 50
    in renal angiography, 1104, 1110
  persistent mesenteric, 1616
  proposed sites of action of, 50
  in renal angiography, 1112–1113
  vasopressin in. *See* Vasopressin
Vasodilation
  drugs in, 57–60
    action of, 52
    in pancreatic angiography, 1385–
      1387, 1392–1394
    proposed sites of action of, 50
    renin determination and, 1306
  in extremity trauma, III:861
  in femoral arteriography, 1711–1713
  proposed sites of action of, 50
  revascularization and, III:230
    infrapopliteal, III:290
  in superior mesenteric angiography,
    1557
  thrombolysis and, III:137–138
Vasopressin, 52, 55. *See also* Vasoconstriction
  in arteriography for gastrointestinal
    bleeding, III:394–400
    anastomotic ulcers and, III:405, III:
      411
    esophageal varices and, III:397
    problems from, III:417–419
  dosage and preparation of, 52
  in hepatic arteriography, 1436, 1450
  in inferior mesenteric arteriography,
    1609, 1611
  in pancreatic angiography, 1392, 1393
  in portal hypertension, III:525
Vasospasm, III:213–214, III:230
  after gunshot wounds of upper extremity
    arteries, 1757, 1758

carotid angioplasty and, III:342
at catheter tip in coronary angiography,
  627
central nervous system embolotherapy
  and, III:767
in cerebral aneurysms, 314, 315
in cerebral artery trauma, 344
in coronary arteriography
  catheter-induced, 685, 731–733
  as pitfall, 731–733
  in Prinzmetal angina, 686, 687, 732–
    733
  of right coronary artery, 564, 565
  spontaneously occurring, 685–686,
    731–733
in epicardial coronary arteries, 731–733
femoral arteriography in, 1733
pediatric angioplasty and, III:916
post-subarachnoid, intracranial angioplasty and pharmacologic vasodilation in, III:753–757, III:758
in renal angiography, 1112–1113
in renal angioplasty, 1041, III:304–307
of renal arteries, 1248, 1249
varicocele embolization and, III:699
Vasovagal reactions, 30, III:489
VCUG (voiding cystourethrogram), III:
  614, III:616, III:618, III:619
  before prostatic urethroplasty, III:629–
    631
VDP (venous dialysis pressure), III:738
Vehicular accidents in liver injury, III:422,
  III:423, III:428, III:430–431
Vein
  in cerebral posterior fossa, 278–279,
    280
  coronary, 590, 591
  course abnormalities of, in tumor, 1782
  damage to, in dialysis fistula thromboly-
    sis, III:736
  of Galen, 275, 276
    malformations of, III:782, III:783,
      III:784
  grafts of
    atherectomy catheter in, III:49
    autologous, sonography of changes
      and complications after, 223–225,
      226, color plates 10 and 11
    venous mapping for evaluating, 1856
  in gray scale imaging, 206
  incompetent, sonography of, 216
  of Labbé, 275, 276
  liver and kidney biopsy through, III:
    195, III:197–199
  pancreatic, 1385–1387, 1389
  of Rosenthal, 274, 275, 276
  suppressing signal from, in magnetic res-
    onance imaging, 193
  thrombosis of. *See* Thrombosis
  of Trolard, 274, 276
  tumor invasion of, 1782
Velocity of blood flow
  in dissecting aortic aneurysms, 516
  Doppler imaging measurements of,
    206–207
  in leg arteries, 212, 213
  in portal circulation, 1500, 1506
  in pulmonary vessels, 856–858, 859
Velocity phase-encoding in dissecting aortic aneurysms, 516

Velocity-mapping in dissecting aortic aneurysms, 516
Vena cava
  inferior. *See* Inferior vena cava (IVC)
  sonography of, 230–231. *See also* Ultra-
    sonography
  superior. *See* Superior vena cava (SVC)
Vena cava clips for partial interruption of
  inferior vena cava, III:982–983
Vena cava filters, III:982–997
  choice of, III:995
  complications of, 1043–1044
  evaluation and comparison of, III:986–
    994
    Amplatz, III:987, III:994
    bird's nest, III:987, III:989–990
    LMG Vena Tech, III:987, III:988,
      III:992–994
    Simon Nitinol, III:987, III:991–992
    stainless steel Greenfield, III:987, III:
      988
    titanium Greenfield, III:987, III:990–
      991
  historical background of, III:982–985
  inferior
    magnetic resonance venography and,
      1852
    overuse of, III:205
    pulmonary arteriography approach
      and, 771
    sonography of, 219, 230
  insertion site thrombosis from, III:95
  placement of
    indications for, III:986
    suprarenal or infrarenal, III:985
    technique for, III:985–986
  in sonography of venous thrombosis of
    extremities, 219
Vena Tech (LGM) filter
  complications with, 1044
  for inferior vena cava, 970
  magnetic resonance venography and,
    1852
Venoablation, penile, III:715, III:720–
  721, III:722–723
Venogenic impotence, III:707–708
Venography. *See also* Angiography
  adrenal gland, 1354–1355
    in aldosteronoma, 1361–1362
    in pheochromocytomas, 1373
  cerebral vascular, 253–254
  before dialysis shunt creation, 1775
  of extremities, 1743–1754
    complications of, 1749–1754
    findings in, 1746–1749, 1750–1752
    history of, 1743
    limitations of, 1749–1754
    magnetic resonance, 1837–1863. *See*
      also Magnetic resonance venography
    normal, 1744
    technique for, 1743–1746
  gonadal, III:682
    in surgical ligation, III:692
  in Klippel-Trenaunay syndrome, III:
    1027–1028
  of lumbar spinal plexus, 933
  magnetic resonance, 1837–1863. *See*
    also Magnetic resonance venography
  pancreatic, 1426–1432
    anatomy of, 1426–1427, 1428
    complications of, 1428–1429

in endocrine tumors, 1429–1431
indications for, 1428
technique of pancreatic vein catheterization in, 1428
pelvic, 1664, 1665
portal, 1422–1426
anatomy of portal vein in, 1422–
1424, 1425
percutaneous approach to, 1424–
1426
transhepatic approach to, 1424–1425
transjugular approach to, 1425–1426
umbilical vein approach to portal vein
in, 1426
renal. *See* Renal venography
in renal transplantation, 1330
spermatic, III:680, III:682–687
after varicocele ligation, III:692
in varicocele diagnosis, III:689, III:
690
in thoracic outlet syndrome, 1007–1008
in venous malformations, III:1023, III:
1024
Venoocclusive mechanism in erection, III:
705, III:706
failure of, III:707
Venosinusoidal leak in corpus cavernosum,
III:707
Venous access catheters, III:969–981
categories of, III:969
complications of, III:979–980
late, III:979–980
procedural, III:979
for dialysis, III:977–978
implantable subcutaneous ports in, III:
976–977
indications for, III:969
malpositioned, III:979, III:980
management and removal of, III:978–
979
nontunnel catheters in, III:978
postintervention care for, III:219–221
radiologic placement of, III:969
technique for, III:969–975
axillary and subclavian vein, III:969–
971
collateral veins in, III:975
hepatic vein, III:975
inferior vena cava, III:973–975
internal jugular vein, III:971–972,
III:973
upper extremity veins in, III:972–
973
tunnel catheters in, III:975–976, III:
977
Venous complications of pulmonary arteriovenous malformation embolother-
apy, III:852
Venous dialysis pressure (VDP), III:738
Venous insufficiency
mechanical embolic agents for, III:76
sonography of, 216, 220
Venous leak in corpus cavernosum, III:707
Venous malformations, III:1022–1029
absolute alcohol embolization for, III:
1013
cavernous, III:1022–1026, III:1027
Klippel-Trenaunay syndrome in, III:
1026–1029
Venous mapping for evaluating vein grafts,
1856

Venous occlusion and stenosis, sonography
flow patterns in, 215–216, color
plate 4
Venous outflow restriction, cerebral plexiform nidus aneurysms and, III:775–
776
Venous phase of renal angiography, 1115,
1118, 1125
Venous plexus, vertebral, 951, 952, 958
Venous pressure
in alveoli, 854–855
arteriovenous fistulas in, III:1001–1002
dialysis (VDP), III:738
Venous ring, persistent circumaortic, 947,
950
Venous sampling
in adrenal gland angiography, 1355
parathyroid, 984–988
in renin determination, 1306–1308
Venous sinuses
occlusion of, in gunshot wound, 351
thrombosis of, 303
Venous stasis
chronic, 1746
in splenoportography, 1506
Venous stenoses in dialysis fistula, III:733–
737
Venous thrombolysis and stenting
in benign obstructions, III:1048, III:
1049–1053
in Budd-Chiari syndrome, III:1052–
1053
of iliofemoral veins, III:1051, III:
1052
of inferior vena cava, III:1051, III:
1052
of portal vein, III:1053
related to hemodialysis, III:1049, III:
1050, III:1051–1052
of subclavian vein, III:1048, III:
1050–1051, III:1052
unrelated to hemodialysis, III:1048,
III:1049–1051
clinical experience and applications of,
III:1048, III:1049–1054, III:1055
complications of, III:1054–1055, III:
1056
historical overview of, III:1046, III:
1047
interventional radiology in, III:1046–
1057
in malignant obstructions, III:1053–
1054, III:1055
of inferior vena cava, III:1053–1054,
III:1055
of superior vena cava, III:1053, III:
1054
postprocedural care in, III:1055
principles of, III:1046–1049
Venous thrombosis. *See* Thrombosis
Venous valves
competent, III:683
incompetent, varicoceles and, III:688
Ventilation, artificial, 36–37, 38, 47–48
Ventilation/perfusion (V/Q) scans, 1837
Ventricle
catheterization of, 558–560. *See also*
Coronary arteriography
coronary arterial branches to, 588, 604
enlargement of, with supravalvular aortic
stenosis, 542, 543, 544–545

function of, contrast agent toxicity and,
27, 28
left
asynergy of, 639–640
catheterization of, 558–560
collaterals at free wall of, 712
equipment for visualization of, 120–
121
function of, 120
ischemic heart disease angiography
and, 120
puncture of, in thoracic aortography,
393
right
collaterals at free wall of, 711
double-outlet, pulmonary valve stenosis in, 826
fistulas of, to right coronary arteries,
742
Ventricular aneurysm, 637
Ventricular arrhythmias, intractable, 638.
See also Ventricular fibrillation
Ventricular asynergy, left, 639–640
Ventricular contractions
left coronary blood flow during, 686
premature, in coronary artery catheterization complications,
575
Ventricular ectopy, sustained, III:216
Ventricular ejection fraction, left (LVEF)
depressed, 574–575
ventriculography in study of, 562
Ventricular end-diastolic pressure, left
(LVEDP), 562
Ventricular fibrillation, 44, 45
angiography in evaluation of, 638
automatic injectors and, 172
contrast agent toxicity and, 27
in coronary arteriography complications,
577
prevention of, in emergency treatment,
39
Ventricular function, global left, 561–
562
Ventricular myocardium, operability of,
689
Ventricular puncture, left, 393
Ventricular septal defect (VSD)
aorticopulmonary window and, 464
central pulmonary artery stenosis and,
831
hypoplastic central pulmonary arteries
and, 831
pulmonary arteriography in, 789
in total anomalous pulmonary venous
connection, 873
truncus arteriosus of, 551
Ventricular systole, compression of septal
branches during, 686
Ventricular tachycardia, 44, 45, III:216
Ventricular visualization, equipment for,
120–121
Ventricular wall
collaterals for, 703, 706, 708–710
left, schematic division of, 626
Ventriculoatrial shunt, broken fragment of,
III:966
Ventriculography
in determining operability of coronary
disease, 689
indications for, 639–640

Ventriculography—*Continued*
left
after coronary artery bypass graft, 760
in coronary arteriography, 560–562
ventricular asynergy in, 639–640
normal, 639
in patent ductus arteriosus, 417, 424, 425
quantitative, during cardiac catheterization, 117
role of, 639–640
Ventriculopleural shunt, 923
abscess formation and, III:948
Venuela catheter, 159
Verapamil, 60, III:216
in emergency reactions, III:216
intraarterial, before thrombolysis, III:138
in pharmacologic erection, III:706
in spasm after renal angioplasty, III:305
Vermian veins
inferior, 279, 280
superior, 280
Verner-Morrison syndrome, 1401–1402, 1405, 1406
Versed. *See* Midazolam
Vertebrae
blood supply to, 363–364, 365, 366
venous system and, 364–366, 367
hemangiomas of, 1804
lumbar, in inferior vena cava obstruction, 958
Vertebral arteries
aneurysm of, III:772–775
angiography of, 933
angioplasty of origin of, III:348–349
blunt trauma to, 348
collateral flow to, 295
extracranial brachiocephalic arterioplasty of, III:347–350
in gunshot wound, 343, 344, 345
occlusive disease of, angioplasty in, III:761–763
in posterior fossa, 277–278
retrograde flow in, 1765
sonography of, 221–222
stenosis in, 287, 290, 295
stroke and occlusion of, 300–301
technique for catheterization of, 249–250
vertebral flow reversal syndrome and, 552, 553
Vertebral and azygos veins, 891–914
with absence
of inferior vena cava, 904–908
of innominate vein, 908
azygos flow in portal hypertension in, 911
azygos rupture in, 911
azygos vein dilatation in, 911
catheter access in, 911
caval obstruction effects in, 910
fistulas in, 911
history of study of, 891–892
left inferior vena cava in, 908–910
metastases of tumors and, 892
methods of study of, 892–893
normal, 893–896, 897–899
unexplained cyanosis and, 911
at upper thoracic level, 894, 898

variations in systemic venous return and, 896–900, 901–910
Vertebral bodies in translumbar catheterization, 1017
Vertebral flow reversal syndrome, 552, 553
Vertebral hemangiomas, 386
Vertebral plexuses, 893, 894, 896–897, 951, 952, 958
Vertebrobasilar arteries
aneurysms of, III:772–775
angioplasty of, 1041, III:347–350, III:761–763
Vertical synchronization (V SYNC) pulse, 141
Vertical vein, left
partial anomalous pulmonary venous connection to, 884
total anomalous pulmonary venous connection to, 875, 876, 877, 879
Verumontanum of prostate, III:622
Very-low-density lipoproteins (VLDLs), 1052
Vesical arteries, 1022
pelvic arteriography of, 1648, 1649, 1660
Vessels. *See also* specific vessel
in arteriosclerosis of abdominal aorta
calcifications and, 1056, 1057
diffuse dilations and, 1058, 1059
tortuosities and, 1058, 1059
caliber of, in coronary arteriography, 641
displacement of, in tumor, 1781
perforation, rupture, and separation of, in superselective catheterization, 166
physiology of, 50–52
Viamonte-Hobbs injector, 173
Vicussens R, 700
Vidal E, III:526
Video camera
digitization and, 142
in vascular intervention angiography, 134–135
pickup tube in, 140–141
Video chain in vascular intervention angiography, 134
Video invert, image display and, 146
Video systems
in cardiac catheterization laboratory, 102–103
for digital angiography, 139–142, 143
camera aperture in, 139–140
pickup tube for, 140–141
target scanning in, 141–142
Videodensitometry, 1125
Vidicon-style tubes, 140
Vieussens arterial ring collaterals, 703–704, 706–708
Viewers, cine, 111–114, 115
Villonodular synovitis, pigmented, 1808–1809
Villous adenoma of colon, 1604
Vinblastine
in hepatic malignancy, III:437
in osteosarcomas, III:1033
Vinca alkaloids, III:81–82
Vincristine, III:81–82
in hepatic malignancy, III:437
Vindesine, III:437
Vinyl chloride, 1450

Violent blunt trauma, 533–535
Viper catheter, III:285
VIPomas, 1402
pancreatic, 1405, 1406
Virchow triad, III:982
Virchow-Troisier node, 1897
Virilizing disorders, 1368, 1369
Visceral angiography
anatomy in, 1087
glucagon and, 61
isoproterenol and, 59
optimal resources for, 133. *See also* Equipment, angiographic
prostaglandins and, 61
Visceral arteries, dilation of, III:336
Visceral-systemic collateral network, 1056, 1061, 1062–1063, 1066–1067
Viscosity, blood
contrast agent effects on, 27
pulmonary blood flow and, 857
Visipaque. *See* Iodixanol
Vistaril in premedication, 1713
Visual perception, magnification angiography and, 178–179
VitaCuff catheter, III:970, III:976
Vital dyes in lymphangiography, 1866
interdigital injections of, 1864, 1865
Vital functions in emergency treatment, 36
Vital staining for lymphangiography, 1864
of arm or foot, 1866
Vitamin K, III:208
VLDLs (very-low-density lipoproteins), 1052
Vocal cords, 983
Vocation nurse in cardiac catheterization laboratory, 131
Voelcker F, 4
Voiding cystourethrogram (VCUG), III:614, III:616, III:618, III:619
before prostatic urethroplasty, III:629–631
Voltage
contrast and, 105, 106
light intensity and, 141
for radiographic tube, 96
Volvulus, 1579
Vomiting
after thoracic aortography, 399
in upper airway obstruction, 36
Von Haller A, 1588
von Hippel-Lindau disease, 1370
von Lichtenberg A, 4, 13, 14
von Schulthess-Rechberg A, 700
VP-16, III:1033
V/Q (ventilation/perfusion) scans, 1837–1838
VSD. *See* Ventricular septal defect (VSD)
Vulva, carcinoma of, 1932–1933

Wagner and Starck modifications of percutaneous suction removal equipment, III:162
Walking saturation band, 193
Wallingford V, 14, 15, 16
Wallstent, 1042, III:90–92, III:93
in aortoiliac disease, III:234, III:237–238
in percutaneous transluminal angioplasty, III:101–108
results of, III:254
balloon-assisted expansion of, III:90–91

in benign biliary obstruction, III:462–464
complications of, III:1054
in coronary angioplasty, III:375, III:376
current use of, III:85
in dialysis fistula stenoses, III:739, III:740
in femoropopliteal percutaneous transluminal angioplasty, III:111–112
history of use of, III:1047
intraurethral, III:633, III:635
in malignant biliary obstruction, III:478–481
in mesenteric ischemia, III:330
in portal vein thrombosis, III:1053
principles for use of, III:1047–1049
in renal artery disease, III:115–116
sizes of, III:93
in transjugular intrahepatic portosystemic shunt, III:532
Unistep, III:92
in urethral procedures, III:619, III:620
Waltman loop, 159
Wandering spleen, 1468–1471
Warfarin, 927
after coronary angioplasty, III:377
in restenosis after balloon angioplasty, III:15
Washout effects simulating filling defects, 971
Water hammer effect of pulses, 528
Watery diarrhea, hypokalemia, achlorhydria (WDHA) syndrome, 1401–1402, 1405, 1406
Watson JC, 68, 76
Waveform analysis in Doppler imaging, 207, 208
WBI (wrist-brachial index), III:858
WDHA (watery diarrhea, hypokalemia, achlorhydria) syndrome, 1401–1402
Wedge filters, 81
Wegener granulomatosis, 1273, 1274
Weinberg catheter, 244
West's model of pulmonary circulation, 850, 851
Whipping of catheter, 166
Whipple disease, 1925
Whipple procedure, III:477
abscesses after, III:934–935
White thrombus, III:124
Wholey MH, 1587
Wiggers CJ, 639

Wiktor stent, III:89, III:90
Williams JR, 768
Williams syndrome, III:911–913
central pulmonary artery stenosis and, 831
hypoplasia of peripheral pulmonary arteries and, 842, 843
Willis, circle of, 261, 280
collateral circulation in, 287, 290–291, 293
Willis T, 891
Wilms tumor, 1132–1137
diagnostic evaluation of, 1134, 1135–1136
extrarenal metastases of, 1133
pathology of, 1132–1133
prognosis in, 1136–1137
symptoms and signs of, 1133, 1135
treatment of, 1136
Winberg T, 1587
Winslow JB, 891
Winslow pathway, 1067–1069
Wire mesh, intraurethral, III:633
Wires in embolization, III:62–63
Wiring, electrical, 130
Wolff M, 1443
Wool coil, III:55, III:56
Workroom for cardiac catheterization laboratory, 89
Wounds
bullet, 1727–1728, 1729
cerebral vascular effects in, 342–353
in extremity trauma, III:858
femoral arteriography in, 1726–1729
infection of, in lymphangiography, 1867
in liver injury, III:422, III:424, III:429
stab
femoral arteriography in, 1726, 1727–1729
of superficial femoral artery, false aneurysm from, 1726
of upper extremities, 1757–1758
Wrist, osteoid osteomas of, 1770, 1789
Wrist-brachial index (WBI), III:858
Wuchereria bancrofti, 1909

Xanthogranulomatous polynephritis, 1276
Xanthogranulomatous pyelonephritis, 1193–1194, 1195
abscesses and, 1187, 1188, 1191
focal or tumefactive form of, 1193–1194
hypertension and, 1276

pyonephrosis and, 1193, 1199
renal cell carcinoma versus, 1154, 1156
Xenetix. *See* Iobitridol
Xenon chloride in laser systems, III:380, III:381
Xenon washout studies, 1245
Xenon-enhanced computed tomography cerebral blood flow measurements, III:768
X-ray apparatus, zero time of, 72
X-ray beam, alignment of, 127
X-ray exposure
versus camera aperture size, 139, 140
peak detected, 139, 140
X-ray film in magnification angiography, 177–180
X-ray grids, 103
X-ray platform, 134
X-ray quanta, sufficient, 89
X-ray tubes. *See* Tube
Xylocaine. *See* Lidocaine

Y-adaptor
in balloon catheter angioplasty, III:37
of renal artery, III:297
in detachable balloon embolization, III:67, III:69
in dialysis fistula thrombolysis, III:729, III:731
YAG in laser systems, III:380, III:381
in femoropopliteal angioplasty, III:280, III:281
Y-grafts, 758

Zahn, line of, III:124, III:125
Z-arm equipment
in craniocaudal and caudocranial imaging, 103–105
radiation safety and, 88, 124, 125, 126, 127
Zeitler E, III:24, III:25
Zero net rotation of magnetization, 196
0 pulse, 196
Zero time, rapid film changers and, 72
Zollinger-Ellison syndrome, 1401, 1403–1405
Zooming, 146
Z-stent
Gianturco. *See* Gianturco Z stents
introduction of, III:1047
in thoracic aortic aneurysms, III:359